T0031175

Ten
Men
Dead

Ten
Men
Dead

*The Story of
the 1981 Irish
Hunger Strike*

David Beresford

Grove Press
New York

Excerpts from *The King's Threshold* by William Butler Yeats
are reprinted with permission of Macmillan Publishing Company.
Copyright © 1934, 1952 by Macmillan Publishing Company.
Copyrights renewed in 1962 by Bertha Georgie Yeats,
and in 1980 by Anne Yeats.

Originally published in Great Britain in 1987 by Grafton Books

Published simultaneously in Canada
Printed in the United States of America

First Grove Atlantic hardcover edition: March 1989
First Grove Atlantic paperback edition: February 1997
This Grove Atlantic paperback edition: October 2022

Library of Congress Cataloging-in-Publication data is available
for this title.

ISBN 978-0-8021-5991-5

Grove Press
an imprint of Grove Atlantic
154 West 14th Street
New York, NY 10011

Distributed by Publishers Group West

groveatlantic.com

22 23 24 25   10 9 8 7 6 5 4 3 2 1

To Ellen and Marianne
with love

"I just heard the news—I'm shattered—just can't believe it. This is a terrible feeling I have. I don't even know what to say. Comrade, I'm sorry, but I just can't say anything else. May God in his infinite mercy grant eternal rest to his soul. Jesus Christ protect and guide us all. God Bless. Bik."

INTRODUCTION
BY PETER MAAS

In their testament to the human spirit, the letters that form the spine of this book are nothing less than the Irish equivalent of the diary of Anne Frank.

That was not at all the original intent of the author, David Beresford, an award-winning correspondent for the British newspaper the *Guardian*. In 1979 he was assigned to Northern Ireland. Two years later a momentous event would unfold in a violent, age-old struggle that has been rather inadequately characterized as the Irish "Troubles."

Ten men incarcerated by the British government—nine of them members of the Provisional Irish Republican Army, the tenth belonging to a radical splinter group, the Irish National Liberation Army—began one after the other to starve themselves to death while a horrified world looked on. They did this not for any personal benefit, but for an ideal.

All of them were quite young. The first and subsequently the best known of the hunger strikers was Bobby Sands, who had started life as an apprentice bus builder before finding an eloquent poet's voice in prison; the others seemed the most ordinary of men, among them a draper's assistant, a mechanic, an upholsterer, a milkman. What made them different was their dedication to driving out British forces occupying Northern Ireland.

Still, what they did, as Beresford writes, "belongs more to humanity than to a limited Nationalist cause, no matter how ancient. It is the stuff of tragedy, of Shakespearean proportions."

The "unbelievability" of it—people ready to die slowly and agonizingly for a principle—held Beresford spellbound.

How could it have happened? "This was, after all," he told me, "not some primitive land, but one of the most civilized countries on earth."

The answer lay in the secret communications—the "comms," they were called—between a select few inside and outside the concrete H-Blocks of the Maze prison just south-west of Belfast, where the hunger strike took place. Beresford learned of the existence of the comms during his interviews with friends and relatives of the dead hunger strikers, other prisoners past and present in the Maze, key figures in the Irish Republican movement, and certain representatives of the British government.

He at once tried to gain access to the comms through the IRA's shadowy ruling body, the Army Council. Negotiations dragged on for months. The war in Northern Ireland is not simply a matter of bullets and bombs. It is also a war of propaganda and intelligence and counterintelligence. Within the Council, a debate raged. The comms contained a great deal of vital security information. But it is a fundamental conviction of the Republican movement that the more people know about the struggle, the more likely they are to come down on the Republican side. And in the end, that proved decisive. That, and a trust in Beresford that he would act honorably. In both instances, the decision was correct.

David Beresford was peculiarly suited to the task, an outsider with special insights. Neither British nor Irish, he was born in South Africa and raised in still another part of a defunct empire upon which the sun never set—Rhodesia, now Zimbabwe. As such, he escaped the snares of romanticism or cynicism that have trapped so many journalists covering Northern Ireland. It was the human dimension of the story that possessed him.

And on a winter's day in 1985, two years after he had started working on the book, he was suddenly brought to an IRA safe house in West Belfast. There, in a child's tiny bedroom on the second floor, were six shopping bags filled with the comms he had sought for so long. He was given twenty-four hours to examine them. It was an impossibility. These messages had been written in the minutest script on thin sheets of cigarette paper before being smuggled out of the H-Blocks in a variety of ways that Beresford graphically describes. And there were hundreds of them.

He insisted on—and finally got—a week's grace. He stayed put, snatching brief periods of sleep, transcribing whatever caught his eye with numbed fingers on a lap-top word processor. The comms, of course, had been composed without the slightest notion that any of them would ever be made public. Still, Beresford was stunned by their intimacy—the black humor in them, the anguish, the pain and fear they contained, their anger and courage, and, most of all, their determination. He had thought that the comms would provide valuable background for him. Instead, as he said to me, "They took over."

The hunger strike that Beresford recounts occurred in the second decade of what modern-day Britons commonly call the "Long War." But what they are talking about is only the last twenty years, when the latest round of the "Troubles" started.

For the Gaelic Irish generally, a better starting date is 1171, when the forces of King Henry II invaded and appeared to conquer Ireland. For self-proclaimed Ulstermen, the largely Scots-Irish majority in Northern Ireland—made up of settlers brought in by London—that swears allegiance to the crown, the issue seemed to have been resolved once and for all in 1690, when the army of William of Orange defeated the deposed Catholic King James II at the Battle of the Boyne.

But for the IRA, which traces its ancestry to the rebel United Irishmen and its founder, Wolfe Tone, the war properly was launched in 1798. Tone, not only a friend and an admirer of America's own revolutionist Tom Paine, but also a Protestant, triggered a war for Irish independence that failed.

After that, you can take your pick. Uprisings were smashed in 1803, 1823, 1848, 1867.

Then came the 1916 Easter rebellion in Dublin and, in 1922, the partition of Ireland. But IRA volunteers, on the cutting edge of combat against the British, refused to accept partition, and savage civil war ensued before the IRA was compelled to go underground.

In 1976 in Northern Ireland, the last chunk of the island where the Union Jack still waved, the British took a drastic step—a final solution. IRA inmates, until then treated essentially as prisoners of war, which among other things permitted them to wear their own clothes, were required to don the uniforms of common criminals. The symbolism was enormous; the H-Blocks rang with songs against Britain's attempt to "brand Ireland's fight 800 years of crime."

The first reaction against the edict was the so-called "blanket protest." For three years, Republican prisoners remained in their cells, winter and summer, huddled naked on bare mattresses with only a blanket to cover them, their excrement smeared on the walls. When this failed, an almost spontaneous, ill-conceived hunger strike erupted.

It also failed, and it is at this point, with the launching of a new, highly sophisticated, profoundly determined second hunger strike—not part of some grand Republican strategy, but one defiantly designed and sustained by the H-Block prisoners themselves—that David Beresford's narrative begins.

And it did not fail. Indeed, what it did will never be forgotten in a war with no apparent end—although one day, some day, that, too, will happen. The wraiths of these ten men bear immutable witness.

September 1, 1988
New York City

Ten
Men
Dead

AUTHOR'S NOTE

There is no neutrality in Northern Ireland, at least in the terminological sense: the use of the term "Northern Ireland" places a writer on one side of the conflict, because to an Irish Nationalist there is no such entity. There are numerous other such ciphers by which the parties to the conflict in Ireland identify the allegiance of a writer or speaker. This book is essentially the story of Irish Nationalist prisoners and I have therefore tended to use their terminology, varying it where the context warrants it. For the guidance of readers more familiar with official terminology the following are the main terms affected: Northern Ireland, or Ulster, is referred to as "northern" Ireland, "the north," or the "six counties"; Londonderry as Derry; the Maze Prison as Long Kesh; the Republic of Ireland is "the south" (the Government of the Republic is, however, the "Irish Government," or merely "Dublin"); prison officers or warders in some instances are referred to, in prison argot, as "screws," and the British authorities sometimes as "the Brits."

The "day in the life" of a prisoner, with which the chapters are interleaved, is a montage based on the reminiscences and writings of prisoners and ex-prisoners, and as a fictional, albeit representational, section is distinguished from the rest of the text by the use of italics. The name Lance Corporal "Kevin Smyth," used in Chapter 4, is a pseudonym.

An important foundation to the book as a whole is the huge volume of "comms"—the smuggled letters sent by the prisoners to the external leadership, many of which are reproduced and others used as a basis on which the story of the hunger strike is constructed. Clarifications of references in the "comms" reproduced are denoted by square brackets.

Apart from the "comms," as published, no attempt has been made to provide sources for information in the book. It is an exercise in journalism, rather than scholarship. But sources include contemporary reports in the national and provincial newspapers of Ireland and Britain, my own recollections, interviews with relatives and friends of the hunger strikers, prisoners past and present, and others involved in the hunger strike—notably members of the Republican movement, clergymen and politicians and, to a limited degree, the Northern Ireland Office. I would like to thank those who did assist, in particular those relatives and close friends of the dead hunger strikers whose contributions to the book were, in many instances, made at considerable emotional cost to themselves. A special thanks is due to Leslie van Slyke, whose loyalty and faith in the project has had much to do with its completion and whose own research contributions have been considerable. Thanks also to the Editor of the *Guardian*, Peter Preston, and the newspaper's Foreign Editor, Martin Woollacott, for their support.

ONE

The Angel was huddled in a borrowed overcoat, but even that and his Arran jersey were not enough to keep out the cold. The car heater was broken and his legs felt numb from the knees down. The snow had him worried as the engine whined its way up the pass: if it got much worse they could get stuck. God help us. Three hours was all they had—and then it would be one dead man, at least.

The driver was concentrating on steering through the drifts: an aesthetic-looking man, almost dapper, with thin face, hair swept back and that solitary air of self-sufficiency which placed him, even without the dog collar.

Then they were over the rise and it was with relief that he saw the snow was thinning. Still, not much time. They swung carefully around the first roundabout and the second. In the distance they could see the bright orange of the security lamps through the black and white of the snow and the night.

He started to worry again when he saw the length of the queue of ten or fifteen cars. The driver dipped the lights and the car heaved over the ramp, the duty soldier reading their number plate into his radio pack. There were cars in the search shed on the side. A moment's tension waiting to be pulled aside, the car heaving over the second ramp, and then they made the third ramp and they were through.

They turned into the car park, the driver plucking the ticket from the machine at the toll gate and the boom silently rising in response. They wasted more time trying to find a space for the car, before hurrying together through the slush to the terminal building.

It was warmer inside, but chaotic with building debris— pieces of plywood scattered everywhere. "Wait for me here," said the Angel, walking on. He went through the brief body frisk and, on the other side, looked anxiously up the stairs. With relief he spotted the man exactly where they had promised, next to the vending machine, the red carnation ostentatious in his button hole. They shook hands at the top and the man said: "This way," striding off. The Angel followed him through the crowd.

"You're on your own," said the man, stepping abruptly to one side. The Angel found himself face to face with the Mountain Climber, a tall, well-dressed man in what looked like a tweed suit, carrying a briefcase. There was the hint of the military in his bearing, he thought. They shook hands, the Mountain Climber making no attempt to introduce himself, just asking: "Would you like a cup of coffee?" The Angel said he would. "There's a quiet place over there," the Mountain Climber said, as they filed through the tables of the cafeteria.

They stopped at a table around a corner from the main part of the big room. As the Angel sat down the Mountain Climber opened his briefcase, took out a sheaf of papers and handed them to him, closed the case and walked off to get the coffee. He glanced down at the top sheet. It was stamped

"Draft." But he could not concentrate on the wording—he was too fascinated by his surroundings.

It looked as though the cleaning staff had been interrupted in their work, but that couldn't be right, not in the evening. There were ranks of chairs scattered around them, but with no tables—nowhere for a stray passenger to sit with his coffee. A cordon sanitaire. There were two watchers sitting up against a wall, one reading a newspaper, the other more alert, looking towards him.

The Mountain Climber came back with the coffee and the Angel swallowed the heat of it gratefully. The Mountain Climber apologized that the final draft was not ready, explaining that the plane had been delayed. It should be with them in a few minutes. Shortly afterwards he came back with it, exchanging it for the original.

"You'd better get that back to your friends," he said.

"Friends?" asked the Angel, nettled by the imputation.

The other man recovered smoothly: "Well, you want to get it into the prison, don't you, and the Republican people will want to look at it."

Conscious of the time ticking away, the Angel said there would be a problem getting into the prison quickly. The Mountain Climber said, "I'll fix that," and went off again. He returned to say, "That's OK, the prison will be waiting for you—as soon as you can." They shook hands and the Angel headed back to the stairs, looking for his driver.

They were there waiting for him, in the safe house on the Falls Road, including the Chief of Staff of the IRA and two members of the Army Council. He handed the document over. Hurried orders were given to run it down the road to the offices, for photostats to be made. When the copies were brought back the men started poring over them. One of the Army Council members said: "It's as full of holes as a sieve." The Angel listened, fascinated by the matter-of-fact discussion.

The door swung open and a bespectacled figure hurried in, panting. He walked over to one of the seated men and handed him a piece of paper. "The hunger strike's over," he said to the room. There was hubbub as they started questioning him.

Three hundred and forty miles away, at the BBC's Television Center in London's Shepherd's Bush, the Secretary of State for Northern Ireland was preparing to speak to the nation. The studio was tense with the nervous energy which always precedes a broadcast. The speech was already on the teleprompt machine. Humphrey Atkins was easy to spot, a tall guardsmanlike figure standing with two of his civil servants. Then someone went to him and said: "Secretary of State, there is a telephone call for you." He was led into an office off the studio and picked up the handset. A voice said: "They've called it off."

One of his officials hurried back into the studio to recover the speech from the teleprompter.

December 18, 1980 was shaping up into a poor news day for the morning papers. President-elect Ronald Reagan was battling to hang on to his nomination of Alexander Haig as Secretary of State, despite criticism of the ex–NATO commander's role in the Watergate scandal. Former Labour Prime Minister Sir Harold Wilson had issued a statement denying suggestions that under his administration classified information had been passed to the KGB through an acquaintance, the jailed textile manufacturer, Lord Kagan. A Swedish pathologist announced that Helen Smith, the British nurse who had died during an illegal drinks party in Saudi Arabia, had been beaten before being impaled on a fence. A story had emerged from Paris of a policeman who had knocked off work early to find his wife and another officer "in an altogether unequivocal situation"— *une affaire d'honneur* resolved unequivocally with pistols at point-blank range, both men miraculously surviving. It was spicy stuff, but none of it worthy of a front-page lead. So when the news broke from Long Kesh prison near Belfast shortly before 8 P.M., the sub-editors were relieved to have a banner headline.

"Hunger strike over," trumpeted the *Irish Times*. "In a dramatic unexpected move the seven Republican hunger strikers in Long Kesh Prison last night ended their fifty-three-day fast—without, it is understood, winning any concessions from the British Government."

In the Irish Parliament deputies were wearily debating the country's economic woes when an Opposition member, Peter Barry, interrupted his speech to announce the news. "I am delighted," he said. "I hope that nothing like it will ever happen in any part of this country again." The Prime Minister, Charles Haughey, issued a statement: "A potentially dangerous and tragic situation has fortunately been averted and all who have contributed to the ending of the strike deserve the gratitude of the Irish people."

North of the Irish border Protestant leaders were exultant. "The ending of the hunger strike has been a great blow to them [the Republican Movement]," said the Reverend Ian Paisley. "They have been made to look mighty small." And the leader of the Official Unionists, James Molyneaux, added congratulations to the British Prime Minister, Mrs. Thatcher, for having "demoralized terrorists generally by making clear that she would not surrender."

Alerted by the jingle of the duty officer's keys in the lock of the perimeter gate, the prisoners crowded up on the heating pipes, eyes straining through the scratched perspex window panels in Long Kesh jail. The gate swung inward and the prison van edged into the courtyard under the overhead fluorescent light. A warder opened the back doors and a slight

figure with mousy-colored shoulder-length hair stepped down.
Wild cheering went up from the cells as they recognized Bobby
Sands. They'd done it! After four and a half years of the
most extraordinary prison protest, they had done it. They'd
won! But as Sands walked across the tarmac yard towards the
double wooden door with his escort at his heels his shoulders
were slumped.

"*Cad e an sceal?*" they shouted, calling for news as he was
led down the corridor to the cell of the "officer commanding"
the IRA in the block. The door was swung open. The two
men greeted each other, shaking hands. Then Sands leaned
forward and whispered in Gaelic: "The hunger strike is over."

"Have we won?"

"We haven't won, but we're not beat yet."

The commanding officer was bewildered. How could it be
over if they hadn't won?

It is an ancient weapon in Ireland, the hunger strike, even more
ancient than the cause in the name of which it was wielded
at the end of 1980. The earlier records place its origins in
medieval Ireland where, as *Troscad* (fasting on or against a
person) or *Cealachan* (achieving justice by starvation), it had
a place in the civil code, the *Senchus Mor*. The code specified
the circumstances in which it could be used to recover a debt,
or right a perceived injustice, the complainant fasting on the
doorstep of the defendant. If the hunger striker was allowed
to die the person at whose door he starved himself was held
responsible for his death and had to pay compensation to his
family. It is probable that such fasting had particular moral
force at the time because of the honor attached to hospitality
and the dishonor of having a person starving outside one's
house.

The tradition found its way into Christianity and there
are legends which have the patron saint of Ireland, St.

Patrick, hunger-striking against God. God always caved in—capitulation in the face of such self-sacrifice being seen by early Christians as a godly quality. A seventeenth-century account of the life of Patrick has the saint ascending the Holy Mount to seek favors of the Lord, only to be told by an angel that he asked too much. Patrick promptly went on a hunger and thirst strike, lasting forty-five days, after which God gave in. In another instance the Irish saint, St. Albeus, dispatched two companions, Lugith and Sailchin, to Rome with a faithful servant, Gobban, with assurances that they would return safely. Gobban died on the voyage, upon which Lugith cried out: "We shall not taste food until the promise made us by Albeus in the name of Christ has been fulfilled." Gobban was hurriedly resurrected. Satan, too, is apparently not immune to the moral force of hunger strikes: a king of Connacht, Conall the Red, and his wife were said to have fasted against the Devil in order to have children.

The tradition of hunger-striking is not confined to Ireland, of course. In British India the ancient practice of "sitting *dharna*," or "sitting down to die by hunger strike," was abolished by government decree in 1861. But it continued to be used as a method of coercion into the mid-twentieth century, peasants often fasting at the doors of moneylenders to try to gain more time to repay their debts. Mahatma Gandhi used the weapon, going on seventeen hunger strikes in his lifetime, to bend the British Raj. And of course it was used to challenge British government authority closer to home early this century by the suffragettes.

In Ireland there was little apparent use of the hunger strike weapon between the Middle Ages and the early twentieth century, when its reintroduction was heralded, curiously, by W. B. Yeats. In 1904 Yeats wrote a little-remembered play called *The King's Threshold*, a story of a confrontation between a poet and his king over the right of poets to take part in government:

KING: . . . *Three days ago*
I yielded to the outcry of my courtiers—
Bishops, Soldiers and Makers of the Law—
Who long had thought it against their dignity
For a mere man of words to sit amongst them
At the great council of the State and share
In their authority. I bade him go,
Though at the first with kind and courteous words,
But when he pleaded for the poets' right,
Established at the establishment of the world,
I said that I was King, and that all rights
Had their original fountain in some king,
And that it was the men who ruled the world,
And not the men who sang to it, who should sit
Where there was the most honour. My courtiers—
Bishops, Soldiers and Makers of the Law—
Shouted approval; and amid that noise
Seanchan went out, and from that hour to this,
Although there is good food and drink beside him,
Has eaten nothing.

The play had no direct relevance to Irish Republicanism, but Yeats, who was something of a mystic, was to take some pride in his prescience when, nearly two decades later, hunger-striking began to dominate the cause to which he had himself become attached.

In 1916 the Anglo-Irish conflict—which had been bubbling on in one form or another at least since Henry VIII proclaimed himself "King of this land of Ireland as united, annexed and knit for ever to the Imperial Crown of the Realm of England"—erupted with the Easter Rising. And the Anglo-Irish War of Independence which followed was marked by a rash of hunger strikes, beginning in 1917 when prisoners at Dublin's Mountjoy jail refused to eat after being brutally treated for refusing to wear prison clothes and to do prison work. Their leader, thirty-two-year-old Thomas Ashe—former president of the Irish Republican Brotherhood (IRB), a forerunner of the IRA—collapsed after forced feeding, dying a few hours later. His funeral, attended by between 30,000 and 40,000 mourners, including some 200 priests, was marked by a brief but well-remembered oration delivered by the IRB leader, Michael Collins: "The volley you have just heard fired is the only speech which it is proper to make over the grave of a dead Fenian."

Even more memorable than Ashe's hunger strike, for Irish Republicans, was the death in 1920 of Terence MacSwiney, then Lord Mayor of Cork and officer commanding the local brigade of the IRA. MacSwiney, a forty-one-year-old poet, playwright and philosopher, had been captured by British troops at an IRA meeting in Cork Town Hall and sentenced by court martial to two years' jail for sedition. He immediately went on hunger strike with sixty colleagues, protesting that the British had no jurisdiction in Ireland and against what he characterized as improper interference in the affairs of a civic functionary.

MacSwiney was an extraordinary idealist in whose little-known writings can be found the philosophical drive which foreshadowed the relish with which he would throw his life and death at England. "One day the consciousness of the country will be electrified with a great deed or a great sacrifice," he prophesied in one political essay, "and the multitude will break from lethargy or prejudice and march with a shout for freedom in a true, a brave and a beautiful sense." In another he wrote: "A man who will be brave only if tramping with a legion will fail in courage if called to stand in the breach alone. And it must be clear to all that till Ireland can again summon her banded armies there will be abundant need for men who will stand the single test. 'Tis the bravest test, the noblest test, and 'tis the test that offers the surest and greatest victory."

It was a test MacSwiney showed himself only too happy to stand. He was transferred after five days from Cork to Brixton prison in London. The British authorities, while experienced in hunger strikes which ended by forced feeding, or—as with Ashe—premature death, had little experience of a fast which ran its full length. Declaring their intention of seeing MacSwiney's protest through, they anticipated that the crisis would take only a fortnight. MacSwiney appears to have shared the misapprehension: announcing his hunger strike at his court martial he had declared, mistakenly: "I will be free alive or dead in a month." After the first few weeks, during which his visitors included five bishops, there was daily anticipation of his death and public excitement reached a feverish pitch which was to be sustained until he eventually expired after more than two months, on his seventy-fourth day without food.

The multitudes lined the streets of London and Cork as MacSwiney's coffin made the journey home; the Pope, Benedict XV, sent an Apostolic Blessing and Plenary Indulgence; four bishops attended a funeral service at Southwark Cathedral and eight accompanied his remains through the streets of Cork. It was a tribute to the principle which MacSwiney had enunciated in his inaugural speech as Lord Mayor and which for decades after was to be a rallying cry for the Republican cause in times of adversity: ". . . the contest on our side is not one of rivalry or vengeance, but of endurance. It is not those who can inflict the most, but those that can suffer the most who will conquer."

Almost forgotten in the publicity surrounding MacSwiney were the deaths of two of his colleagues back in Cork prison, one of them, Joseph Murphy, on his seventy-sixth day without food—the longest fast on record.

Partition and the Anglo-Irish Treaty of 1921 were followed in Ireland by the civil war in which the pro-treaty forces—although heavily outnumbered by the anti-treaty faction, which had the support of the then 100,000-strong

IRA—were, with English help, eventually victorious. In 1923 anti-treaty prisoners staged a massive hunger strike which started at Mountjoy jail and spread to other prisons, involving at its peak about 8,000 prisoners. The strike was for their release and in protest against Partition. There were at least two deaths and possibly three. It appears to have achieved little, apart from creating bitter divisions among the prisoners themselves, although several thousand were released shortly after it ended.

Most of the southern Irish accepted the Partition compromise and set about building their idiosyncratic society, on the principle of a bird in the hand being worth two in the bush—in this case a state of twenty-six counties being worth more than continued warfare over thirty-two counties. The anti-treaty forces split, the majority subverting their Republican ideal for political power and entering the new Dublin parliament as "Fianna Fail," the "Soldiers of Fortune." They took power in 1932 with the active support of the IRA, but feuding developed between them in which the Fianna Fail government executed and jailed many of their old comrades in arms. Several hunger strikes were launched over prison conditions and IRA demands to be treated as prisoners of conscience. After early successes the government began dealing with them ruthlessly. Two IRA men, Tony D'Arcy and Jack McNeela, were allowed to die in Mountjoy in 1940, the impact of their strikes limited by government censors who restricted press coverage. In 1946 Sean McCaughey, the IRA Chief of Staff at the time of his arrest, went on hunger strike for political status. He was allowed to die after twenty-two days—hurrying his end by refusing water as well as food in the final days.

The next significant hunger strike came nearly three decades later, by which time the Irish conflict had assumed a new dimension.

By the late 1940s the IRA was virtually defunct. It reorganized and rebuilt during the 1950s, launching a new campaign in the north, but was again effectively suppressed by security forces on both sides of the border. It formally abandoned military operations in 1962 and drifted into a state of somnambulance, to be awakened, with the rest of Northern Ireland, by the growth of the Civil Rights movement at the end of that decade.

Northern Protestants—self-described "Loyalists" (loyal to the Crown) or Unionists (committed to the union of the UK and Northern Ireland)—had exercised the option to "remain British" in terms of the Anglo-Irish Treaty, but they were left largely to their own devices by Westminster. They enjoyed a large degree of self-rule, with their own parliament and government at Stormont—a flamboyantly baronial castle just outside Belfast—and were assured of a built-in majority against the Catholic population which had been reduced, by the deliberate design of the border, from an all-Ireland majority to a northern Ireland minority. The Loyalists further entrenched their control of government by gerrymandering constituency boundaries, giving them representation in the Stormont parliament out of proportion to their numbers, and indulged their power by widespread discrimination against Catholics, particularly in employment and housing.

The winds of change started to blow over the north of Ireland in 1968, precipitating marches and agitation for civil rights by the Catholics. A Protestant backlash ensued and as the territory staggered towards civil war Britain was forced to move in with troops, suspending the Stormont parliament and eventually imposing direct rule from Westminster.

Gunmen and bombers on both sides of the sectarian divide hastily organized. On the Loyalist side vigilante groups merged into the huge Ulster Defense Association, operating in tandem with the Ulster Volunteer Force. The IRA, caught unprepared, suffered a split over ideology with a minority of hard-liners forming a "Provisional" leadership. Bloody feuding followed between the "Official" and "Provisional" IRAs, together with tit-for-tat exchanges with the Loyalist paramilitary groups and attacks on the "British forces of occupation"—the army and police. In 1972 the Officials declared a ceasefire, effectively surrendering the mantle of the IRA to the Provisionals. And gradually the conflict settled down into its present-day confrontation between the militant Republican Movement—the IRA, together with a small splinter group from the old "Officials," the Irish National Liberation Army (INLA)—and the forces of the Crown with the occasional and embarrassing assistance of the UDA and the outlawed UVF.

The British Government's response to the undeclared war with Irish Republicanism was a massive deployment of manpower and resources to the security front. And it was in this battle with the new "terrorism" that Long Kesh came into being: first as an internment camp for men held in detention without trial, and then as a jail for prisoners convicted of terrorist-related offenses.

In those early years the Kesh—established on the site of a World War II aerodrome—was run on the lines of a prisoner of war camp. The inmates—whether Republican or Loyalist— lived in dormitories in Nissen huts, segregated according to paramilitary allegiance. They organized and disciplined themselves with military-style command structures, drilled—with dummy guns made with woodworking equipment supplied by the prison—and held lectures on revolutionary politics and guerrilla warfare. The IRA's prisoners constituted the Fourth Battalion of the Belfast Brigade—falling under the authority of Belfast "Brigade Staff" in operational matters, such as the organization of escapes, and under the ultimate control of the supreme seven-man "Army Council."

Initially the convicted prisoners were refused the privileges of those being held without trial, but in June 1972 forty IRA prisoners, led by a legendary Republican figure, Billy McKee, launched a hunger strike for POW status. During the strike rumors circulated in Belfast that McKee had died, and rioting ensued. The rumors proved to be untrue and the Government granted "special status"—essentially POW status—after thirty-seven days, before any deaths did take place. It is debatable how far the prison action influenced the decision of the Government, which made the concession, at least in part, to secure a short-lived ceasefire which was being negotiated with the IRA at the time.

There was another well-publicized hunger strike in southern Ireland, in 1972, by the Chief of Staff of the IRA, Sean MacStiofain, in protest when he was arrested moments after being interviewed for the Irish state broadcasting corporation. He abandoned the fast after fifty-seven days, allegedly on the orders of the Army Council, but amidst some derision. The episode helped destroy his Republican career.

The following year two sisters, Dolours and Marian Price, and two men sentenced with them for a car bombing in London went on hunger strike for the right to serve their sentences back in Ireland. After a fast interrupted by forced feeding, which lasted more than 200 days, the Government capitulated and they were repatriated. In 1974 and 1976 two more IRA men, Michael Gaughan and Frank Stagg, died on hunger strike in English jails in unsuccessful bids for political status. Gaughan died of pneumonia and complications apparently caused by forced feeding, a brutal process in which the prisoner's jaws are clamped open and a greased pipe is pushed into the stomach—sometimes going down the windpipe by mistake. Gaughan's death was a major factor in the Government's subsequent decision to avoid forced feeding when dealing with hunger strikes. Stagg was on hunger strike with Gaughan, but abandoned it after his death, on promises of repatriation. When the repatriation failed to materialize he staged a further series of hunger strikes and returned to Ireland in a coffin, following his death on February 12, 1976, after a continuous sixty-two days without food. He was laid to rest after a bizarre battle over his body with the Irish authorities, during which his coffin was hijacked at Shannon airport by the Special Branch and interred under six feet of concrete some distance from the Republican plot where he had asked to be buried. After six months, when police had tired of standing guard at the cemetery, the IRA with a priest in attendance tunneled under the concrete, removed the coffin and reburied Stagg beside Michael Gaughan.

Detention without trial was an obvious embarrassment to Britain—which, after all, prides itself on having introduced the concept of *habeus corpus* to the world—and it was eventually phased out in 1975. But simultaneously it reversed its position on special category status, announcing that such prisoners convicted of offenses committed after March 1, 1976 would be treated as ordinary criminals.

With this decision Long Kesh divided into what were essentially two separate prisons, surrounded by seventeen-foot-high, two-mile-long concrete security walls overlooked by a dozen ostrich-like sentry boxes. The Maze (Compound), with its Nissen huts—popularly known as the "Cages"—continued to hold the dwindling numbers of special category prisoners convicted before the cutoff date. For the new wave of inmates the authorities built the Maze (Cellular), a complex of blocks whose characteristic shape brought a new term to the Irish political dictionary: the H-Blocks.

The H-Blocks, as the Government was so often to boast, comprised the most up-to-date and luxurious prison in Western Europe. Eight of the single-story gray-brick blocks were built at a cost of about £1 million apiece. Each of the wings—formed by the four uprights of the "H"—contained twenty-five cells, a dining room, exercise yard and "hobbies room." The central bar of the H, known paradoxically as the "Circle," held classrooms, offices for the warders, a medical treatment room and stores. Other facilities within the complex, but outside the blocks, included industrial workshops, an indoor sports hall, two all-weather sports pitches and a well-equipped hospital incorporating a dental surgery. Inmates were offered sporting activities ranging from snooker to basketball; vocational training from motor vehicle maintenance to horticulture; and classes from art and music to Irish language and Braille. Imprisonment in the H-Blocks was a status tens of thousands of prisoners around the world would have envied. But it was not special category status.

The phasing out of special category status in 1975 was an integral part of a new security strategy devised by a high-powered government think-tank—which included representatives of the army, police and the counterintelligence agency, MI5—in an attempt to break the IRA and end the fighting in Ireland. Known as the "criminalization," or "normalization," policy, it was essentially an attempt to separate the Republican guerrillas from their host population, the Catholics; depriving the fish of their water, to echo Mao Tse-tung's famous dictum.

In terms of this policy the conflict was to be portrayed as a law and order issue, rather than a war. In addition, the Government began a strategy of "Ulsterization." Troop levels were wound down, as far as army commanders considered safe. Recruiting was stepped up for the police, who took command of anti-terrorist operations. And great emphasis was placed by the authorities on the "criminality" of terrorism, with a stream of rhetoric from politicians and police commanders referring to the "godfathers" of the IRA, to "gangs," "thugs" and "racketeering." And, of course, special category status was abolished, to remove the formal distinctions between paramilitary prisoners and "common" criminals.

The new policy, quickly recognized by the IRA, presented the Republican Movement with an emotional problem in addition to the obvious tactical issues. Despite the refusal of British leaders and public opinion to recognize the fact, there was no difference in the minds of a substantial proportion of the Catholic population between Robert Emmet, martyred on an English gallows in 1803, and James Connolly, the leader of the 1916 uprising, shot by an English firing squad, after whom Dublin's main railway station is now named; between Connolly and Tom Williams, an IRA man hanged in Belfast in 1942 by a "Protestant government for Protestant people"; or between Williams and Sean McKenna who, as Republican epitaphs have it, "died of in-depth interrogation, Long Kesh, 5/6/75." Criminalization was a denial of a belief held dear by Republican Ireland—that husbands, wives, boyfriends, girlfriends, parents, grandparents and great-grandparents who had suffered and died for Irish independence had done so in the high cause of patriotism. And so it was that on September 16, 1976, when a squabble started between warders and a prisoner being admitted to Her Majesty's Prison Maze (Cellular), the ghosts of an ancient cause were looking over the shoulder of the convicted man.

The prisoner, a bull-necked young redhead named Ciaran Nugent, had been sentenced to three years for hijacking a van, and chanced to be the first IRA man convicted of a "terrorist" offense committed after the cutoff date for special category status. Asked for his clothes' sizes for a uniform, he said: "You must be joking me." It was a moment which set in motion events that were to come to an extraordinary conclusion more than four years later.

In those four years after Nugent's defiant statement the confrontation between prisoners and the Government became, symbolically at least, the testing point for the Government's criminalization policy.

Nugent was placed in a cell without any clothes, forcing him to cover himself with a blanket. Prison rules required an inmate to wear clothes when leaving his cell, so Nugent and the IRA and INLA men jailed after him found themselves confined to their cells twenty-four hours a day. The breach of prison discipline, by their refusal to cooperate with the authorities, carried further punishment. Under northern Ireland's parole system prisoners are entitled to fifty percent remission of sentence for good behavior. Non-cooperation therefore had the effect of doubling their sentences. Cooperation would have entitled them to four visits with family or friends a month. Non-cooperation cost them the three "privileged" visits, while the requirement that they wear a uniform to go to the visiting area cost them the fourth, "statutory" visit. This virtually isolated them from the outside world, with contact limited to one censored letter in and out of the prison a month. After furniture had been smashed in confrontations with the warders, their beds and footlockers were removed, leaving them to live in their dreams and memories, or the reality of life in a seven-foot by eight-foot concrete box, with a Bible, mattress, three blankets and a cellmate for company. The "blanket protest" had started.

After several months of this the protesting prisoners compromised on their monthly visit, opting to wear the uniform for the trip to see friends and relatives. It was as much for operational reasons as out of loneliness, because it was the only way of liaising with the outside leadership. But otherwise the confrontation steadily escalated, the authorities content to engage in a trial of strength which they seemed certain to win in the long term.

In 1978 a dispute started over the circumstances in which the prisoners were allowed to wash and go to the toilet. They were allowed down the corridors provided they covered themselves with a towel. But they were refused a second towel to wash themselves and, on the principle that they should not be forced into nakedness even in the washrooms, they refused to leave their cells. The "no wash protest" had begun.

Brawls ensued with prison officers over the emptying of their chamber pots and they started slopping out by throwing the contents through the spyholes and windows, the warders sometimes throwing it back. The openings were then blocked, so the prisoners resorted to pouring the urine out through cracks and dispersing the excrement by smearing it on the walls. The "dirty protest" was under way.

Despite their isolation and the tight security control, the prisoners quickly organized themselves, helped in part by some fortuitous transfers within the Long Kesh complex. The first came in early 1978, when a prominent IRA figure, Brendan Hughes, was moved into the H-Blocks.

Hughes, popularly known as "Dorcha" or "the Dark" for his dark complexion, was Officer Commanding (OC) the IRA's Fourth Battalion, formed inside the prison with nominal command over both the "Cages" and the H-Blocks. He had first arrived at Long Kesh back in 1973 when he was interned, at the age of twenty-five, after being badly beaten during interrogation. Within two days of his arrival in the Cages he was involved in an attempted escape—a scheme to hook himself under a truck in a parachute-type harness. That particular plot was abandoned. But, after several other attempts, he succeeded by hiding himself in a mattress thrown on to the back of a refuse truck which dumped him on a rubbish tip at the nearby village of Hillsborough—the residential home of the British Cabinet minister responsible for the Province under direct rule, the Secretary of State for Northern Ireland.

Hughes was recaptured seven months later in a police raid on an ivy-clad house in the fashionable Malone area of Belfast. He was dressed appropriately for the area on his arrest, if not for the part; he was by then Belfast commander of the IRA, but was found wearing a three-piece pinstripe suit. The contents of the house made an even greater impact than the discovery of Hughes himself. It turned out to be the Belfast headquarters of the IRA and documents seized included what the then British Prime Minister, Harold Wilson, was to claim were plans to precipitate a sectarian civil war. In fact they were contingency plans in the event of such a civil war developing.

Hughes was sentenced to fourteen years for possession of arms found in the house. He returned to Long Kesh as a special category prisoner, but in mid-1977 was involved in a fracas between prisoners and warders and was jailed for a further five years for assault. Because the new offense was committed after the 1976 cutoff date for special status, he was transferred to the H-Blocks, immediately taking over command of the protesting prisoners. Quiet-spoken, easy-going and much admired, he was a highly popular leader. Described by the British press as one of the "godfathers" of the IRA, he was invariably cast as the "fairy godfather" in the Christmas pantomimes the prisoners staged in the blocks, shouting his lines down the corridors with an Italian accent, in imitation of the Mafia.

In January 1979 the prison administration, in an attempt to "isolate" the leadership, transferred thirty-two men identified as the top IRA figures into one wing of H-Block 6. It was equivalent, in prison terms, to setting up an officers' training academy, and the men, many of whom had served time together in the Cages, set about developing a philosophical and strategic approach—including a refined training course for prisoners. In September the administration redistributed the thirty-two men among the main protesting blocks, H3, H4, and H5, effectively diffusing the reinvigorated leadership.

The H-Blocks are intended to facilitate control by restriction of both movement and communication. So the IRA leadership put a priority on the organization of communications, developing a highly efficient system. The monthly visits were to some extent under the control of the prisoners, who were required to submit requests to the governor stipulating what person was to be invited and on what date. The applications were carefully staggered so that, as far as possible, each wing of each block had a prisoner meeting a visitor every day. Family and friends—mainly women—acted as couriers, carrying the steady stream of tiny "communications" or "comms," etched on cigarette papers and wrapped in household cling-film, in their mouths, in their bras, under their breasts, in their panties, sanitary napkins and vaginas. The prisoners carried them to the visiting area in their backsides, tucked behind their teeth, jammed up their nostrils, or in their foreskins. The payloads could be formidable—one prisoner was reputed to have set the record by carrying over forty cigarette papers in his foreskin. The system became so efficient that on occasion the external leadership could expect to get a message in, a reply out and a second message back in a single day.

Leading figures in the blocks regularly sacrificed contact with their families to invite senior Republicans in for strategy discussions. Communications between the wings of the H-Blocks were by shouting; designated prisoners boasting particularly strong voices and knowledge of Gaelic acted as "scorcher" (shouter), bellowing messages late in the evening—when most of the warders had knocked off for the day. More sensitive messages were relayed between blocks by being recycled through visits.

But, while the communication lines were there, the strategy debate conducted along them as to how the prison issue could be won, or at least defused, was inconclusive. And the problem was becoming a nightmare for the IRA.

With the introduction of the criminalization strategy, Britain had done away with internment without trial in northern Ireland, but had restructured the legal system—abolishing juries and diluting the rules of evidence—to make it easier to obtain convictions. With increasingly sophisticated surveillance techniques and the development of what was euphemistically called "interrogation in depth"—methods ranging from simple beatings to sensory deprivation, a form of psychological torture—the security forces were making heavy inroads into the ranks of the IRA and INLA. The number of sentenced prisoners in northern Ireland's jails had risen from 745 in 1972 to nearly 2,300 in 1979. In Long Kesh, by late

1980, there were 1,365 prisoners, 837 of them Republicans and 341 on the dirty protest (the numbers fluctuating as new prisoners arrived and joined in, while others broke and opted to conform). Tensions inevitably existed between conforming and non-conforming prisoners and, as morale sank with continued failure to resolve the crisis, divisive pressures were building up in the Republican Movement, which had always been susceptible to schism. The problem for the Movement was compounded in February 1980 when thirty-two IRA prisoners at northern Ireland's women's jail, in the county of Armagh, went on a dirty protest after several had been beaten in scuffles with warders—including male officers drafted in from the Kesh for the occasion—during a search for uniforms the girls had worn for a defiant paramilitary parade.

The prisons had been symbolic in the Irish Republican psyche throughout the twentieth century, and collapse of the protest would symbolize, for many, a collapse of the Movement in the face of criminalization. As accounts emerged from Long Kesh of the horrendous conditions the prisoners had boxed themselves into, together with stories of vicious beatings by warders, their families added to the pressure for action.

The IRA leadership tried to resolve the dispute both by political agitation and by more violent means. The arguments publicly mounted for a return to special category status—that the men had been convicted by special courts, under emergency legislation which specifically recognized the political nature of their offenses—were cogent, but not widely compelling. The Catholic population, as well as the Protestants, were tired of a decade of violence. The refrain constantly hammered out by political leaders and security force chiefs, that the men of violence were mere parasites on the rump of the communities they purported to serve—thugs led by godfathers sending the young and the innocent to their deaths for personal gain—was making inroads on the Nationalist psyche.

The IRA launched a campaign of selective assassination against the prison service, killing warders—many of them "fingered" by the prisoners for alleged brutality. By January 1980 they had killed eighteen, including one woman prison officer. But the killings merely reinforced the abhorrence of violence outside the Maze and heightened bitterness within the service, exacerbating tensions between prison staff—numbering about 875 in the H-Blocks—and prisoners. By 1979 the prisoners were putting pressure on the Army Council to be allowed to use their weapon of last resort. Hunger strikes had won them special category status in 1972, they argued, so why not now?

Serious talk of a hunger strike to resolve the jail dispute had been under way as early as mid-1978—it had been much discussed by the leaders of the Republican prisoners who had been transferred to H6 that year in the attempt to isolate them. But it was opposed by the IRA outside the Kesh. In a sense prisoners were a millstone around the necks of the external leadership. It was a millstone which had to be borne, out of both sentiment and practical necessity. Most obviously, failure to support the prisoners would quickly alienate the Movement from the families which formed the core of its support in the Catholic community. But it was a heavy burden to bear, because from the point of view of the Movement at the time the prisoners, or at least the funding and organization which had to be devoted to them and their families, were a drain on the limited resources they had with which to pursue their "war" against Britain. It was a basic tenet of the Provisionals that victory in the war would resolve their other problems, including the jails; the prisoners would of course be released with British withdrawal. So priority had to be given to the military effort. A hunger strike would necessitate a major diversion of resources. Everything else would have to be subordinated to it. And it could trigger an emotional outburst in the Nationalist community which the IRA did not have the capacity to control, which could force it to overextend itself—a fatal mistake in terms of military strategy. Never-theless the prisoners were an important constituency in the organization—there were more members of the IRA in the Kesh than there were active volunteers outside. And while the fourth, "prison" battalion fell under the command of the Army Council, the inmates were a tail capable of wagging the dog, at least on the prison issue.

At one stage planning got under way for a hunger strike in the late summer of 1979, at about the time Pope John Paul II made the first-ever papal visit to Ireland. The prisoners even sent out the name of ten volunteers, but on the decision of the Army Council they were persuaded to give Sinn Fein—the political wing of the IRA—one last try at bringing about a settlement through protest action. In October a broad-based campaign had been launched for the restoration of special status by the National H-Block/Armagh Committee, which included members of Sinn Fein, the Irish Republican Socialist Party (IRSP)—political wing of the INLA—and others sym-pathetic to the prisoners and their cause, such as Bernadette McAliskey, the fiery Republican left-winger who, as Berna-dette Devlin, had a major impact on Irish politics in the early days of the "Troubles."

The H-Block Committee launched an international protest campaign to try to swing the Government, helped by the prisoners who busily churned out smuggled letters by the thousands to VIPs around the world, appealing for help. The Catholic Primate of All Ireland, Cardinal Tomas O Fiaich, was persuaded to throw his weight into the search for a settlement. He held a series of meetings through 1980 with the newly appointed Secretary of State for Northern Ireland, Humphrey Atkins, as well as meeting secretly with top Sinn Fein officials. To try to encourage the talks, the IRA called off the attacks on prison warders. But by mid-1980 it was becoming obvious that little ground had been gained through negotiation. And then the Government strengthened the prisoners' hand, in demanding a hunger strike, through a development in Wales.

In May 1980 Gwynfor Evans, the President of Plaid Cymru, the Welsh Nationalist Party, threatened to go on hunger strike in protest against the refusal of the Conservative Party to honor a manifesto pledge to give the principality a Welsh-language station on the new, fourth television channel. The sixty-seven-year-old MP announced that he would start a hunger strike to the death on October 6 unless Government met the pledge. On September 17 the Home Secretary, William Whitelaw, capitulated, announcing that Wales would get the service. In Ireland the lesson seemed clear and the prisoners in the Kesh renewed their pressure on the Army Council.

"The Dark" was particularly vehement in his demand for a hunger strike, on one occasion having a stand-up row with a Sinn Fein official visiting him, saying the leadership just did not appreciate what was happening inside, the savagery of it all. The National H-Block Committee had had its chance, he said, the bishops and the cardinals had made their approaches. Now only one thing was left to bring it to a head: hunger strike.

While the Army Council was agonizing over the decision, another IRA hunger strike started which did not have their authorization and which was to have damaging consequences. It was staged by Martin Meehan, a former IRA commander who had been sentenced to twelve years' jail for conspiracy to kidnap. It was a dubious conviction—based largely on the uncorroborated evidence of a teenaged informer and petty thief paid by the army to "target" Meehan. Although Meehan's involvement with the IRA was well known, he was so infuriated by the conviction that he announced that he would hunger-strike until either his release or his death. He stayed on his fast for sixty-six days, culminating with a thirst strike, before allowing himself to be "persuaded" off it by Cardinal O Fiaich. His colleagues in the IRA were incensed by his action. What he had effectively done was to provide the authorities with a "practice run" for the mass hunger strike which now looked increasingly inevitable—it gave the Government's medical advisers a chance to assess the likely course of a fast to the death and to construct a psychological strategy to deal with hunger strikers. Despite this, the Army Council gave the prisoners their go-ahead and on October 10 Sinn Fein announced that the hunger strike would be launched seventeen days later.

The agreement of the Army Council meant that the prisoners had gained the support of probably the most important individual thrown up by the Republican Movement in the present "Troubles," Gerry Adams.

Adams was born in 1949, into an old Republican family, although he was not aware of his ancestral credentials in his childhood; one of his early memories was of an earnest discussion with schoolmates as to what "IRA" stood for—they agreed on "Irish Rebel Army."

He did get involved at a comparatively early age, however, joining up in his teens—well before the new round of troubles broke out in 1969. At school he passed his O-levels and started studying for his seniors, but finding all his friends were getting jobs and earning money he left school at the age of sixteen, much to his father's disgust. In the IRA he threw himself into political activity—notably agitation for improved housing conditions—which had become the focus of the Republican Movement since the collapse of the 1956–61 campaign. He was always considered left of center in his politics, so it came as something of a surprise to colleagues when he left the "Official" IRA to join the Provisionals after the 1969 split. He rose quickly through the ranks, to battalion commander in the Belfast Brigade at the time of his internment in Long Kesh in March 1972. Or so the press claimed. Certainly he was considered important enough by the IRA leadership to demand his release in June of that year to fly to London with a delegation for secret talks with the Home Secretary, William Whitelaw, which led to a short-lived ceasefire. He was interned again in late 1973, by which time he was said to be Officer Commanding the Belfast Brigade. In December 1973 he was jailed for eighteen months for trying to escape from internment with three other IRA men—attempting to cut their way through the wires with bolt-cutters. It was during this jail term that he developed a reputation as one of the main intellectual forces in the Movement, writing a book, *Peace in Ireland*, and a regular column under the pen name "Brownie" in *Republican News*, the weekly journal of Sinn Fein. In 1978 he was arrested and charged with membership of the IRA. There was little evidence to sustain the charge, but he spent seven months on remand before the case was dismissed. It was to be an important period, because while awaiting trial Adams was held in one of the H-Blocks set aside for remand prisoners, and he joined in the "no-wash protest." It was also his first experience of cellular confinement. He found it frightening at first and it changed his approach to the prison. In the Cages they had had an escape mentality—it was felt that you could not fight within the prison, because the prison would always win; if a warder wanted to move a prisoner from A to B he would, eventually, reach point B, no matter how much he fought at point A. So there seemed little point in fighting. Instead resistance was expressed by trying to escape, to rejoin the fighting outside. In the H-Blocks, where escape seemed impossible, Adams began to realize that it was possible to fight inside—witnessing with amazement the determinedly cheerful and aggressive attitude of his fellow inmates. In one memorable instance he watched with amazement two young lads calmly putting on heavy boots in anticipation of an expected punch-up with warders in which they would inevitably take a heavy beating.

He also had a chance of seeing many of the "blanket men." As a high-risk prisoner he was subject to special treatment, taking his visits in the blanket men's visiting boxes which were emptied for him, but he often met them on his way out. They struck him as figures out of a Solzhenitsyn novel, with their angular gauntness, wan skins, assortment of beards, long, matted hair and ridiculously ill-fitting uniforms. The experience was important, because Adams's influence on the Movement was growing. By 1980 he was not only a member of the Army Council, but in practice the most senior figure in the Republican leadership. A lean, almost skinny man, 6 feet 1 inch tall, Adams was a contradictory figure: obviously ruthless in planning yet, as his writing showed, a sensitive personality; often remote but charming in conversation. He was a born leader, but in his efforts to bring the Movement into the political arena—believing that Britain could not be defeated by military means alone—he was intensely disliked in some sections of the IRA. Invariably puffing on a pipe, he would remain aloof in discussion before intervening to make a considered, incisive and usually decisive contribution. His cool in times of crisis was almost frightening. And he was well qualified to deal with the prison crisis, not only because of his brief experience of the blocks, but because he knew the Dark well—the two of them had shared a cubicle in the Cages—as well as Sands, whose immediate commanding officer Adams had been in the Cages. With those ties and experience he felt bound to do something about what was happening in the H-Blocks. He had opposed a hunger strike, on tactical grounds, but had finally capitulated in the face of the Dark's insistence that they had a moral duty to the prisoners, particularly to the younger men who were coming in with little experience for life in such horrendous conditions.

Hunger-striking, when taken to the death, has a sublime quality about it; in conjunction with terrorism it offers a consummation of murder and self-sacrifice which in a sense can legitimize the violence which precedes and follows it. If after killing—or sharing in a conspiracy to kill—for a cause one shows oneself willing to die for the same cause, a value is adduced which is higher than that of life itself. But the obverse is also true: failure to die can discredit the cause. To scream for mercy at the foot of the gallows—or nod at the saline drip as kidneys and eyes collapse and the doctor warns of irreversible damage—is to affirm that there is no higher value than life and none more worthy of condemnation than those who take it.

For the IRA, failure to resolve the prison dispute could have horrendous consequences. As one young prisoner who had a gift for the telling phrase, Bobby Sands, kept putting it, "The H-Blocks could become the knacker's yard of the Republican Movement." But the consequences of staging a mass hunger strike in Long Kesh and seeing it collapse would be catastrophic. It would not only reinforce the Government's criminalization policy—for who could be more criminal than those who would take life without justification—but it would also destroy morale both within the prison and outside. It could break the Republican Movement.

And that was what seemed to have happened on the night of December 18, 1980. To the despair of the IRA commanders, in their safe house on the Falls—and to the relief of Humphrey Atkins, taking that call at the BBC—the hunger strike had collapsed after only fifty-three days. The prisoners had been outmaneuvered, although the cleverness with which it had all been done was lost on all outside the main parties to the conflict.

From the start of the 1980 hunger strike, the Government had taken a tough and uncompromising line in public. "The Government cannot concede on the principle that is at stake here," the Secretary of State for Northern Ireland, Humphrey Atkins, had declared at the outset. But in private the British Government's position was not as unshakable as the rhetoric made it appear.

Although Mrs. Thatcher made much of the principle that "we don't talk to terrorists," the realities of government do not allow for such hard and fast rules. Throughout the present Irish "Troubles," negotiations, secret or otherwise, have been conducted between the IRA and successive British administrations, and one of these lines of communication was reopened in anticipation of crisis as the Dark and his six colleagues began their fast. The channel was an old one, dating back to the early 1970s when it had been established by the Foreign Office with the help of a Catholic businessman living in the north. The businessman was a buffer between a senior civil servant at the Foreign Office in London and—in 1980—the IRA Chief of Staff. Contact between the businessman and London was usually by telephone. Transcripts of the messages were then passed to the IRA Chief of Staff who relayed them to Gerry Adams in Belfast. Replies went back by the same route. The Foreign Office contact was code-named, by the IRA, the "Mountain Climber."

Hunger-striking is, at least when pursued seriously, a psychological battle which pivots on the anticipation of that "moment of truth"—the immediate prospect of death. The buildup to that moment is marked by the two sides to the dispute maneuvering to heighten the psychological pressure on the other. And the groundwork for this was carefully laid for the 1980 hunger strike.

The Government, for its part, had made a last-minute "concession" on the clothing issue, announcing that prison uniforms were to be abolished. It transpired that they were simply being replaced by prison-issue "civilian-type" clothing, which was effectively another uniform, but it was presented as a concessionary move and followed by Humphrey Atkins's firm statement of unalterable "principle." The prisoners had, for their part, selected seven men to take part in the strike, the number seven having—as so often in Irish Republicanism—historical and political significance, the "Proclamation" of a Republic, with which the IRA had launched the rebellion of 1916, having been signed by seven. Six of the chosen prisoners—representative of the six counties of northern Ireland—were from the IRA, the seventh from the INLA. The Dark, inevitably, was the leader, standing down as commanding officer of the IRA in the Kesh in favor of Sands, who had been his deputy. Sands had volunteered for the hunger strike and had even told his parents he was going on it, but it was decided that he was needed for the leadership position.

As the fast progressed the Republicans escalated the pressure on the Government, three women in Armagh jail joining in on December 1 followed by another twenty-three prisoners in the Kesh on the 15th.

It had been decided that the Republican Movement as such would present the prisoners' demands as being for political status, but that the National H-Block Committee—conducting a broader-based campaign on the prisoners' behalf—would avoid the terminology, calling instead for the so-called five demands so as to give the Government some room to negotiate on a "reform" basis. The five rights demanded were: to wear their own clothes; to refrain from prison work; to have free association with other prisoners (a right implying freedom to be separate from other paramilitary groups); to organize recreation and leisure activity—with one letter, parcel and visit allowed per week; and to have remission lost, as a result of the blanket protest, restored. A suggestion that demands for the reform of the Diplock court system—the system of trial without jury and related dilutions of the rules of evidence—be included was vetoed by the external leadership as being too ambitious.

In the psychological battle with Government the Republicans suffered two critical weaknesses, although they were not appreciated by them at the time. The first was the frame of mind with which they launched it. Although hunger-striking to the death had a long tradition in the Movement, those epic fasts—like that of MacSwiney—were long buried in history. Even the Gaughan and Stagg deaths in the 1970s were, in a sense, remote to Republicanism in Ireland itself, because they had occurred in England. Hunger strikes which had taken place in the north—and there were many little-recorded ones—were more symbolic, aimed at gaining publicity for particular complaints with no real intention of going to the death. This led in 1980—despite the seriousness of the issue over which they were now hunger-striking—to a fatal tendency to see the fast as another such symbolic action. The attitude was reflected by what was to prove the second cardinal weakness of the 1980 hunger strike: the use of seven men fasting simultaneously. It made sense publicity-wise—a "mass" hunger strike sounds more dramatic. But in practical terms it was riddled with weaknesses. First of all, if the action was seriously intended, it meant that they were only as strong as the weakest of their number. It was also inevitable that there would be divisions between seven, each of them with their lives on the line, wondering if the others were prepared to go the distance. And, by necessarily having a leader in such a group, he would be subjected to additional pressure when that "moment of truth" did arrive, because he would be faced by not only his own death, but that of his comrades.

These factors were brought to a disastrous head for the Movement after the fast had run for fifty-three days, with the help of a brilliant finesse on the part of the authorities. The weak link in the seven—physically—turned out to be Sean McKenna, a twenty-six-year-old serving a twenty-five-year sentence for attempted murder and membership of the IRA. On December 18 McKenna became critically ill. The Dark was *au fait* with the Mountain Climber initiative and knew that a document was on its way from the Foreign Office in London, which might contain enough for a settlement. The ground rules under which he was operating were that no decision would be taken on the abandonment of the fast without consultation with Sands—who had taken over from him as officer commanding the IRA prisoners—who was being allowed in from his wing to see the hunger strikers in the prison hospital, and who was in continual contact with the outside leadership through channels which included a lawyer acting as a courier. But in the early evening the authorities struck, dramatically transferring McKenna to the Royal Victoria Hospital in Belfast "to die" and blocking frantic requests by Sands to see the hunger strikers again—cutting the Dark off from the outside world. In the belief that McKenna was on the verge of death, amidst angry argument between the other five and faced by the possibility that the Foreign Office document—at that moment in the hands of the courier, the Angel, and on its way from Aldegrove airport outside Belfast—offered a possible settlement, the Dark ordered an end to the hunger strike.

TWO

*"They were quite unlike the population of
any prison in England or Wales in their dan-
gerousness, their allegiance to a paramilitary
organization, their cohesiveness, their common
determination to escape and their resistance to the
efforts of the prison authorities to treat them as
ordinary criminals."*

—Report of an Inquiry by
HM Inspector of Prisons

The Angel stood in the corner of the room in the prison hospital, anxious not to get in the way. He could not see tears,
but he suspected the Dark was near crying. Bobby Sands, in a
chair next to the bed, was trying to comfort him, reading from
the Mountain Climber's statement brought in by the Angel
and repeating, reassuringly: "We can make something of it."
But then he got up and went over to the Angel and said: "It
wasn't what we wanted." The warder cut in and said: "OK,
you're finished . . ." And Sands was led away on his rounds of
the blocks, to break the news to the waiting prisoners.

By the time he arrived back in his own cell late that night he
was furious. The document was as "full of holes" as one of
the IRA leaders had said earlier in the Falls Road. It could
have been used as the basis for further negotiations, but it
was obvious to Sands that with the hunger strike over they
had nothing with which to negotiate.

A desperate exercise in damage limitation had already begun. By the time Sands got back to his cell a statement had been put out by Sinn Fein on his behalf—the Angel had brought a copy of it for his clearance—saying: "Dependent upon a sensible and responsible attitude from the British Government in implementing their proposals, the blanket men will make a positive response. We are satisfied that the implementation of these proposals meets the requirement of our five basic demands. Republican prisoners will not be wearing any form of prison uniform and will not be participating in any form of penal work." But Sands knew that only an unusually generous interpretation of the "proposals" by the Government would satisfy the five demands and that, on past form, would not be forthcoming.

The next day he started to send furious requests out to the Army Council, demanding to be allowed to restart the action immediately himself. Messages came back, ordering him to cool it; the Movement was not ready for another hunger strike. He was instructed to treat the ending of the first hunger strike as if there had been a settlement, to see what the authorities were willing to concede now that they were no longer having to act under "duress." But planning for the second strike began almost immediately.

After Christmas, belated moves were made by the authorities to avoid another confrontation. On the morning of January 5, during wing shifts—when the cells were hosed down—the prisoners were told that if they kept their cells clean this time they would be given furniture in twenty-four hours. But no mention was made of clothes and the prisoners ignored the gesture. Simultaneously some "comms" being smuggled out, dealing with planning for a second hunger strike, were intercepted by warders. They made it clear that the prisoners were in earnest.

Sands had already decided in outline how he was going to handle a new hunger strike. He had decided on four men, or five if the INLA prisoners were going to take part. He called for volunteers. The names poured in, although they were fewer this time than for the first hunger strike: it was clear to the prisoners that this time it would be a fight to the death. Sands already knew which prisoners he wanted; it had just been a question of waiting for them to submit their names, which they did.

The authorities, after the first abortive move, started another initiative. On Friday, January 9, the new "civilian-type" uniforms were brought into the prison. The prisoners had decided to wear them for visits, but nothing more. On the Sunday the Governor, Stanley Hilditch, saw Sands and the officers commanding the protest blocks, outlining to them a proposed step-by-step procedure by which they were going to bring about normalization. A wing from H5 would, on an experimental basis, move into a clean and furnished wing on the following Thursday. As the next step they would be issued, simultaneously, with their own clothes and prison clothes. The shift went ahead without any difficulties. Then Hilditch came in again to see Sands. In anticipation of a new hunger strike Sands had already stood down as commanding officer and the position had been taken over by a prisoner in the cell adjoining his, Brendan McFarlane—"Bik," to everyone who knew him. McFarlane scribbled a note that night to Gerry Adams—"Brownie"—describing what had happened.

To Brownie from Bik 15.1.81
Marcella [Sands] has no lights so this is forced upon me. Here goes, Sunshine. Marcella saw 'Rat' [Governor Hilditch] this afternoon for a five minute yarn—it was friendly, though cautious. Rat said that more time was needed for him to think on the next step (i.e. simultaneous issue of clothing) because, quote, 'the consequences and implications of this are great, serious and far-reaching'—he said we should therefore approach this aspect carefully and

slowly and asked for one week of a break in any moves to consider the situation. He also said he would stop further wing shifts to furnished cells just to freeze things for this one week. Marcella told him we were considering washing and informed him that as an indication of our good will and willingness and sincerity we had decided that either tomorrow or Saturday ten men from here and ten from H5 would wash, shave etc. This will now be held back till next Tuesday in keeping with AC [Army Council] directive to seek a principled settlement. The Brits may be stalling. We believe they wish to compromise us on the principle of clothes and, by a week's respite, they may gain some ground. However we feel that we could use the time to examine our position thoroughly, unless of course there are dangers which would dictate that we shouldn't stall and perhaps we don't see these yet. You can let us know your attitude on this. Marcella will comm you tomorrow in detail on today's developments. 'Rat' also said to Marcella that 'prison regime was not static and was indeed developing.' There ye are now! We feel that the best thing to do is to pause till next Thursday (we just decided this minute on Thursday as opposed to Tuesday. Sorry!) We should release a statement that morning as to what the crack is. Now if families of twenty men could be quietly informed on Wednesday evening to get clothes ready for Friday morning to be left in, that would be sound. Incidentally, Marcella told the 'Rat' that in the light of what he was saying we would give him a week's grace. Index [Fr. Toner, the prison chaplain] was in and also said we should go slowly and carefully on this and even suggested that maybe some men wearing prison sweaters wouldn't be too bad. HA! HA! Marcella will see Pennies [Danny Morrison] on special visit tomorrow and give him the heap. We will comm other blocks on situation, but if you feel that another AC job is necessary bang one in. Marcella is hoping to see the Block O/Cs tomorrow and will explain things then. I think that's all. So take yourself off, you horror picture. See you around. Take care and God Bless—Bik.

The delays were proving damaging to the prisoners. Morale had plummeted as it became apparent that the first hunger strike had resolved nothing. There was a steady drift of men abandoning the blanket protest and conforming. There were other problems as well, one of them being a prisoner, Michael Logue from Downpatrick, who was pressing to be allowed to go on his own hunger strike. Logue had been jailed for two and a half years in late 1976 for possession of incendiary bombs and armed robbery. The explosives charge had related to a fire-bomb attack on a drapery shop in Dromore, Co. Down, in April 1976, in which three people had been killed—a married couple and their daughter. When Logue was released in 1979 he had failed to report back to the IRA—effectively dropping out of the Movement. But in 1980 he had been arrested again and after interrogation had signed a "confession" to the 1976 killings. When the case came to trial he had pleaded not guilty, but was found guilty on three counts of manslaughter and sentenced to twenty years. He insisted that he was innocent of the killings and now wanted to go on hunger strike in protest, despite warnings that such individual protests at wrongful conviction never worked. For a while it looked like a repeat of the Meehan episode, but eventually he was persuaded to postpone it until the special status issue had been settled.

Outside the Kesh a sudden blow befell the prisoners' cause when Protestant gunmen made a bid on the life of Bernadette McAliskey, the spokeswoman and most outstanding personality in the National H-Block/Armagh Committee. The two main Protestant paramilitary groups—the huge Ulster Defense Association and the small, outlawed Ulster Volunteer Force—had been planning to kill her for weeks, scouting out possible lines of attack on her isolated home near Lough Neagh in Co. Tyrone. Unknown to the paramilitary groups, army intelligence had got wind of their plans and an under-cover patrol was keeping watch on the house from a small clump of trees nearby when, on Saturday, January 11, three gunmen from the UDA burst in, smashing the front door down with sledgehammers in conventional commando style. Bernadette's husband, Michael, tried to block them, throwing himself at the door, and they shot him four times. Then they ran into the bedroom where Bernadette was trying to hide her two-year-old son, Fintan. The lead gunman pulled the boy aside and emptied his 9 mm Browning pistol into Bernadette, six of the shots going straight through her, a seventh hitting her in the back of the head and passing through her body to emerge from her left leg. A second gunman fired another two shots into her with his .38 pistol. Bernadette, still conscious, pretended to be dead. The gunmen, satisfied their mission was accomplished, ran for their Avenger car waiting outside, only to be met at the door by the undercover army patrol. The gunmen surrendered without a fight. Incredibly, Bernadette and her husband survived.

> 19.1.81 To Liam Og [a Sinn Fein official] from Bik Comrade, enclosed a short note to Bernie. Hope to God she recovers. Stick a few cards along with the note from all of us . . .

She was the sixth H-Block activist to be shot in six months in what appeared to be a concerted effort by the UDA to intimi-date campaigners. Five days later the IRA responded in ruthless fashion, dispatching eight gunmen across the border from Co. Monaghan in an attack on Tynan Abbey, a battlemented Gothic pile and home of the former Speaker of the defunct Stormont parliament, Sir Norman Stronge. The "active service unit" blew in the door of the mansion with explosives. They rushed into the library and shot dead Sir Norman, aged eighty-six and holder of the Military Cross, and his son James, forty-eight—a former Unionist MP at Stormont—with one bullet each in the head. Then they set fire to the 239-year-old building with incendiary bombs. Police racing to the scene in armored Cortinas, after hearing the explosions, blocked the end of the abbey's mile-long drive. One of the getaway cars, a Lada hijacked earlier for the attack, crashed into it. The gunmen leaped out and opened fire on the officers in the car at point-blank range, but the shots were deflected by the armored glass. One of the gunmen tried to open a door of the Cortina to get at the officers, but the driver slammed the car into reverse. Out of reach the police began firing at the gunmen, who fled on foot across the fields of the 800-acre estate.

Local Protestants were incensed by the killing, blaming it partly on government security deficiencies in the border region. They sent a personal message to Humphrey Atkins—who counted himself a personal friend of Sir Norman—informing him he was not welcome at the funeral. A message of condolence was sent by the Queen.

Back in the Kesh the step-by-step attempt at a settlement was proceeding. The prisoners taking part in the experimental clean-up were finding it difficult to get used to their new "normality."

21.1.81 From Marcella [Sands]
Comrade, got the Big Efforts comm today and I also saw Angel briefly . . . bed's breaking my back, we're not used to such comforts . . . writing on a table is strange, sitting on a chair. Men saw themselves in the mirror last week for the first time in almost three years. It was frightening, especially for Rasputin, or I mean Bik . . .

The authorities were stalling again on the next step. On Friday, January 23 they had refused to issue the ninety-six prisoners now cooperating on an experimental basis with their own clothes. So the decision was taken to bust up the clean cells the following Monday. Over the weekend the leadership outside changed its mind and sent a message in to Sands, instructing him to postpone the action for twenty-four hours. But Sands could not get a message across to H5 fast enough to pass on the order, so he decided he would have to ignore it. The prisoners proceeded to smash up the cells on Monday night.

From Seanna [Officer Commanding] H5 28.1.81
. . . At about 9 o'clock the lads gave the furniture the message. About 9.30–10.00 the screws moved the lads from their own wing into a wing that was in the process of being cleaned. Shite all over walls, water over floors. They didn't allow them to walk over. Instead they grabbed them by the hair and run them over, kicking and punching the whole time. Sean McPeake from Bellaghy has a wooden leg. They tried to make him run, dragging by the hair and hooting etc. So Sean sat down on the floor and refused to get up. They got around him and gave him a rough kicking. The PO [principal officer] was the main man in beating him. They eventually had to drag him over. Eamonn Digney Andersonstown was tripped while running. He saw medic who told him he had fractured arm. Eddie Brophy took a heart attack and was given tablets. The lads were kept lying in a dirty, empty wing with no bedding or blankets. Just a skimpy towel round the waist until 11.30 this morning when the whole wing was moved to H6 . . .

From Marcella 28.1.81
Comrade, Firstly you may have been shocked by last night's events. Sorry if you're shattered, but comrade for once we got into mix-up in communication . . . Now here is the full crack; by the way I'm in [the dark] to write this and I'm

leaning on a poe [chamber pot]!! We moved at 9 P.M., wrecked the place, right, our reasons petty harassment and humiliation of men—similar to that which helped prompt the no wash protest three years ago. At ten P.M. the screws arrived. We halted and we were moved in twos from B wing to C wing. Now comrade, C wing has just been vacated by the wing that remain on no wash, the cells are bogging covered in excreta, also puddles of water on cell floors where the cleaners had begun work. Six men, T. Louden Unity Flats, M. Devlin Ardboe, Kieran McKenna S. Derry, B. Forman New Lodge, K. Lynch and Liam McCloskey Dungiven, they all were fired over a table and the cheeks of their behinds torn apart by the screws' hands. Comrade, this is sexual assault. The filthy cells in which we were left were in darkness and there was no water to drink, no beds, blankets, not even a bloody blanket. All we had was a towel. Comrade, there were govs. and POs in the block, but no one would come when we rang bells. Now we sat all night naked up until five minutes ago, before the bastards found it in themselves to give us blankets and mattresses. Now we didn't sleep, we were frozen etc. Big Gerry McNally took sick twice in the middle of the night, they wouldn't give him a blanket!! The whole 47 of us stick our names down for Gov. today, firstly six men went to doctor and said, we've no water, we've no clothing or beds, we've been fired into dirty cells which we did not mess, what are you going to do about it? He said he'd see but it was not a medical matter. We got the hold of a PO at 10 A.M. this morning and he issued us with 'half a fucking blanket each.' Bik told him they were torturing us for furniture being broke. We also at 10 A.M. got water. We saw Gov. at 11 A.M. every man asked for board form [complaint form] to get signer [lawyer] to see governor and Northern Ireland Office for breach of prison rules. We may have chance of a signer. Play this up, of court case over torture. To rub it in they put our dinner out, left it sitting for half an hour, then gave us it freezing cold. The boys are exhausted, the wing's like a morgue—all asleep. Bik, me and the lad waiting on the bad reports coming in from H5, expecting more trouble here. Remember the main point: they put us back on no wash again by putting us in filthy cells to try and sicken us. Only we [If we had not] moved on court issue we'd have been sitting fuckin' foundered till tonight. Man near collapsed here with cold and exhaustion. Sorry about the balls up, but we'd have had a bigger one if we had have moved. Okay comrade, two dales [radios to be smuggled in] for Elephant Friday!! I'm away for a sleep, think I'm sleeping now! Marcella.

Preparations for the hunger strike had been continuing all the while. Sands had finally decided to start it with three IRA men, including himself, and one INLA representative. He was planning to choose twelve men in all and anticipated two women from Armagh jail would join them. On Sunday the 25th the Army Council had sent in formal comms to the two other IRA prisoners chosen, Frank Hughes and Raymond McCreesh, asking for confirmation that they had volunteered and were prepared to follow it to their deaths if necessary. On Friday the 30th both men, who shared a cell, sent their formal replies in the same wording: "Yes, I am prepared to see it through." The following day McFarlane received a smuggled comm from the officer commanding the INLA in the prison, Patsy O'Hara, confirming that he would be their first man on.

Among the prisoners in general, Monday night's bust-up of the cells brought home what was happening—that they were heading for a second hunger strike, which many had thought would never take place. Frantic efforts began to prepare the ground, including another letter-writing campaign, messages going out for the names and addresses of newspaper columnists, professors, universities, trade unions, politicians, filmmakers—even the American hostages being held in Iran, if some way could be found of getting letters to them through Republican contacts with the Khomeini regime.

But if the prisoners were preparing for another hunger strike with determination, the IRA Army Council was viewing the prospect with some trepidation and sent in a last, eleventh-hour appeal to them to consider what they were doing, stressing the possible consequences and stipulating that this time there would be no holding back on military operations outside, as had been done during the first hunger strike for propaganda purposes.

31.1.81 To Army Council
Comrade, we received your comm (dated 30.1.81). We have listened carefully to what you have said and we recognize and accept the spirit in which it was wrote, likewise in view of the situation we do not deny you or criticize your extreme cautiousness. But, however distressing it may be, we regret that our decision to hunger strike remains the same and we reconfirm this decision now with the same vigor and determination. We fully accept and in full knowledge of what it 'may' entail, the right of the army to carry on unlimited operations in pursuance of the Liberation struggle and without handicap or hindrance. We accept the tragic consequences that most certainly await us and the overshadowing fact that death may not secure a principled settlement. So comrades, in all respects we recognize and respect your problems. We realize the struggle on the outside must also continue. We hope that you accept that the struggle in H-Blocks, being part of the overall struggle, must also go on in unison. We reconfirm and pledge 'our' full confidence and support to you and march on with you to the Irish Socialist Republic.

From Marcella 31.1.81
Comrade, find enclosed confirmation of hunger strike.
We need that hunger strike statement that fast comrade.
The delay is damaging us, i.e. men will think we're telling
lies. Lost a half a dozen comrades in the blocks yesterday
[conforming]. Even a hunger strike won't hold some, for
some it means three months' remission . . .

On Thursday, February 5 the announcement was finally
made. The second hunger strike would start on March 1—
the fifth anniversary of the date on which the Government
had started phasing out special category status. In the House
of Commons Atkins declared: "The principles by which the
Government has stood in the face of the protests at the Maze
and Armagh prisons still stand. It will not concede that it
should now establish within the normal Northern Ireland
prison regime a special set of conditions for particular groups
of prisoners." A few days later word was leaked by Sinn Fein
that the prisoners would be going on hunger strike one by one
and that the leader this time would be Sands.

For the Republican prisoners of Long Kesh the choice of Sands
as commanding officer was an instance of the moment producing the man. It was not as if he were a natural leader.
Superficially he was a fairly ordinary prisoner.

From Marcella
Comrade, here goes with all my details. I'm 27 on 9 March
coming (swear to God) i.e. 9.3.54. Born in Belfast. Went
to Stella Morris Primary School and secondary school
(Rathcoole). Also attended Newtonabbey Tech for about
9 months. Worked as apprentice coach builder for about
three years or more. Was in Union (whichever one that
comes under). Now was also fantastic sports man. Ha!!
Well, when I was young I was very much involved in soccer,

athletics, swimming and about ten thousand other sports.
Think there's merit in that? Was not really in any Gaelic
football club. By the way, I used to run for Willowfield
Temperance Harriers (real black [Protestant] place) in all
the leading races in the north for boys; couldn't run fast
enough on the two occasions I was snared ya!! (Take a
redner [blush] says you) . . . I was caught the first time in
October 1972 in Lisburn and genuinely on the run. I was
then 18 and very naïve. Got bad time in [police] barracks
and I did sign a statement which was basic (i.e. not bad).
Was convicted by a Judge Higgins late March, early April
'73, to five years for possession of 4 shorts [pistols] which
were stored in a place I was staying (they weren't in a good
state which is why I got a light sentence). The woman of the
house sold her soul for £300 and shot to England leaving
the Brits in the house to wait etc. (you crying?). Also was
done with two or three petty robberies which were fashionable in them days. I refused to recognize [the court] etc.
You should get Judge's summing up that was in the paper,
i.e., 'young man never in trouble, no criminal record, from
good family'—okay, take the point? Now I was released
on 13.4.76. Hold on, forgot to mention I was going with
a girl before I got lifted and was going to get married. She
was pregnant, I got married in gaol on remand, it's not
a well-known fact. Anyway, comrade, as I said I got out
13.4.76 and lived in Twinbrook with wife and child and
was snared again on 14.10.76, six months later, outside
a furniture showroom in Dunmuray in which were four
ticking bombs. You'll get all the crack on that somewhere,
it was pretty fierce—two or three comrades were shot, I
was caught in a car with three others and a gun. Anyway I was took eventually to Castlereagh [interrogation
centre] and got very bad time, but gave (this time) only
name, address and said I was looking for a job. Anyway,
I didn't sign and at the end of 11 months of remand (four

of which were in H-Block) I got sentenced to 14 years for possession with intent. Refused to recognize [the court]. We beat stack of bomb charges 'cause we'd kept quiet. Four of us got 84 years between us for one gun. You should see signer [lawyer] and he'll get you 10 page statement I wrote on the six days we spent in Castlereagh. [Fr.] Faul might have it also. The judge on that occasion was 'Watt.' The trial, true to form, was a farce etc.!! There was a ruckus after we were sentenced which we didn't start, screws got into us, three of us got boards [sent to punishment block] and six months loss of remission. I spent first 22 days of sentence on boards in Crum[lin Road jail]. 15 days I spent totally naked in front of hundreds of crims [ordinary criminals]. I was subjected to No. 1 starvation diets [bread and water] every three days etc.! Must have wrote you articles on that at one time. The blanket men down there at that time used to get 3 days of every two weeks, we got 15 days in a row (I'll write you an article on this again 'cause it was really bad). Anyway I came on the blanket late Sept. '77 and began writing articles and stuff right away and I never really received any bad beating. But in Jan. '79 I was really bad with flu and was carried out to hospital on a stretcher. They tossed me in the air while on it, hit me and dropped me naked on the snow and threw me into the back of a van like a bag of rags. I was forcibly bathed the same night. (That was the third forced bath I got I think.) Anyway sagarts [priests]: I'm friendly with [Frs] Faul, Reed and Mahon, ha!! Not much use that, is it? The sagarts in Twinbrook, you know them. Stay clear there—i.e. Rogan. If he weighs in I'll ask him to leave, for he'd say things that weren't OK. I've a cousin who is a nun and who visits me. Also am friendly with other nuns. She's dead sound, i.e. passively radical ha!! I've no criminal record. I'm great admirer of your dog and Ethna Carberry [an Irish poetess]. Back to wife: I'm now separated (that's the way it goes) but I will see her during the hunger strike. She's in England. Bear this in mind comrade. Make it a point to get word to her that I want a visit, or she will be dangerous loose end for the press, okay. See my ma on that. You should know that that is my principal excuse for signer: she asked for a separation, I agreed and it was done in court. My wee lad is eight in May. Anyway for what it's worth I'm well known in Twinbrook, Andersonstown, Short Strand, Bawnmore, Unity Flats and the Markets. I've done roughly 8 years in gaol. 3 and a half in cages, 4 and a half this time. I spent nine consecutive Xmas's [inside]. My birthday will fall in later stages of hunger strike no matter. In regard to my family: My mother and father are like all mothers and fathers, very vulnerable to the press. They won't be of use for interviewing, okay? They'd get murdered, so look after them. I've a sister who is married. 'Marcella' is her name, so now you know who that [his penname] came from. She, if groomed, might be sound okay? Cara [friend], she's 26. I've a brother who plays traditional music. He's about 20 . . . I've another sister who is 21 and single. She's in Dundalk [south of the border—on the run]. Fire bombs went off in her pocket. She can't come up here, but if again groomed would do down there. She's been there for 3 years, okay. I haven't seen her in over three years. Because of her (and I'm not trying to be smart or stupid or mimic anyone) I wanted buried down there. To be honest I think I'm going to die and again I'm not playing at bravado or egotism. You understand, I'm sure. Anyway I've relatives in USA and England (see my ma), probably other countries too, because I've lost touch. My wife lost a child the second time I came in. I was in two and a half months when it occurred. I got hospital parole in the High Court, the first person to get it I believe, and I of course honoured it . . . With the exception of a broken heart I'm healthy (I think). Have been interrogated in Castlereagh,

Crumlin Road, detention center, Black Road, Musgrave billet, Dunmurray Bks, Lisburn Rd and Fort Monagh. The latter being the only one where I wasn't assaulted. I'm fairly fluent in Gaelige (big head). Well that's about the heap, comrade . . . Marcella.

He was born in Rathcoole, in North Belfast, and spent his formative years in nearby Abbot's Cross, part of the predominantly Protestant suburb of Newtonabbey. His parents, John—a Post Office worker—and Rosaleen, were a shy couple who kept very much to themselves, so it was not well known in the neighborhood that they were Catholics. But when one of the neighbors did discover it she began a vicious campaign against Rosaleen Sands—simply by mimicking her. When Mrs. Sands went to hang her washing out, the neighbor did the same, hanging similar pieces of laundry. If she cleaned the windows, there the neighbor was, doing it herself. And from time to time the neighbor would start hammering on her wall. Mrs. Sands broke under the strain and went to a doctor, who advised her husband that he would either have to take the neighbor to court, or move. They moved, to Doonbeg Drive in Rathcoole—another predominantly Protestant area—when Bobby was seven years old.

He was a stubborn child and protective of his two sisters, as well as of his mother's peace of mind. He left school at the age of fifteen and joined a coach-building firm in a nearby industrial estate as an apprentice. The "Troubles" were just beginning. Their street had six Catholic families in it. One day the Ulster Defense Association (UDA), the Protestant paramilitary group which was later to make the botched attempt to kill Bernadette McAliskey, staged a march down it. The Sands family kept their lights out, Bobby sitting in vigil on the top of the stairs, clutching a carving knife, his sister Marcella beside him with a pot of pepper. Another day he was coming home when two men called to him for a light and, when he stopped, one lunged with a knife, cutting him. It made a flesh wound and he went to great lengths to make sure his mother did not find out, getting Marcella to wash his clothes and a friend, with some knowledge of first aid, to patch him up. His experience as a cross-country runner began to be of use to him, as he ran for his life to escape local Protestant gangs. The intimidation steadily worsened. Youths began to gather outside the Catholic houses, chanting "Taigs out." A story circulated that a woman living around the corner, working for the UDA, was touring the area with young Protestant couples, inviting them to choose Catholic houses for occupation. Bobby's younger sister, Bernadette, saw the woman in front of their house with a young couple. The next week a rubbish bin came flying through their living-room window. It was their notice; new tenants had been found.

His mother went down to the Housing Executive—the local housing authority—the next day with the story and a plea for another home. The answer was indicative of the times: find an empty one and move right on in. So that was what they did, moving to Twinbrook, a Catholic estate on the outskirts of West Belfast, in June 1972. It was like moving to another world. Shortly afterwards Sands joined the IRA.

Serving his first five-year sentence as a special category prisoner, Sands found himself in compound number 11—Cage 11. And that was important, because shortly afterwards the officer commanding the Belfast Brigade of the IRA, Gerry Adams, was picked up by the security forces and interned in the compounds. Adams was promptly made officer commanding Cage 11.

The Cage quickly gained a reputation among the other Republican prisoners as a bunch of renegades. The IRA was still, in those days, conservative—the "rosary beads wrapped around a .303 brigade." Cage 10 next door, nicknamed "Sandhurst" because of their passion for parades and military discipline, had even staged a book-burning ceremony, destroying copies of such books as *Das Kapital,* the *Communist Manifesto* and *Thoughts of Mao* as subversive and alien influences. At one stage battalion staff—most of them in Cage 10—even considered standing down Cage 11, after word spread that they had conducted a series of lectures entitled "Celtic Communism," a Marxist analysis of early Celtic society.

It was a young crowd in Cage 11. Adams, who was himself only twenty-four, used to call them "the childer with a Park Drive behind their ears"—young men with old heads on their shoulders, Park Drives being a particularly noxious cigarette favored by old men in the Catholic ghettos. But it was an exciting group to be in, its members regularly cramming themselves, up to thirty at a time, into a small wooden "study hut" for lectures which usually turned into heated debating sessions.

Sands, at nineteen, was made officer commanding one of the three huts in the Cage and subsequently training officer. He showed himself to be a prolific as well as politicized writer. He read voraciously—his favorites including Frantz Fanon, Camilo Torres, Che Guevara, Amilcar Cabral, George Jackson and, of Irish writers, Connolly, Pearse and Mellows—keeping a fast-growing pile of exercise books full of political analyses, quotations and notes. He was planning to write a book with it all, but they were destroyed in 1974 when the IRA in the compounds burnt their huts in a dispute with the administration over rights and privileges.

Despite the scornful attitude shown towards the Old Guard among the prisoners, Sands was committed to the point of being overbearing where the Movement and politics were concerned. If he lent another prisoner a book he was likely to cross-examine him when it was returned and, if not satisfied that he had absorbed the contents, insist on his reading it again. He was immensely irritated by the "watch-the-dots"— prisoners so absorbed by television that they would watch with rapt attention even the dwindling dot as the set was turned off at the end of broadcasting. Always conscious of his own dignity, he was hammer direct in argument, quick-tempered, loath to concede a point and intolerant of others he felt were not taking issues as seriously as he did. But for all that he was a talented young man who could not only write striking poetry and speak increasingly fluent Gaelic but could play the guitar—"Bobby Magee" was a favorite—bodhran drum, tin whistle and banjo. And on the soccer field he was surprisingly good—for a poet, at least. A natural tactician.

There was a widespread belief at the time, both inside and outside the prison, that the "Troubles" were moving towards an end—that the British were looking for a withdrawal and it was only a matter of time before they went. Sands did not believe it. But to the more hopeful the signs seemed to be there, in the frustration of British attempts to normalize the Province: there was the collapse of Sunningdale—a scheme hatched by the British and Irish governments, providing for an All-Ireland representative assembly and joint law-enforcement agencies and judicial system—in the face of a Loyalist strike in 1974; there were ceasefires and secret talks between the IRA leadership and senior civil servants and, so it was said, there was a rundown of industry which showed the "Brits" were withdrawing their imperial interests. But in 1975 cranes were busy on the far side of the prison complex, hauling huge building blocks, and one day Sands grabbed a young teenager, Jake Jackson, saying passionately: "Come here, see that fucking wall? Do you see those cranes? Do you know what they're building? I don't know, but I'll take an educated guess, they're phasing out status and that's where we're going."

He was right, of course, generally as well as specifically. Instead of pulling out, Britain dug in even deeper, reimposing direct rule after a brief experiment in power-sharing and devising the three-pronged strategy—Ulsterization, normalization and criminalization—which found one form of physical expression in the building of the H-Blocks. And in 1977 Sands fulfilled his own prediction with his arrival in the H-Blocks, a few months after young Jake Jackson.

He had enjoyed only six months of exuberant freedom, a time when he had a considerable impact on the Twinbrook Estate where his parents lived and where he now set up house with his young wife, Geraldine, and their son, Gerard. He threw himself into community work with the almost frenetic energy which distinguished him, joining the local tenants' association and persuading taxi services to run in the area; getting a local branch of Sinn Fein going; launching his own Republican newsletter, *Liberty*, which he sold around the estate; and starting social and cultural evenings in the local parochial hall.

Apart from the overt political activities, Sands was of course still involved in the covert operations of the IRA, heading a newly formed Twinbrook active service unit. They had outside help, from other longer-established units, for the attack on the Balmoral Furnishing Company, a double-story sales room at Dunmurray near Twinbrook, on the outskirts of Belfast. Nine volunteers were involved, including one girl. It was a straightforward "commercial bombing." They drove in through the front gate, held up the security man who came to question them and marched him into the store at gunpoint. All the staff and customers were rounded up and taken into the basement, where they were ordered to lie on the floor while the bombs were planted upstairs. In the company's offices, across from the showroom, staff realized what was happening and telephoned the police. One of the staff moved his car across the access road. The active service unit ran out of the showroom to find their getaway blocked and military police down the road, heading towards them. They split up and ran in all directions as the bombs began to explode. The military police opened fire, wounding two of them. Sands and three others, none of whom was hit, jumped into a parked car where they were all arrested. They denied any knowledge of the bombing, claiming they had simply taken refuge from the shooting—Sands insisting he was in the area looking for a job. But a gun was found in the car and, after the Crown had failed to prove their connection with the bombs, they were all convicted of "possessing" the firearm, each getting fourteen-year sentences.

His arrest wrecked Sands's marriage. Geraldine did not share her husband's dedication to the cause and when she had a premature delivery shortly afterwards—losing the baby—she blamed it on the trauma of his arrest and the subsequent army raid, which half wrecked the house.

Back in the Kesh, in the H-Blocks, Sands became "public relations officer"—effectively secretary to the Dark, with whom he shared a cell—taking responsibility for communications both between the blocks and with the outside. The Dark himself was not one for writing. In some ways Sands was fussy about his duties, almost bureaucratic, refusing to hand on tidbits of gossip until they had been cleared for dissemination by the Dark. And he still had that old disputatious strain. The argument over what was the capital of Cambodia was particularly memorable . . . he had got it wrong, but it took ages to persuade him. But the humor was always there, as when they disagreed over whether some birds in the distance were sandpipers or wagtails.

"They're sandpipers," said Sands.

"How d'ya know?"

"Stands to reason, there's a river on the other side of that wall."

"How d'ya know there's a river on the other side of the wall?"

"Because those are sandpipers there."

There was the all-day argument about the height of the cell doors: Sands said 6 feet 3 inches, because screws were on average 6 feet 2 inches tall, he said, so it stood to reason they would have given them an inch clearance. It was eventually proved to him that it was 6 feet because the flyleaf of the Bible gave its own exact dimensions and the door was carefully measured with it. At which Sands crowed: "How can you believe the Bible?"

And then there was the debate over what flag should be chosen when the IRA finally established the new workers' republic. One suggested it should incorporate a hammer, another an axe; Sands declared it should be green, white and gold with a lunch box in the middle to represent the workers. It all helped to pass the time.

Despite the idiosyncracies he was again a fairly popular figure, busying himself late into the night writing articles—under the pen name "Marcella" in tribute to his sister—to be smuggled out for use in the Sinn Fein newspaper, *Republican News,* and experimenting with his poetry. He was teaching himself as he went along and his poems were often imitative—of Oscar Wilde's *Ballad of Reading Gaol,* among other works—and his prose marked by overstatement. But it was still powerful. Rehearsing his newly completed stanzas down the wing, he often stunned the other prisoners with the strength of his imagery. He had a talent as well for one of the most popular forms of entertainment in the blocks, "telling" books. The more articulate among them would take turns recounting a book—sometimes a film—which they remembered. Sands, with an immense imagination, care for detail and apparently exhaustive memory, made a deep impression with a blockbuster, Leon Uris's Irish novel *Trinity,* which took him several nights to relate. He also made an impression with an account of nineteenth-century coal-mining life in Wales—the forces of the state being used by the coal magnates to stamp out worker organization—and another about Red Indians fighting for their traditional way of life in the face of an advancing tide of land- and money-hungry palefaces. Another, called *Jet*—about the freewheeling life of a hippie—had such an impact on his listeners that he had to do *Jet II*. Several were to make vain efforts after their release from prison to find a copy of the original. There were suspicions that he made a lot of it up, Republican values making appearances in the most unexpected places . . .

He was also writing music, with the help of the most talented musician in H3, Brendan McFarlane, who shared a cell next to Sands with baby-faced Jake Jackson.

McFarlane was an extraordinary character in his own right. Born in Belfast in 1951, he did well at school, where he got the name "Bic" from a popular brand of biscuits, McFarlane's—"Bic" developing into "Bik" as he grew older. He went on to study for the priesthood and was in the final year at a seminary in Wales when the "Troubles" broke in northern Ireland. After much agonizing he abandoned his calling and went to join up with the IRA. He married, but the marriage broke up, and then he was jailed for the bombing of a Protestant bar in Belfast's Shankill district. The bar, the Bayardo, was a haunt of the Ulster Volunteer Force—a small Protestant paramilitary group which specialized in random sectarian killings—and the attack was in retaliation for a previous UVF gun attack on a Catholic bar in the Ardoyne area of Belfast. Five people died in the Bayardo blast, which made McFarlane a sectarian mass murderer . . . or at least that was the tag which could easily be attached to him by a hostile press. This was why he was never chosen for a hunger strike—he was potentially a one-man public relations disaster.

McFarlane inevitably identified with Camilo Torres, the Latin American revolutionary priest killed in Colombia in 1966, who had asserted that he had "taken off his cassock to be more truly a priest." McFarlane was well steeped in the theology of liberation which emerged in the wake of the Second Vatican Council and remained a devout Catholic. Every morning in the H-Blocks he would go through the same routine, pulling his mattress against the wall and opening his Good News Bible—given to him by a woman on the prison's Board of Visitors—to Psalms 51, 52 and 103 . . . "Let me hear the sounds of joy and gladness; and though you have crushed me and broken me, I will be happy once again."

He was a stocky and hirsute man, nearly 6 feet tall, and good-looking, although a youthful accident—he had been hit in the left eye by a hurling stick and had scar tissue and trouble with an inward-growing eyelash—gave him a hooded look. Behind it was a surprisingly gentlemanly character who was highly regarded by the other prisoners; one who liked being liked too much to happily accept command positions, although he had been Officer Commanding the Crumlin Road jail during his remand.

It was an ideal combination, Sands and McFarlane in their adjoining cells. Sands shared his now with Malachy Carey and McFarlane with Jackson. There was a constant flow of chafing and practical joking between them.

To Liam Og from Bik 4.2.81
. . . Enclosed you will discover a letter to one Jacqueline Mason from Malachy. It is in reply to a 'letter' he received from her. Under no circumstances must you deliver that letter. The Jacqueline Mason who wrote to him is in this cell. I want you to reply to the letter, or one of the girls in the office—smother it in scent and send it through the censor. You should have heard him when he received the letter from 'her.' He's crazy. Anyway, can you please help us out in our devilish scheme? It's right up your street, comrade . . .

Liam Og from Bik 5.2.81
. . . By the way Charlie [Sands] is well into poetry—he read one out last night and wrecked the wing. A work of art, though I'll be cutting it to ribbons when I hear it the

second time. Daren't let him know I actually appreciate his stuff. Sin e. Good night and God bless. Bik.

On Thursday, February 5 the new hunger strike was announced in a statement from the prisoners, saying they had abandoned the previous fast because they had been "morally blackmailed" and demanding of the Catholic Church and politicians: "What did your recommended ending of the last hunger strike gain for us? Where is the peace in the prisons which, like a promise, was held before dying men's eyes?" In the House of Commons Humphrey Atkins replied that "the Government will not surrender control of what goes on in the prisons to a particular group of prisoners. It will not concede the demand for political status, or recognize that murder and violence are less culpable because they are claimed to be committed for political motives."

The prison staff were showing no let-up in the aftermath of the cell bust-up on January 27. A steady stream of comms went out, detailing both fights on the wings and the disappearance of more prisoners to the conforming blocks.

Liam Og 5.2.81 8 P.M.
... A few points here that occurred today. During a cell search in the other wing Brendan McClenaghan (Ardoyne) was battered over the mirror—he was punched in the kidneys and kicked on the legs. His head was also battered off a concrete wall ...

Liam Og 6.2.81
Comrade, one man put the gear [prison uniform] on yesterday, Hugh Malone Lower Falls, and with Tommy Gorman out [released] today that leaves us with 125 in this block. This morning when the screws were collecting the breakfast dishes one screw went into the cell as Tommy was lying on his mattress and gave him a pretty bad beating.

He was pulled out of the bed by the hair, punched and kicked. He was bruised on the back and quite a bit of hair pulled out. He made a complaint to the Principal Officer and had the notes marked by the doctor. He should see you later today so you should be in the complete picture then. This is just in case he was held back until this afternoon. Slan leat comrade. H4, 10 A.M.

In the early hours of Friday morning, February 6, on the side of a mountain in the Antrim hills north of Belfast two hooded men opened the back of a van, its rear windows masked by black polythene. Five journalists stumbled out and looked around them. In the distance below they could see the lights of the town of Ballymena. It was cold, the wind sweeping across the exposed hillside as they were led, stumbling, through the heather before hearing a familiarly bellicose voice in the distance. They came into a clearing to find a bizarre scene: 500 men standing under a flapping Union Jack, being addressed by the huge figure of the Reverend Ian Paisley, Member of Parliament, Member of the European Parliament and leader of the second largest Loyalist party in the country. A whistle blew and the 500 men, in rows of ten, raised their right arms, brandishing pieces of paper above their heads. They were firearms certificates. Another whistle and arms were lowered. "Big Ian" led the journalists on a tour of inspection of his "troops" and then back to the blacked-out van. Then he launched into a tirade. The British and Irish governments were conspiring in secret towards Irish reunification and these 500 men were a token of the thousands "prepared to defend their province and their rights in exactly the same way as Lord Carson and the Ulster Volunteer Force," he declared in his booming voice. "We will shortly challenge the Government to interfere with us and our province if they dare and we will with equanimity await the result. We will do this regardless of the consequences of all personal loss or of all inconvenience. They may tell us if they like that that is treason. It is not for men who have such stake as we have to trouble about the costs."

The performance brought a new dimension to the ancient art of saber rattling. Reminiscent of the fabled exercise in military futility of the Grand Old Duke of York, it had on this occasion more to do with politics than military matters. Paisley was launching a new bid to become undisputed leader of Ireland's Protestants and was trying to do so by assuming the mantle of one of the most famous political figures in Irish history, Sir Edward, later Lord, Carson.

Carson, a brilliant barrister, was the man who destroyed Oscar Wilde in the witness box during the famous criminal libel case which led to the poet's incarceration and the writing of *The Ballad of Reading Gaol*. Carson was also a leading light in the Conservative Party at the turn of the century. In 1912 he launched the "Ulster Covenant," a petition signed by 400,000 men protesting against the inclusion of the Protestant north in government proposals to grant Home Rule to Ireland. He established a 100,000-strong Protestant militia, the Ulster Volunteer Force—"Carson's Army"—which created fears of civil war, leading to the Government's capitulation on the Home Rule issue and eventual partition. Paisley, whose father, a Baptist Minister, had signed the Ulster Covenant, was brought up in the Evangelical tradition. Ordained a Minister in 1946, he quickly established a reputation for himself in the mission halls of Belfast—once dubbed "a city of religious night clubs"—as a scourge of Roman Catholicism, of the "Whore of Rome" as he was wont to refer to the Pope. With the explosion of the Civil Rights movement in 1968 he threw himself into the political arena. Identifying with the Protestant working class, he established himself as an alternative to the Loyalist establishments of the time—the dominant and monolithic Ulster Unionist Party, the masonic-style Orange Order and the majority Presbyterian Church—setting up his own Democratic Unionist Party, Independent Orange Order and Free Presbyterian Church. A mesmerizing orator, "Big Ian" combined an awesome bigotry with a paradoxical sense of humor and shrewd political sense. Elected to Stormont in 1969 in what was known as the "revolt of the bucket carriers," he had gone on to take seats at both Westminster and the European Parliament in Strasbourg, becoming the single most important Protestant politician in the north. But he had never quite realized his ambition of overtaking the "Official" Unionist Party to become undisputed leader of Ulster's Protestants and was always on the lookout for the opportunity to do so. Now he believed he had found it.

In the closing stages of the 1980 hunger strike, in early December, Mrs. Thatcher had traveled to Dublin with her Foreign Minister and Chancellor of the Exchequer—the most high-powered ministerial team ever to take part in an Anglo-Irish summit. The Irish Prime Minister, Charles Haughey, ignoring Mrs. Thatcher's passionate devotion to the unity of the United Kingdom, had persuaded himself that he was about to win a glorious place in the history books by bringing about a settlement of the Irish question. At the other end of the Irish political spectrum Paisley decided that for once he agreed with the Irish leader. Seizing on a section of the joint communiqué issued by the two Prime Ministers—which announced the establishment of joint working parties to study "the totality of relationships between the two islands"—Paisley declared it was a plot for reunification. And so on the Antrim mountainside he collected his latter-day version of Carson's Army and announced his plans to fight the threatened destruction of Irish Protestantism. His voice reverberating in the back of the blacked-out van, he told the shivering journalists: "Just as in the past, at a parallel time of imminent constitutional danger, the men of Ulster pledged, organized and prepared themselves to resist to the death any attempt to hand them over to their enemies then, so at this time of equal danger the men of Ulster are preparing to resist and destroy the process of ongoing all-Ireland integration intended to flow from the Dublin summit. Before you tonight you see a token of that preparation."

In Long Kesh life went on as usual for the men who had committed themselves to the cause of all-Ireland integration.

Liam Og from Bik 7.2.81
... This morning more than 33 men were beaten during a wing shift—all were beaten twice while being forced over the mirror. S. Finucane has bruises on his legs. He is the only man who is marked ...

Liam Og from Bik 8.2.81
Comrade, enclosed are a few wee items for everywhere. Just see that they are delivered or I'll kick you to death. Just a quick comment on events in this block since last week's. They have (the screws that is) been harassing us pretty constantly. Keeping us waiting for visits for refusing to give [identity] number. Our people are waiting for an hour or so down at those visits. The grub has been receiving the good old ration treatment. There has been a marked cut down since arriving here. Cell searches are on a daily average three per day and any food (bread) left in the cell is confiscated. Bloody annoying business altogether. That's about the heap ...

14.2.80 From PRO H3 1.30 P.M.
A chara, This morning at approx. 11 A.M. as Liam Ferguson from Co. Fermanagh was returning from a visit the wing class officer and another screw hit him roughly 7 times across the face because his trousers were ripped at the crutch, as everyone in the wing did last Sunday.

Sands, meanwhile, was worrying about his parents. They seemed cynical about the planned hunger strike and Mrs. Sands in particular was in a highly emotional state about it all. It was beginning to look as if he would not be able to depend on them to back him. He tried to take his mind off his worries by busying himself with "Mrs. Dale."

Mrs. Dale was the code word in the blocks for a radio, *Mrs. Dale's Diary* being a popular BBC soap opera. They were tiny crystal sets, built into plastic medicinal tubes, which were smuggled into the prison in the traditional way, up the rectum. A wire to the window acted as an aerial and another to the heating pipes was the earth. The Kesh was only a few thousand yards from the BBC's local transmitting aerial and the sets easily picked up the fourth—current affairs—channel, Radio Ulster. They found that by manipulating the crystal set aerial—putting it in their mouths was one way—they could get other stations as well. They tried to keep two in their wing, one a spare in case a prisoner carrying one was taken to the punishment block, or there was a breakdown. Sometimes they had as many as five. Sands proved adept at mending them. They had to be carried with everything else of course, up the backside, in case of cell searches. But that did not discourage ambitions for bigger things.

Liam Og from Marcella 15.2.81
. . . I got Mrs. Dale to talk to me you know, after five or six operations. This is the 'six million dollar Mrs. Dale' I ask you!! I made it with the old ones and spare parts. It's in four or five bits. We wrap it up like a fish supper. Reckon if I'd had worked on it a bit more I could have phoned you with it (Big Head).

Liam Og from Bik 17.2.81
. . . Re the recording device—well if you let me know exactly what size it is I'll be able to tell you whether we can

hold it or not. Also re the statement you want Charlie to record. Do you intend to send us in a prepared statement or do you want us to do one ourselves? Let me know as soon as possible. Just while we are on the topic of technology, do you reckon there is a chance of boxing off a miniature two-way receiver, might as well go the whole way to MI 90 while we are at it . . . By the way Charlie, Teapot and Hector are exercising their vocal chords for recording. Sounds like Carrick House [a local doss house] . . .

Planning for the hunger strike in Armagh women's jail was running into problems. The Republican women in Armagh were passionately committed to the cause: at the end of the 1980 action their three hunger strikers had been so skeptical of a "settlement" that they had refused to come off their fast, only agreeing to do so twenty-four hours after the men in the Kesh, after a courier had been sent in to persuade them. But there were only thirty-two IRA prisoners in Armagh and a number of them were unsuitable for physical and other reasons, so they were having difficulty finding candidates. Two of the girls who had taken part in the first strike had been ruled out, together with a third volunteer who had changed her mind. Another volunteer was considered too underweight. And then another girl changed her mind, leaving the officer commanding the prison, Sile Darragh, making a passionate plea to be allowed on hunger strike herself. Sile, twenty-three years old and doing five years for membership of the IRA, herself weighed in at little more than eight stone.

Liam Og from Armagh [women's prison] 18.2.81
Comrade, what I am about to tell you may come as no surprise. Lynn O'Connell has also reconsidered her decision. I talked to her this afternoon and she told me that she felt she could carry on the hunger strike, but tonight she came to tell me that she is not confident now and

wants to withdraw. Now I have something more to say on Armagh's position. I think I know what the initial reaction is going to be, but please hear me out comrade. I propose that I represent Armagh on the hunger strike. Now I may be wrong, but I think the first thought that comes into your head may be that I am reacting to emotionalism because of what has happened over the past week, but I assure you that is not the case. I have been thinking along those lines I admit for the past few days, but my decision is neither rash nor light. I have thought of all the factors involved and my own position and believe as regards our Movement. I firmly believe that no matter what Silver [Fr. Murphy, deputy prison chaplain] said on the matter, Armagh must take a position on this hunger strike. For Armagh to pull out now is already defeating our Movement who have committed themselves to standing by us in our hunger strike decision and have already declared that Armagh will embark. If there is no hunger strike here it will be seen by the British as weakness. Comrade I cannot accept a defeat, my belief in the Republican Movement, my principles and my hatred for the British are too strong. A great Movement like ours cannot be put in that position. I know what the consequences of this hunger strike are going to be and I know what the consequences to our Movement will be if it fails. I have been stressing all this most profoundly to the others who came forward for hunger strike and who can know this better than I? Remember too comrade that this is not the first time I came forward for hunger strike. I put myself down for the last one. I'm not sure if you're aware of what happened then so I will explain—at that time I had nine months of my sentence left to do. The arguments put to me all concerned that fact. They were that I, through embarking, could put lives in danger as the British may not have taken the hunger strike seriously. If a girl with only nine months embarked, that they would not believe I was prepared to die and may have kept holding off to see how long I would last and that if I were to embark they would then think that Armagh did not have the backing or the strength to carry on a hunger strike. Nothing now comrade is more apparent than this last sentiment. Armagh has no hunger strike and that's it in a nutshell. The present situation cancels out the other two arguments. I would not be writing this comm if I were not prepared to die. My sentence can have no bearing now. I can't see how I would be putting any lives at risk because of it. Hunger strikers are going to die and that is reality so I will make no difference. I am the person who wrote those comms to AC [Army Council] pushing for hunger strike, if I cannot stand behind my own words I had no right to send those comms. I now propose to stand behind them. I have committed myself to this step and to the aims of our Movement and the well-being of that Movement is my only concern. I ask you to put my proposal to the Army Council and seek clearance. I am prepared to embark on the 8th March and will try my utmost to have everything sorted out as soon as possible.

Pennies from Bik 18.2.81
Dirty Coat, a chara, got your comm today. Must admit I was slightly taken aback by the news of the two girls withdrawing their names. However as you said, rather now than at a critical period. They must be commended for this . . . I informed Liam Og that we now believe that no-wash protest would be terminated the day the hunger strike commences. If we acted prior to this it may provide an opportunity for the Brits to attempt an outflanking move with irrelevant concessionary measures which could well appear positive to the public (a positive response, that is) . . .

Liam Og from Bik 18.2.81

... Last night the 'Elephant' had his medication confiscated by a screw. It's the type of gear one inserts into one's rectum. Anyway the screw told him to squat over the mirror and insert the efforts in his presence (perverted bastard). The Elephant refused and the gear was confiscated. He saw the quack this morning who ate the clamms off the screw ...

[From] PRO H3 18.2.81

... Colm O Neill (Armagh) was pulled out of the cell and dragged by hair up wing to Class Office to see Gov. He was charged with attempting to smuggle letter out on his visit (he was wearing a towel). The Gov. sentenced him to 4 closed visit. While he was being dragged out he was punched on face, head and body (no marks) ...

Bik to Liam Og 19.2.81

... Charlie [Sands] has me wrecked with the traditional music reports Mrs. Dale keeps telling him about. He enjoys tormenting me the sadistic B. ...

The dearth of volunteers at Armagh was not the only problem facing McFarlane and the external leadership. They were still trying to decide the formula by which they would phase on the hunger strikers: should replacements only be brought on after death, or should a second four join before a death? If before a death, it gave an impression of solidarity, but at the same time it could have the effect of weakening the resolve of the first hunger striker—knowing there was someone already in the public eye to fill the gap if he pulled out. It was ruthless thinking, but then it had to be—the stakes were just too high now to make mistakes. There was also the question of what the other prisoners should be doing during the hunger strike, whether they should continue with the dirty protest. There were differences of opinion between the prisoners, but it was decided that the protest was overtaken by the hunger strike and there was nothing to be gained by maintaining it. Everyone knew that the hunger strike was their last chance; if it collapsed, protesting would all be over. But to avoid any misunderstanding outside, and in case the Government tried to exploit it, they decided to postpone calling off the dirty protest until just after the hunger strike had started.

There were also rumors reaching the blocks that the six earlier hunger strikers still in the prison hospital had resumed their fast. That was a worry as well; some of the six were quite capable of it. The rumor turned out to be false, but then Sands got a comm from one of the seven, Tom McFeeley, asking to be allowed to join the second hunger strike. McFarlane replied, flatly refusing. And down in Armagh women's jail Sile got a message from the Army Council vetoing their participation.

Attention now was on Sands, in more ways than one. First there was Father Denis Faul, a visiting chaplain to the Kesh. A fervent Nationalist, but one strongly opposed to the use of violence and highly suspicious of the "Marxist" strain in the modern-day Republican Movement, he was— as the nickname bestowed upon him, Denis the Menace, suggested—both distrusted and liked by the prisoners; distrusted because of his frequent denunciations of the IRA, liked because he had done more than any other individual to expose security force brutality in northern Ireland. He had been involved in attempts by the Catholic Church to resolve the prisons dispute and was now strenuously trying to get a postponement, arguing with Sands over the morality of hunger-striking, pointing out the impact it would have on both his family and the community. Sands threw scripture at him: "Greater love than this hath no man than that he lay down his life for his friend." Faul said resignedly: "Bobby, there's no answer to that."

To Liam Og from Marcella [Sands] 21.2.81
Comrade, how are you? Was visited today by the Menace down on the visits. Again he went through the rigmarole of what the Bishops are doing behind the scenes and the amadon [fool, a reference to Irish Prime Minister Charles Haughey] and of course wanting a six month delay to allow these to work whilst the Menace and others would mount a Civil Disobedience campaign etc. Again I disappointed him and criticized the bishops and Sagart Mor [Cardinal Tomas O Fiaich] very strongly. He questioned the unity of the men and I left him in no doubt to the unified attitude here and I deliberately told him that this was amplified by people who had been on hunger strike wanting to go on again . . . I told him the only thing that would stop hunger strike would be an assurance of previously negotiated and guaranteed settlement to be implemented on an agreed date. I believe the six months delay is designed to fit in with the opening of Magaberry [a new prison being built in the north] and that would only be a nonprincipled solution. Anyway he now knows how determined we all are and more so me personally. See ya, Marcella.

Liam Og from Bik 21.2.81
Comrade find enclosed comms for officer commanding Crum[lin Road prison] and Armagh NSHBC [National Smash H-Block Committee] and short letter to the families of those kids who died in that fire at Dublin disco . . . Charlie [Sands] is getting special humiliation treatment over the mirror after his visits. I'm worried at him sticking his boot in a screw. He'd get murdered, no problem. He came very

close to banging one the other night. I'll have to calm him down a bit. That's all for now. God Bless.

Liam Og from Bik 23.2.81 7 P.M.
Silvertop [Fr. Murphy] was just in a few minutes ago with Charlie [Sands]. Never said anything direct, but just said rather cutely that he was praying the Brits gave us our own clothes. Charlie said that if they did we aren't taking them. We want the heap [everything]. Silvertop referred to lock-up in our cells with our own clothes and any marginal privileges etc. Charlie told him that this might have been alright a few weeks ago, but not now . . .

The days fled to the end of the month, Saturday the 28th. That night the prisoners received their weekly ration of fruit. For Bobby Sands it was his last food. It was an orange and it was bitter.

The crows woke the prisoner, assembling on the razor wire and the towering security lights. But it was to the cold he woke, hugging the three tattered army blankets closer to his body, knees tucked up into his belly for warmth. The crash of the bucket echoed down the corridor. Frankenstein was night guard. He must have slept over; usually he beat the crows to it.

The bucket clanged its way at the shove of the guard's boot down to the blue box in the wall at the end. The click of the red button being pushed sounded clearly before the bucket started clattering its way back. In the distance the hum of cars was starting along the motorway. The prisoner began dozing again and then woke to the parade.

"Yeoww, 'tenshunnn!" The boots stamped.

Twenty-five cells listened for the words "wing shift" in the distant murmurs. But it was all prison widows and Prison Officers Association bulletins. No Mountbattens dead outside, no batons being warmed today. The strumming on the grilles, the morning after Governor Miles had been shot, flitted through the prisoner's mind: the scrape of the table down the wing; the banging of the locks being shot; the splash of bare feet and boots running through the pools of urine; the grunt as hard wood slammed into bare hips . . . Sounds, always sounds. Sounds of fear, sounds of safety.

"Bears in the air." The doors rattling open and booming shut, to the cry of the head count: ". . . two, two, one, two, two . . ." The prisoner tensed as he heard a break in the rhythm, the grunt of the guard heaving at a mattress. A shout: "It's all right, he's alive." The prisoner relaxed as the rhythm picked up: someone had failed to show his face. But there was no fight. He pulled his own blanket down and looked into the pallid face of his cellmate, sunken eyes and jaws framed by greasy, matted hair, an eight-inch beard, with filthy fingernails clutching the top of the blanket: it was difficult to believe the face was of a twenty-two-year-old.

As the banging came closer the prisoner mechanically fumbled for the tightly rolled package tucked into the blanket next to his shoulder, reached between his legs, probed and thrust it home. His own door swung open and out of the corner of his eye he caught a flash of Mengele's white coat, behind the long nose and flushed face of Sherlock, calling "Two." Sherlock Holmes, the amateur detective—always finding plots that were not there.

"CD Grille, C Wing numbers, 45."

"CD Grille, C Wing, 45?"

"Correct."

"Carry on C Wing."

It sounded like Don Quixote was on the grille, the Spanish expert. Tuesday. The greyhounds could count on some yellow cake tonight.

Medical examination. He probed tentatively at the molar, hoping to God it wasn't toothache.

His cellmate pushed himself upright and he followed suit. He carefully pulled the torn blanket over his head, poncho-fashion; carefully, because he was not too sure that yesterday's stitching with his chicken-bone needle would hold. Time he found another staple, they were much more effective.

"Hope it's cornflakes," he said, feeling the craving of his stomach after last night's "Ulster fry"—boiled egg, half a soda bread and a piece of hairy bacon at 5 P.M.

"Maybe, it's been porridge three in a row," his cellmate said.

The prisoner stood and wrapped the second blanket around his waist, propped his sponge mattress up against the two heating pipes and started making his runway with the third blanket, folded twice to the center to give his bare feet protection from the asphalt floor. He started his pacing: six paces up, six back, six paces up, six paces down, figure of eight to break the monotony, six paces up, six paces down. His cellmate was already sitting, his mattress folded into a chair against the wall, concentrating on the Bible.

The breakfast trolley rattled its way down. The door opened, the orderly lifting the tray over the thin bread barrier that the prisoner had built to stop up the gap under the door. Porridge. It was the tea urn, thank God, it would be hot today.

He held the two plastic mugs under the tap and the orderly filled them to the top. Good man. That put a bit of cheer on the day. He placed them, hurriedly but carefully, on the pipes and went back as the door slammed. Hastily he snatched the two slices of bread off the plates and tore away the soggy portions, slinging them into the garbage corner. He tossed the oatmeal against the wall, momentarily glancing down as he did so, checking if the scar had gone and remembering the pain when he had slipped on his runway, gashing his arm on the porridge and potato pebbledash. But at least it annoyed the screws—even with the steam hoses they had trouble lifting it off the wall.

It was a good block of margarine today and they already had extra wrapped in the parable of the fishes and loaves.

"Here's extra buioch, what'll we do with't?"

"We've enough, throw it on the wall."

He cut it carefully with the plastic knife and then slapped it on the metal plate above the pipes; handy for throwing to the birds. And greasing your arse.

He evened out the two slices of torn bread, spread marge on both portions and passed one over. Sitting crosslegged on his runway, he sipped gratefully at the hot tea.

"Think the marge's good for the birds?" he asked.

"Good enough for Commie crows."

The prisoner grinned. The crows had been Commies since Bob had "told" a Ludlum book, recalling a line about crows migrating to Moscow. Their commune was down in the woods next to the river; their contribution to the Cause the daily raids on the rich barley and oat fields of Hillsborough.

The cell door opened twice more—plates collected, water container refilled. Three pints today, he estimated. Then he heard a bunt of excited chatter a few cells away and clambered on to the pipes, clinging to the wire mesh and peering past the two concrete bars and through the clear perspex at the top of the window box. Flakes of white were hushing their way down into the gray yard, a few bumping against the perspex. In the distance he could hear the traffic on the motorway. Outside. His stomach tightened as he suddenly remembered. The visit. He stared out into the white chaos.

THREE

SOLDIER: *You mean to starve? You will have none*
   of it?
I'll leave it there, where you can sniff the savour.
Snuff it, old hedgehog, and unroll yourself!
But if I were the King, I'd make you do it
With wisps of lighted straw.
                    —The King's Threshold, *by W. B. Yeats*

The day was marked by Sinn Fein with a march through West Belfast. It was a cold Sunday and it was raining. Four months before, about 10,000 had taken part in the march which had marked the beginning of the first hunger strike; Bernadette McAliskey, watching it, had had tears running down her face, of pride and excitement, believing she was watching the birth of another mass movement like the Civil Rights demonstrations eleven years before. Today only 3,500 were taking part and giving little cause for excitement, more for regret at lost opportunities, and a reflection of the sense of déjà vu in a tired community. There were some fine statements, of course. One was read out to the demonstrators on behalf of the prisoners, declaring: "We have asserted that we are political prisoners and everything about our country, our interrogation, trials and prison conditions show that we are politically motivated and not motivated by selfish reasons for selfish ends. As further demonstration of our selflessness and the justice of our cause, a number of our comrades, beginning today with Bobby Sands, will hunger-strike to the death unless the British Government abandons its criminalization policy and meets our demands."

Inside H3 Sands was preparing his statement for posterity, a diary which the external leadership had asked him to try and keep. "I am standing on the threshold of another trembling world," he carefully wrote on a scrap of toilet paper. "May God have mercy on my soul."

He also made a present for one of his friends among the prisoners, Ricky—in the Irish, "Risteard"—O'Rawe, who had taken over as public relations officer for the IRA men. The gift was the lyrics of a song he had written, which he carefully etched on cigarette paper. "A Sad Song for Susan," it was called—a song replete with his own feelings of emotional loss.

> *I'm sitting at the window, I'm looking down the street*
> *I'm looking for your face, I'm listening for your feet.*
> *Outside the wind is blowing and it's just begun to rain*
> *But it's being here without you that's causing me such*
>   *pain.*
> *My mind is running back again to when you were here*
> *And I wish I had you now, I wish you were near.*
> *Remember the Winter nights when you warmed me*
>   *from the cold*
> *And the Spring when we walked through green fields*
>   *and skies of gold*
> *You're gone, you're gone, but you live on in my*
>   *memory.*

At the end of it he scribbled a note to O'Rawe: "There you are Risteard, fresh from the heart for what it's worth. I wrote it one rainy afternoon on remand in H1 when I had the fine company of a guitar to pick out the tune. So Sine e."

[From] H6 Sun 1.3.81
While Mass was in progress cell searches were carried out.
During these searches disinfectant was thrown around all
cells. It was also thrown over 4 mattresses and also two
pillows, two mattresses were torn in half and three pillows
destroyed. Sin e.

The following morning the prisoners ended their no-wash
protest, as planned. It passed off peacefully enough, but the
enthusiastic response of the warders was unsettling. They were
moved to clean cells, provided with new bedding, allowed
haircuts and shaves and were told that loss of remission for
failing to conform would be cut by half and that they would
be getting fruit parcels once a month. It appeared the authorities were under the misapprehension that they were engaged
in another step-by-step attempt to resolve the dispute. Time
would tell them. The blanket protest would continue.

The INLA prisoners were getting worried about terms of
reference for negotiations. Their commanding officer, Patsy
O'Hara, told the IRA commander in his block, H5, he had
received orders from the INLA Army Council that nobody
could negotiate on their behalf. Their main worry was that
their men would not get segregation from the IRA prisoners—
being swamped by big brother was a perennial INLA concern.

Sands found that particularly generous portions of food
were being offered to him. So his cellmate, Malachy Carey,
was having a feast. He deserved it. Because of Sands's pivotal
role, first as officer commanding and then as lead hunger
striker, Carey found himself something of a beast of burden,
carrying supplies and comms. He had staggered out of one
Mass, where smuggled items were usually exchanged between
prisoners, with a wad of comms, tobacco, a camera, a radio
and "Rennie Barker"—a Parker pen refill—inside himself. It
had earned him the nickname "The Suitcase."

On the Tuesday Sands had a visit with an Irish and an English journalist he had invited in. The English reporter asked him if he thought he was going to die. He said he did. There was a sense of luxury to it all for him. A table was brought into the cell and his food placed ostentatiously on it, with the odd jibe as to whether he was still not eating. He was smoking—"bog-rolled blow"—and had been allowed newspapers and a book of Kipling's short stories. There was a touch of irony in that, of course: Kipling, the bard of British Imperialism. There was an introduction by W. Somerset Maugham and one line leapt out at Sands: "It is true that the Irish were making a nuisance of themselves." Indeed. But he got a lot of satisfaction from the book.

On Wednesday he was feeling great. There was even jam with the tea.

Liam Og [Sinn Fein official] from Bik [McFarlane] 4.3.81
. . . I saw Charlie [Sands] out at the showers this morning. He shaved off his beard and is just now having his hair cut. He saw the doctor and had medical run-down—weight 63 kg, blood pressure 110/72, pulse 72 . . . He has no complaints whatsoever and is sleeping well at night though not at all during the day. He spends the day yarning with the guy next door, reading and doing a bit of walking in the cell which is now completely furnished. He got everything he wanted on request and is visited by a Governor (McCartney, I think his name is) each day. He reckons this Gov. is the main man to monitor the hunger strike. The reasons for asking for books, papers, furniture is to simulate normal cell conditions so that if they try to move him he can insist that there is no reason so he will be in the exact same conditions as he is at present. It can then be seen for the move it is—i.e. isolation. We hope to maintain this current position for quite some time. Index [Fr. Toner] was in last

night and spent most of the time talking about religion. Charlie reckons he was just trying to get deeper insight into him. Anyway Index remarked that he thought his spirit was very high. Incidentally Silvertop [Fr. Murphy] made the same comment on Monday evening . . . Now generally, Charlie is in good form and is not as yet experiencing any weakness, dizziness, tiredness, pains and nothing at all. He is not taking salt tablets, but he has raw salt in his cell. The doctor was telling him that this was a better way to take it as it meant the water was fresh and not distasteful, which he believed was the cause of sickness among the last hunger strikers. So he takes a little raw salt each day and is drinking in the region of six pints of water . . . I got a glimpse into his cell and he looks pretty comfortable. He has sheets and an extra blanket and one blanket hanging over the grille on the window . . . Now Oliver dear chap, I know I am regarded as a religious freak, but my faith does not extend to withering fig leaves that don't bear fruit, or raising the dead, or my fine fellow, producing sheets of S&S [Stretch and Seal plastic, to wrap smuggled items] from fresh air!! I beg, plead, implore, beseech thee is there any bloody chance of lots and lots of lovely fresh S&S very very soon—Please? I mean what did I ever do to you? . . . Take care and God Bless.

[Unsigned] 5.3.81
Bobby's weight today is 62 kg. His heart beat is 88 and blood pressure 112/70 . . . He requested blankets. Said he felt the draft coming in the windows. So the screws put a blanket on the windows during the night.

The other prisoners' thoughts were constantly on Sands. Food had been dropped as the favorite topic of conversation—no more cries went up of "Here comes Henry VIII," no more guessing games about what was for dinner.

They had started saying the Rosary twice a day. Bobby himself was saying his prayers, and castigating himself as a crawler. He found he could ignore the food put out for him easily enough, but he kept longing for a piece of brown wholemeal bread, butter, Dutch cheese and honey. "Well, there will be a great feed awaiting me above—if I get there," he thought. "But what if there is no food up there?" On Friday he was beginning to get brief spells of energy loss. He had dropped 6.6 lbs. by Saturday.

He stumbled across some articles about wildlife in the newspapers; he had been passionate about birds since childhood. He had been listening for them, curlews flying past the cell windows, the croak of the black crows, waiting for the sound of the lark and spring.

Monday the 9th was his birthday. He was twenty-seven.

Liam Og 9.3.81 from Marcella [Sands]
Comrade, how are ya? I'm still in the wing with the lads and how long that will last is uncertain. I'm feeling physically alright, I've had no headaches or even minor medical complaints. There are I believe several tactics being deployed at present, foremost is I believe a deliberate policy of false disinterest that is 'we couldn't care less' type of thing to make me feel small or insignificant and to try to create the impression in my mind that the hunger strike is merely confined to my cell. But I can see that. Secondly (and I must say first that I have no trouble in resisting the temptation of food because of my frame of mind) my opinion is that there has been a vast improvement in the quality and quantity of food. Stew is the best food here, we've had it 3 times in seven days . . . It appears that the seven comrades are still a bit down. I was disappointed that I never even got a note from the Dark even if it was just to say goodbye, but I hope they'll be alright . . .

To Liam Og from Marcella 9.3.81
Comrade, Just some worrying thoughts that are in my mind. As you should know, I don't care much to entering any discussion on the topic of 'negotiations' or for that matter 'settlements' but what is worrying me is this: I'm afraid that there is a possibility that at a crucial stage (which could be after death) the Brits would move with a settlement and demand Index [Prison Chaplain, Fr. Toner] as guarantor. Now this is feasible, if a man is dying, that they would try to force Bik to accept a settlement to save life which of course would be subject to Index's interpretation. And we know how far that would get us. It wouldn't make any difference if it were he and Silvertop [Assistant Prison Chaplain, Fr. Murphy], the same would occur. I've told Bik to let me or anyone else die before submitting to a play like that. Well that's what was bugging me—silly old fool aren't I!! . . . I was wondering (here it comes says you) that out of the goodness of all yer hearts you couldn't get me one miserly book and try to leave it in: the Poems of Ethna Carberry—cissy. That's really all I want, last request as they say. Some ask for cigarettes, others for blindfolds, yer man asks for Poetry.

In the evening, when the dinner plates had been cleared away and the night guard had settled down, the "scorchers" shouted the news across the courtyard between the two facing wings. Jake Jackson, with his fluent Irish and strong young voice, was the scorcher for A wing and he yelled that Sands was all right and his weight—132 lbs. At the end of it Spotto Devine in D wing shouted: "One more thing." And then their wing roared in Irish: "Happy birthday, Bobby."

They celebrated with a concert which followed a now familiar form. "Teapot" and "Hector" were the impresarios. "Teapot" was Jimmy McMullan—he got the name because a British army patrol had shot the top of his ear off and filled him full of holes back in 1975. He was the second IRA man sentenced under the criminalization policy, after Kieran Nugent, and was now the longest-serving blanket man. "Hector"—Jim McNeil—had a gammy leg and used a walking stick; he had been shot up after opening fire on an army patrol in 1976. The two of them were always vying, jovially, for ascendancy. Hector was a couple of inches shorter than Teapot and used to stand on an upturned chamber pot to get above him.

Bik McFarlane kicked off the concert, with a rendering of "Big Yellow Taxi." Jake sang "Skibereen," Bobby his own haunting composition, "Back Home in Derry," and Blessed Noel Quinn from Bellaghy "My Little Armalite":

> *I was stopped by a soldier, said he you are a swine,*
> *He beat me with his baton and he kicked me in the*
> *   groin*
> *I bowed and scraped, sure my manners were polite,*
> *Ah, but all the time I was thinking of my little*
> *   Armalite.*

The song was in sharp contrast with the name: he had got the "Blessed Noel" because he walked with an almost pious hunch, had a beard which parted in two peaks, and resembled a biblical figure in a rosary book the prison chaplain had brought into the wing—or at least that was what Teapot said.

Hector gave a song about the murderous B Specials which went on and on and had everyone yawning ostentatiously at their doors and Teapot blowing raspberries. Big Tom McElwee down at the end of the corridor was called and he said: "You'se all know I can't sing, so I'll do this poem," which had them all jeering: "Not that one again." But he persevered, in his big countryman's voice, with the tale of the rock flowers spellbound by the mists from the sea. The evening ended with Bik playing requests, singing another of Sands's songs,

"McIlhatton"—the tale of the poteen maker in the Glens of Antrim—whistling jigs and reels to the rhythm of the bodhran drum played on the steel door of his cell.

9.3.81 [unsigned]
. . . [Bobby] says that there is not a thing wrong with him and is in pretty cheerful spirits. He seems to have totally accepted the fact that he will die, this has come across in his speech. He has mentioned it a few times in a quite matter of fact manner . . .

Over the next few days birthday greetings came trickling into Sands's cell—some published as adverts in a local newspaper, others in conventional cards, or smuggled comms from other parts of the prison.

Liam Og from Sin Sin 14.3.81
Bobby's weight 58.25 blood pressure and heart beat normal. The screws turned his cell lights on 3 times last night wakening him on every occasion. Times 10.00 P.M., 2.00 A.M., 6.00 A.M. No other details.

Sands was becoming increasingly tired. He very much wanted to try writing some more poetry—he had ideas for some on the hunger strike—but decided that he just did not have the energy. Better to concentrate on keeping going. The daily diary was taking too much out of him as it was. He stalled ten days before taking another bath, to avoid the risk of a cold. On Sunday the 15th he got company, at least in the abstract, with the announcement that Francis Hughes had joined the hunger strike in H5. The next day Sands had a visit with his family. He was concerned about the loss of energy involved in taking the walk to the visiting block, but was looking forward to the open air. He wrapped up warmly.

To Liam Og from Bik 16.3.81

... Bob had a very good visit with his family and feels much happier at seeing them in a more contented frame of mind. They were very sound indeed he says. He got some verbal abuse from screws at visits—usual rubbish about food etc. He did not get a search, out or in, apparently this is to do with screws working to rule. This morning they were informed by Hilditch since no-wash protest was terminated, they were now back to normal good time and normal wages—i.e. no bonus for kicking blanket men to death. One of them said to Ricky the NIO were no longer paying them to do the mirror search so they weren't going to do it. We don't think the Administration have put a stop to it—just the screws' work to rule OK!

Marcella to Liam Og 16.3.81

Comrade, how are you? It's me. Well I'm alright. I had a visit with the family today. I was apprehensive going out (know what I mean) but I must say my ma, da and Marcella were just fantastic (circumstances considered). The visit really boosted me (not that I was in dire need of a boost—Sherlock!!) but it did do the heart good of course. My Ma's still a wee bit inquisitive on 'are you doing this of your own free will son' and has now accepted that I am; with me reassuring her of that. They were most interested to know what they can do to help me ... they're sound enough. They have a wee bit of hope and I didn't say anything to wreck that hope. Now some wee points (I will mention them to Bik tomorrow). Silvertop and Index still come in. Silvertop is alright (well not devious) the other effort is overtly cordial and like a jackal waiting on prey to physically weaken (well dare 'em). Silver is Sagart Mor's [Cardinal O Fiaich's] man. Sagart Mor was going to make statement following end of no wash to put the ball in the

Brits' court, by saying the prisoners have moved with a show of flexibility, now Brits should make a return step-by-step gesture in granting clothes (and petty things). Sagart Mor thought this is a good move and was enthusiastic, but Silvertop put a halt to it saying that I did not want this, pointing out to him (1) I would not accept any petty concessions which would only serve to undermine 'once again' the true issue at stake i.e. status. (2) My advice is Sagart Mor is to take a political redner [blush] and speak out with clarity and with vigour against the Brit intransigence to solve this issue. (3) Sagart Mor also knows that only a public declaration from Brits or direct negotiations with guarantees leading to package of five demands will solve this issue okay. Now that Bik is OC only he, me and OC of Armagh (with other additions I didn't elaborate on) will negotiate and no one else and if (when) I die Bik will (and at all times) be in control okay. Comrade now here's a point that's worrying me: in the event of me, Frankie or Raymond dying you'll have no one left to work with and you know who'd be left [presumably the INLA representative, O'Hara] and what could happen. Just thought that someone behind him would be a safeguard. Let's face it comrade it may well happen like that. Sorry to be so cryptic but think about it . . .

While Sands and the leadership were worrying about the larger issues, other prisoners had their own problems.

H4 16.3.81 [unsigned]
On Sunday 3rd March a wing was moved from H4 to H6. There was no trouble. The wing was moved back from H6 to H4 on Friday 13th. This time there was trouble. The screws told the men to take their cell cards while moving from block to block. The men refused and a few beatings were handed out. Most of the beatings weren't

too bad. Only a couple were slightly bad. One man's nose
was bleeding and he had a swollen lip. Another man had a
couple of bruises. Most of the men were running down the
wing and through the circle with their arms up their backs.
One man was kicked in the testicles. All of this trouble
took place in H6. When the man who was kicked got back
to H4 he saw a medical officer. One of his testicles had
went inside him and the area was swollen. He was taken
out the same day again and went to hospital. He is now
in an outside hospital. His name is Owen O'Boyle, South
Derry . . . Sin e H4

Outside the prison it was all fairly quiet. In the House
of Commons the Secretary of State, Humphrey Atkins, had
declared yet again his Government's determination not to
concede special status to the prisoners. MPs on both sides of
the floor appealed to him to stop making such statements,
because it was only giving the IRA publicity. Better to let them
fade into obscurity, said one Conservative MP, John Farr.
But on the very same day they were speaking a man died of
a heart attack in Ireland; a death which would soon put an
end to talk of obscurity.

His name was Frank Maguire. Big Frank Maguire. He ran a
pub in Lisnaskea, Co. Fermanagh, in the southeast corner of
northern Ireland. More importantly, he was a member of the
House of Commons.
    Fermanagh has an idiosyncratic Republican ethos among
the counties of Ireland, which dates back to Partition and the
Anglo-Irish Treaty. The Irish delegation to London which
signed the Treaty believed—and indeed were encouraged to
do so, with apparent good faith, by Lloyd George—that the
border which would be delineated by a proposed boundary
commission would make the northern statelet unviable as
an economic or national unit, with the major Nationalist

population groups in Fermanagh, south Derry, Derry City and South Armagh going to the south. The sense of betrayal when they were incorporated in the Protestant north was felt particularly in Fermanagh, the only one of the six counties where there was an overall Nationalist majority. This, together with the scars of the civil war which followed the Treaty, created in Fermanagh a disillusionment with party politics, coupled with an almost paradoxical Nationalist unity. In the mid-1920s a Nationalist Registration Association was formed in the county to make sure that they maintained a majority in any elections and they were successful in that until the start of the Civil Rights movement in the late 1960s, which threw up a new and powerful political grouping, the Social Democratic and Labour Party (SDLP). But even then, despite the intrusion of party politics into Fermanagh, Nationalist unity was the overriding political consideration among Catholic voters. And it was to resolve a split between rival Nationalist politicians that Frank Maguire emerged as a compromise candidate for the second of the two general elections in 1974, beating a former leader of the Official Unionist Party, Harry West, to take the seat.

Born in 1929, into a family of four children—three boys and one girl—Frank had worked at the Lisnaskea pub for his uncle, John Carron, who had been a Nationalist MP at Stormont before it was prorogued. He had been involved in the Republican Movement in the 1950s campaign and had been interned without trial for two years, acting for a time as Officer Commanding the IRA in the Crumlin Road jail. But he had turned against the physical force tradition and was vehemently opposed to violence.

At Westminster, where he was rarely seen, he was regarded as a mildly eccentric character who, at the time of his death, had still to deliver his maiden speech. He made one critical nonappearance in 1979, when his absence contributed to the narrow defeat of the then Labour government of James

Callaghan which brought Mrs. Thatcher to power. But his great interest, in pursuit of which he would go to considerable lengths—even making a reluctant appearance in Parliament—was in prison welfare: not just Irish prisons, but anywhere in the world where he felt there was penal injustice. He lent his name, for instance, to any group campaigning for prisoners of conscience behind the Iron Curtain. In Fermanagh itself he was an extremely popular figure, involved in GAA (Irish) football and always an easy touch, in his office above "Frank's Pub," for a quick loan which as likely as not would be spent in another pub down the road.

When Frank died it was assumed his seat would be taken over by his brother Noel, who, at forty-nine, was just two years younger than he. Noel, too, had been closely involved in politics. He had been particularly close to John Carron—had in effect been brought up by him and his wife—and had worked for him for a while as a political secretary at Stormont. When Frank became MP, Noel became his right-hand man, doing much of his constituency work for him. Politically he was like Frank, although he had a wider experience of the world. He had read history at Trinity College in Dublin, abandoning his studies to wander abroad. He had ended up in the United States where he worked as an archivist in Washington and as a ghost writer, attaching himself to a number of geographic expeditions, including one to Antarctica. He looked a bit like a sailor—a Captain Nemo figure, almost, with graying hair, blue eyes and nautical beard.

Certainly Sinn Fein posed no threat to the Maguire succession. The organization did exist at the time in Fermanagh, but only just, and largely in the diminutive figure of Owen Carron.

Owen Carron was just an ordinary member, virtually unheard of outside the county, even within the organization. He was a bachelor, aged twenty-six, with a potentially powerful face—piercing blue eyes, jet black hair and aquiline features—which was compromised by a shy manner and small stature; he stood about 5 feet 5 inches tall. Trained as a teacher in Manchester, he had taught history, religion and English at a Catholic secondary school in Armagh, but had given it up because it was too far to travel from his home, a ten-acre farm near Enniskillen where he lived with his seventy-five-year-old father. He had started a local H-Block Committee and had arranged some fairly successful meetings, marches and pickets in support of the first hunger strike. When that collapsed nobody even told the Committee—they heard about it on the radio like everyone else. When the second hunger strike started they found it almost impossible to generate any local interest.

Shortly after Frank Maguire's death Carron had a telephone call from the President of Sinn Fein, Ruairi O Bradaigh. There was a monthly meeting pending of Sinn Fein's national executive and the organization's attitude towards the election—who they should support—was likely to come up. O Bradaigh, who was wanted by the security forces in the north, asked Carron if he would come down and meet him in Carrick-on-Shannon, to advise him. Carron went down and told O Bradaigh that the possible rivals to Noel Maguire were Bernadette McAliskey and a former boy scout leader in the area, Bernard O'Connor. McAliskey had signaled her apparent interest in the seat by attending Frank's funeral on crutches—her first public appearance since the bid to assassinate her. But, although she was one of the most outstanding political speakers and thinkers on the island and greatly admired for her pluck, conservative Ireland had never quite got over the shock of her having had a baby out of wedlock while an MP. And, despite a brief flirtation with the IRSP, she did not have the organizational backing to overcome the prejudices. O'Connor was a small gadfly on the rump of the establishment and liked for that; he had once run a local version of *Private Eye*, with scurrilous attacks on various dignitaries, and had stung the establishment even more tellingly in 1980 when he had been awarded £5,000 by the High Court in Belfast against the police for badly beating him up during interrogation. But he was not seen as a serious candidate and Carron's advice to O Bradaigh was that Sinn Fein should just stay well out of it all.

At the Executive Committee meeting in Dublin the following Saturday the issue was raised. Gerry Adams, Vice-President of Sinn Fein, had realized that something was needed to raise public consciousness, which had been so deflated by the anticlimactic ending of the first fast. He floated the idea of putting Sands up in Fermanagh–South Tyrone. The idea was backed by the second vice-president, Daithi O Conaill, another former Chief of Staff of the IRA. There was some argument over whether it was too great a risk, putting Sands forward and then having to withdraw. But it was agreed in principle that if they could persuade the other Nationalist candidates to give him a clear field he should go forward.

They called a meeting of Republicans from Fermanagh–South Tyrone to put the idea to them. It was held again south of the border, in the Swann hotel, in Monaghan. About 150 people turned up. The Sinn Fein leadership was on the platform in force—Adams, O Bradaigh, O Conaill, Joe Cahill, former Quartermaster General of the IRA, and John Joe McGirl, another one-time Chief of Staff. Opinion, on the floor, was obviously strongly against a prison candidate and it was confirmed on a vote, with an overwhelming majority against Sands. As the meeting broke up Carron was asked to stay behind, to meet the leadership. He waited in the lobby while they had an impromptu meeting of the Sinn Fein executive. While he was waiting he talked to some friends from Fermanagh and they agreed among themselves that the Movement should press ahead with Sands as a candidate regardless of the vote at the meeting. Then the executive came out and Carron told O Bradaigh their thinking. O Bradaigh said the executive had just come to the same decision.

Adams headed for the telephone to tell the Belfast headquarters to issue a statement, with an appeal to other possible candidates to give way. What Adams and company had not told the meeting was that they already had undertakings of sorts from both McAliskey and Maguire. McAliskey had not hesitated; asked to come in to the Belfast offices to see Adams, she had walked in and said "I know what you're looking for and that's OK." Adams and another Sinn Fein officer, Jim Gibney, had gone down to Lisnaskea to see Maguire. They had a long chat with the family which was inconclusive until Adams ended it with the blunt question: "You wouldn't stand against a hunger striker, would you?" To which Noel replied: "No, if a prisoner stands I would withdraw. I think it would be a mistake . . ."

In the prison Sands was having trouble with the cold. He wrapped himself as tightly as he could in blankets, but he had difficulty keeping his feet warm. By the 16th he had lost 12.65 lbs. After seventeen days he gave up his diary, it was too much effort. He ended on a defiant and passionate note: "They won't break me because the desire for freedom, and the freedom of the Irish people, is in my heart. The day will dawn when all the people of Ireland will have the desire for freedom to show. It is then we'll see the rising of the moon." The "rising of the moon" was a quotation from a poem celebrating the great rising of 1798 written by a young Fenian, John Casey, who died in 1879 at the age of 24, of ill-health partly attributed to his harsh treatment in prison:

> Well they fought for poor old Ireland
> And full bitter was their fate
> (Oh! what glorious pride and sorrow
> Fill the name of Ninety-Eight.)
> Yet, thank God, e'en still are beating
> Hearts in manhood's burning noon,
> Who would follow in their footsteps
> At the risin' of the moon!

Poetry, as ever, was Sands's passion. And McFarlane did all he could to satisfy it.

Pennies from Bik 19.3.81

. . . Bob was pleased you managed to get that book for him. I told Liam Og to leave it up on Saturday. But you know that while we were in H6, during 1979, he sent up to me and told me after reading some of Ethna's [Carberry's] work that he had written her a wee note and 'you never know', sez Bob, she might just do something on the blocks. Did he take a red face when I informed him that she'd been dead more than 10 years. [In fact she had died in 1902.] He has been extra careful what he says to me since then. Anyway, will you do your best to get some more stuff like that for him. He's mad about poetry as you know . . .

The following Saturday, his twenty-third day without food, Sands started developing a sore throat. The doctor said he might have to take some medicine for it, but Sands said he was not prepared to do that. The doctor said it would only be penicillin and it did not have any vitamins in it, so Sands said he would think about it. The next day it seemed to be improving, although he could feel he was getting weaker. It was arranged for another prisoner to slop out for him as he did not feel up to it any more.

In Dublin, in room 3074 of the Arts Block at Trinity College, the thirty-five-year-old Director of Employee Relations and Services from British Leyland in Coventry, Geoffrey Armstrong, was delivering a paper to sixty-four members of the local Junior Chamber of Commerce. At 2:20 P.M., in the middle of this talk, the doors at the back burst open and three men in combat jackets, masked by balaclavas, marched to the front. Some of the audience thought it was a student prank, but then two of the hooded men produced guns. "Everybody freeze,

nobody move, this action is in support of the H-Blocks," one
of them shouted. For a moment it looked as if they were going
to shoot a woman in the front row. But a gunman turned back
to Armstrong, who had retreated from his podium, and shot
him three times in the flesh of his legs. Armstrong turned pale,
started shaking and collapsed. The gunmen ran out.

The title of the paper Armstrong had been delivering was:
"Managing change in an uncertain climate."

Frank Hughes and his cellmate, Raymond McCreesh—who
had by now joined the hunger strike with the INLA commanding officer, Patsy O'Hara—were in high spirits. They
had a concert for McCreesh in H5, during which he delivered
a speech, entirely in Irish, on the meaning of the hunger
strike. Frank was so lively they had to stop him singing and
later he sent out a request for the latest issue of *Republican
News*, because he had heard there was a photograph of him
in it. The newspaper, a weekly, was a fairly thick tabloid, but
Sinn Fein had perfected a method of reducing it in size, with
the help of a photostat machine, and smuggling it inside in
the normal way. Their smuggling was getting ever more ambitious. They tried to get in a camera—code-named Iris—but
the prisoner who was due to collect it on a visit blanched at
the sight of it, as McFarlane explained in a comm written
with a new pen.

Liam Og from Bik 23.3.81
Comrade, as you will note, I have acquired a new pen—
Bob's in fact!! Did you know that I had that blue Parker
since the middle of the last hunger strike. Bloody marvellous job it was—took heart attack last night . . . Big Tom
is shattered—nearly shit himself when he saw 'Iris.' Said
a girl like that could never have a successful relationship
with shy chappie like him. So comrade it's curtains for
Iris . . .

McFarlane had got the pen as a farewell gift from Sands. On the morning of the 23rd Sands was taken away to see a specialist. The warders said he would not be coming back, he would be taken directly into the prison hospital, a small clinic adjoining the H-Blocks, with eight single-bed wards. Sands passed the pen on to McFarlane through Jake Jackson, who was being allowed by the warders to clean out Sands's cell. Jackson was given his hairbrush as his memento.

Liam Og from Tony H5 25.3.81
. . . Patsy was out washing. Screws sent orderly to clean out his cell. Patsy told him not to do it and asked for his neighbours to do it. Screws didn't allow it. Governor told him that he is allowed one visit per week, but only for his family, 'no gangsters or reporters we would only turn them away'. Said he wouldn't get a radio, because 'you are still on protest and you would only turn it up for the other NCPs' [non-conforming prisoners]. You are allowed two letters per week, but if 7 or 8 come the system will allow you them. On the Irish News 'there is no great demand for it, but we'll see'. On books from outside we wouldn't give straight answer. Doctors checked his stomach and chest told him he was sound. All 3 have to wait 10 minutes at grille before seeing doctor. All in good spirits. That's it for now.

To O/C Blocks H3—O/C H5 26.3.81 From Tony H5
. . . Now our propaganda is going OK, but seemed to slow up a bit. We put out 305 [comms] during the fortnight ending 21st . . . Here are their weights when they started and last night. Frank 71.60–60.67: Ray 63.20–61.70: Patsy 76.76–75.35.

On the 26th Sinn Fein announced that Sands would be standing for Fermanagh–South Tyrone. But the field was still not clear of Nationalist candidates, as they had originally hoped. Word had come up from Enniskillen that Noel Maguire was having second thoughts—the local clergy appeared to be pushing him and he had deposited his nomination papers. And to complicate matters another possible candidate had appeared. The Social Democratic and Labour Party (SDLP), led by John Hume, decided to opt out, but a leading member, Austin Currie, was rebelling. Currie had been the youngest MP ever elected to the old Stormont parliament. He was a Nationalist, but strongly opposed to the IRA, and he let it be known that if Maguire did not stand, then he would do so to block Sands.

Inside the Kesh the prisoners had mixed feelings about the decision to put Sands up, but generally supported it. Developments were watched closely from the cells.

Liam Og from Bik 29.3.81
. . . Looks as though there is plenty of devious activity afloat with the election, just as you said—it makes me throw up. One thing is very clear—the Brits fear us taking this seat, hence the SDLP opposition. If Austin Currie runs against Bob the split vote will allow West to take the seat. The other Nationalist MPs won't want this and will of course seek agreement on a sole candidate. This means that Bob would have to slide out, if SDLP consent was to be gained—devious pro-Brit bastards!! No doubt, Maguire would be suitable to them and other Nationalists. Now I was just thinking—Bob would hammer Currie but not necessarily win the seat. Regardless of this it would be a blow to the SDLP and a boost of sorts to us. Currie is the weakest of any of the potential candidates but is holding the heap to ransom for the Brits (not forgetting the Church and Free State). I think we should not allow ourselves to be intimidated or bluffed out of this election. I reckon we should tell Maguire that we are going to run—just put it

to him straight what Currie and that shower are up to and ask him to back us. If we get the seat then he can have a crack at it shortly. If West takes it, then it will only be a short period until a general election and it can be regained no problem. Maguire should be asked to adopt Bernie's [McAliskey's] line and shelve his political career for a short while in the interest of men's lives and what is at stake. If he and Bernie are behind us we will take that seat, even if Currie does run.

It was a bad time for Noel Maguire—probably the worst in his life. The previous year he had lost both his parents. His mother had phoned him one day to say his father had collapsed and had been taken to the hospital. He got to the hospital to find them both lying in the morgue—she had died as she put the phone down. In January his aunt—John Carron's wife, who was almost a mother to him—had also died. And then there was Frank in March. Now he was suddenly being presented as the man who stood between life and death for Bobby Sands. Letters poured into the Stag's Head pub, which he was running, and his uncle's home where he was staying just outside the town. Old-time Republicans made personal appeals to him and calls came in from as far afield as America, pleading and demanding that he stand down. He could not understand the pressure. He had no intention of standing against a prison hunger striker—Frank would never have done that and nor would he; the unity of the people was what counted. But he just did not believe that Sands would stand and he would not believe it until his nomination was in.

Owen Carron was frantically collecting signatures for the papers—of a proposer, seconder and eight nominees. He collected the last of them shortly before midnight on Sunday, with McAliskey as proposer, getting everyone to sign two sets of papers, because he was terrified there would be a technical hitch when he handed them in: the returning officer would no doubt be a Loyalist.

On the Monday Carron met Adams and Gibney at the house of an ex-prisoner, Jimmy McGivern, on the Catholic Ballygawley estate, in the town of Dungannon, where the returning office was situated. He went to lodge the papers with Gibney at about 11 A.M. There were no problems. Maguire had already lodged his papers. The question was whether he would now withdraw before the 4 P.M. deadline.

They went back to the Ballygawley house and the anxious wait began. Tension mounted. McGivern was pacing backwards and forwards, cursing under his breath. Gibney was making worried phone calls. Adams was being his usual cool self, puffing on his pipe, making occasional entries in his ever-present notebook. At about 3 P.M. McGivern said: "Christ, he's not going to do it." At 3:45 the telephone rang.

Noel Maguire was in his office above the Stag's Head, preparing his campaign with his agent, Michael Cunningham, when they got the news that Sands's nomination was in. His two nephews, Frank Og (Junior) and Martin, were in the house next door and Noel raised them on an intercom system from the office: he did not feel in a state to drive, they had only fifteen minutes to get to the returning office in Dungannon; would Frank Og drive him? The two boys agreed to come. They jumped into Frank's old blue Ford Granada—Noel, the two nephews and Cunningham—and headed off.

At McGivern's house in Dungannon Adams and company began cheering: Maguire was on his way. They ran for their Ford Escort.

They parked the car around the corner from the office and Carron and Adams stayed in it—they did not want anyone to think they were prepared to withdraw Bobby. In fact Adams had already written a statement announcing Sands's withdrawal and had tucked it away in his pocket; he had already decided that if Maguire did not make it he would be pulling them out. McGivern and Gibney with another Republican who had joined them, Francis Malloy, went to see what was happening. The press was already there, waiting. There were only ten minutes to go and there were fears Maguire's car had got stuck in a traffic jam. Then the Ford Granada was sighted.

Cunningham got out first and walked to the stairs where a local Republican began to abuse him for his part in encouraging Maguire to stand. Cunningham walked back to the car. The Sinn Fein trio held their breaths; was this the proverbial straw; would Maguire get angry and drive off? Then the familiar figure with his white beard clambered out of the car and walked, with distinctively delicate steps, up to the stairs. Reporters called out, asking whether he was withdrawing. He ignored them and went inside. A few minutes later he emerged carrying his nomination papers and made a brief statement: "It has now become a question of conscience with me. I have been told the only way of saving Bobby Sands's life is by letting him go forward in the elections. I just cannot have the life of another man on my hands. I am calling my supporters to throw their weight behind Bobby Sands." Carron and Adams walked over and shook his hand.

In the Kesh the prisoners had been given their own, limited opportunity to make a political gesture—warders had presented them with government census forms. Outside the prison a campaign had been started to disrupt the census, by refusing to complete the forms, as a demonstration in favor of the hunger strikers. There was a debate among the prisoners as to how the papers should best be used—as toilet paper, or for cigarettes. Eventually they decided to play "weddings," tearing the forms up and tossing the confetti out of their windows and around their cells.

In Anderson Crescent, in a Catholic enclave within Derry's predominantly Protestant area of Waterside, Joanna Mathers was going from door to door, collecting census forms. An honors graduate from Belfast's Queen's University and married to a farmer, she had given up a job with the Town and Country Planning services in the city to bring up her two-and-a-half-year-old son, Shane. To make some pin money, she had volunteered to help with the census. She had just got up to Patrick McLaughlin's house in Anderson Crescent when a masked man danced up to her, snatched the clipboard she was holding with one hand, put a gun at her head with the other and fired. The girl squealed and ran past McLaughlin, who was standing at the door. He slammed it shut, but the gunman crashed through it and, waving the gun, grabbed the census forms before disappearing. Inside the house Joanna was dead.

In Belfast the Reverend Ian Paisley was galloping on down the Carson trail, without very much success. After his military-style parade on that Antrim hillside in February—in protest against the Anglo-Irish talks the previous December—he had decided to emulate Sir Edward Carson's "Ulster Covenant," a petition signed by nearly half a million Protestant men in 1912 to protect against Home Rule for Ireland. Dr. Paisley had announced that, in imitation of Carson's Covenant campaign, he was staging a series of rallies around northern Ireland, culminating in a monster rally at Stormont—underneath a statue of Sir Edward himself. The campaign turned out to be a pale imitation of the Carson campaign, fewer than 10,000 people turning up for the final "monster" rally on Saturday, March 28. But the blow was softened for Dr. Paisley by the police, who put the figure at between 28,000 and 30,000. Dr. Paisley told the crowd he had information that British Intelligence was planning to assassinate him.

In the Kesh prison life continued in its rut.

Liam Og from PRO H4 30.3.81
Owen O'Boyle from South Derry came back to H4 today.
On Tues 13.3.81 he was taken to the City hospital [after a
punch-up with warders] until 15.3.81 then he was moved
to Musgrave hospital where he underwent an operation
on his scrotum to replace his testicles back in place. Altogether he got 15 stitches. On the 26th he was moved to
the prison hospital until the 30th when he was moved
back to H4.

From Pat to Liam Og
Bit of crack here today. John Cassidy from Derry has a
nervous breakdown and was taken out to hospital. He's
been on the blanket from 1977. He's in a bad way. (He's
doing 12 years.) Also do you know 3 ex-blanket men
are already in psychiatric ward in hospital camp. Alex
Comerford (Clonard) F. Hanley (Lower Falls) Gerry Murphy (Dundalk). Good PR point. Everything else sound.
Pat H6.

"The doctor wants to see you to tell you when you are
going to die," a warder muttered as he walked into Patsy
O'Hara's cell in H5.
O'Hara walked out and came back later, telling the warder
he was a "slabber."
"I'm no slabber; I speak the Queen's English," said the
warder, following him into the cell.
"When you open that door I don't want any snide remarks,"
said O'Hara.

Sands, in the prison hospital, had lost 24.8 lbs. after thirty-two
days without food. He was still downing pints of water, but
finding the liquid increasingly repulsive. He reacted cautiously
to the news from Dungannon.

To Brownie from Marcella [Sands] 2.4.81
Well Comrade Mor, How are ya! Got your note. Seems
we've well and truly entered new realms. Hopefully we'll
be successful if only for the Movement's sake. I'm just
getting the days in, they fly in. Feel myself getting naturally
and gradually weaker. I will be very sick in a week or two,
but my mind will see me thru. I've no doubt about that.
Seen ya on TV, ya big ugly hunk, you haven't changed a
bit. I'm not at all building hopes on anything. I'm afraid
I'm just resigned to the worse, so sin sin. People find this
hard to grasp altho' I'm ensuring I give my family some
hope to hold on to. I've been reading poetry and Gaelige
in the papers and listening to whatever traditional music
there is on the radio and generally carrying on—so for a
change I'm taking it easy (such an excuse, are ye jealous?).
Watch your big self and Beannacht de ort comrade. Marcella XXXXXXX

That evening McFarlane was trying to figure out what
longer-term strategy to follow if deaths did take place. The
hunger strike committee—an informal group of Sinn Fein and
IRA officials, headed by Adams and set up to handle short-
term planning of the hunger strike—had ruled out replacing
the present four with a separate and second "squad"; it would
be too much like starting a third and then fourth hunger
strike. Instead they had agreed with the prisoners that if a
hunger striker did die he would be replaced with another on
an individual basis. But if the present four did die they would
effectively have another squad of replacements. So would it
be worth going beyond the four? McFarlane figured not. If
public pressure failed to move the Government by the time
the first four died they would have effectively shot their bolt.
And after four, with the authorities still adamant, more deaths
would start to look like suicide, which would be damaging
for the Movement. But if they were to abandon the hunger

strike after four deaths, what then? If the protest continued it would dwindle in size and just be a millstone around the Movement's neck, hampering the war effort. Far better for everyone to move off the protest as one unit, and then devote their energy, so far as the cellular system would allow, to training and politicizing the men for a return to the war. But if they were going to do that the men would have to be prepared for the decisions—they would have to start debating it in the wings soon. But how could he get such a debate going without encouraging a defeatist attitude, without destroying morale? They were tough decisions.

To Brownie Thursday 2.4.81 8.30 P.M.
... Do you mind you told me about lonely posts?—well you were dead right—I feel like an Arab in a synagogue!! Why me eh? It's all your fault, you know! Do you remember?—'Child, how would you like to take on a wee job—PRO?' 'No,' sez I—'Child, you are now PRO.' Hope you're satisfied. I'm away to cry. Take care and God bless.—Bik—

Suddenly Carron had found himself centerstage in one of the most extraordinary political dramas witnessed by a country well used to drama. He was made election agent, which meant he would effectively have to play the part of the candidate. The Northern Ireland Office had refused to allow Sands any freedom to campaign, such as the right to be interviewed on television, despite a threat by the H-Block Committee to take them to court under the Representation of the People Act. So Carron had to go up to the Kesh to get Sands to sign papers appointing him his spokesman for election purposes.

It was the first time he had met Sands. Carron wore his customary blue, pinstripe suit—an unusually dapper figure for a Movement whose followers tended towards the proletarian uniform of anorak and jeans. In Sands he expected to find the long-haired and chubby person familiar to Republican posters and was mildly surprised by the frail figure with short, fair to ginger hair in pajamas and dressing gown who got up to greet him as he walked into the ward at the prison hospital. They adopted the small talk of strangers who knew of each other. Carron awkwardly said that if at any stage Sands wanted to opt out of the hunger strike he should not worry—he would handle things with the people outside. Sands said there was no question of that.

Although they had got a clear field for Sands in the by-election it was going to be no easy ride. The Loyalists also had a single candidate in Harry West, a local farmer and the Official Unionist who had held the seat before Frank Maguire. Sectarian rivalry in Fermanagh–South Tyrone had always ensured a big turnout on polling days—it had repeatedly scored the highest percentage poll in the United Kingdom at general elections. The constituency was reckoned to have a built-in majority for the Nationalists of about 5,000 votes, which meant that if the Nationalists got a unity candidate they could generally expect to win. This time, however, there was no such certainty: Sands could lose through abstentions, largely by Nationalists who might still see a vote for him as a "vote for violence." There was also much antagonism at Maguire's treatment.

Carron and his fellow campaigners quickly discovered the strength of that antagonism when they went hunting for a campaign headquarters in Enniskillen. There was an empty shop in the town which would have been perfect, but when they went to see the owner, a local Catholic businessman, he threw them out indignantly. Eventually they found a little terraced house on the edge of the town center which was awaiting demolition and squeezed into that.

They had only nine days to campaign, before polling day, and the pace was frenetic. Republicans poured into the constituency from all parts of Ireland to help. It had an extraordinary impact on the Catholic community. Fermanagh and South Tyrone was an area where Nationalists were not accustomed to public demonstrations of support for the Republican cause—it was too quick a way of landing up in a police interrogation room—so the sight of convoys of five or six cars flying tricolors and posters, blaring Republican songs from loudspeakers as they roared through little hamlets, created a sense of euphoria. There were problems, of course. Reports came in that the predominantly Protestant Ulster Defense Regiment—successors to the old "B Specials"—were taking a hand in it, harassing canvassers and pulling down posters. At one stage campaigners reported that they had worked through to 4 A.M. putting up posters along a ten-mile route through the constituency, only to find they were all gone when they drove back again. They had gone back to the office, loaded up and started all over again . . . But the wrangling over Noel Maguire seemed to have been forgotten and the canvassers were increasingly encouraged by their doorstep soundings.

Polling day arrived. The booths had their impersonation agents from the two sides, watching eagle-eyed for dead citizens whose passion for voting from the grave was a byword in Fermanagh–South Tyrone. Adams did a tour of all the booths and was startled by the animosity shown by Loyalists—living in something of a political cocoon, in the "ghettos" of West Belfast, he had had little to do with ordinary Protestants since the "Troubles" had started and had not fully appreciated the depths of hatred felt towards the IRA and its associates.

In the House of Commons the Labour spokesman on Northern Ireland, Don Concannon, made an impassioned bid to swing the vote, warning: "A vote for Sands is a vote of approval for the perpetrators of the La Mon massacre, the murder of Lord Mountbatten and the latest brutal and inhuman killing of Mrs. Mathers."

The ballot boxes were locked in the evening and flown by army helicopter to Enniskillen for the count the next day.

Adams slept overnight in Enniskillen and the next morning drove off alone across the border, on his way to report to O Bradaigh. In the Fermanagh College of Further Education the count went on, Carron and West watching the quick-fingered clerks going through the bundles of ballot papers, journalists peering in through the door, a small crowd gathering as the afternoon wore on. Up in the Kesh the Republican prisoners were huddled over their little crystal sets; McFarlane had warned them that if Bobby won there was to be no cheering—it would alert the warders to the fact that they had radios and precipitate searches. Shortly before 2 P.M. the screws in the circle in H5 started yelling and cheering and the prisoners' hearts sank. But it turned out to be only Alex "Hurricane" Higgins, the darling of the Irish snooker fraternity, sinking a corker on television in a world professional championship match against Steve Davis.

At the Fermanagh College of Further Education in Enniskillen the returning officer took the microphone: "Sands, Bobby, Anti-H-Block-Armagh, Political Prisoner . . ."

On the Slane Road to Dublin the red Ford Escort started weaving between the hedgerows as Adams pounded on the steering wheel, shouting: "Fuck it, we've done it, we've done it, we've done it . . ."

In H5 the prisoners could not contain themselves and the roar of triumph, "Bhi An Bua Againn"—Victory is Ours—brought the warders running.

Sands had won 30,492 votes to West's 29,046.

Liam Og from Bik Friday 10.4.81 8.30 P.M.
Comrade, What a day—a real super effort!! Don't know whether to laugh shout or cry. The news was greeted here in silent jubilation (we are very security conscious you see!!) Now I wonder will the opposition be just as quick to declare that the IRA have that popular support they were claiming would be seen if we won this seat. Good old

Austin [Currie] was quick to say we hadn't and it wasn't a vote for the RA [Republican Army]. Up yours too, Austin my boy. Just looking at the figures; it would appear that our honourable opponent, farmer West, received an amount of Nationalist votes—fair play to the dear sensible bastard. Up theirs too!! Onward to victory. Hope you have sobered up sunshine, I'm sitting here picturing the heap of you swilling down loads of black brew and making right idiots of yourselves and boy am I jealous?? . . . I'm away here to relax for a wee while. The strain of this last week has been too much man!! Congrats to one and all you wonderful people. We really showed them. Take care and God Bless . . . Up the good old RA and other such outrageous outbursts. Nite, nite and God Speed. Bik.

Liam Og 10.4.81 from Tony H5
. . . Fr Murphy was in his (Ray's) cell tonight and told him he was talking to Bobby this evening after the election result. Bobby was having a bath and was overjoyed. Fr Murphy was saying that he thought that there was a good chance that the British Government will act on the issue now seeing as we got 30,000 people to stand behind us. He added that he was also talking to Frank and he was very happy with the result . . . comrade I find words hard to describe the jubilation felt here this evening. With the result of the election there is a feeling here tonight which has not been here in a long time. The screws are visibly shattered already—just great.

The warders were not the only ones "shattered" by the result. It undermined the entire shaky edifice of British policy in northern Ireland, which had been so painfully constructed on the hypothesis that blame for the "Troubles" could be placed on a small gang of thugs and hoodlums who enjoyed no community support. Of course it was a shaky edifice in the first place; there had been plenty of evidence to discredit it before the Fermanagh–South Tyrone by-election, at least for those interested in looking for it. In fact it was not even the first time a jailed Republican had taken the seat. In the early 1920s an internee, Cahir Healy, had won it no less than twice and in 1955 Phil Clarke, serving time for an IRA raid on an army barracks, had taken it. But in the polarized circumstances of the north in 1981 you were either a believer or not and the word of the believers—of the security forces, the Government—had come to be accepted far beyond its disputed borders. It was, after all, the foundation of the Government's entire criminalization strategy, the central plank of security policy. And now more than 30,000 Catholics, in just one out of twelve constituencies in the north, had—if Don Concannon was to be believed—voted for "the perpetrators of the La Mon massacre, the murder of Lord Mountbatten and the latest brutal and inhuman killing of Mrs. Mathers." The contradictions and confusion created in Britain were captured in a headline in the Tory-supporting *Daily Express:* "Elected: The Hon. Member for Violence." The *Sunday Express* followed with a blanket condemnation of the voters: "Their attendance at Mass this morning is as corrupt as the kiss of Judas."

But governments, of course, do not lightly give up their misconceptions. Public policies are made up of interlocking structures and interests which over the years develop a momentum of their own; the ship of state is not easily diverted from its course—not even by 30,492 voices out in what for Britain was, after all, the wilderness of Fermanagh–South Tyrone. And so the Government sailed blithely on. In far-off Riyadh, in Saudi Arabia, Mrs. Thatcher emerged from a royal banquet to insist that the result changed nothing. "A crime is a crime is a crime," she said. "It is not political, it is a crime." At Westminster the Leader of the House of Commons, Francis Pym, started sounding out MPs on support for a move to

summarily expel Sands. But it quickly became apparent that
the Government would not get the support for it, not simply
because it would open them to the charge of hypocrisy—in
allowing Sands to stand and then disqualifying him because he
had won—but because there was nothing to stop the Republicans immediately putting him, or another hunger striker,
forward again in the ensuing by-election.

In the prison the hunger strike was continuing inexorably. As
the count had got under way down in Enniskillen, Hughes
was being moved to the prison hospital. Patsy O'Hara was
beginning to feel the effects, telling the doctor that when he
touched his left side, or his stomach, a pain shot up his body.
The doctor said it was to be expected and would only get
worse. A few days later, on the 15th, both he and Raymond
McCreesh followed Sands and Hughes to the hospital, both
of them getting rousing send-offs in their wings.

Quite apart from the overall political significance of the election
result, it had destroyed the Government's short-term strategy
for handling the hunger strike. It was obviously no longer possible to continue trying to ignore it. Instead it was decided to
present a reasonable front—to be seen to be doing everything
possible to resolve the dispute, short of meeting the demands.
So when Sands put in a formal request to be allowed a visit
from three members of the Dublin Parliament, it was quickly
granted; so quickly that Sands himself was caught short—the
outside leadership had not got around to telling him what was
the purpose of the visit. He was getting short-tempered by this
stage and was irritated by the lapse. He had had the last rites
on Saturday the 18th. Medical staff had begun rubbing cream
into his body and checking his condition every two hours. He
was sleeping on a sheepskin rug, on a waterbed, to try and
protect his skin. His eyes were hurting all the time and he was
finding it difficult to read the smuggled comms.

The three Irish Parliamentarians were also members of the European Parliament: Sile de Valera, a statuesque blonde and granddaughter of the founder of the present Irish Republic, Eamon de Valera; Neil Blaney, a former Irish Cabinet minister slung out of government after a scandal over alleged gun-running to the IRA; and John O'Connell, a medical doctor, editor of the *Irish Medical Times* and son of a British soldier.

They met at the Fairways hotel in Dundalk, just south of the border in the early hours of Monday morning, having been told that the RUC wanted them across the border by 7:30 A.M. for security reasons. Owen Carron and Danny Morrison met them at the hotel and they piled into Carron's car. On the other side of the yellow line marking the border the police were waiting. Two armored Cortinas loaded with officers pulled out, one in front and one at the back, and they roared up the A6 to the Kesh.

As they went into the prison hospital John O'Connell turned to the other two and said that he was planning to ask Sands to end the hunger strike. They walked into the cell, looking dapper—all three of them wearing suits—as the warder said: "You've got visitors, members of the European Parliament." Sands was lying on the bed looking gaunt, his face marble white, almost blending with the white sheets; he was very different from the chubby-faced picture everyone knew on the election posters and in the media. His eyes seemed glazed at first, but he brightened and sat up when he saw them. O'Connell looked at him critically, as a patient; he had little experience of starvation, only a couple of patients suffering anorexia nervosa, but the diagnosis he offered up mentally was easy: emaciated, needs nourishment fast, intravenously. They took his hand in turn—Sands too feeble to lift his—and introduced themselves. O'Connell made a quick medical check before they started talking: eyes shrunken and sight fading. He flashed a hand in front of his face: wink reflex going. The pulse was weak and, slipping a hand into his pajama jacket, he felt the heart was feeble. About five or six days to live.

They sat down on the right-hand side of the bed. How could they help? they asked. Sands launched into an account of the hunger strike, explaining why the five demands had been devised and how they could be met by Britain without loss of face. They listened intently, struck by the clarity of his thinking. Then O'Connell appealed to him to come off, telling him that he had proved his point and that all three of them would fight for him and demand that Thatcher make the changes. It was right to stand and fight for what you believed in, but there was no use dying for it. Surely it was better to live and fight than to die. Sands smiled: "I knew you would say that," he said. No, he would not be coming off. They talked for about forty minutes—no limit had been set on the visit—when O'Connell decided Sands should be allowed to rest and said they had better be going. He took Sands's hand in his own, putting the other on his shoulder, and said: "We'll do everything we can to help." De Valera had tears in her eyes and put a hand behind him; for a moment O'Connell thought she was going to sweep him into her arms, like a mother cuddling a child. Blaney, big and tough of reputation, bent over to say goodbye and caressed Sands's face with the back of his hand in a gesture of intense gentleness. As they looked back from the door all three knew they would not be seeing him again: there was no doubt in their minds that Sands was going the distance. De Valera turned to the warder and asked why they kept food at the bottom of the bed. "In case he wants to eat," said the warder.

They were taken out of the prison through a side gate, because there was a Loyalist demonstration taking place at the front against their visit. They had planned to go to Belfast to hold a press conference, but their police escort insisted they had to return south. So they headed back to Dundalk to organize an alternative press conference in Dublin and dispatch a telegram to Thatcher, appealing for a meeting to discuss the prison dispute. Mrs. Thatcher, still in Saudi Arabia, retorted at a press conference: "It is not my habit or custom to meet MPs from a foreign country about a citizen of the UK, resident in the UK."

Desperate moves were afoot in Dublin. The Papal Nuncio, Monsignor Gaetano Alibrandi—the Vatican's ambassador to Ireland—dispatched a telegram to the Pope, outlining the growing crisis. The Prime Minister, Charlie Haughey, was becoming increasingly anxious. He had planned to hold an election in May and the groundwork was well advanced; the campaign song, "Arise and Follow Charlie," had even made it into the pop charts. But if he held an election with the hunger strike still on, it could be disastrous for him. Sands had shown the impact the H-Blocks could have on an election and a few thousand votes stolen from Fianna Fail—the "Republican Party"—by the prisoners could be enough to give FitzGerald power. He called in the British Ambassador for half an hour for discussions. Haughey, together with John Hume and the Bishop of Derry, Dr. Edward Daley, was busily trying to arrange for an intervention by the European Commission for Human Rights. The European Commission had been involved in the H-Block issue before, although in completely different circumstances.

The commission was established to monitor and act under the European Convention on Human Rights, enacted and signed by twenty states in 1953. Staffed by about twenty lawyers, housed in a modern building behind the Council of Europe Assembly in Strasbourg, their brief was to investigate complaints, mediate between complainants and, where they were unable to resolve the issue, to refer the matter to the European Court of Human Rights for a ruling, or to the Council of Europe's Foreign Ministers for diplomatic action. In June 1980 they had rejected a complaint over the H-Blocks issue, brought by Kieran Nugent and three other prisoners, ruling that there were no grounds under international law for the claim to political status and that conditions in the prison were self-inflicted, and therefore no cause for complaint against Britain. But at the same time they had criticized Britain, expressing concern "at the inflexible approach of the State authorities which has been concerned more to punish offenders against prison discipline than to explore ways of resolving such a serious deadlock." It was the phrase which Haughey and Hume believed could give the opening to Britain to now act—because it could be presented as a reaction to the commission, rather than to the hunger strike. The problem was that the commission's constitution specified that complaints could only be lodged by signatories to the Convention, or "any person, nongovernmental organization, or group of individuals claiming to be the victims of the violation." So the complaint had to come from the prisoners—preferably Sands. Hume, with his powerful contacts in Europe, had nearly persuaded the commission to allow two members, the Danish acting president, Professor Carl Aage Norgaard, and a Norwegian, Professor Torkel Opsahl, to act as mediators. But a row had ensued at the commission's Strasbourg headquarters, with other members protesting that such an informal initiative might damage the commission's standing. So Haughey decided he would have to get a formal request out of the Sands family for the commission to intervene.

He had an hour-long meeting with Bobby's sister, Marcella, and their mother, at which he told them the only chance for him was to get the commission into the Kesh. Britain was looking for an opening for a settlement. It was a formality. He produced a prepared document—a complaint to the commission over the treatment of Sands in prison—and persuaded Marcella to sign it. It was a three-point complaint against Britain, for violating Sands's rights to life, to protection from inhuman treatment and to freedom of expression—the last a reference to the refusal of the authorities to allow him access to the media before the election and to have normal contact with his constituents since becoming an MP.

Within hours Professor Norgaard and Professor Opsahl were on their way, together with two commission officials, Mr. Michael O'Boyle and Dr. Hans Christian Kruger. They stopped off at London and had a ninety-minute meeting with Foreign Office officials, agreeing that while Marcella Sands's complaint was sufficient grounds for them to make the journey, it would have to be confirmed by Bobby Sands himself if they were to take it any further.

They went into the Kesh on Saturday the 25th, and ran straight into problems. Sands, through his lawyer, Pat Finucan, flatly refused to see them unless his "advisers"—McFarlane, Gerry Adams and another senior Sinn Fein official, Danny Morrison—were present. The commissioners asked if they could see McFarlane to discuss it and he was brought across to the hospital to meet them. They asked him if there was any way they could get in to see Sands on their own, just to get confirmation of Marcella's complaint. McFarlane said that the conditions had already been agreed among themselves and would have to be met before Sands would agree to see them. The commissioners said rules of procedure by which they were bound would not allow it. The commission always conducted its business in confidence and the presence of "witnesses" had a ring of publicity about it which worried them. McFarlane, as always looking for the opening to wrong-foot the Government, asked who had prevented them from bringing in Adams and Morrison. Professor Opsahl said it was the Government, but Dr. Kruger cut in, saying the Government would prevent them if asked. McFarlane said that was only an assumption until they made the request. Kruger said that was correct, but they did not feel able to make such a request. McFarlane said they had already set the precedent by asking to see him. There was no question of his asking Sands to change the preconditions. O'Boyle said talk of preconditions indicated inflexibility. McFarlane retorted that they had made attempts to settle the issue in the face of British inflexibility.

With the argument unresolved McFarlane went in to see Sands for ten minutes. Sands could hardly talk. He was not incoherent, but his speech was slurred and slow, as if he was running up a hill. McFarlane outlined what was happening and Sands told him to stand fast. McFarlane went out to see the commissioners again, reaffirmed Sands's position and told them that if they could get permission to have Adams and Morrison in, it could lead to talks. He was taken back to his cell.

After eight hours in the Kesh the commissioners gave up. They slipped out of the prison through a side entrance, avoiding a demonstration by 200 followers of the Reverend Ian Paisley, who were waving placards demanding: "Did 2,000 dead have human rights?" and brandishing hangmen's nooses. Later the commissioners issued a three-paragraph statement, pedantically headed: "Marcella Sands v. United Kingdom (Application number 9338/81)." It said Mr. Sands did not wish to associate himself with his sister's complaint, although he was prepared to see them in the company of three colleagues. "After further consultations the delegation concluded that in the circumstances it was not possible to see and confer with Mr. Sands and accordingly no meeting took place."

That night Sands had a crisis. His family were called up to the prison hospital and for a while it was touch and go whether he would make it through the night. Outside tensions rose. Bakeries in Catholic areas reported a run on bread supplies as stockpiling began. The IRA staged a show of strength in Armagh, setting up a road block with fifteen masked men carrying Armalites and submachine guns. The "Ulster Army Council," a defunct umbrella organization which had been created to coordinate Loyalist paramilitary action, was revived and met to agree on strategy for the defense of Protestant areas if civil war broke out. The UDA announced it was mobilizing 2,500 men in Belfast to protect Protestant areas. In Andersonstown, West Belfast, the INLA dumped a hijacked lorry in the middle of a road, blocking traffic. A police patrol arrived and Constable Garry Martin, aged twenty-eight and the father of two baby sons, climbed into the cab to move it, dying instantly as it exploded. Near the town of Castlewellan, in Co. Down, IRA gunmen opened fire on an unmarked van carrying three soldiers. The driver lost control and the vehicle turned over, killing Lance Corporal Richard McKee of the Ulster Defense Regiment. Across the Province police started rounding up H-Block campaigners for "questioning." In Belfast 13,000 took part in a march, showing the strength of Nationalist emotions. In London one end of Downing Street was padlocked as police discreetly began introducing tighter security measures. The Government seemed resigned to the death of Sands and the ensuing mayhem.

But at 4:30 P.M. on Tuesday the 28th the twice-hourly shuttle service to Belfast took off from Heathrow with another VIP on his way to try and settle the dispute at the Kesh: this time it was the Pope's secretary.

Fr. Magee was an Irishman, born in Newry in 1936. He had studied philosophy in Cork before going out to Nigeria, working there for six years as a missionary teacher. In Nigeria he had been befriended by Cardinal Sergio Pignedoli, then papal delegate in Lagos, under whose patronage he was to have a meteoric career in the Church. Ordained in Rome in 1962, he was invited by Cardinal Pignedoli to join the Secretariat for the Evangelization of Peoples in Rome. In 1975 he had been appointed personal secretary to Pope Paul VI, a personal friend of Cardinal Pignedoli. Fr. Magee established a close relationship with Paul VI, who mentioned him in his will, but after his death was asked to remain secretary to

John Paul I. It was Fr. Magee who found the pontiff dead in his bed, thirty-three days later. When the Polish John Paul II was elected he also asked Fr. Magee to stay on, explaining: "I don't know anyone around here at the Vatican." Later the Pope appointed a Polish priest to share the secretarial duties with him.

Fr. Magee had discussed papal intervention in the hunger strike with Cardinal O Fiaich, by phone to Armagh, a few days earlier. The Irish Cardinal was not particularly enthusiastic, feeling that it was too late and that to have an emissary come over from Rome in a blaze of publicity and then fail to settle the dispute would be worse than nothing. But the Pope and the Vatican's Secretary of State, Cardinal Casaroli, after consultations with the Catholic hierarchy in England as well as the Irish Government, decided the intervention was worth it. Fr. Magee phoned Cardinal O Fiaich again on Tuesday, April 28 to say he was on his way. The British Embassy in Rome was advised of the priest's plan and it was agreed that no announcement would be made until he actually got to Belfast and into the Kesh, to avoid Loyalist demonstrations on his arrival. But when he arrived on his Alitalia flight at Heathrow en route for Belfast he found the press had been alerted and the airport was swarming with journalists. He was met by the Minister of State at the Foreign Office, Peter Blaker, and had a brief talk with him in an airport lounge before taking the flight to Belfast.

In Belfast Cardinal O Fiaich had discovered that the police were arranging to pick Fr. Magee up at the airport. He tried to persuade them not to, because it might identify him too closely with the authorities. But the police insisted, on security grounds. At the airport the cardinal suggested to Fr. Magee that he go to Fr. Murphy's home and then into the Kesh under the aegis of the prison chaplain. Fr. Magee agreed, but police insisted on his making the trip to Fr. Murphy's in a bullet-proof limousine. So they set off in convoy, the cardinal in his car, Fr. Magee in the police car and press cars tagging along behind. It was turning into a circus. At Fr. Murphy's house, a few miles from the Kesh, they had to talk in the bedroom, to avoid the heads peering in through the windows downstairs. Fr. Magee went into the Kesh twice, seeing Sands three times as well as meeting Hughes, McCreesh and O'Hara, making a personal appeal on the Pope's behalf to them to try to settle the dispute. He also spent an hour with Humphrey Atkins, finding the Secretary of State surprisingly hostile. He left Northern Ireland with nothing achieved, issuing a statement to "assure all that the efforts of the Holy Father will continue in seeking ways to help people in Northern Ireland, indeed in Ireland as a whole, to work out solutions to their communal problems in accordance with Christian teachings."

The tension continued to rise, with some help from the Secretary of State, who announced he had knowledge that the IRA was planning to try and start sectarian warfare in the event of Sands's death; he claimed that in one area of Belfast they were intending to evacuate residents and burn their emptied houses, blaming it on Protestant paramilitaries to fuel sectarian conflict. When it emerged that the area he was referring to was the Short Strand—a Catholic enclave in Protestant East Belfast—the claim was met with ridicule; one community leader in the area, making the point that virtually every family there had IRA connections, asked sarcastically: "Whose house will they burn first?"

In Rome the Pope called on Roman Catholics to "pray for our Catholic and non-Catholic brethren in Northern Ireland in the time of grave tension they are going through, which it is feared may again erupt in new and most grave acts of fratricidal violence."

In the village of Toomebridge Bernadette McAliskey was appealing for calm. "In the event of Bobby Sands dying we do not want a single riot, a single stoning or a single petrol bombing," she told several thousand demonstrators at an H-Block rally. "If Bobby Sands can die for the five demands, we can hold our tempers."

Inside the Kesh the tension was having its effect on McFarlane. He had anxiously asked the Falls Road for advice on what would happen if a settlement were reached while Bobby was in a coma. Would doctors be able to intervene, legally, if they had not had his prior permission? On the Monday night, after the commissioners had gone, he dreamed he was talking to Cardinal O Fiaich. The cardinal was giving him a verbal lambasting. Adams was standing behind the primate, pissing against a wall and glaring at McFarlane menacingly over horn-rimmed glasses. It was beginning to dawn on McFarlane that maybe the Brits were not going to do anything: they were just going to let Bobby die.

Brownie [Gerry Adams] 29.4.81 from Bik
Comrade, Mor, got your very welcome comm today. Good to hear from you. This is really some situation isn't it? A terrific thought struck me two days ago and that was that there was every possibility the Brits will not say anything at all or make any attempt at dipping in attractive offers, but just stand back and let things run their course. I think your analysis of the Brit mentality is about as close as anyone can come i.e. their stupidity is unbelievable. I still don't think they have learned that oppression breeds resistance and further oppression—further resistance!! As for their arrogance—I never saw the likes of it (of course I'm not a much travelled individual but I reckon I'd have to go a long way to meet persons of a similar 'superior' nature). However, as you said, they will regret their stupidity. How I wish I were out—just to light the blue touch paper and retire if you know what I mean!! Old habits die hard though some of mine had to be re-directed as you well

know. Anyway, one day I'll make a few noises in the right
sectors. Now, where was I? Yes, Brit arrogance. I mind
Tom McKearney quoted me a bit of Rudyard Kipling (I
think that's the guy who makes exceedingly good cakes!).
According to old Rudy the British are immune to logic—a
sensible enough assertion I would say. They're the only
people I know who are perfectly correct when they are
entirely wrong. I was over there a couple of years and found
that this attitude was prevalent among all classes. Though
I suppose it's wrong of me to generalize in such a manner.
Oh balls to the British—why waste skibs and ink? As you
know I saw Bob on Saturday—it was quite an experience
and in all honesty I haven't felt the same since. I just had
a short yarn with him and when I was preparing to leave
he said quietly: 'I'm dying Bik.' Don't think I can describe
how I felt just then. I couldn't say anything except God
Bless. I told him I'd see him again very soon and he just
gave me a quiet laugh. Man, what a feeling!! . . .

To Liam Og 29.4.81 12.30 A.M. (of 30th)
. . . I think it's becoming increasingly more obvious that
the Brits are going to hold fast. It's a nightmarish thought
comrade which is taking on the form of cold hard reality
with each passing day . . .

Liam Og from Bik 30.4.81
Comrade, just after reading your comm for the third time.
What can I say? You should have been a psychologist—that
was an invaluable therapy session on three skibs. The truth
is you are perfectly correct in drawing the conclusions you
did from my last comms as I have been worried of just such
a situation you mentioned, i.e. a last minute life and death
struggle, with the Brits trying to panic me. There is only
one answer I suppose and that is to be strong—stronger
than the Brits in fact and to have faith in oneself and

those pulling with you. As you say—maintain the line and refuse to be panicked. I know Bob will see it through so I reckon 100 per cent effort must be forthcoming from the rest of us. It's just that this situation is exactly what you said it was—overwhelming—and it takes a bit of effort staying with it. However your comm had a sound effect on me—reassuring and solidifying I would say. You're really quite a chap you know and you needn't apologize for things which may hurt—very often they prove the only recipe for success. By the way it didn't hurt. Try harder next time (Ha). You're not really the 'B' you say you are though there are those who would say you were worse. Just on what you say about other men going on hunger strike—I take your point about committing the Movement on men's personal opinions and agree that only the best interests should dictate our actions. You already know my feelings about replacing a dead comrade—I still feel we should do this though I did accept last week's decision of the Army Council. I believe that this situation has become even bigger than we imagined it would and therefore we should examine all strategies which may help to achieve a victory. I know we are speaking here of a terrible cost in terms of men's lives. Anyway the first four hunger strikers and then a possible repetition with those who follow. But high stakes will demand a high price. I know all the arguments against protracted hunger strike and basically speaking I have been in agreement with them. However if changing circumstances offer us other avenues which at one time considered infeasible are now thought feasible we should explore them. That's about it I reckon. I've enclosed the names of the first four replacements from my original list. I'll get them to comm you as soon as possible. They are 1. Joe McDonnell H5 Lenadoon. 2. Brendan McLoughlin H5 North Derry. 3. Kieran Doherty H6 Andersonstown. 4. Kevin Lynch IRSP H3 Dungiven. There are others which you won't need at present—just the first four OK. I haven't much else for you just now . . .

Jim Gibney, a senior Sinn Fein official, had just been in to see McCreesh. He was in good shape. Gibney was walking down the corridor when he saw Sands's door open. His mother, father and sister, Marcella, were alongside the bed. Bobby was wearing a crucifix given to him by Fr. Magee on the Pope's behalf.

"How are you?" asked Gibney.

"Is that you, Jim?" asked Sands.

"It is, Bobby." He took his hand.

"I'm blind. I can't see you. Tell the lads to keep their chins up."

With speculation in the media that the end was only hours away for Sands, the Province settled into a deathly wait. On Thursday night he slept in snatches, from hour to hour. He had been managing to hold the water down, but was battling to get it out again. His hearing was going as well as his sight—noises seemed to echo in his head. Pain in his stomach and chest was constant. Friday was May Day and Labour's spokesman on Northern Ireland, Don Concannon, chose the occasion to fly over from London for a hurried visit to the Kesh, to inform Sands of his party's backing for the Government on the whole issue. Concannon, who as former minister at the Northern Ireland Office responsible for prisons had presided over the withdrawal of special category status, explained afterwards that he had gone in because he did not want Sands misunderstanding the Opposition's position.

Later in the day Carron was allowed in for the last time. He found Sands in no shape to talk. He was lying on the waterbed, his left eye was black and closed, the right eye nearly closed and his mouth twisted as if he had suffered a stroke. He had no feeling in his legs and could only whisper.

Every now and then he started dry retching. He managed to ask Carron if there was any change. The Fermanagh man said no, there was no change. Sands said: "Well, that's it." He told Carron: "Keep my Ma in mind." Carron bent over the bed, hugged him and kissed him.

"Do not tell me the IRA represents people in Northern Ireland," said the Foreign Secretary, Lord Carrington, on Independent Radio. "They have no status, they are not accepted by anyone," he added.

Over the weekend one last, despairing bid was made by Haughey and the Church. Fr. Murphy went in to see McFarlane to relay the suggestion, from Cardinal O Fiaich, that if the prisoners would compromise with two or three demands—say their own clothing, the right not to work and perhaps free association—it would give Haughey more leverage in dealing with Mrs. Thatcher. The Government had been insisting that the five demands amounted to political status, so that they could not claim that three demands also amounted to status. It would put them in an embarrassing position. McFarlane replied sarcastically: "Why was it only at the last minute that everyone wanted to put pressure on the Brits?" There was no way that they were going to provide escape hatches for "Amadon"—"the Fool," as he called Haughey—in his dealings with "Tinknickers," Mrs. Thatcher. Obviously Britain did not want a settlement, so it did not matter whether there were fifteen demands or one demand. They were using the prisoners to try and break the IRA and were prepared to let men die to achieve that. And if that was the case then men would die, because they were not surrendering.

"You are looking for a victory over them and they the same over you, which means someone loses," said the chaplain. "What I'm looking for is a settlement whereby the prisoners get basically what they want and the Brits don't come under the accusing finger of surrendering to terrorism, which they won't do anyway."

McFarlane said that if the Brits really wanted a solution they would agree to fifteen demands and call it Man on the Moon Status. The prisoners were sticking by their five demands.

"I hope you win," said Fr. Murphy, as he left.

On Sunday Sands lapsed into a coma. His parents, brother Sean and Marcella were with him to the end, which came at 1:17 on the morning of Tuesday, May 5, 1981.

It was announced by the Northern Ireland Office thirty-five minutes later with a terse statement: "He took his own life by refusing food and medical intervention for sixty-six days." The Speaker of the House of Commons, George Thomas, rose to tell Parliament with the words: "I regret to have to inform the House of the death of Robert Sands Esquire, the Member for Fermanagh and South Tyrone." He pointedly failed to extend condolences to the family, which are traditionally offered by the Speaker on the death of a Member.

Reaction flooded in from around the world. The U.S. Government issued a statement expressing deep regret. The Long-shoremen's Union announced a twenty-four-hour boycott of British ships. The New Jersey state legislature voted 34–29 for a resolution honoring his "courage and commitment." More than 1,000 gathered in St. Patrick's Cathedral to hear New York's Cardinal Cook offer a Mass of reconciliation for northern Ireland. Irish bars in the city closed for two hours in mourning. The New York Times said: "Despite proximity and a common language the British have persistently misjudged the depth of Irish nationalism." In San Francisco's Irish community the mood was reported to be "subdued, courteous enough, but curiously menacing, as if everyone is waiting for a message as yet undelivered." In Rome the President of the

Italian Senate, Amintore Fanfani, stepped into the breach left by the British Speaker, expressing condolences to the Sands family. About 5,000 students burned the Union Jack and shouted "Freedom for Ulster" during a march in Milan. In Ghent students invaded the British consulate. Thousands marched in Paris behind a huge portrait of Sands, to chants of "The IRA will conquer." The town of Le Mans announced it was naming a street after him, which the British Embassy said was "an insult to Britain."

The Hong Kong *Standard* said it was "sad that successive British governments have failed to end the last of Europe's religious wars." The *Hindustan Times* said Mrs. Thatcher had allowed a fellow Member of Parliament to die of starvation, an incident which had never before occurred "in a civilized country." Tehran announced Iran would be sending its ambassador in Sweden to represent the Government at the funeral. In Oslo demonstrators threw a balloon filled with tomato sauce at the Queen, who was on a visit to Norway. In India Opposition members of the Upper House stood for a minute's silence in tribute. Members of Indira Gandhi's ruling Congress Party refused to join in. In Portugal members of the Opposition stood for him. In Spain the Catholic *Ya* newspaper described Sands's hunger strike as "subjectively an act of heroism" while the conservative *ABC* said he was a political kamikaze who had got his strategy wrong. *Die Welt* said in West Germany that the British Government was right and he was simply trying to blackmail the state with his life. In Russia *Pravda* described it as "another tragic page in the grim chronicle of oppression, discrimination, terror and violence" in Ireland. In Poland Lech Walesa paid tribute. In Toulouse a bomb exploded in a warehouse used by the British tire firm, Dunlop, and a slogan was found sprayed on a wall saying: "English power kills." A second bomb blew a hole in the door of the British Chamber of Commerce in Milan and a third exploded outside the Royal British Club in Lisbon. In

London a parcel bomb addressed to the Prince of Wales was intercepted at High Holborn sorting office.

On the streets of West Belfast the women took to the streets, banging dustbin lids—in the days of internment used as the alarm to signal the troops were coming. By 2 A.M., as the news had spread throughout the ghetto areas, barricades were burning and Molotov cocktails arching their way towards police and army bases and patrols.

In cell 6, D Wing, H3, baby-faced Jake Jackson lay on his back in the top bunk, staring at the ceiling. He was remembering a day back in December 1965. He had been six years old, living with his granny in the Ardoyne. It had been snowing outside, which had added to the feeling of desolation. He had gone downstairs to his Aunt Mary and said: "My Granny won't wake up." Then Mary was crying and neighbors were running in and out. On the day of the funeral his mother had come back without his father and he'd said "Where's daddy?" and his sister had said "Your dad fell down the hole and they filled it in" and he had cried and cried and cried. And on his bunk he cried quietly in the silence of the H-Block. Below him Bik was scribbling.

To Brownie 2.15 A.M.
Comrade mor, I just heard the news—I'm shattered—just can't believe it. This is a terrible feeling I have. I don't even know what to say. Comrade, I'm sorry, but I just can't say anything else. May God in his infinite mercy grant eternal rest to his soul. Jesus Christ protect and guide us all.
God Bless.
xoxo Bik xoxo

Liam Og Tue 5.5.81 8.00 A.M.
Comrade, this grief is unbelievable. I know you all must be wrecked out there. Words fail me to tell you the truth.

I always was prepared for this and thought it would come but I was always praying and hoping that we could avoid it. When it did come it stunned me and I still feel numb. I can't really say much at present. I've enclosed a short note to the Sands family and Ricky has done one from the blanket men OK? Let's stay together comrade and hammer the bastards into the ground. I'll be in touch again soon. Could you get the signer [lawyer] up on Thursday just to get me out of this concrete box. God bless. Bik.

5.5.81 from Seanna H6
Got words on visits about Bob. No need to tell you how we feel. Also we got comm from you this morning. Screws not saying anything to lads, but slobbering and cracking jokes amongst themselves. Just before lock-up tonight they searched a few cells and wrote slogans on the walls. Screws weren't regulars . . . A few of the things they wrote, 'Goodbye Bobby, Bobby Sands RIP etc.' . . .

To:—Frank—Ray + Patsy—Hospital
Comrades, the death of our comrade Bob has left us all in great sorrow and though we had prepared for such a tragic event it nevertheless stunned each of us. I feel a great sense of personal loss also—in fact we all do—blanket men are more than comrades—they are brothers. Therefore our loss is all the greater. We all feel a bitterness of immeasurable depth and a very great anger at this callous act by the British Government. From this has come an even greater determination, to resist and to fight back harder. It is a time for total commitment by each of us as we think on the ultimate sacrifice Bob made and of the torture each of you are enduring this very instant. We have taken strength from his death and from your resolve and I can tell you now that these men have responded in a true Republican spirit—totally disciplined and determined. We all stand

with you and we shall not be shaken. We can succeed and we will succeed. May God take care of each of you and Bless you.—Bik—

To Liam Og from Bik 5.30 P.M.
Comrade, I've been following all the news and trying to keep a clear head at the same time. Things must be hectic out there. In here its quiet—no trouble—no talk from screws—no problems. Hope you got all my stuff today. There's not a lot I can tell you at present—I'm ready and waiting for any moves anyone may make, but I don't reckon they are coming—not just now, anyway. I hear Frank is in a bad way now. Dear God what a place!! Your advice re people trying to put pressure on me, and what way I should get was sound. That's what Index was at this morning in his bungling fashion. I paid no heed comrade—such tactics aren't worthy of a reaction. Well mate, it's been a heartbreaking day for us all. We lost someone we all loved very dearly and we can't cry in case someone is looking. Who made these rules, eh? Love to all.

To Liam Og from Bik 5.3.81 1.00 P.M.
Comrade, got your comm a few minutes ago—sound enough. Not really much to say. My sorrow is now paralleled by an extreme bitterness comrade, but I'm sound enough. I've kept the lads on a tight rein and they have responded well. It's now 1:30 and Index has just left me. We didn't talk much though he asked if there was anything in my power to prevent the Hughes family going through the same agony next week. I told him that power lay with the Brits and if they didn't implement a solution then there would be more deaths and as far as I could see this was on the cards. He said a prayer for Bob and just after he started he turned to me and said—'we're praying for two Roberts

aren't we?' (referring to my father)—I just said—that's correct. That's the heap. I'll get back to you tomorrow. Take good care and God Bless. Bik.

6.5.81 From Riasteard PRO
Alright comrade? Will you put an insertion in the paper on behalf of the blanket men using the following verse. 'They have nothing in their whole imperial arsenal that can break the spirit of one Irishman who doesn't want to be broke.' That's it cara, it is of sentimental importance to a lot of us for Bobby more or less adopted it as his motto . . .

To Liam Og from O/C H5 6.5.81
. . . The tension in the block prior to Bobby's death was running very high. There was an incident on Monday concerning a petty screw and one of our lads (Paddy O'Hara, Tyrone). There were words exchanged and when the screw started into Paddy's cell he was clocked. The screw got a black eye. Paddy at this point was alright, but he was then put between the grilles with the same screw and we heard scuffles there and believe Paddy may have received a severe beating. The men are now stunned and shocked at the reality of Bob's death. The tension is still there and the screws are not taking any chances, letting too many out at the same time . . .

His body was brought home the following afternoon, to his parents' house on Laburnum Way in Twinbrook Estate where it lay in state in an open coffin under the front window of the drawing room. Local youths built a shrine out of boxes across the road, with a crucifix painted black—the words "peace," "justice" and "freedom" inscribed in white—a tiny statue of Christ in Glory and, fluttering above in the slight wind, the tricolor and the flags of the ancient kingdoms of Ulster,

Munster, Connacht and Leinster. Relays of young IRA men and women in black masks, IRA uniforms and dark glasses stood guard of honor night and day, one at each end of the coffin, watching as neighbors, friends and the curious walked through to pay their last respects. Several top IRA men who had never personally known Sands slipped by, kissing his cold and rouged face.

A Sinn Fein official whispered to Rosaleen Sands that there was an English journalist outside who wanted to see him. She did not want him in, but then someone said, "Why not, let them see what they've done." So he came in and stood uncertainly by the coffin, nodded to Mrs. Sands who stared implacably back, and hurried out . . .

A news agency photographer offered the Sands family £75,000 for a picture of Bobby in his coffin. During his time in internment a group photograph had been taken of him and fellow prisoners, with a smuggled camera, and the blurred picture had become one of the most famous in the world. His family turned down the offer of a new one.

The funeral was held on the Thursday. The Sands family had been refused a "concelebrated Mass"—the Church did not want to make a fuss about Sands's death. The people did.

It was pure guesswork as to how many attended, but the general estimate was that more than 100,000 people lined the route from St. Luke's church, a few yards from the Sands home, to Milltown cemetery. It was the silence of the numbers which made the deepest impression—not frightening, but awe-inspiring. The tricolor and gloves and a white rose were pinned to the coffin. It wended its way down the Stewartstown Road, past the army base at Lenadoon, where huge screens had been erected to protect a nearby Protestant housing estate from the sight of an IRA martyr's funeral. The procession was led by a piper, playing an H-Block song:

But I'll wear no convict's uniform
Nor meekly serve my time
That Britain may call Ireland's fight
Eight hundred years of crime.

It was raining and at Milltown the red clay was being churned by shuffling feet between the dangling Christs and the marble Marys watching over the tombstones. Mourners had ducked under their umbrellas and television cameramen and photographers from America, Europe, Japan and even Thailand clung to a scaffolding erected to give them a bird's eye view of the grave. The coffin was carried with the pomp of the slow march, eight-year-old Gerard smart in brown jacket with a Beatle-style haircut, clutching his grandmother's hand and following behind, looking bemused by the funeral rites for a father he had not known.

In the crowd a middle-aged woman in black leather coat and boots, her hair done up in loops, craned to try and see Mrs. Sands. Peggy O'Hara whispered to her daughter, Elizabeth, in explanation that she was trying to see what a mother looked like who could stand by and let her son die.

They played the Last Post, rolled up the tricolor and gave it to Mrs. Sands with the beret and the gloves. Owen Carron delivered the oration. He was tired—he had been up all night at Liam Og's house, writing it—but he said the required things, ending with the declaration: "Bobby Sands, your sacrifice will not be in vain." The coffin was laid in the grave. The family took turns shoveling in a symbolic clump of earth. Gerard had to be helped with the heavy spade.

The Secretary of State marked the day with a statement defending the Government against the charge of inflexibility. "Is murder any less murder because the person responsible claims he had a political motive?" he asked. "The answer is no," he said.

The army's Spearhead battalion, on standby in Britain for emergencies, flew into the Province.

In Dublin there was a knock at the door of Garret FitzGerald's home. Mrs. FitzGerald opened it and saw a beggarman. English newspapers said the beggar was a gunman dressed in paramilitary uniform, come to assassinate Garret for criticizing the IRA.

Inside the Kesh, after the dinner dishes had been cleared away and the warders had started the night watch, McFarlane called down the corridor: "Parade, fall in!" Behind the steel doors bare feet stamped to attention. "Stand easy!" Jake Jackson had been working on the oration since the day before. Now he started reading from the four sheets of toilet paper he had used to write it on: Comrades, we are gathered here to commemorate the death of a friend and a comrade and a great Irishman . . ."

"Snowing."

His cellmate put down the Bible and clambered up beside him. The prisoner stepped down and began his circuit on the runway. He stopped, leant over his bed and dug into the foam, straightening up with the tiny square of paper, which he began to unfold. It was frayed and smudged and the blue ink had softened to cloudy mauve where dampness had crept in. At the top, barely legible, was the title: "Mo Chraoibhin Cno" ("My Brown-Haired Girl") and the name of Ethna Carberry. The poetess from Rathcoole, from where the dog chased its tail and he had once played kick the tin. He picked out the brass link from the rosary, cradled in the center of the paper, and searched the yellowing wall for yesterday's scratching, among the brown smears and Gaelic phrases. He found it:

A sword of light hath pierced the dark, our eyes
    have seen the star.
Oh Eire, leave the ways of sleep now days of
    promise are,
The rusty spears upon your walls are stirring to
    and fro,
In dreams they front uplifted shield, then awake,
Mo Chraoibhin Cno!

Carefully he began etching: "Within the gloom we hear a voice that once was ours to know . . ." On the next wing shift it would all be gone, washed and melted into curled-up wisps of paint by the steamhose, the scalding water and bleaching detergents. But now at least it was a distraction. What else was there, but the brown-haired girl upon the wall?

The prisoner's arm was aching by the time he had finished. Carefully he folded the paper again and buried it back in the mattress. He began pacing the floor for warmth, falling into a rhythm with his cellmate, walking parallel. Six paces up and six paces down. What would be the circumference if it was the diameter? He'd worked it out before, argued it out, but couldn't remember the answer. He grunted with impatience and stopped to peer out the window again. Two sparrows were truding in the snow.

He turned to the rubbish pile and sorted out some bread, putting that day's slices on one side; maybe he would try again at molding a chess set. He had stamped the last set flat, crumbling on the heating pipes. Become a Grand Master. A game a week, that would be fifty-two a year, 1,040 in twenty years, how many in twenty-two? He lost the calculation. Twenty-two years. He grunted. His cellmate stopped the pacing.

"What d'you think things will be like in twenty-two years? Think we'd have robots for screws?"

"Aye, with the Red Hand of Ulster engraved on their arms."

"Singing 'The Sash.'"

"Knowing my luck when I'm let out I'll be flattened by an automated bus at the front gate."

The prisoner climbed back on the pipes and flung the bread out. One sparrow caught the movement, fluttered briefly in the air, dropped down and began pecking. The other quickly joined in. Not as excited as with the maggots.

Resting his head against the grille again, the prisoner remembered his panic the morning he woke up to find mattress, blankets, hair and beard crawling with the white slugs; their tiny rustles at night as they shoved the paper in the corner; the crunch under his bare feet when he got up. But the birds had loved them. So what did you do for the summer? Collected maggots for the birds . . . His mind started its familiar wandering. Have you read the Bible? No, but I smoked the Ten Commandments. Not true. He'd been through it twice now. That was a Right. A Bible for "spiritual consolation." And to wipe your arse. The thought seemed to trigger his stomach.

He went over to the plastic chamber pots and took the lid off. Full. Christ, hope the other lasts until lock-up. Otherwise it will be out the window, with piss down the wall. Or general slop-out. The yellow stream slowed and stopped.

"Need a shit."

"Right on," said his cellmate, moving to the window and staring studiously out.

The prisoner slid the packet out and put it aside with his blanket, before squatting. Inevitably the story of the Secretary of State's wife flitted through his mind; the screw swinging the door open for her at just that moment. And Wee Lennie: "How's about you then." The screw frantically swinging the door.

Finished, the prisoner picked up the piece of sponge torn from the mattress and began the ritual smearing on the wall. Then he picked up his package.

"You'd better bangle it now," he said, carefully peeling back the clingfoil. He picked out the two tiny packages, rewrapped the little clump of tobacco and Parker pen refill and handed it to his cellmate who quickly slipped it up inside himself.

The prisoner stared at the two packages, still hesitant. He hadn't opened them, but knew what was written inside, in tiny scrawl on carefully creased cigarette papers. One was from his commanding officer to the Belfast Brigade. A list of names and home addresses of screws for stiffing, culled from sympathetic "crim" orderlies. There'd be a duplicate going out. But it was a critical comm: critical for him if he was caught with it. The thought, if any of the names were hit while he was on the board for carrying the list! The rule was: no chances with critical comms. No letters to increase the risk. But the letter was important. It had been slipped to him at Mass by a friend—serving life for the murder of two policemen—whose wife had decamped with their child and, what made it worse, another member of the Movement. The letter was begging for information. Would he still get the child up for visits? Would she be raised by his parents?

"D'you think it'll be all right?"

"Ah, sure, two's not much different."

They'd discussed it the night before, so there wasn't much point talking any more. He slipped back his foreskin and carefully molded in the packages before covering them up. Then he slicked some of the birds' margarine off the wall and greased his anus, ready for the quick switch. There should be some more tobacco. He didn't expect the visit until the afternoon, but it was as well to be ready. He pulled his blanket around him.

FOUR

"The legends represent the imagination of the country; they are that kind of history which a nation desires to possess. They betray the ambitions and ideals of the people and, in this respect, have a value far beyond the tale of actual events and duly recorded deeds, which are no more history than a skeleton is a man."

—Standish O'Grady (1832–1915)

At 8 P.M. on the night of March 16, 1978 an undercover unit of the army's elite Special Air Services took up a position on the south side of the Ranaghan Road, about three miles from the little village of Maghera in Co. Londonderry. It was freezing cold, but the sky was clear and there was little wind.

Lance Corporal David Jones and Lance Corporal Kevin Smyth were wearing balaclava helmets, camouflage tunics with fishing jackets over the top and black "Doc Marten" boots—favored footwear with gunmen on all sides of the Irish conflict. Smyth was carrying a Sterling submachine gun and Jones an SLR—a 7.62 mm self-loading rifle. Both had night binoculars and 9 mm pistols strapped to their sides. Jones had a Pye Westminster radio in his rucksack.

They were watching a farmhouse belonging to the family of Barney Cassidy. It was a five-bedroom house, with an asbestos roof and walls covered in pebbledash, known locally as "Darach"—the "Copse." The land had been in the Cassidy family for as long as anyone could remember; Barney's grandfather had owned it for sure and before him there were Cassidys living there. Barney lived there now with his wife, four daughters and a son, farming a small herd of beef cattle on the twenty-two acres of land. There was no Republican tradition in the family, but Barney, like so many others in the area, was a known sympathizer and the house a welcome haven for the young boyos who sometimes came out of the night and were grateful for a plate of food and some warmth by the peat fire, with no questions asked. On this particular night, it being a Thursday, Barney was looking forward to a few drinks at the Ponderosa pub, up the hill. But he had to check the cattle first. He wandered idly down the driveway.

The two soldiers shifted over to a manure heap on the edge of the field, giving them a view up the drive. Jones moved a few yards, behind a piece of corrugated iron, and put the radio on the ground. Tuned into a military frequency it was their lifeline. The two men switched every five minutes, one of them watching, the other squatting by the radio. At 9:10 Smyth, whose turn it was at the radio, reported movements at the farm. About one and a half minutes later they heard a noise off to the left. Smyth pivoted and raised his night binoculars.

There seemed to be two men, wearing berets and combat jackets and carrying guns in a semi-alert position, butts at the right shoulder, muzzles down to the left. In the dark they looked like soldiers. He called out to them.

One of the men had dyed his hair light blond and darker roots were showing. He had a small badge on the left breast pocket of his Irish army surplus combat jacket, with the word "Ireland" and a small tricolor. He was carrying an M14 rifle and two magazines of twenty rounds each taped together—so that when one was emptied the other could be loaded with a quick, reverse movement. He had a nickel-plated .38 Special in a leather shoulder holster which had been made for him by a young admirer while staying in a safe house about six months before. The other gunman was wearing a beret and carrying a rucksack on his back. He also had a semiautomatic rifle, the small, light and deadly Armalite—again with two magazines of thirty rounds each bound together—and a 9 mm pistol.

Inside the rucksack there was a do-it-yourself kit for killing cops: an Irish tricolor, a switching mechanism, a pressure mat, wires and some pieces of wood to help hang the flag. It was a favored booby trap and one with political significance. Back in 1954, under the old Stormont rule, the Protestant government of the day had introduced the Flags and Emblems Act which made it illegal to interfere with the display of the Union Jack, but gave police powers to pull down any other flag on public or private property which they considered might give rise to a breach of the peace. By now Stormont had fallen, but the predominantly Protestant police force could still be counted on to react predictably to the flying of a tricolor. The pressure pad connected to a small block of commercial explosive could be counted on to make any such policeman's fate equally predictable.

There was a tin of sardines in the rucksack, with a couple of apples and bars of chocolate—enough to take the edge off the hunger during the long nights that they were on the move; daylight was reserved for hiding and sleep. There was also a spare pair of jeans. The bigger man liked wearing combat trousers on operations—he considered himself, after all, an Irish soldier—but he had to take them off in built-up areas.

They were alert, but not really nervous. Half an hour before they had heard a helicopter hovering in the area, which was always a danger sign—it could have been off-loading a patrol. Then they heard a murmur in front of them; it sounded like "OK fellows," spoken in an Irish brogue. Soldiers! And twenty or thirty yards beyond them another group. Simultaneously and without a word the two men swung the muzzles up.

A bullet hit Smyth in the stomach, just below his navel. The force of it knocked him over on to his back. Jones was hit in the chest and started screaming. Smyth pulled himself to his knees, cocked his submachine gun and let loose a long burst of automatic fire at the running men. He dropped the Sterling and crawled to the radio. He fumbled, but finally got it working and called for help. Then he pulled himself over to Jones, who was continuing to scream. Smyth tried to open his first-aid kit, but was too weak. Scared of his own loss of blood, he rolled on to his back and tried to press the exit wound into the grass. He could feel it was not working, so he turned back on to his belly, hoping that the smaller entry wound would not leak the precious fluid so fast.

The two guerrillas were backing away desperately as they fired. The smaller of them felt something warm on his left hand. He thought he had been hit, but it was a blood splash. They both turned to run and the bigger man gave a groan and fell. His companion began to spring, hoping to draw the fire, and then felt warmth on his leg; this time he had been hit, about two inches above his ankle, but the bullet had gone straight through—missing his shin bone by a fraction of an inch. He zig-zagged across the field, head down. He heard screaming and the bullets zipping overhead—it sounded like a heavy machine gun. "I'll never make it to the end of the field," he thought to himself. The blood was soaking into his sock. He scrambled through one hedgerow and then a second, the pocket of his jacket ripping open as he went, strewing ammunition on the ground. About three-quarters of a mile from the shooting he stopped, gasping for breath, the rucksack still on his back. He looked back. Headlights showed the reinforcements were arriving. He limped on, his leg getting stiffer.

Back in the field Jones's condition was obviously critical. He was thinking of his girlfriend, Anne Mannering, a nurse from Pudsey, near Leeds in Yorkshire. They were due to get married in a fortnight's time. He had taken four weeks' leave for it. The wedding invitations had already gone out and the previous week he had made a dash home to his mother's house in Bromsgrove, near Birmingham, to get his birth certificate. His mother, a char at the local hospital, had just got the invitation the morning he arrived. He had been in a mad hurry, but when she said she did not know if she could make the journey all the way to Leeds—you never knew what would happen on these trains nowadays, did you—he promised he would come and pick her up.

Jones was a veteran; seconded to the SAS from the 3rd Parachute Battalion, he had seen active service in Ireland before as well as overseas postings, like Belize and Cyprus. So he knew enough now to know that he was probably dying. And as he lay waiting for the ambulance, he whispered to two fellow officers attending him, Patrick Macleod and David Brewin: "If I don't make it, make sure Anne gets all my stuff. She would have got everything if we'd been married. I want her to get it all anyway."

The brief gunfight had broken out at 9:16 P.M. At 9:41 the "quick reaction force" of six men, stationed at nearby Kilrea police station, roared up in two Land Rovers. An ambulance nearly beat them to it. The injured men were rushed to the Mid Ulster hospital, at nearby Magherafelt. Surgeons operated immediately on Jones, but the single bullet—entering between the eighth and ninth ribs on the left and penetrating his stomach and liver—was fatal. He died the following evening from shock and uncontrollable infection. Smyth survived.

At the scene of the gun battle troops swung into the routine of a follow-up operation. They blocked the Ranaghan Road, threw a cordon around the Cassidy farm and surrounding area and sealed off the field with the rolls of white tape that have become the flags of disaster—threatened or present—in northern Ireland. Captain Michael Martin of the 1st Gloucestershire Regiment set up an incident control point on the road. At 11 P.M. he was joined by his commanding officer, Lt. Col. Firth, and police. They agreed to keep the cordons in place until dawn when they could start the search.

The debris of the gunfight lay strewn in the field at first light. The soldiers quickly found the M14 rifle lying in the grass with seven rounds of ammunition still in it. Empty cartridge cases lay around. They spotted a blood trail going off into a hedgerow in the direction of the Glenshane Pass, towards the west. Following it they picked up a beret, a pair of gloves, a packet of Gold Bond cigarettes and a tube of Blisteze lip salve, the Smith & Wesson loaded with another six rounds and two more full magazines for the M14. The blood trail ran about 600 yards, across the Ranaghan Road, through three hedges to a water hole where a leather belt with holster was spotted. An army tracker dog led them across three more fields. The animal lost the scent briefly, but two spots of blood were found on the doorstep of a farm building. The searchers began a sweep, to try and pick up the trail again. One of the searchers, Pvt. Geoffrey Cheshire, came up to an old stone wall and spotted a man's shape in a nearby clump of thorny bushes. He was sitting, with his legs in front of him, wearing a combat jacket, army-style trousers and the ubiquitous Doc Marten boots. His left thigh was covered with blood. Cheshire called out to him twice, asking who he was. The man did not reply. Pvt. Michael Downes joined Cheshire. They cocked their rifles together and the man lifted his hands, saying: "You've got me." Then he put his hands back on the ground behind him, threw back his head and started coughing. Downes asked him if he was in pain. The man looked at him and smiled. Cheshire asked his name. "Seamus Laverty," said the man. Other troops and police arrived at the scene. The man had blond hair and a moustache, but it was obviously dyed—dark roots were showing. Detective Denis Murray asked him again who he was and he said: "Eamon Laverty." Murray said: "I think you're Francis Hughes." He spoke hopefully, but with confidence. The man's face was on notice boards in every police station in northern Ireland.

*   *   *

Five miles to the east Cathy was on her way back from St. Patrick's Day Mass, driving along the old Scribe Road, when she spotted Margaret at the bottom of the drive of Deed View House, admiring a clump of daffodils. She stopped her car and went over to the older woman. "It was a bitterly cold night," said Margaret. "I was wondering where Francis was." "You may keep the prayers up," said Cathy.

The Hughes family had lived in the country area of Tamlaghtduff, about half a mile outside the small village of Bellaghy in Co. Derry, for as long as could be remembered. Joseph and Margaret Hughes were both born and brought up in the Scribe Road; when they were married, in 1939, she had to move only a few yards across the road to set up home with him in Deed View House. Nobody is sure where the name came from, except that the field in front was called The Deed. There were more obvious views to be celebrated—to the west the Sperrin mountains, to the east Lough Beg, Lough Neagh and in the distance, on a clear day, the hills of Antrim.

The land was good, although it was only with the arrival of motorized plowing that much of the hilly ground could be cultivated. Deed View was fairly typical of the area; twenty acres of land on which they kept "a wee bit of everything"— growing some potatoes and corn, fattening a few pigs for the bacon, dairy cows and beef cattle. They weren't poor, but they were certainly not rich.

They reared ten children in the four-bedroom house, heated by its single peat fire. Joseph was hard working, as one had to be to bring up a large family on a smallholding, and Margaret, an intensely religious woman, was a conscientious housekeeper. There were four boys and six girls. Four of the girls were to go into nursing and three of them were to marry Protestants. Of the boys one was to become a building contractor in Dublin, a second a joiner in London and the third was to stay in the Scribe Road, building his own bungalow next to Deed View House and setting up a small auto-electrical business there, servicing the local farming community.

There was little to distinguish Frank, except perhaps that, being the youngest of the boys, he was particularly close to his mother, regularly helping her with the housework—unthinkable among the other boys. He went to St. Mary's primary school in Bellaghy and then to Clady Intermediate, some three miles away, where he failed to distinguish himself either academically or athletically—preferring the customary pursuits of country boys, playing in the bogland a few hundred yards from the house with his friends Ian Milne and Seamus Bradley, messing around on old cars with his cousin Tom McElwee and going to disco dances and Irish folk gigs. He fared well with the girls—a handsome lad, standing nearly 6 feet tall with strong features and dark blond hair. He left school to start working for a brother-in-law, as an apprentice painter and decorator.

Frank had his first taste of the "Troubles" as a fifteen-year-old schoolboy. The Hughes family were well known to be Republican-minded; Joseph had fought for the IRA back in the 1920s, although he never talked much about it, and at least one uncle had carried arms for the Movement. So the boys were obvious targets of suspicion for the security forces when the violence started again in 1969. And early one chilly morning in 1971 there came the pounding at the door which signaled a raid.

The police were after one of Frank's big brothers—Oliver. The two of them were sharing a bedroom at the time—Oliver was due to move out ten days later, when he was getting married. The police charged into their room and told Oliver to get dressed, he was going with them. He dressed, but despite the cold deliberately did not reach for his jacket, hanging behind the door—it had a clip of ammunition in the pocket. Then his mother came in and, as mothers do, started fussing—insisting it was too cold to go out without a jacket. A policeman standing by joined in the argument, supporting her, and Oliver reluctantly pulled on the jacket, with a ten-year jail sentence lurking in his pocket. Fortunately for him the police, determined to take the family by surprise, had left their vehicles down the road and, as he trudged down the driveway, he furtively flicked the offending bullets into the dark.

The sight of a brother being hauled away to an internment camp—Oliver was to spend eight months in detention without trial—is a formative experience for any young boy, but family tradition has it that another experience, some two years later, launched Frank's career as Ireland's most famous gunman. He had been to a dance with a friend at Ardboe, down in Co. Tyrone, and came home late and apparently in some pain. He told his family he had backache and retired to bed. After he had been laid up for a couple of days his father confronted him and the story came out: he had been picked up by a patrol of the predominantly Protestant Ulster Defence Regiment and badly beaten. His father told him to go and see a doctor and report it to the police. Frank refused, declaring: "I'll get my own back in my own time."

He did, of course: with a vengeance. The precise toll he wreaked will never be known—the security forces were later to suggest about thirty policemen and soldiers died at his hands, but they had their reasons to portray him as a mass killer at the time; his colleagues, sensitive for the same reason, concede about a dozen. But mere vengeance was not the driving force.

Frank Hughes was fairly typical of the rural Republican tradition: unsophisticated in political terms, with a taste for cliché—"I die in a good cause . . . for mother Ireland . . . that others may be free . . ."—which would set their urban contemporaries ashudder, but with a simplicity of mind and directness of purpose which left them largely untouched by the bloody, ideological schisms which repeatedly rent the Movement in the cities. As the clothes he was wearing when he was captured testified, he considered himself an Irish soldier and as such regarded it as a point of honor to wear what approximated a uniform whenever he could.

He joined the Republican Movement as a member of the Official IRA, under the command of a local veteran who had done time in jail for "the cause" and who was something of a father figure for Nationalist youth in the area. When the "Officials" declared their ceasefire in 1972, Frank and his friends formed their own group, calling themselves the "Independents." The following year they threw their lot in with the "Provisionals," as it became apparent they had assumed the leadership of the physical force tradition in Irish Republicanism.

Frank himself had a mechanical aptitude which well qualified him for guerrilla war. He was competent with a gun and if not the inventor—as he was widely credited—he at least showed himself adept at constructing one of the most effective booby traps of the period. It had a trigger made of a clothes peg with two metal contact points in the jaws, held open by a small piece of wood tied to a piece of fishing line, the other end of which was hooked to an object likely to move independently, such as the tire of a car, a gate or a door. When the tire turned, or the gate or door opened, the line pulled the wood out of the clothes peg, allowing the contact points to snap together to close the circuit and trigger the explosion. It was deadly simple.

But Hughes's most effective weapon was psychological, a state of mind familiar to stories, in the more "legitimate" theaters of war, of holders of the Victoria Cross or the Congressional Medal of Honor—what is described, somewhat tritely for lack of a fuller explanation, as fearlessness. As one senior IRA commander was later to say of Hughes: "He was the sort of man who would shoot up a few policemen on his way to a meeting to plan our next attack on the police."

The tales of his coolness in tight corners were legion. While he was resting in the kitchen of a safe house, there came a knock at the door. The householder opened it to an army officer, the farmyard beyond him swarming with soldiers. While the householder was reassuring the officer he had seen nothing suspicious—praying that he would not search the house—Hughes, wearing his customary army trousers and combat jacket and carrying his rifle, calmly brushed passed them, muttering apologetically: "Nothing inside."

Crossing a field with two other IRA men, carrying a concealed pistol, they ran into an army foot patrol. Questioned, they explained it was a short cut. The soldiers hesitated, then waved them on. As they walked away tensely the two other men were horrified when Hughes stopped, turned and called out: "Got a light?" A soldier nodded and Northern Ireland's most wanted man strolled back to them for a smoke and a bit of a chat.

A friend, cajoled into giving him a lift with his rifle, looked ready to break into perspiration all over again at the memory of the road block they ran into: "It was a narrow road, no room to turn. Frank said: "Keep driving. If they do put up the gun I'm smashing the windscreen first and keep you driving on. We'll take the one down the road and not to worry about the road block." That's what he said. I put up my hand like this—I'll never forget it in my life, the sweat was just running down. He reached across and saluted them. He had the butt of the rifle ready to go through the window. Now the boy was so badly taken aback, or whether he thought we were police, or what he believed, I don't know; but we went sailing through. Unless he was blind he could see the butt of the gun."

At times he exasperated IRA commanders. "Resting" in Donegal on one occasion, he got into a heavy drinking session with another well-known gunman and together they set off to "capture" an Irish police car, tying up the occupants after stripping them of their uniforms and returning home to present their hostess with a police whistle as a "trophy of war." On another occasion he went off for a joyride in an IRA "staff car," hurtling around a beach in it before crashing, writing it off.

He could also be an embarrassment to his family: after he planted bombs in two shops and a filling station in Bellaghy itself—on the grounds that the owners had links with the security forces—yelling "Up the Provies" as he raced through the village, they found it expedient to make detours to avoid some Protestant neighbors.

It has been said that courage is resistance to fear and mastery of fear, rather than absence of fear. And the apparent lack of fear displayed by Hughes leads one to question his courage and search for traces of the psychopathic. But there is nothing else in his behavior to sustain the suspicion. And one is left rather with the judgment that his was that paradox of courage which, as G. K. Chesterton once said, lies in the necessity to be a little careless of one's life in order to keep it. Certainly it was Hughes's readiness to fight, rather than his wish to survive, which appears to have given him a vital edge in confrontations with the security forces. It was displayed in one of his narrowest escapes, in the incident at Moneymore.

On April 8, 1977 four police constables were on routine patrol in southeast Derry, traveling in a silver-colored Mark 3 Cortina. At 2:30 P.M. they were just leaving the town of Moneymore, on the road to Magherafelt, when a blue VW Beetle came out of a side road, forcing the police driver, Constable Sheehan, to brake. "That boy will have to be spoken to," said Sheehan as he put the siren on.

They overtook the VW, waving at it to pull up. The other driver braked heavily and the police overshot, pulling up twenty yards further on. The VW reversed, trying for a three-point turn, and ran into a ditch on the side of the road. The engine raced. It was stuck.

Hughes and two colleagues jumped out of the VW and opened fire. The four policemen scrambled to get out of the patrol car. Sheehan was hit almost immediately and fell back. The other three ran for cover. A second officer, Constable McCracken, fell mortally wounded. Constable Allen ran back to the car to try to get out Sheehan, who was still alive and groaning. He pulled him over the passenger seat and then grabbed an SLR in the back seat, swung it around, pulled the trigger and realized the magazine had fallen off. He grabbed a Sterling submachine gun, cocked and pulled the trigger, but it was jammed. Desperately he radioed for assistance.

At Draperstown police station Sergeant Peter McKernan heard the SOS and, picking up a Sterling, ran for a car with two constables. Listening to the radio transmissions they guessed at the gunmen's possible escape route and swung off the Moneymore road into Carmean Lane, to try and head them off. They spotted three men 100 yards ahead, jogging towards them. The police car braked violently. Two of the gunmen leapt over a barbed wire fence, on the edge of a quarry, while the third, Hughes, covered them, exchanging shots with the police—blasting the windscreen of their car in the process—before vanishing after his comrades. Sgt. McKernan ran twenty yards back down the road, where he would get an overview of the quarry, and spotted the three men heading towards Moneymore. One of them would drop out, fire back at the police, rise and the second would drop and fire and rise, followed by the third and then the first again—the classic military technique of covering by "leaps and bounds." They were about three to four yards apart and the tactic was so effective the sergeant never saw a firing position and kept losing them as he tried to aim. But he blazed away nevertheless, firing forty-eight rounds without any sign of a hit. Eventually he lost sight of them and the firing died away.

As police and army reinforcements poured into the area the three gunmen ran into an open field. There were some woods in the distance, but on the assumption these would be the first targets of the hunters they made for a solitary clump of bushes in the middle of the field, in the hope they would be too obvious to be searched. Crouched among the branches they heard the arriving troops setting up their command post on the other side from them. An agonizing wait for discovery followed. At one stage they heard men being detailed to check the other side of the bushes and braced themselves for what seemed inevitably their final shoot-out. But the soldiers, out of sight of their officers, sat down for a smoke just around the corner from them. As daylight faded the three decided they'd have to make a break for it. In the dark they slipped away, taking turns to cover each other in the same way as had impressed Sgt. McKernan a few hours earlier. The hunt went on the next day, but by then the three gunmen were well away and news was circulating among the Nationalist population that Frank Hughes had done it again.

It was after Moneymore that the police took the unprecedented step in Northern Ireland of naming Hughes as their most wanted man, circulating posters to the public with pictures of him, Milne and another Republican who sometimes operated with them, Dominic McClinchey. Milne was captured with Bradley in August 1977 and McClinchey was arrested in the Irish Republic in the same year. And then, on St. Patrick's Day 1978, it was Hughes's turn.

He was in horrendous pain, but he considered himself lucky in a way that it did take fifteen hours before he was discovered—he believed he was hated enough by the security forces to be finished off on the spot, but by the time he was found there were too many involved for a quiet execution. They were in no hurry to help him, though; they posed him for a photograph before loading him on a stretcher. He shouted "Up the Provos" as they carried him away.

He was flown by helicopter to Musgrave Park, the top security hospital in the southern suburbs of Belfast. Surgeons had to battle to save him, with two operations—the second to halt bad hemorrhaging. His hip was badly shattered and a steel pin was inserted to hold it together, leaving one leg noticeably shorter than the other. His family were told he refused a general anesthetic for fear he would talk while unconscious.

When Oliver was allowed in to see him his first words were: "How many did I get?"

"One," said Oliver.

"I thought it was two," he said.

He could not be interrogated or charged until he had recovered, and the recuperation was to take ten months. His family was allowed in on regular visits and his mother, Margaret, was relieved to find he was not in pain. But as his Aunt Cathy discovered, he was just being the youngest son again; on one occasion she went into his ward as Margaret left and found him cursing. He said he had nearly failed to hold out for his mother's visit and he undid the bandage to show Cathy the protruding bone.

There were fears at one stage that he was losing his mind— prompted by extraordinary letters he was sending out to them, badly spelled and full of bizarre remarks. Like the one he sent Cathy on May Day: "You were asking me did I watch TV. Well times if there was something good on I would watch it. I would rather listen to the radio. There was a Western on TV one night and to tell you the truth I was scared stiff, because there was a lot of shooting in it. And I was feared one of the cowboy bullets would come through the TV and hit me in the leg . . ." Relatives decided it was an attempt to persuade the authorities, through the censors, that he was mentally disturbed.

In January 1979 he was judged fit and on the afternoon of Wednesday the 24th he was taken to Castlereagh, Belfast's main interrogation center and one of three in the territory. He was an important catch and two senior interrogators, Detective Chief Inspector Francis E. Dempsey and Detective Inspector Hamilton Houston, were first in to interrogation room 13B. They took their seats behind the low wooden table in the windowless white cell, laid out their file on Hughes—a large "secret" ostentatiously stamped on the cover—and got to work. "Are you going to talk to us?" asked Dempsey. "I don't talk to strangers," said Hughes.

Under the Prevention of Terrorism Act they had seven days to try and break him. They used fourteen interrogators working in relay—mostly two-man teams—and questioned him for a total of thirty-nine hours and thirty minutes. Hughes was ready for it.

He refused to take food or water from staff, for fear they would slip him drugs—drinking water only from a tap when he went to the washroom, munching a few chocolates slipped to him by his lawyer and eventually eating only when he was allowed into the kitchen to watch the preparation of his meals.

"Could you tell us how you came to be shot?" he was asked. "I'll see my solicitor about that," he retorted. It was to become his refrain. At times he showed stress—banging his feet against a table leg, shifting uneasily as the leg would hurt and at one stage blowing up when an officer pointed a pen at him—threatening to push it down his throat. He occasionally lapsed into expletives—"You bundle of whores . . . You fucker, you, away and fuck yourself . . ."—and at other times laughed and sang to himself. But he developed a taste for that stock answer as the officers battled to find any lead-in to get him talking. Asked if he wanted a sweet and offered a Polo mint, he said: "I'll have to ask my lawyer about that." He repeated it when he was offered a glass of water and a cigarette. Taken out into the corridor to exercise his leg, he was asked how it was feeling and countered, with a smile: "You'll have to ask the doctor about that."

If there was a sign of anyone breaking it was the police, and it came when the head of the CID, Detective Chief Superintendent Bill Mooney, broke in and delivered a twenty-minute homily. He told Hughes that they had evidence to connect him with serious offenses. Hughes burped, smiled and said: "Do you reckon?" Mooney told him his laughing and bad manners were a facade and when he faced up to his responsibilities he would not be laughing and mocking them. Hughes laughed and repeated: "Do you reckon?" Mooney told him to think over things and consider his position. Hughes asked with relish: "Is that a question?" Mooney said, resignedly, no, it wasn't—it was just good advice.

At 10 P.M. on January 29 the interrogation finally ended as Sergeant Arlow read the charges to him: Murder of David Anthony Jones "contrary to the common law" and causing an explosion at Tamlaught in Co. Londonderry on January 25, 1977—a fishing line bomb which had failed to kill a police officer in his home. "Not guilty to any trumped-up charge," said Hughes.

It took a year before he was brought to trial, appearing before Mr. Justice Murray in Belfast Crown Court. The forensic evidence—the blood and traces of his hair at the scene of the shooting and his fingerprint on the bomb—were enough for a conviction. "The view that I have formed of the case and all the matters before me is that you are a dedicated and hardened IRA terrorist," said Murray. He gave him concurrent sentences including life and twenty years. With full remission he could not hope for release, at best, until 1990, but probably not until the turn of the century.

He was taken to Long Kesh and put in cell 3, D wing, H-Block 5. There were forty in the wing at the time and he was given an enthusiastic welcome, with the banging of chamber pots, clapping and cheering. They had a sing-song that night and he showed that he had a good voice, with renderings of "Kevin Barry"—celebrating another legendary IRA figure, from the War of Independence—and "Tom Williams," whose hanged body still lay in the yard of the Crumlin Road remand prison Hughes had just left. He also showed an unexpected talent for storytelling, with fairy tales of the wee folk and others culled from Irish mythology.

He was known as "Francie" in the prison, or "Bootsie"—having been allowed to keep his Doc Marten boots, one of which had been built up for his shortened leg by a friend while he was on remand. His crutch was regarded as a potential weapon, so it was kept in the Circle, but he was allowed it when he had to move, for wing shifts or visits. He was also exempt from the hated mirror search, because his leg made it impossible to bend. He was not only a heroic figure among the prisoners, but a popular one, although he was not an obvious leader in jail conditions and was not given any special position in the command structure. Inevitably he volunteered for the first hunger strike, but failed to make the first seven, because the leadership had tried to make it representative of the different areas of northern Ireland and wanted Co. Derry represented by a man from Derry City, rather than the country. He was among those who joined in at the end of that fast and it was a measure of his standing that, when Sands briefed the officers commanding each block at the end of that hunger strike, he also obtained permission to brief Hughes personally; there were fears he would refuse to come off.

H5 Block. Friday night 30.1.81
Comrade,
    In answer to AC [Army Council] comm of 25.1.81
regarding my position on the h.s. my decision remains
the same—Yes—I am prepared to see it through.
                        Slan.
                    Francis J. Hughes,
                        Bellaghy
                        Co. Derry

27.2.81 H-Block 5, Long Kesh, 10:15 P.M.
Dear Oliver,
    I hope this finds yourself, Ann and family in good
health and in good spirits as it leaves me much the same.
I think. Ha! Ha! It's just a small note to tell you that I
will be going on the hunger strike on Sunday the 8th . . . I
have a pass sent out for a Belfast fella called Jim Gibney
plus yourself and John for Wednesday the 11th. I have to
have that Jim fella up on every visit, but if I can get off
with it I will only be getting him up on a couple. He's
supposed to be a good sound fella and if he can give me
a good enough reason for wanting to be up so often then
I'll have to change my mind. I'll explain all to John in the
morning, but in case I don't get a visit I will be sending
this out to you with K. O'Neill tomorrow. Don't say to
anyone other than John that I don't want this Jim boy up
on every visit. OK. It's probably all for a good reason, but
I'd much rather have my family up on each visit, so if my
wee plan doesn't work out to get him away out of my road,
please understand that it must be vitally important that I
get him up . . . Here, before I sign off it's best to tell you
what I personally think of the situation at present. In short
things are very bleak and unless there be dramatic changes
soon things will get even bleaker. Oliver, hope for the best,
but expect and be ready for the worst. I pray constantly

for yous all, so please don't break down and remember, keep the spirits up. Tell mammy, daddy and everyone else I was asking. Take extra care, good luck and God Bless.
Frank.

On February 28 Hughes celebrated his twenty-fifth birthday and his mother and Aunt Cathy came up to the prison to see him. Margaret was looking smart for him, in a sheepskin coat and a pleated woolen skirt. "God, Mother, those clothes are very expensive, where did you get all the money from?" he teased her. And then later he said, "I've something to tell you. There's another hunger strike starting—there's a fellow on it tomorrow and I'll be starting it too." There were tears, but no attempt to persuade him against it. "You'll be up soon again?" he asked her as they said goodbye. "No, I'll be up after the hunger strike is over," Margaret replied defiantly.

He was scheduled to start the strike on Sunday, March 15, two weeks after Sands. On the Friday night he had a nightmare, dreaming that he was already on hunger strike, but that he had forgotten and had eaten his breakfast by mistake. He felt shattered when he woke up.

They had beans and pie for his last supper, on Saturday night. When he had finished he rapped on the cell wall and called out to "Donkey Head" next door: "That's the last meal." After the warders had knocked off they had a sing-song for him and demanded a speech, clapping and cheering and banging their pisspots as he went to his door. It was a countryman's speech, the sentiments predictable, but obviously heartfelt. He told them that he wanted to be in the front line of the war. He had been, when he was roaming the fields of Derry, and he had been there again when he joined the blanket protest. And now he was taking the fight to the enemy again with the hunger strike. He recalled the story of his capture and confided how he had agonized, just after being wounded, over whether to hold on to his M14 for a final shoot-out, or abandon it and try to get away. Sometimes he had regretted the decision he had taken, but now he was being given a weapon again and this time he was going to use it to the end. If he died, he told them, they should listen out for the sound of his crutch tapping down the corridors, because he would be back to keep an eye on them. As he finished the wing exploded with cheering.

He ignored his breakfast the next morning and then went out to Mass with his cellmate, Raymond McCreesh, and the other lads. There was a wing shift immediately afterwards, which passed without trouble, and then dinner. When the warder, "Plastic Face," came around for the dishes in the early afternoon he asked who had failed to eat his dinner. "I didn't, I'm on hunger strike," said Hughes. "And when did you start this so-called hunger strike?" asked Plastic Face. An exchange of obscenities followed.

On Monday morning he was called in by the doctor, examined and weighed—he was underweight, at 156 lbs. They separated him from Raymond, putting him in a cell on his own, with a locker, chair, the daily newspapers, books and a few religious magazines. He seemed in a good mood as the days went by, shouting items from the newspapers to the other lads and joining in the crack. They smuggled lots of cigarettes in to him, but he stopped smoking after two weeks, because he thought they might catch him in the chest and reduce the time he could last. He was worried about that—the leg wound was giving trouble and he suspected he might beat Bobby to the death.

Pennies from Seanna 18 March 1981
Frank is 100 per cent. Re his leg wound, he said he never said anything about it before in case he would be knocked back. The whole problem is internal—the bone mainly. He gives himself 45 days. After that with the leg etc.,

he'll either be dead or that far gone that it won't make any difference. Those are his own words. Also no matter what he won't let anyone down. He'll not be ending it, regardless who tells him . . .

His eyes were beginning to hurt after four days, as was his tongue, and he had stopped passing solids. They had outside medical advice to drink as much water as possible—five pints a day was his target—and to take salt. But Frank wouldn't take the salt in the water, he insisted on eating it separately, which was what made his tongue hurt. He was sleeping all right at night, but found it difficult during the day; he wanted to rest as much as possible. He tried to exercise as well, limping around the cell. A prisoner from the next cell was allowed in to slop out for him and mop the floor. The Governor called in every day to check on him and said he would see if he could do something about the broken window. They seemed to have more screws on the wing.

At Mass on April 5 the lads could see that he was a lot thinner, his eyes seemed a little glazed, his speech weaker, slurred and slow. But he showed there was still lots of strength there, by slugging one of the other prisoners playfully in the stomach, nearly laying him out.

That night they gave him a farewell concert, assuming he would be off to the prison hospital, like Bobby, after twenty-one days. He was in good form, getting up and singing at his door for a good three-quarters of an hour—his old favorites, "Kevin Barry," "Tom Williams," "Four Green Fields." The next day he was obviously feeling the weakness; while out washing he had a dizzy spell and had to sit down. His tongue and eyes were hurting again. But when the Governor made his daily visit, and Frank asked him to arrange for his family to drop a radio in so that he could use it in the hospital, he was told not to bother, he was not being moved yet—they had decided that Bobby had been moved a week too early.

It wasn't until the twenty-sixth day that they moved him, just after lunch. The lads gave him a rousing send-off, cheering and shouting their best wishes. Over the noise, as he went through the grilles, they heard him shout: "Up the Provos."

Liam Og Wednesday 15.4.81 Camp Hospital
Comrade, Just a couple of lines to let you know how I'm keeping etc. Firstly my weight today was 61.25 blood pressure 100/50 and my pulse was 48. I am keeping very well and in good spirits etc. My oul legs are getting very weak, but can still walk with no great problem. The leg that I got shot in is giving me slight pains around the fracture itself and the aul knee. Nothing to worry about for it's not all that bad yet. That's about it for now comrade and until I'm back on paper again, good luck and God Bless and take care. Tell Bik, Sid and all the lads in the block that I was asking. I'll write soon again.
Francis Hughes

He got worried, inside the hospital, about a rifle he had hidden in South Derry. He wanted to make sure the lads had it before he went—it would be a waste, otherwise—but they could not find it. Eventually, in frustration, he drew a detailed map which he had smuggled out and the rifle was found.

To Liam Og from Raymond [McCreesh] Prison Hospital 26.4.81
Frank is sick at present and has been for three or four days. He is throwing the water up all the time. His eyes and head are sore all the time. He is getting examined every 2 hours. I will try and get more exact details of his health this evening and put them in this comm. He is not fit to come out for association and wasn't able to come out for Mass

this morning . . . There is talk of Frank starting daily visits soon. Frank is on spring water throwing it up—weight 56 kg blood pressure 100/70. Constant headaches and sore eyes. Professor Love said this morning that he was a week to 10 days before his time. Has to use wheel chair. That's about it, Liam, for the minute. (Frank is in bad shape.) Slan.

To Liam Og from Raymond McCreesh 30.4.81
. . . Frank was anointed this evening. He is still throwing up constantly and having the same trouble with his eyes. The Priest is afraid of him going into a coma and there is a chance he could die before Bobby . . .

On May 8 Margaret Hughes was up early. She had arranged an appointment in Toombridge with her hairdresser, who was opening the salon specially for her at 9 A.M. It was the day of Bobby's funeral, but it wasn't for that she was having a perm—as always she wanted to look good for a visit to Frank. She felt she had a duty to look good for him. Just as he felt the duty to tell his mother how lovely her hair looked when she came in with his younger sister, Noreen, a pretty nurse who worked at the Royal Victoria Hospital. But, as he confided to Noreen later, it had only been with luck that he had focused his eyes enough to spot the hairdo. He told them he had heard Bobby's family praying and then the sound of the metal trolley being wheeled in, which signaled he had gone.

The hunger strikers' lawyer, Pat Finucan, was allowed in to see them on the same day. O'Hara told him that the prison chaplain, Fr. Toner, had asked him: "Are we going to have another coffin going through Derry?" He said one of the medical consultants, Professor Love, had given him seven to nine days. "But I don't believe him. I think I've got longer," said O'Hara.

Hughes told Finucan to give a message to the Republican leadership. "Tell outside that I won't be letting anyone down.

I don't mind dying, as long as it is not in vain, or stupid. Bobby's people being there was the worst thing," he said, "knowing mine will have to go through the same thing." He gave a clenched-fist salute as Finucan left.

Across the Irish Sea, a builder and football enthusiast, David Brooke, was heading home with his wife and eight-year-old son after watching the FA Cup Final in London. They had just pulled out of a garage in Essex when the car was surrounded by police brandishing pistols and rifles. A helicopter hovered overhead. Simultaneously other police were raiding their home in Blackthorn Crescent, an officer putting a gun to a neighbor's head and handcuffing him to the steering wheel of his car. After the Brooke family had been interrogated for five hours they were released. An ex–army officer had reported seeing them loading a Sten gun into their car in London and had said they had Irish accents. The gun was the car jack and the Irish accent Devon.

The Hughes family started getting daily visits. Frank's face was yellow, his eyes were going and he was obviously in pain when his father went in on the morning of Monday, May 11.

"Do you see me, Francis?" asked seventy-two-year-old Mr. Hughes.

"I see the shape of you, but I can't see your face," said Frank. He fell asleep for a while and then they talked some more.

"You're not too bad," said his father.

"Ah, now, tomorrow or Wednesday will see the finish of it," he replied.

Noreen was in again that night and he told her, just before she left, that she had better get going, or her car would be locked into the prison car park for the night. "Drive carefully," he said. She turned and said, laughing: "I'm going home on two wheels." "I mean that," he said. "Drive carefully." She would always remember that: "Drive carefully"—her brother's farewell.

During the night, with another sister and a brother, Dolores and Meagher, at his bedside he slipped in and out of consciousness. In one lucid spell he managed to say to them: "Take care of mammy and daddy." They were his last words. By the time Noreen got back in the morning, with her mother and father, Oliver and her fourth brother, Roger, Frank was in a coma. The warders would only allow four into the prison at a time, so their mother went in for a couple of minutes and then left with Dolores and Meagher to make way for the others. Oliver was acting as spokesman and it was acknowledged by the family that he would speak for them in dealing with the authorities as well—if they decided to pull Frank off, for instance. But when he went in this time he knew there was no longer any such role for him; it was too late for medical intervention. The life of Frank Hughes was ending, even if the legend was only just beginning. Oliver started to cry.

They left Patrick, Noreen, Roger and another sister, Vieyra, with him. The four of them attended his bedside in relays, two of them with him while two rested in the small waiting room. At about 4 P.M. the prison chaplain, Fr. Murphy, came in and told Noreen: "I think he's near the end." She went through and found he was cheynestoking—the erratic breathing that signaled the end was near. Then a prison officer came in and told her they were locking the car park and she would have to move her VW.

It was an agonizing walk to the car park, impatiently watching the warders fiddling with the locks on the gates as she was escorted through. And while she was moving the Beetle another sister, Marie—a nurse in Scotland—arrived. So there was an argument at the gate, the warders insisting that there were already four inside, so Marie couldn't get in. Eventually their seventy-two-year-old father decided to leave, to make way for the girl.

They all stood at the bedside, praying with Fr. Murphy. At about 5:30 P.M. he seemed to have gone. Noreen took his wrist and couldn't feel any pulse. It was Tuesday, May 12. He had lasted fifty-nine days.

The warders asked them to leave so they could tidy up. They all went into the waiting room and milled around, not sure what to do—wanting to make some sort of protest, but unable to think of anything except to insist they would be staying put until Oliver was allowed back. A medical orderly came in and asked Noreen to formally identify the body. She did so, mechanically, and as she was coming out of Frank's room again she asked if she could see Raymond and Patsy. To her surprise he said she could and she was taken through to a sitting room where the two men were sitting in wheel-chairs, watching TV in their dressing gowns. She walked over and said: "I'm Noreen, Francis's sister. I just want to tell you Francis has died." There was nothing else to say. She put out both hands and they took them in theirs. For a few seconds she stood there silently, clutching on to them. The sadness was there, of course, but her overwhelming thought was: "Thank God, it's all over. Someone else's turn now."

Liam Og Tue 12.5.81
Comrade, I've just learned of Frank's death. Suffering Jesus—those bastards are really going to town on us. There's nothing I can say comrade—just nothing at all. This is one hell of a place. I'll get back to you tomorrow. Maybe I'll get the signer [lawyer] before the weekend. I've just told the lads the news and there's unnatural silence hanging over the wing—the other wing as well. I just want to scream or kill somebody. I'm deadly serious, comrade. If there's anything on earth that can harden a man's heart to such a degree—then it's this devil's tomb. I'll sign off here mate. Take good care and God Bless. Bik.

It wasn't quite over. There was still the funeral and that turned out to be dramatic; inevitably, since they were not only burying a body, but raising a legend.

It was arranged that the family would collect the body from the morgue at Foster Green Hospital, in predominantly Protestant South Belfast, at about noon the next day. The plan was to take the body over to Catholic West Belfast, where thousands were gathering along the Falls Road to say goodbye, and then out along the motorway to South Derry—through the little village of Toombridge where another Catholic crowd was waiting. But they arrived at the hospital to find that the police, waiting in their fortified Land Rovers, had decided they were going to take charge of the body and the procession. Frank was to be "arrested" one last time.

The tension built up as family and Sinn Fein leaders argued with the officers. At one stage a rumor did the rounds that the body was going to be kidnapped and then the family rushed into the morgue and surrounded the coffin. It was while they were standing around that word came that Pope John Paul II had been shot in Rome. The day was taking on a surreal quality.

Eventually the family agreed to head straight for Derry and the coffin was loaded into the hearse under the close supervision of Danny McCusker, the undertaker. Two police Land Rovers led the way, followed by the hearse, Noreen in her blue VW, and her father and mother in the car, then another Land Rover and Oliver in his Renault 18.

Just as Noreen was driving through the hospital gates the lead Land Rovers slowed down. A crowd of Protestants, mainly women, threw themselves at the VW, hammering the windows and roof. Time seemed frozen amidst the hatred as Noreen waited frantically. Finally the procession eased forward.

They had just got on to the dual carriageway when she realized that the police behind her were trying to overtake.

Irrationally, she felt she would be abandoning Frank if she let them get between her and the body, so she clung determinedly on the hearse's tail. But the Land Rover cut in, forcing her to stop or collide with it. Danny McCusker, watching in the hearse's rearview mirror, braked to a halt as well. There was pandemonium, shouts of "We'll take the Fenian bastard and burn him in a ditch." Noreen started screaming hysterically and a friend slapped her in the face. Her father was knocked to the ground. An officer tried to open the back of the hearse, but Danny had locked it, popping the keys into his mouth.

Eventually all calmed down and the procession got going again. As the police led them through a Protestant housing estate Union Jacks were waved and stones were hurled. Then they were on to the motorway and running smoothly, until they got to the Randalstown/Portglenone slipway, where police called another halt. Owen Carron came over to the VW and told them the police wanted to go through Portglenone, avoiding the Nationalist crowds waiting at Toome. "Let them take it," said her father. "You can't let them take it through Portglenone, the Loyalist mobs are out," said Carron. The old man was silent. Back in the Renault Oliver told them to get on with it—he just wanted to get Frank back home. But as the hearse went down the slipway police blocked off the route. Frank was going home without his family.

At Deed View House there were hysterical scenes as they waited for the coffin, the eldest of the sisters, Philomena, bursting into tears, crying that she had heard police say they were going to throw him into the River Bann. A priest comforted her. And then the hearse was spotted coming up Scribe Road.

The coffin was unloaded and carried the last quarter of a mile in the rain, watched by about 3,000 people crowded into the narrow lanes.

The old folk slept separately in the house and they each wanted their son in their own room. They compromised, agreeing to take turns on the two nights he would be lying there. Patrick got him the first night, but of course they never did get to move him to Margaret's room.

And so he lay there, for a lying in state that would have done any guerrilla proud. And they poured in, a steady stream of mourners, to say goodbye to the rouged face of a legend. And the heavens opened up and it thundered and it rained and people said that was appropriate to the death of Francis Hughes.

They buried him on Friday, May 15, but not before a final confrontation with the police, who blocked the road into Bellaghy—making sure that the village he had bombed with such gay abandon years before would not have to see him again. Oliver protested that it was the way Francis had gone to church every Sunday, but the police were not impressed. So, after a farewell volley had been fired by three masked men at the bottom of the Hughes' driveway, they straggled their way over the extra two miles to St. Mary's parish church.

"Imagine living away out here on your own," said a city boy, from Belfast's Short Strand, looking at a fine new bungalow in a field. "You'd get a right biff from the Brits there with no one to notice."

At the church Fr. Michael Flanagan recounted the tale of Lazarus being raised from the dead and asked whether it was not time for peace—for the forgetting of all those unforgiving memories. The answer came outside in the graveyard as three army helicopters roared overhead and the IRA's one-time Director of Operations, Martin McGuinness, delivered the funeral oration, predicting that the spirit of Francis Hughes would live on in South Derry, in East Tyrone and in the Bogside, in the little streets of Belfast and those of Crossmaglen.

And while it was all going on, a man from Crossmaglen down in County Armagh was furiously scribbling a telegram to the Prime Minister, beseeching her to give the prisoners their clothes. "In God's name don't allow another death," wrote the Irish primate, Cardinal Thomas O Fiaich.

". . . the one who died last was a murderer, let's not mince words," Mrs. Thatcher was saying in exchanges in the House of Commons.

The prisoner was brought out of his doze by the clang of the grilles again and the call of "Bears in the air," over the neverending sound of construction work outside. Would they never finish building this bloody place? Mutters wafted down the corridor. Cellular confinement time. Must be nearly 10 o'clock.

"Your fourteen days up?"

His cellmate nodded.

The prisoner sat on his runway, picked up the Bible and stared moodily at the opposite wall. He quickly looked down as the door swung open, not taking in the print. The class officer rattled his way through the list.

". . . d'you want to put on prison clothes and go to work? No. Brush? No. Exercise? No. Shave? No. Shit? No. What about a radio? No. What about a bit of ice cream? No. What about a big woman?" The prisoner snorted, but his cellmate flared. "Ah, fuck off."

"Knock that off," came the shout from the commanding officer. The door boomed shut, the boots clumping back towards the circle.

"CD Grill . . ."

First visit of the day. But not him; the Geek. The slagging started:

"Hey, you make sure you brush your teeth . . ."

"You want a shower . . ."

Then the wing went quiet, waiting to see if it was going to be rough. It would set the pace for the day.

The prisoner pressed his eye against the slit at the side of the door, but there was just a flash of naked skin and towel going by. Murmurs from cell 26—the search room. He let out his breath as the cry in Gaelic echoed down from the grilles: "It's not too bad."

A few minutes later the slagging started again, the boyos on the other side of the wing, overlooking the yard, shouting from their perches on the pipes. He could imagine the scene as he listened to the cat calls: trudging through the snow, the lead figure with his long, matted hair, baggy uniform with ripped crutch and, a few paces behind, the smartly turned-out and bored screw.

"Look't the state of that there."

"Yaah"—the screw falling for it.

"Not fuckin' him, you, walking behind him . . ."

"Hey, you taking that for a walk?"

"Aye, giving it a breath of air." The click of fingers and the taunt to the screw: "Here, boy. Here boy. Good boy."

The shouting died down as the duo disappeared through the first set of compound gates. Then the rhetorical shout, aimed at the prisoner, from the next cell.

"Hey, who's that supposed to be having a visit with the Kitten?"

"Oho! Stood up. She's heard about you."

"Ah, fuck off."

He grinned to himself, wondering what she would be like. It would be odd, greeting a strange girl with an open-mouth kiss. And him stinking, like he did. Like they all did. She was Sinn Fein and should know to take his comm first. But it could always go wrong: two tongues simultaneously pressing two packages, locked in labial combat in the middle of the room. And if he dropped the comm! The screams from

*the womenfolk in the scramble for it. He'd head butt the
screw and they'd wrench his mouth open, trying to stop him
swallowing. The beating and the silence of the Boards. The
prisoner shook his head clear . . .*

It was nearly an hour later that the bellow of "Big Bear
in the air" started the awful cacophony of chamber pots,
lids, fists and feet pounding on steel doors and incoherent
shouting. The prisoner and his cellmate dived for their mattresses and Bibles. Their door swung open to an assistant
governor—Pinocchio today—with his entourage of chief officer, principal officer and class officer; two screws guarding
the door, one dangling the keys.

Pinocchio's voice could just be heard above the background noise: "Class officer, prefer the charges, please."

"I state, sir, that I did on the twenty-first day of the month
charge this prisoner with refusal to wear uniform, refusal
to do prison work, contrary to rule forty-four and contrary
to rule sixty-three. I referred the charges to the prisoner at
breakfast time this morning. The prisoner refused to answer.
I took this refusal to answer as refusal to comply with prison
discipline and in accordance charged the prisoner with the
said articles . . ."

The Brits and their bloody formalities, thought the
prisoner.

"Have you anything to say in your defense?" asked
Pinocchio.

With studied nonchalance the prisoner's cellmate turned
the page of his Bible to II Chronicles, 10, his eyes caught
by the heading: "Ten tribes revolt." *Revolting tribes.* For a
moment his attention became real: "And King Rehoboam
took counsel with the old men that had stood before . . ."

"In the absence of a plea from you I order you, prison
officer, to enter a plea of not guilty on his behalf."

"I enter a plea of not guilty on his behalf, sir."

"Have you anything to say on your behalf? Having heard the evidence and read the charge preferred against you I make you an award of fourteen days' loss of privileges, fourteen days' loss of association, fourteen days' loss of earnings, fourteen days' loss of parcels, fourteen days' loss of visits, fourteen days' loss of . . ."

With a final: "Good morning," *the Governor strode out. As the door boomed closed behind him the two prisoners grabbed for the chamber pot lids and joined in the hammering.*

"Big Bear off the air!" The prisoner looked at his cellmate and shook his head—it sounded like Don Quixote, trying to pull a fast one. They redoubled the banging until the code for the day—four taps from the end cell—could just be heard down the pipes. The noise reluctantly tailed off, followed by the shout of confirmation: "Big Bear off the air."

FIVE

News of Francis Hughes's death was broadcast in the late afternoon and picked up on a car radio near Dundalk. In the front passenger's seat was a short and stocky priest with florid face and receding hair. He was a man in whose company others instinctively felt comfortable, a gregarious soul with a penetrating sense of humor and a rumbustious laugh which would have made him the center of most social gatherings even without the status of his office: Prince of the Roman Catholic Church, 112th successor to St. Patrick in the See of Armagh, Primate of All Ireland.

The hunger strike was, for Cardinal Tomas O Fiaich, the realization of long-held fears and often expressed warnings. It had presented him with a political, moral and theological dilemma. With the death of Hughes it was all coming closer to home for the man from Crossmaglen.

Crossmaglen has a particular place in the Irish political directory. As villages go there is nothing in the world which stands comparison. It looks ordinary enough at first, with its single- and double-storied pebbledash buildings clustered around a dusty and potholed market square. But on one side of the square the front wall of a derelict building is pockmarked with bullet holes. In the center, in sharp contrast to the mundaneness of the cattle pens a few yards away, an angular, bronze giant stands on a rising phoenix. The inscription on the granite plinth below offers: "Glory to all praised and humble heroes who have willingly suffered for your unselfish and passionate love of Irish Freedom." The giant has clenched fists and glares across the square at another monument: an ugly, roof-high pillbox enclosed in a wire cage and bedecked with aerials, a concave mirror and closed-circuit television cameras which pivot slowly under remote control, following the movements of villagers and visitors.

It was always a troublesome village for authority, right back to the days when, as Crois Mhic Lionnain, or MacLionnain's Cross, it was famous for its fairs, or at least the "undesirables" who attended them. It became even more troublesome with Partition, which gave it place as one of the most southerly — and therefore, of course, most Republican—villages in the north. The surrounding countryside of South Armagh, with its hills, winding lanes, hidden culverts, Nationalist population and a degree of sanctuary south of the nearby border, made it a haven for the IRA. It was bandit country. And Crossmaglen was the capital.

The cardinal was born just outside the village, at Cullyhana, in 1923—the youngest of two sons of Patrick Fee, a schoolteacher. The name of O Fiaich, anglicized in the seventeenth or eighteenth century, is one which can be traced in Irish annals as far back as the thirteenth century. The family seems to have come from Co. Fermanagh, where they were Erenaghs or Herenachs—often an hereditary office, carrying responsibility for the collection of tithes and dues and the administration of the parish. His grandfather later moved to Co. Armagh to work as a laborer for a Protestant farmer in the area.

The cardinal entered the Irish national seminary, St. Patrick's College, Maynooth, at the age of seventeen and proved an outstanding scholar, specializing in Celtic studies and taking his B.A. with first class honors in 1943. He then nearly died of pleurisy and pneumonia, but recovered to be ordained in Armagh in 1948. He continued his academic career, taking a Master's degree with first class honors in early and medieval Irish history and, after two years at Louvain University in Belgium, a licentiate in historical sciences "avec la plus grande distinction" in 1952. Establishing himself as an authority on early Irish missionaries, he was appointed a professor at Maynooth in 1959 and President of the College in 1974.

He was a good friend of the then Primate, Cardinal Conway; they traveled together, on one memorable trip, to Calcutta, touring the slums with Mother Teresa. In 1977 Conway died of cancer. It was generally assumed the position would be filled by a bishop transferred from another diocese, but on August 22, O Fiaich became the first man for more than a century to fill St. Patrick's seat without already being a bishop.

In that seat he was widely regarded as the leader of the Catholic Church in Ireland, but the belief was founded on something of a misapprehension. In the Catholic hierarchy he had no more authority than any bishop, although as chairman of the episcopal synod in Ireland he was first among equals. There was even a rival primate: in olden days the position was contested between the Armagh and Dublin archdioceses, so in a compromise worthy of the Vatican—at some time in the Middle Ages, the precise date of which has never been pinpointed by historians—Dublin was pronounced the seat of the Primate of Ireland and Armagh that of the Primate of All Ireland. With Partition—the border happening to divide the Armagh diocese, as well as the rest of the country—the phrase "All Ireland" took on an added connotation, reinforcing the belief, however erroneous, that its bishop was the spiritual leader of the whole island.

O Fiaich was a Republican—one could hardly imagine a man from Crossmaglen being anything else—but strongly opposed to the physical force tradition of the IRA. He chose as his episcopal motto "Fratres in Unum"—Brothers in Unity—a

phrase taken from the 113th Psalm: "How good, how delight-
ful it is for all to live together like brothers." At his ordination
as Primate in St. Patrick's Cathedral he declared: "Brotherly
love, peace, harmony, reconciliation, mutual forgiveness, an
end to past dissensions and a new beginning in the practice of
justice and charity towards all, these will be the objectives of
all my work in Armagh, whether it lasts for a year or a day."

But within a year he had been drawn into a political row,
over an interview with a Dublin newspaper in which he argued
that there should be a declaration of intent by Britain to withdraw from Ireland. He had gone on to make an unprecedented
declaration of faith in Irish Protestantism, saying: "I would
trust the Protestants in the event of withdrawal . . . I would
have enough confidence in the Protestants to take independence as an interim solution . . ." But in all the fuss the flavor
of that was lost. He was confirmed in Protestant eyes as the
harbinger of Fenianism; the "Chaplain-in-Chief of the IRA"
as elements of the British press would come to portray him.

Perversely, that reputation was to grow in the face of his
clear commitment to the ecumenical cause and his repeated
denunciations of political violence: "No cause is advanced by
murder and no Irish cause can receive anything but dishonor
from the slaughter of a brother Irishman, Protestant or Catholic," he declared at the 1978 funeral of a postman, killed by
the IRA as a suspected informer. But who could believe the
words of a man from Crossmaglen?

There was little doubt, in the mind of the man from
Crossmaglen, about the threat to the cause of reconciliation
posed by the prisons dispute. And soon after his ordination
as Primate he was lunching with the Secretary of State, Roy
Mason, and appealing for compromise. There was a Labour
government in power at the time, but Mason—a one-time
coal miner, nicknamed the "Barnsley Brawler" in recognition both of his constituency and of his reputation—was
even more heavy-handed in dealing with insurgency than his

Conservative predecessors and successors. He insisted there could be no concessions. It was at this meeting that O Fiaich also pleaded for the royal prerogative to be exercised for the release of two prisoners. One of them, Henry Gerald Heaney, was an elderly man imprisoned with his sons over an arms cache found in his house. Priests had reported that he was sick, a loner and, they were convinced, completely innocent.

The next month, in January 1978, O Fiaich made his first visit to Long Kesh. He was surprised both by the respect with which he was treated by the Republican prisoners and by the strength of morale among them. He thought afterwards that it had been like saying Mass in a bush station.

Six months later, on Friday, July 28, he saw Mason again and once more pleaded for concessions—arguing that the isolation of the prisoners, both from other people and from books, radios and newspapers, posed a danger to their mental as well as physical health. A civil servant sitting in on the meeting cut in, to say that any concessions at all would be claimed by the Republicans as political status.

On that Sunday O Fiaich made his second visit to the Kesh. By this time the dirty protest was under way and it horrified him. He was met by the prison governor who told O Fiaich that he had turned down his request to see Gusty Spence—the best-known UVF prisoner, who had been sentenced to life back in 1966 for murdering a young Catholic barman. It was not a good start to the visit, but it got worse.

In the first cell he visited, the stench robbed him of speech and he stood silently for a couple of minutes. Gradually he got used to it, as he moved around seeing the prisoners from his diocese. But when he came back to them after a break for lunch—to the cell of the brother of a fellow student at Maynooth—he found himself battling not to vomit. The prisoners added to his distress with horrific tales of beatings, the humiliation of their nakedness and the routine searches of their anuses. He was already bitter with Mason over Heaney—who had been refused the royal prerogative on the grounds that he was not terminally ill, and had died in prison in June. Now the cardinal was furious.

He returned to Armagh and summoned the Church's chief public relations officer, Jim Cantwell, up from Dublin. Together they drafted the statement which was to be a landmark in the long-running dispute:

> There are nearly 3,000 prisoners in Northern Ireland today. This must be a cause of grave anxiety to any spiritual leader. Nearly 200 from the Archdiocese of Armagh are among the total of almost 1,800 prisoners in the Maze Prison at Long Kesh. This is the equivalent of all the young men of similar age groups in a typical parish of this diocese.
>
> Last Sunday I met as many as possible of these Armagh prisoners, as the bishop appointed to minister to themselves and their families, conscious of Christ's exhortation about visiting those in prison. I am grateful for the facilities afforded me by the authorities.
>
> On this my second visit as archbishop to Long Kesh, I was also aware of the grave concern of the Holy See at the situation which has arisen in the prison, and I wanted to be able to provide the Holy See with a factual account of the present position of all prisoners there, something I shall do without delay.
>
> Having spent the whole of Sunday in the prison I was shocked by the inhuman conditions prevailing in H-Block 3, 4 and 5, where over 300 prisoners are incarcerated. One would hardly allow an animal to remain in such conditions, let alone a human being. The nearest approach to it that I have seen was the spectacle of hundreds of homeless people living in sewer pipes in the slums of Calcutta. The stench and filth in some of the cells, with the remains of rotten food and human excreta scattered around the walls,

was almost unbearable. In two of them I was unable to speak for fear of vomiting.

The prisoners' cells are without beds, chairs or tables. They sleep on mattresses on the floor and in some cases I noticed that these were quite wet. They have no covering except a towel or blanket, no books, newspapers or reading material except the Bible (even religious magazines have been banned since my last visit); no pens or writing materials, no TV or radio, no hobbies or handicrafts, no exercise or recreation. They are locked in their cells for almost the whole of every day and some of them have been in this condition for more than a year and a half.

The fact that a man refuses to wear prison uniform or to do prison work should not entail the loss of physical exercise, association with his fellow prisoners or contact with the outside world. These are basic human needs for physical and mental health, not privileges to be granted or withheld as rewards or punishments. To deprive anyone of them over a long period—irrespective of what led to the deprivation in the first place—is surely a grave injustice and cannot be justified in any circumstances. The human dignity of every prisoner must be respected regardless of his creed, colour or political viewpoint, and regardless of what crimes he has been charged with. I would make the same plea on behalf of Loyalist prisoners, but since I was not permitted to speak to any of them, despite a request to do so, I cannot say for certain what their present condition is.

Several prisoners complained to me of beatings, of verbal abuse, of additional punishments (in cold cells without even a mattress) for making complaints, and of degrading searches carried out on the most intimate parts of their naked bodies. Of course I have no way of verifying these allegations, but they were numerous.

In the circumstances I was surprised that the morale of the prisoners was high. From talking to them it is evident that they intend to continue their protest indefinitely and it seems they prefer to face death rather than submit to being classed as criminals. Anyone with the least knowledge of Irish history knows how deeply rooted this attitude is in our country's past. In isolation and perpetual boredom they maintain their sanity by studying Irish. It was an indication of the triumph of the human spirit over adverse material surroundings to notice Irish words, phrases and songs being shouted from cell to cell and then written on each cell wall with the remnants of toothpaste tubes.

The authorities refuse to admit that these prisoners are in a different category from the ordinary, yet everything about their trials and family background indicates that they are different. They were sentenced by special courts without juries. The vast majority were convicted on allegedly voluntary confessions obtained in circumstances which are now placed under grave suspicion by the recent report of Amnesty International. Many are very youthful and come from families which had never been in trouble with the law, though they lived in areas which suffered discrimination in housing and jobs. How can one explain the jump in the prison population of Northern Ireland from 500 to 3,000 unless a new type of prisoner has emerged?

The problem of these prisoners is one of the great obstacles to peace in our community. As long as it continues it will be a potent cause of resentment in the prisoners themselves, breeding frustration among their relatives and friends and leading to bitterness between the prisoners and the prison staff. It is only sowing the seeds of future conflict.

Pending the full resolution of the deadlock, I feel it essential to urge that everything required by the normal man to maintain his physical and mental health and to live a life which is tolerably human, should be restored to these prisoners without delay.

The reply from the Northern Ireland Office was equally furious:

> These criminals are totally responsible for the situation in which they find themselves. It is they who have been smearing excreta on the walls and pouring urine through cell doors. It is they who by their actions are denying themselves the excellent modern facilities of the prison. It is they and they alone who are creating bad conditions out of very good conditions.
>
> Each and every prisoner has been tried under the judicial system established in Northern Ireland by Parliament. Those found guilty, after the due process of law, if they are sent to prison by the courts, serve their sentence for what they are—convicted criminals.
>
> They are not political prisoners: more than 80 have been convicted of murder or attempted murder and more than 80 of explosive offences. They are members of organizations responsible for the deaths of hundreds of innocent people, the maiming of thousands more and the torture, by knee-capping, of more than 600 of their own people . . . No one who is convicted of a crime carried out after 1 March 1976—and that includes those involved in the 'dirty' protest—will be given any form of special status. As soon as this decision is understood and accepted, conditions in the cell blocks can return to normal.

Criticism of O Fiaich poured in. The Governing Committee of the Presbyterian Church issued a statement accusing him of "grave moral confusion." The *Church of Ireland Gazette*—journal of the Anglican Church—said it "left the rest of us in little doubt about where his loyalties lay." And even the journal of the Catholic Church in England, *The Tablet,* declared: "We hope the leaders of Irish opinion . . . disassociate themselves from a statement which can do no good to the cause

of peace in Northern Ireland." It was being said widely that
O Fiaich had lost any chance of winning a cardinal's hat. He
pressed ahead, though, writing a highly critical report for the
Pope. But on the day that he delivered it to the Papal Nuncio
in Dublin—the Vatican's ambassador to Ireland—Pope Paul
VI died. And John Paul I, who followed him, lasted only
thirty-three days; by one account he was reading O Fiaich's
report the night before he died.

In March 1979 the Labour government in Britain collapsed
and Mrs. Thatcher came to power, appointing a new Secretary
of State, Humphrey Atkins. Inevitably Atkins brought hopes
of a fresh approach to the prisons issue. O Fiaich, who by now
had received his cardinal's hat, met Atkins in February 1980
in Armagh. He was encouraged by the new man's apparent
flexibility. The cardinal suggested to the Secretary of State
that he might talk to Sinn Fein. Atkins said he would consider
it. Later he wrote to say he had decided against it—the first
inkling O Fiaich was to have of Atkins's weakness. Mason,
for all his "toughness," had at least been his own man.

In August 1980 O Fiaich was back in the Kesh again and
this time he was allowed to see Spence, who bade him "caed
mile failte"—"a thousand welcomes"—as they were introduced in the UVF compound in the Cages. In an Irish context
it was an extraordinary meeting—between the folk hero of
a gang of sectarian killers and the man who represented the
"Red Whore of Rome," the first target of their hatred. What
was even more extraordinary to the cardinal was that Spence
complained the authorities would not allow the president of
the Gaelic League into the prison to present several of his men
with the Fainne, a medal for fluency in Irish. Spence himself
had studied the language.

At this stage, talk of an impending hunger strike was
beginning to circulate and O Fiaich decided he had to move
to cut it off. He asked to see Atkins again and on March 5
he had the first of a series of meetings with the Secretary of

State which were to run through 1980. At the third meeting, on June 20, he thought he was about to make a breakthrough when the chairmen of the Boards of Visitors of both the Kesh and Armagh prison joined them and backed the cardinal in appealing for a concession on the clothing issue, arguing that it would not amount to the granting of special status. The two chairmen, a west Belfast dentist, Kevin Johnson, and a prominent trade union leader, Joe Cooper, both Catholics, also argued that penal work was not really an issue, because they did not have the facilities to offer the prisoners work even if they did agree to do it. Afterwards the cardinal kept up the pressure, sending Atkins a list of alternatives to "penal" work which could be offered to the prisoners—including the construction of a Roman Catholic chapel in the prison.

At his fourth meeting with Atkins, on July 28, he found the Secretary of State in a friendly mood—he appeared ready to make concessions. But nothing happened. In September the cardinal had to go to Rome for an episcopal synod. Rumors of a hunger strike were rife by then, so before he left he issued a statement stressing that negotiations had not broken down— hoping that would stave off the fast until he returned and had a chance to try again. But the synod lasted longer than he had anticipated and while he was in Rome—on October 10—Sinn Fein announced the hunger strike would be starting on the 27th. So O Fiaich called his secretary in Armagh and instructed him to organize an emergency meeting with Atkins. The Secretary of State agreed to see him in London on the afternoon of the 23rd; he would be at a Cabinet meeting in the morning.

The cardinal left Rome early on that Thursday morning and was met by a Kerry priest at Heathrow. Bishop Daly had come down from Derry to join him. He had arranged to stay at the Westminster home of his English counterpart, Cardinal Hume, and was driven straight there. During lunch a note was passed to him from clergy house, next door, to say it had just been announced on the radio that prison uniforms were being abolished in the north. Jubilant, he telephoned Fr. Murphy, the assistant prison chaplain at the Kesh, asking him to go in and assess the reaction of the prisoners.

He met Atkins as arranged, at 4:30 P.M. at the Northern Ireland Office in Whitehall. The Secretary of State started with a long-winded summary of the concessions which the authorities had already made to the prisoners—such as the granting of compassionate parole. The clerics began to get impatient. Then a typed document was brought in and handed to them. It was headed: "Final Version." The cardinal and Bishop Daly hastily scanned it, looking for the reference to prison clothes. It was in paragraph 8: "The Government has decided to abolish prison uniform as such and to substitute civilian-type clothing." It was meaningless—the substitution of one type of uniform for another. An argument started. The churchmen insisted it would have no effect. Criticism of the concessions—based on the news broadcasts, that the prisoners were to get their own clothes—had already started coming in. It wasn't looking too bad. So why not stick to it? But the Secretary of State was obdurate. It appeared that he had had his instructions at the morning Cabinet meeting.

Bitterly disappointed, Cardinal O Fiaich headed out for Heathrow again, telephoning Fr. Murphy from the airport to tell him what happened. He flew back to Rome and on October 27, the day the hunger strike started, he was invited to supper with the Pope. He spent nearly an hour telling the Pontiff the story of the prison dispute. The Pope asked him what he could do. The cardinal asked him to make a private appeal to Mrs. Thatcher. The Pope told him to give him an *aide-mémoire* . . .

For the Church the hunger strike was proving damaging internally, as well as hurting relations with the state. Clear divisions were developing between the hierarchies in England

and Ireland, particularly over the theological issue of whether death in such circumstances amounted to suicide. Cardinal Hume had started the controversy over the issue during the first hunger strike when, on a visit to Derry in November 1980, he had described it as an act of violence. He had also circulated a pastoral letter, read out at all Masses in England and Wales, denouncing it as suicide. O Fiaich and Hume usually got on well together and, while the Irish cardinal disagreed strongly with the Englishman on the issue, he decided not to reply, both to protect the friendship and to avoid the spectacle of cardinals squabbling in public. But his priests in Armagh were not so reticent and, collectively, they sent off a protest to Cardinal Hume.

One man who quickly spotted the division between the hierarchies—leaping into the breach with a call for a statement from O Fiaich endorsing Hume's position—was the West Belfast MP, Gerry Fitt, one of the most curious public figures in Northern Ireland. Born and brought up in Belfast, he had started his adult life as a soap boy in a barber's shop. During the war he had served as a merchant seaman, sailing on convoys to Russia, and then entered politics, winning the Dock seat—the constituency covering the capital's dockside area—in the Stormont parliament in 1962. Four years later he took the Westminster seat of West Belfast. He was a colorful and witty man but, for a political leader, highly idiosyncratic. He led the Province's main Nationalist party, the Social Democratic and Labour Party (SDLP), from its inception in 1970, holding the position with the strength of his personality while being substantially out of step with grassroots opinion. He resigned as party leader in 1979, denouncing it as too nationalistic, and became an Irish totem for the English political establishment, with increasingly bitter attacks on Republicanism. He had made one such attack shortly before his attempt to exacerbate the divisions between the cardinals, describing the hunger strikers as "brutal murderers," and saying: "You will hear that the hunger strikers have made their wills and sent them to their relatives. But a lot of their victims did not have an opportunity to write a will, or to decide whether or not they wanted to live or die—that decision was taken for them."

As the news of Hughes's death was being broadcast, on Tuesday, May 12, the man in whose favor Fitt had abandoned the leadership of the SDLP was preparing himself for a meeting with the Prime Minister. John Hume was as worried as the cardinal, even if the perspective of the man from Derry was at variance with that of the man from Crossmaglen.

Even though he had to wait a decade to be confirmed in that position, Hume was the natural leader of the majority of Catholics in the north, both because his personal beliefs coincided with the middle ground of moderate Nationalist opinion and because he was one of the most outstanding politicians produced by that population. Previously a history teacher who had studied under O Fiaich at Maynooth, he had been raised in poverty, his father a riveter in the local dockyards. He came to prominence as a leader of the Civil Rights movement of the late 1960s, and it was to that tradition that he belonged. He combined a degree of social puritanism—he was a founder in Derry of the Credit Union, a self-help community banking system—with a Pepysian taste for good company, good food and good whiskey, resulting, later in life, in a constant battle to fend off corpulence. An enchanting raconteur at the dinner table, a powerful orator on the platform and an outstanding debater and performer in front of the television cameras, he was a formidable politician. And he had no time for Republicanism, or political violence. Which is where the conundrum of John Hume lay—in the paradox that, as leader of the minority community in the territory, his political strength stemmed from Republican violence. While he denounced it, it in fact gave him clout with the political establishments of London, Washington and Strasbourg. In Washington he was a hero of the Irish-American establishment, claiming personal friendship with the Kennedys and from time to time boarding the Kennedy children, on summer jaunts to Ireland, in his Bogside home. In Strasbourg, where he was a member of the European Parliament, he was considered a voice of Irish socialism and of moderation from the mayhem of Ulster. In London he was the man Government was constantly looking towards in their despairing attempts to find a constitutional solution.

But, if the Republican violence gave him political clout across the water, he needed to demonstrate his influence with those establishments to reassure his own supporters of the virtues of political moderation, particularly with local government elections imminent in the north—they were scheduled for May 20. And so it was that he sought a meeting with Mrs. Thatcher and got an appointment on Wednesday, May 13.

Liam Og [Sinn Fein official] from Bik [McFarlane] 12.5.81 4:30 P.M.

. . . this morning Kevin Lynch (IRSP) had a visit with a Fr McEldowney from Dungiven who admitted he had been sent to see Kevin (wouldn't name who sent him). He asked Kevin if the first two of our demands would settle the issue, whereupon Kevin referred him to me, saying that if anyone wanted to discuss the demands they should see me and no one else would be talking about them. He referred to tomorrow evening's meeting between Jack [John Hume] and Tinknickers [Mrs Thatcher] and said he was looking on an answer before this occurred. So we take it that Fr McEldowney came on Jack's business with the Sagart Mor's [Cardinal O Fiaich's] blessing. He was also looking up to see Frank in hospital . . .

On Tuesday Hume had flown to Dublin and met Haughey, as Prime Minister, Garret FitzGerald, as leader of the Opposition, and Frank McCluskey, leader of the Irish Labour Party, to brief them on the line he intended taking with Thatcher. They all gave him their backing. Then he flew to London. The appointment had been set for 5 P.M., but soon after his arrival at the Irish Club, where he was staying, he had a call from the Northern Ireland Office to say the appointment had been postponed for four hours. He assumed it was a public relations decision—it meant any statement he might make after the meeting would be too late for the evening television news and at least for the early editions of the next day's national newspapers. He made his way to the Houses of Parliament, killing time, and managed to see Michael Foot, the leader of the Opposition. Foot appeared uneasy; he was maintaining the bipartisan stand on Ireland with the Conservatives; but taking flak from some backbenchers. Hume urged him to intervene. Foot was noncommittal. As Hume left he ran into Fitt, on his way in to see Foot. Later Fitt issued a statement, saying that the Labour leader was standing by his position rather than Hume's.

At about 9 P.M. Hume strolled over to the little cul-de-sac which had been the home of British political power for nearly a quarter of a millennium. As he went up to the bobby at the door of No. 10 the irony of the moment struck Hume; in the early days of the Civil Rights movement he had staged a forty-eight-hour token hunger strike in Downing Street. As he had left that demonstration he had told a friend, Paddy O'Hanlon, that when he came back to the street it would be to go into No. 10. Since then he had been in twice, to see Harold Wilson and subsequently to attend a party thrown by Ted Heath.

The door opened as he approached and he was greeted by the Prime Minister's private secretary. Derrymen, it seemed, got everywhere; the secretary confided to him, as he conducted Hume upstairs to a sitting room, that they had been to school together, at Foyle College in Derry.

Thatcher was waiting in the sitting room with Atkins. She offered Hume a drink and he asked for an Irish whiskey. She confessed she only had Scotch. "I'm not a bigot, I'll have a Scotch," he said. She invited him to speak, pouring a Scotch for herself as well. He launched into his prepared monologue. The deaths were threatening to destroy the "democratic" Nationalist parties both north and south. Moderate Nationalists in Ireland were opposed to the IRA, but felt that the young people in the prisons were victims of the situation, rather than the source of the problem. That sympathy with the prisoners was a fact, whether the British Government recognized it or not. The Government could defuse the whole problem by granting minor concessions, including giving the prisoners their own clothes, without conceding political status. Atkins asked if he could guarantee a settlement with those concessions. Hume said he could not guarantee it, but he was sure of it. Thatcher said the deaths were self-inflicted. A crime was a crime and she was going to treat them as criminals. She was not going to intervene. Hume began to get angry. She was completely misreading the situation, he said. Moderate Catholics were shocked by her intransigence. She was destroying democratic politics in the Province. But the Iron Lady was not for bending. After an hour she conducted him to the door and said goodbye, asking Atkins to stay behind, she wanted a word with him.

Having seen off Hume, Mrs. Thatcher turned her sights on his American allies, the so-called "Four Horsemen"—the leaders of the Irish-American community, Senator Ted Kennedy, Senator Daniel Moynihan, the Speaker of the House of Representatives, Tip O'Neill, and Governor Hugh Carey of New York. After Sands's death the four had sent a telegram to Downing Street, accusing Mrs. Thatcher of inflexibility and urging her to compromise on the practical issue of prison administration to end what they said was an unnecessary crisis. Now Mrs. Thatcher released her letter of reply:

HM Government has, in fact, acted with great flexibility. We have offered a series of improvements in conditions to all prisoners—most of which the protesters have rejected. We have also facilitated visits to the hunger strikers by the European Commission of Human Rights, by members of the Dublin Parliament, by the representative of the official Opposition here and by the personal representative of the Pope. None of these actions has had any effect on the prisoners whose sole purpose is to establish a political justification for their appalling record of murder and violence.

She followed up with a telegram to Cardinal O Fiaich, in reply to his appeals and complaints, declaring: "The solution does not lie in our hands. It lies with the hunger strikers themselves, their families and advisers. More directly, it lies with the leadership of the Provisional IRA, who have taken a cold-blooded decision that the unfortunate men now fasting in prison are of more use to them dead than alive."

In New York, Kennedy issued a statement retorting: "The Prime Minister's response shows only the shadow of flexibility without the substance. It ignores possible initiatives which could resolve the current dispute over prison conditions."

In Dublin, Charlie Haughey, still desperately trying to find a solution to pave the way for a general election, was busy once again with an initiative that had failed—the European Commission on Human Rights. His government had been trying, unsuccessfully, to find a prisoner at the Kesh who would make the application that Sands had refused to make. On Thursday, May 11 his Foreign Minister, Brian Lenihan, in Strasbourg ostensibly for a meeting of the Council of Europe, had discussions with the Minister of State at the British Foreign Office, Douglas Hurd. The next day the European Commission announced it was reopening the 1978 McFeeley case.

*   *   *

In Belfast, meanwhile, a voice of Ulster Loyalism, the *News Letter*—the north's largest morning newspaper—was waxing lyrical about English cowardice. The newspaper's agitation was over a decision by the English Football Association to call off a scheduled match in the north, on security grounds. Describing the decision as "contemptible," the *News Letter* said that in the world wars thousands of Ulstermen had gone voluntarily "to help defend Britain's existence and they did not hold meetings and decide not to go." The newspaper suggested that white feathers should be sent to the English football authorities, "preferably bedraggled ones from long-used pillows as it would not be right to ask local hens to make any better ones available."

"No special consideration is the British line," said an editorial in the *Irish Times*. "For God's sake, has not everything in the North in the last decade been special?"

Two squat police Land Rovers were on patrol in West Belfast when a rocket-propelled grenade hurtled through the night, hammering through the armored back of one vehicle before exploding. The blast killed twenty-three-year-old PC Samuel Vallely, son of a clergyman and father of a sixteen-month-old daughter. He had been planning to emigrate to Canada.

On his last visit to Long Kesh, on August 3, 1980, Cardinal O Fiaich had nearly committed a monumental error; as he was leaving the blocks and examining his list of Armagh prisoners he realized he had forgotten to see the brother of Brian McCreesh, one of his priests in the diocese. He told the warders he had to go back. And so it was that he saw Raymond McCreesh for the last time. As he went into the cell Raymond was lying down and looked up at him from under his blanket. He shared his brother, Brian's, boyish face and what the cardinal couldn't resist describing to himself as an angelic smile. A quiet, soft-spoken, reticent lad. He was not looking very well.

H(5) Block Friday night 30.1.81
Comrade,
    In answer to A/C [Army Council] comm of 25.1.81 as regards my position on the hunger strike. My answer is yes. I am prepared to see it through.
Slan,
Raymond McCreesh
South Armagh

To Liam Og 13.2.81
Name: Raymond Peter McCreesh—address 33 St Malachy's Park, Camlough, Newry, Co. Down. D.O.B. 25.2.57. Telephone no. don't know. Schools Camlough Primary, St Coleman's College, Newry. Employment: Served two years' apprenticeship as sheet metal worker. One year in Newry GTC and one year in Gambel-Simms factory in Lisburn. Worked as milk man for a while. Qualifications Junior Certificate—3 O-levels in Irish, French, English and City and Guilds 200 in practical and theory (sheet metal working). Trade unions: was in same union in Gambel-Simms. Think it was called Sheetmetal Workers and Boilermakers Union—not sure of name and was never really involved in it except for getting name put in book. GAA very slight involvement. In Garrick Crudden GFC when younger. Contact Tommy and Paddy Lynch in Camlough and they'll see you right. Tommy is former chairman of Armagh County Board. Doctor—new family doctor recently, don't know his name, no medical complaints. Captured 25.6.76 taken to Bessbrook Barracks, usual interrogation methods. Charged 29.6.76. Conspiracy to kill British soldiers, attempting to kill British soldiers,

possession with intent, possession and membership—
sentenced on 23.3.77 by Judge Watt. Refused to recognize.
Solicitor Rory McShane, Newry. Came on blanket 24.3.77.
Got slapped about a couple of times, but got no beatings
worth talking about. A chara . . . Slan Raymond.

Raymond was another country boy, like his cellmate,
Frank. They had been a family of farmers for six or seven generations, but his father had run a taxi business at Cullyhana,
just outside Crossmaglen, which is where they had first got
to know the cardinal's family. They had moved to Camlough
back in 1953, into a neat little council house—a pebbledashed
two-up, two-down—just outside the village. Raymond was
born there, in February 1957, the second youngest of eight
brothers and sisters. They had a sound upbringing, in an
intensely religious household, and the children did fairly well
for themselves in adulthood. There was Brian, a priest, and
the others an accountant, a teacher, a bookie, a linguist, a
computer programmer and a secretary. Raymond joined the
IRA in South Armagh at the age of seventeen, using his job as
a milkman to gather intelligence in his area. He operated for
two and a half years without being suspected by the security
forces.

On the morning of June 21, 1976 a routine army patrol
dropped in on a public house, the Mountain House Inn, near
Belleeks in Co. Armagh. The corporal leading the patrol
became suspicious, because the proprietress was not very
friendly and although the pub was closed he could hear men
talking inside. The patrol left, but then circled back to watch.
Shortly afterwards they spotted three men leaving, one of
them an IRA suspect, Paddy Quinn.

When the patrol reported back to base at nearby
Bessbrook—headquarters at the time of the 3rd Battalion of
the Parachute Regiment—eight men were sent out to keep
a watch on the pub. Four men set up an observation post

about thirty meters away from the building. They included the patrol leader, Colour Sergeant Malcolm Baughan, and Lance Corporal David Jones. The sergeant sent the other four to a position on high ground about half a mile away to provide cover. They patiently watched the inn, photographing and logging movements. After four days a little boy spotted them and was seen going into the hotel. So Sgt. Baughan moved his four men to some other high ground to the south, had a drink and then with Lance Corporal Jones moved down the hill to set up a new observation post. Half an hour later, at 9:30 P.M., they spotted four men getting out of a blue Peugeot Estate on a side road, off the main Belleeks–Camlough road, about 450 meters away. They were all carrying guns and were wearing hoods. They walked, military style—covering each other—across fields to a nearby farmhouse.

Raymond McCreesh and Paddy Quinn were at their homes when they got word to get ready for an operation; an army observation post had been spotted watching the Mountain Inn and they were going to mount an attack on the troops. They were picked up at about 7:30 by two other men in a saloon car, Daniel McGuiness and a fourth man, "Malachy." They switched cars, getting into a Peugeot in which guns had been left for them—Quinn got an Armalite, McCreesh a Garand rifle, McGuiness another Armalite and "Malachy" a Sten submachine gun—and then headed for the farmhouse near the Mountain Inn. They got out of the car on the side road and headed across the fields to Paddy Mackin's house.

Sgt. Baughan whispered to Lance Corporal Jones to stay where he was and to start shooting if he could get a clear line of fire on the masked men. He went back up the hill to rejoin the rest of his section and radioed Bessbrook for support. Then he called his other section across, ordered his radio operator to stay where he was and led his men back down to Jones. They were about seventy-five meters from Jones when they heard him opening fire.

McCreesh and Quinn took cover behind the hedge and Danny McGuiness ran for a bunker in the fields. McGuiness could hear machine-gun bullets hitting the wall next to him. He tried to fire back with his Armalite, but the first few rounds were duds. He hurriedly ejected them and started blazing away, triggering off over fifty shots until the army stopped firing. He thought he was surrounded and the others probably dead, so he just lay down and waited for them to come and get him.

As bullets hammered into the hillside near the troops, Sgt. Baughan told his men to split up along the ridge and start shooting. Seeing one of the gunmen sprinting out from a hedge and across the field, Sgt. Baughan shouted at one of his men to get him with his light machine gun and it began its chattering. The running man seemed to have been hit and fell. But he crawled on, to another hedge, slid over it still carrying his gun and got up to stumble down the farm track on the other side. The sergeant bellowed to all his men to concentrate their fire on him. But the gunman made it to the gatepost at the entrance of the house and disappeared. Overhead came the clatter of helicopters. Reinforcements had arrived.

Behind a hedge McCreesh and Quinn, hearing the helicopters, began running like hell across a hayfield to the house of Pat O'Neill. Quinn banged on the door, but nobody seemed to be in. So he smashed the bathroom window and clambered in, McCreesh just behind him. They ran into a front room. They could see soldiers surrounding the house. Covert army patrols were reputed to carry out roadside executions when they caught IRA men red-handed. So they were terrified the troops would kill them out of hand. McCreesh grabbed a phone and called the police station in Bessbrook, shouting what was happening and that they were prepared to surrender to the police, but not to the army. Quinn called his sister, Roisin, and told her to get help. She could hear shooting in the background.

Three helicopters of reinforcements had arrived at the scene. The largest, a Puma, landed a patrol of eight men led by Lieutenant Simon Barry. Orders had been radioed to him to deal with the men in the house before it got dark. The lieutenant crept up to the front of the house and broke a bedroom window with the butt of his rifle, shouting to the gunmen to come out and surrender. A voice shouted back that they would only surrender to the police. Barry bellowed back that he would throw a grenade in if they didn't surrender. A voice shouted at him to fuck off. He fired two shots through the window towards the ceiling of the bedroom. A shout came from the house that they were surrendering.

McCreesh came out first, but another two shots were fired from outside so he retreated into the house again. Then they heard a soldier shout that they had one minute to come out and there would be no more firing. Quinn led the way this time, McCreesh following—leaving their guns in the house. The troops made them lie spread-eagled on the tarmac outside until the police arrived.

Over near the Mackins' house McGuiness was pretending to be asleep—the Armalite and its four magazines by his side—waiting for the troops to come and get him. They found him there on the floor of the bunker shortly after 5 A.M., the next morning.

To Liam Og from Raymond 16.3.81
A chara. There is a couple of things I want to get cleared up here. Firstly I got the Army Council comm dated 6.3.81 confirming my date for embarking upon the hunger strike. I'm sorry for the delay in replying, but I only got the comm on Sunday 15.3.81, that's the way things are in here . . . Jim Gibney was saying that you were looking for a more detailed run-down on me. Well I'm sorry but I can't think of anything else other than what I have already given to you. I'll give you a few more details—about my stay in

Bessbrook barracks after I was captured, if that's any good to you. I was held for three days from Friday night 25.6.76 until Tuesday 29.6.76 when I was charged at a special court in Newry. During my time in the barracks I was subject to the usual interrogation techniques. I was forced to exercise including press ups, jumping up and down off a chair for long periods of time (must have thought I was a kangaroo). Standing spread-eagled against a wall for long periods with my finger tips barely touching the wall. One [security] branch man spat in my face several times. Pressure was asserted at the back of my ears using fingers. I was subject to the usual verbal abuse. I was punched about the body and head. It was mostly thumps with the flat of the hand and on the top of the head. On several occasions the butt of a cigarette was held close to my chin but they made sure not to leave any marks, although I could feel the heat. On one occasion the light in the interrogation room was put out and the branch man told me to make a go for it and see how far I would get. This was after they had shown me a loaded short arm [pistol] one of them was carrying at this time. This is the procedure they went through. I don't know if it is of any use to you, but I'll give it to you anyway. The lights were out. One branch man stuck his finger into my side, another flashed a lighter without a wick, causing only a bright spark from the flint and another banged the table to produce the noise of a shot. All this was done at one time. I was probably supposed to fall dead at this stage of the game, but something must have gone wrong. I'm still here anyway . . . As I said there is nothing else I can think of about myself which would be of any help to you. I'm sorry about that. But I'm not much use at it come to writing things like that . . .

Raymond and Quinn were flown back from the scene of the shooting by helicopter to the Bessbrook police station, arriving at 2 A.M. The interrogators started on Raymond first. They had been caught red-handed and there did not seem to be much point in refusing to admit it. By 3:30 A.M. they had a three-page statement from him, telling the story. Then they moved on to Paddy Quinn. "We were caught with the guns and the ammunition and that's all I want to say," said Paddy. But they took a five-page statement from him as well. Both Raymond and Quinn refused to make written statements, or sign them. When McGuiness was brought in the next night he did make signed statements.

The three of them refused to recognize the court when they came up for trial, making their conviction even more certain. Once inside the Kesh, Raymond refused to don the prison uniform for the monthly visit and—despite his deep religious streak—refused to even put on the trousers to attend Mass.

The choice of Raymond McCreesh to follow Hughes on the hunger strike came as a surprise to some. He was a quiet and introverted figure whose religious passion—regularly during the day he would go on his knees on the concrete floor of his cell—made him appear a little strange among other prisoners, accustomed though they were to the grip of the Roman Catholic faith on their rural comrades. It was a factor which might have made him vulnerable to pressure from the priests. But he had been chosen on the recommendation of Sands, who had known him for a while on the same wing and valued his determination.

Coincidentally McCreesh had shared a cell with Frank Hughes. And it was not the only coincidence, because the same man had been instrumental in the capture of both of them. Corporal David Jones, the SAS man killed by Hughes in the 1978 shoot-out, was the same soldier who, as a member of the Parachute Regiment, had opened fire on McCreesh and his colleagues down in South Armagh two years previously.

There was a further ironic twist to that coincidence: because Jones's last words, as he lay dying near Maghera in Co. Derry, had led to a court action turning on the very question over which Frank Hughes himself had died and Raymond McCreesh was now putting his life on the line—whether there was a state of war in Northern Ireland.

Under English law there are two circumstances in which a verbal—as opposed to a written—last will and testament can be binding. The first is if it is made by a sailor at sea. The second is if it is by a soldier during a state of war. Which raised the question, after Jones's death, as to whether his last words to his two fellow officers—". . . make sure Anne gets my stuff"—constituted a will.

The issue was referred to the High Court in London two years after his death, in July 1980. Delving into ancient precedents—one going back to the Middle Ages, others involving the death of a cook in India in the eighteenth century, an Egyptian uprising in the nineteenth century and the fate of an Australian soldier in Malaysia in the twentieth century—Mr. Justice Arnold concluded that Jones had been engaged in active military service against "a conjuration of clandestine assassins and arsonists," and that was enough to validate his will. So Jones's fiancée, Anne Mannering, got his £3,000 death grant and belongings, in the face of bitter protest from his mother.

Judge Arnold was not, of course, required to delve into precedent on the reverse question, as to whether "a conjuration of clandestine assassins and arsonists" on active service were entitled to special status.

McCreesh's determination, as recognized by Sands, was shared by, among the rest of his family, his mother Susan, behind whose shy exterior there was a will as steely as that of Mrs. Thatcher. But another mother, who was to share Mrs. McCreesh's coming ordeal day by day, had sworn to herself— from the day that her son told her of his decision—that she was going to bend.

After Sands's death Peggy O'Hara had asked to see the IRSP. A leading figure made the trip up to Derry from Dublin. She told him bluntly that she would not allow her son Patsy to die. It was a serious blow for the organization, but the official had no choice but to say they would support her come what may.

The IRSP was born of a second split in the old Official IRA, in 1974, precipitated by the expulsion of one of its leading members, Seamus Costello—the leader of an IRA flying column in the 1950s campaign. It was formally established in December 1974 and, as had happened at the time of the Provisional breakaway, feuding ensued in which five men were killed and more than seventy wounded. It was during this fighting that the IRSP established—initially without the knowledge of many of its members—a military wing, the People's Liberation Army. It grew rapidly, drawing support from members of the Officials who objected to the ceasefire, as well as some members of the Provisionals who left that organization during their ill-fated truce with the British Government in 1975. In June 1976 it changed its name to the Irish National Liberation Army. The IRSP and INLA were dominated by Costello until he was shot dead, at the age of thirty-eight, by an unidentified gunman in a Dublin street in 1977. Over 5,000 attended his funeral and the INLA did him proud, with a full guard of honor. The commander of the guard was a twenty-year-old youth out on bail on charges of holding an Irish police officer at gunpoint: Patsy O'Hara.

In private the IRA dubbed INLA recruits "space cadets"—implying they were "spaced out"—and referred to their stronghold in the Divis Flats complex in Belfast as the "Planet of the Irps," a play on the acronym IRSP. The INLA was a small organization: before the hunger strike it had roughly 100 members, a quarter of them "active," concentrated in the cities of Belfast, Derry and Armagh as well as Dublin. It was less disciplined than the IRA and therefore less predictable. There were divisions within it, between members north and south of the border, the Belfast leadership suspecting that the Dublin grouping was holding back arms shipments for fear of future internal feuding.

The INLA was little known outside Ireland until it leapt into the British public consciousness on March 30, 1979 with an explosion in the precincts of the House of Commons. A bomb had been planted by the INLA in the car of a Conservative MP, Airey Neave. Triggered by a mercury trembler switch—the same sort of switch which activates a two-tone door gong—it exploded as he drove up the ramp from the Commons car park, killing him instantly. Neave, a British war hero—he was the first officer to escape from the Colditz POW camp—was the Tory spokesman on Northern Ireland at the time. More importantly, he was a close personal friend of Mrs. Thatcher and was responsible for the 1975 party coup which gave her the leadership. In Ireland her inflexibility of the prisons was widely blamed on her relationship with Neave and bitterness over his death.

Costello was succeeded, at least as leader of the IRSP, by Miriam Daly, who lectured in political studies at Queen's University, Belfast. Her husband, Jim, was a Queen's philosophy lecturer. One of Jim Daly's party duties was to edit the *Starry Plough*, the official journal of the IRSP, traveling to Dublin to prepare each issue with the help of Patsy O'Hara.

Patsy was born in 1957 in Derry, where his father owned a public house and a small grocery shop. The premises were blown up early in the "Troubles" and the family lived on the small compensation payment made by the Government, on the dole and then on some money Peggy made working as an attendant at public lavatories in the city. Patsy was to nickname his father "Steptoe," because he used to eke out some money by ripping out wires and lead from derelict houses.

The family did have a Republican background. Patsy's grandfather was wounded fighting for Britain at Ypres in the First World War, but he returned to Ireland to join the IRA, transporting weapons and men along the Foyle in the 1920s. The eldest of the boys, Sean, was interned for two years from 1971 and the second eldest, Tony, was jailed in 1976 for five years for robbery, serving his time on the blanket protest.

Patsy, the youngest of the boys, had his first sight of the "Troubles" in October 1968, when he watched the Civil Rights marches with his family. His first taste of the violence came at the age of fifteen, in 1972, when he was shot in the leg by a British patrol—in cross fire, according to the army—in the Bogside area of Derry. He had already joined the Fianna Eireann, the youth wing of the IRA, two years previously.

Interned for six months from October 1974, he joined the INLA shortly after his release. He was arrested again in June 1977 and charged with possession of a stick of gelignite, only to be released after ten months on remand amidst suspicions that the explosives had been planted on him. He was arrested again in September 1976 and acquitted four months later on a second possession charge; arrested in Dublin in 1977, for allegedly holding a police officer at gunpoint, only to be acquitted once again in January 1978. Then, on May 7, 1979, he ran into a four-man patrol of the Royal Hampshire Regiment in Derry and was seen to throw an object into some nearby bushes as he ran from them. He stopped when they shouted they would open fire. In a search of the area the soldiers found a Soviet-made F1 fragmentation grenade hidden in a purple-patterned sock. They raided his house and found a matching sock in his bedroom. On January 15, 1980 he was sentenced to eight years and immediately went on the blanket protest.

Patsy was an intelligent left-wing ideologue, shy but obstinate and puritanical within the organization about dedication and discipline. Small as a boy, he sprang up in adulthood to a slim 6 feet 2 inches tall. He made a striking figure in his black ceremonial uniform with white belt, as a staff captain in the INLA. He had been elected to the Ard Comhairle—the Executive Committee—of the IRSP in 1977, and when he was committed to Long Kesh he was the obvious choice as commanding officer of the small group of INLA men being held there. He was nicknamed "Scatter." It was something of a family name. Originally it had been bestowed on one of his two brothers who, so the story went, had stepped out of a rioting crowd in Derry wielding a "Chicago Piano"—a Thompson machine gun—and had shouted "scatter" before opening fire on the security forces. Patsy was renowned for a love of singing, but had a hideous ear for tone and his contributions to concerts tended to be met with roars of abuse. He had been scheduled to be the fourth INLA replacement on the first hunger strike, but decided he would lead on the second.

The relationship between the IRA and the INLA was fraternal—both had suffered enough from Republican feuding—but uneasy. They cooperated to some extent operationally—sharing the same enemy it would be foolish to do otherwise—but to the INLA the IRA was big brother, always threatening to swamp them. For the IRA the INLA was a recruiting competitor, however small; one which would benefit from any divisions in the larger group's ranks. More seriously, their comparative lack of discipline and "mad dog" tactics, together with confusion in the public mind between the two groups, posed a threat to the IRA's military and political planning. The tensions between them were not so pronounced inside the Kesh, although there was ceaseless banter between them: "D'ya hear the news, the Irps are going to step up their protest, they're going to slop out the top of their doors." But because they were so small in number they tended to passively accept the IRA command structure, although they were likely to fly their own flag when any major moves were afoot, as they were doing by insisting on taking part in the hunger strike.

There was uncertainty in the IRA leadership, however, as to how reliable they would be on the hunger strike. So while they had agreed to INLA participation they covered themselves by matching O'Hara, putting McCreesh on the same day—the twenty-second of Sands's fast.

Although Patsy had started on the same day as Raymond, the O'Hara family were convinced he would last longer—he was obviously the stronger of the two. The youngest of the family, Patsy's sister Elizabeth, had been down to see Charlie Haughey and reported back to the family that he was insistent no more of the hunger strikers would be allowed to die. And he was the Irish Prime Minister, after all—he should know. So Mrs. O'Hara felt pretty confident; there was lots of time to play brinkmanship with the Brits.

McCreesh's deterioration was sudden. Fr. Brian, his brother, visited him on the afternoon of Saturday, May 16, with their mother, sister Bridie, and brother Malachy. Raymond's speech was slurred and his eyesight had almost gone, but he appeared mentally bright and lucid. They had told him about Frank's funeral and he was obviously upset about the death of his old cellmate.

A Protestant gunman from the outlawed Ulster Freedom Fighters crept into the bedroom of a Catholic butcher, Pat Martin, in the Ardoyne area of North Belfast, and pumped four bullets in his head. Pat, aged thirty-eight, had been targeted because he was identified at Sands's funeral. His fifteen-year-old daughter, Elaine, found him and shouted down the stairs: "Daddy's lying in a pool of blood." It was Saturday, just in time for the Sunday newspapers, which announced he had been killed for refusing to close his shop for Frank Hughes's funeral.

*   *   *

The McCreeshes went back to their home at Camlough and in the early evening got a call from the prison doctor, asking them to come back. He wouldn't tell them what it was about, but said there was no cause for alarm—it was not what they thought. So they got back into Brian's Opel Kadett and roared up the A6 to the Kesh. This time they were hurried through the formalities of the search and when they got to the prison hospital were conducted into the doctor's office. A medical orderly came in and explained what had happened: they had asked Raymond if he wanted some milk after the family had gone and Raymond had said he didn't know. Obviously if he drank milk that was the end of his hunger strike, so they had decided the family should come up before they gave him some. Perhaps they would like to go in and check? They could take their time—spend as long as they wanted. The authorities didn't want to get it wrong, you understand.

Bewildered, the family went in and found Raymond in a confused state. He seemed to think he was in a hospital in Scotland. Fr. Brian leaned over him and said, "Raymond, you are not in Scotland, you are in Long Kesh. Do you know what Long Kesh is?" Raymond smiled in recognition and said: "A concentration camp." It reassured them. But he still seemed totally confused. He said the doctors had told him he was in Scotland and that he hadn't eaten. Fr. Brian said: "You've been on hunger strike, this is your fifty-seventh day on hunger strike." He tried to get his brother's mind working, mentioning Bobby's name, but it didn't seem to mean anything to him. Then he said of Frank Hughes, whose cell he had shared for a year before the hunger strike, "Do you remember Frank?"

"Where is Francie?" asked Raymond. "Is Francie dead? Who killed him?"

Then the hospital staff came in and said that's it, they would have to go. So they went back into the doctor's office and told him they had no reason to believe he had changed his mind, there were no grounds for intervening. Why, asked

Fr. Brian, had they offered him milk in the first place? The orderly shrugged.

On Sunday the family were told they could start their bedside vigil. Before he went up Fr. Brian sent a telegram to the Prime Minister, begging for concessions to save his brother. When he got to the prison hospital he found Raymond comatose.

He came out on Monday to find a public furor was starting over the milk his brother hadn't drunk. The Northern Ireland Office had put out a statement saying, "There was an indication on Saturday night that he wished to end his hunger strike. However he is still refusing nourishment." They added that they could not comment about the family's visit. It was carefully phrased; the NIO was not making any allegations against the family, they were not commenting at all. And if anyone wanted to draw any conclusions from the sequence of events—hunger striker wants food, family visits hunger striker, hunger striker decides he doesn't want food—that was their business. And of course the conclusions were drawn. By Monday night the BBC reports were suggesting Fr. Brian had persuaded his brother to die.

In South Armagh on Tuesday a ten-ton, six-wheeled Saracen armored car was driving along a winding country road a couple of miles from Raymond's house, when 1,000 pounds of explosives hidden in a culvert underneath it went off. A twenty-five-foot-wide crater in the road and the armored turret was all that was left to mark the place. One of the Saracen's huge tires, weighing four cwt., had flown right over a farmhouse nearly 200 yards away. Five soldiers had been inside the vehicle: Paul Bulman was the youngest of them. He would have been twenty on the Saturday. He had telephoned home on Monday night to say not to worry, everything was OK with him. He said he was a bit too old for birthday presents. His dad, a forty-seven-year-old shipyard worker at Wallsend, said he'd send the lad some money instead. "Man that is born of woman has but a short time to live," the chaplain, Rev. John Harris, intoned at his funeral a week later on Tyneside. And one of his mates confided: "He seemed to be enjoying it out there. He said there was plenty of action and it was better than just hanging around in Germany doing exercises and all that."

On the same day, in Belfast's Twinbrook Estate—just across open ground from the Sands' front door—twelve-year-old Carol Anne Kelly was walking back from the corner shop. She had reason to be pleased with herself, having just bought the last pint of milk in stock. Down below the hillock on which the houses were built four army Land Rovers roared along the road. There was a crack. The baton round, five ounces of hard plastic, left the riot gun at a speed of 180 mph. Carol stopped and then said "Someone help me" as she slowly toppled. A housewife standing on her doorstep just a few yards away stared in disbelief; she thought the girl was joking—you know how kids will do stupid things. Carol died in hospital two days later, the fifth child to be killed by a plastic bullet in the north.

In Long Kesh Patsy O'Hara was living up to his mother's hopes; while Raymond had been lying semiconscious he had even been able to take part in a propaganda stunt. He was sitting in the television room with another patient, Seamus Ferguson—a conforming Republican prisoner who happened to be in the hospital with a leg injury. Suddenly Patsy pulled a miniature camera out of his pocket and whispered to Seamus to take his photograph with it. They opened a door of a metal cabinet in the corner of the room, so that Seamus could be blocked off from any warder who might glance through the observation slit. He began snapping away at Patsy in his wheelchair. Finished, Patsy took the camera back. The film was smuggled out and a blurred picture of Patsy was published in an Irish newspaper a week later, but in a routine search warders discovered the camera, together with a tiny tape recorder, in McCreesh's room.

Although Patsy seemed all right, his mother Peggy decided she wanted to be close enough to intervene if he took a sudden turn for the worse, and she moved down from Derry to Belfast with her husband, Jim. At first they stayed at the home of an IRSP member, Sue Bunting. The house had uncomfortable associations. The previous October, just before the first hunger strike, Sue had been living there with her thirty-two-year-old husband, Ronnie—a Protestant and son of a prominent Loyalist figure, but nevertheless a member of the IRSP. An IRSP colleague, Noel Lyttle, was staying with them; he had just been released from Castlereagh interrogation center. At about 4:30 A.M. the two Bunting children, aged seven and three, were wakened by shots. Gunmen using sledgehammers had smashed their way through the front door, shooting Ronnie and Sue at the top of the stairs and Noel as he lay in his bed. Noel and Ronnie had died; Sue took a bullet in the face, but survived.

Later Peggy and Jim moved to the home of Patsy's old mentor, Jim Daly, on the Andersonstown Road. He moved out of the master bedroom to make them comfortable. But there was something about the room which also made them a little uncomfortable—a feminine touch, including talcum powder on the dressing table and dresses in the wardrobe. It was something of a shrine for Jim Daly. Less than a year before his wife, Miriam—who had succeeded Costello as chairperson of the IRSP—had been killed in the house. Jim had been down in Dublin at the time, when gunmen had broken in and tied Miriam to a chair at gunpoint in the hallway. They gave up waiting for Jim to come home and made do with Miriam, finishing her off by firing through a cushion to silence the shots. Their ten-year-old daughter, Marie, came home from school to find her mother lying there with her head blown in and ran from the house, screaming: "There's something wrong with my Mummy."

It was a wise move by Peggy, coming to Belfast, because on the Wednesday Patsy had a heart attack. Her husband had gone to Derry that day, to try and find some old photographs of Patsy for the newspapers, and she had gone up in the afternoon. She wanted to reassure him that he wasn't going to die, so as she was leaving she suddenly turned back, put her arms around her son and said: "I don't care about Ireland, or the world, but I'm going to save you." And with that she hurried out.

On her way back to Daly's home she made a detour, to the Sinn Fein office, to tell them what she planned to do. And then she went back to the house in Andersonstown Road. The telephone rang and it was one of the prison chaplains, telling her of Patsy's collapse. Back she went to the prison, to find Patsy unconscious with two priests in the room, praying. She took his hand and wet his lips with some water from a carafe next to the bed. It was time to act, but she was frightened. Then a doctor came in and cuffed his face to bring him around, saying: "Patsy, your mother's here." His eyes opened on her and he whispered: "I'm sorry, Mammy, we didn't win. Let the fight go on," before drifting off again.

In a state of frenzy over the decision facing her, Peggy asked for a pen and, going into the rest room set aside for the family across the corridor, scratched his words on a cigarette packet. She needed to talk to someone and asked permission to see Mrs. McCreesh. The request was refused. It was going to be a long and lonely night.

The next morning her husband came up with Jim Daly, to relieve her. Jim was posing as an uncle to gain entrance to the prison. She told them the story of Patsy's last words and of her decision.

Liam Og from Bik 9.30 P.M. 19.5.81
. . . Personally I'd whack the Concorde with a Sam 7. Then where would we be, sez you? Oh, I don't know!! Did you

ever feel totally frustrated? No, don't answer that. I've a blinding headache just now—a rarity for me which makes it all the more annoying . . . You know something—I feel really terrible just sitting here, waiting for Ray to die. I haven't prayed too much since Bob died—I don't know what it is. Perhaps I should try harder. Love to all. Take care and God Bless.

PS Have just heard about that cunning little operation in S. Armagh. Oh, you wonderful people!! Far from home they perish, yet they know not the reason why! Tis truly a great shame. They kill and die and never think to question. Such is the penalty for blind folly. God Bless. Bik.

Down the corridor Raymond was nearing the end. Fr. Brian was celebrating Mass at his brother's bedside on the Tuesday when he suddenly recovered consciousness, sat up and said: "Is that you, Mammy? It's great to see you." They talked with him for a while before he slipped back again. On Wednesday they said Mass again and once more he seemed to recognize them. He died in the early hours of Thursday morning, after sixty-one days without food.

To Liam Og from Bik 21.5.81
Comrade, just got your stuff a few moments ago. As you say, the heartbreak gets worse. No matter how much one expects the worst it doesn't help soften the blow. I managed to get a verbal to O/C H6 this morning to instruct Big Doc to go ahead tomorrow. There's a comm here from him anyway, just to confirm it. The O/C of H5 informed me that Brendan was finding it hard to keep the water down . . .

To Liam Og Thursday 21.5.81
. . . Here are some names of volunteers who are on my short list in numerical order of preference: Tom McElwee (Bellaghy—H3); Lawrence McKeown (Randelstown—H3);

D. Nellis (Derry City—H3); M. Hurson (Tyrone—H5/6?).
Those were the next four men I had picked. Now both
Tom and Lawrence have approached me of late to reaffirm
their commitment to hunger strike and were fighting for
a place further up the list. Anyway I'm just letting you
have these names in case the worst comes to the worst
with Brendan. If he did happen to die in the coming days
or next week we would need to replace him. This is cruel,
comrade. Really cruel. I was pretty much stunned today at
Index's [Fr. Toner's] news—visibly stunned and he knew
it. Sorry mate, but what with Ray dying this morning
and then getting whacked up the kite with Patsy about
to go any minute the thought of Brendan not lasting past
the weekend was somewhat staggering even for someone
who is trying his best to 'stay solid'. Such a bastard of
a day. What I want to do right now is kneel down and
cry myself to death. I picked up a Sun dated Friday 8th
that I hadn't seen—when I saw the photo of Bob and his
young lad I was shattered. Funny, I was just thinking last
night about him and how much he wanted a visit with
the young lad. This is a rough life, old friend . . . Patsy is
now in a coma, so I suppose it's only a matter of hours
now. God help their families. Take good care of yourself
mate and God Bless. Bik.

McCreesh and O'Hara had started together and they were
to die within hours of each other, Patsy's turn coming later
that night. They were waiting for the arrival of Patsy's girlfriend, Edel, a beautiful young girl who lived in Dublin and
with whom he was deeply in love. She was catching the last
train up to Belfast to try and see him. Two of the menfolk were
in the room—Jim Daly and Mickey McCaffrey, the fiancé of
Patsy's sister, Elizabeth—when his breathing seemed to stop.
His body was icy cold. A doctor and an orderly examined him
and pronounced him dead. Jim Daley and Mickey McCaffrey

started to cry. The rest of the family—Peggy and her husband and Elizabeth—were called in from the rest room. A priest had started the obsequies—"dear brother departed"—and someone murmured it was a pity he had not lasted until Edel had got there. At that moment the body gave a gasp and Patsy started breathing again. He seemed to take a breath every twenty minutes. Peggy couldn't stand it and she left the room again. Then the door swung open and in came Edel, an entrance worthy of Sarah Bernhardt. With a tooled sheepskin coat slung over her shoulder she strode to the bed, sat herself down, took Patsy's hand and began talking to him, telling him not to die, asking him if he wanted to eat. Patsy stopped breathing. The doctors said he was dead again. But his dad knew about death—as a small boy he had watched both his sister and brother die, the girl of peritonitis, the boy of fast-developing tuberculosis. The girl's had been a horrific death; she had squealed and squealed until she was exhausted. But in the end both of them had made that curious noise—the death rattle. And until he had heard his son make that noise he wouldn't believe he was dead. So he bent over Patsy and shouted his name in his ear. And the young man gave a heave and made a noise and his dad was convinced. Patsy O'Hara had finished his war.

Outside the prison the fighting went on. The cardinal issued an anguished statement: "I shared the family's joy in 1973 when a t-Ath Brian (Fr. Brian McCreesh) was ordained priest for this diocese. It would be unthinkable of me, therefore, not to be willing to share their burden now in the hour of their greatest need," he said. "I repudiate unequivocally this recourse to arms, but I well remember how easy it was in the mid-'70s for many young men on both sides to become convinced that this was the best way to defend their own community. Raymond McCreesh was captured bearing arms at the age of nineteen and sentenced to fourteen years' imprisonment. I have no doubt that he would never have seen the inside of a jail but for the abnormal political situation.

"Who is entitled to pronounce him a murderer or a suicide?"

In London a leading Catholic, Lord Rawlinson—a former Attorney General—felt entitled, declaring himself "ashamed and distressed" by the cardinal's stand. The Primate's position on whether the hunger strike deaths were suicide was "extraordinary," he said. The prisoners had deliberately killed themselves. "I have always understood as a Catholic that to do this was a mortal sin." Another prominent English Catholic and former Minister of State, Shirley Williams, joined in, referring to the deaths as suicide and saying: "It is not sacrifice, it is a sort of sacrilege."

In New York Ted Kennedy said it was time the British Government ended its "unseemly posture of inflexibility."

In Dublin Charlie Haughey had made no advance with the European Commission and had decided electoral procrastination was no longer viable. He announced the general election would be in three weeks' time—the shortest notice of an election allowed by law. In the north the electorate had gone to the polls the previous day for the local government elections and the results which were just coming in underlined the polarization which was taking place. It was summed up by the defeat of the former SDLP leader, Gerry Fitt, who had been thrown off the Belfast City Council after holding his seat for twenty-three years; a clear rejection of his anti-H-Block stance. The SDLP itself had lost nine seats—three percent of its votes—while on the other side of the sectarian divide the Rev. Ian Paisley's Protestant extremists, the Democratic Unionist Party, had almost doubled its representation, from seventy-four seats in the 1977 local government election to 142.

The milk incident was not allowed to die its own death, either. At the weekend the *Sunday Times* published a bizarre report, with what it claimed were excerpts from a tape recording of Fr. McCreesh and his mother, egging Raymond on to his death. "Now Raymond, you're going back on your word," Mrs. McCreesh was quoted as telling a recalcitrant son. The Northern Ireland Office issued a statement denying any knowledge of such a tape, but added disingenuously that they had found a tape recorder in McCreesh's room.

Patsy O'Hara was brought home to his parents' house on the edge of the Bogside. The INLA guards stopped photographers going in, but when his father saw Patsy's body he insisted on a cameraman being called, to take pictures of what looked like cigarette burns on the corpse and its broken nose.

They buried Raymond McCreesh on an Armagh hillside the following Saturday. A lone piper led thousands of mourners, including sixty priests, through the hedgerows to the gates of St. Malachy's chapel. There they stopped and at a command three men in IRA uniforms stepped out of the crowd and fired a volley of shots over the coffin with .303s. Inside the church Fr. Brian led the Mass, assisted by the prison chaplains, Fr. Toner and Fr. Murphy—Index and Silvertop, as Bik would have had them. The Mass was sung in Irish and, as the procession of priests came down the aisle hand in hand, one could be seen to have tears in his eyes; tears of happiness at the piety and at the language—Church and Republicanism for once being woven smoothly together. At the graveside, within sight of the McCreeshes' front door and under circling army helicopters, Ruairi O Bradaigh, President of Sinn Fein—defying arrest by being in the north, from which he was excluded—asked derisively of Britain: "Where now is their normalization policy, their Ulsterization policy and their policy of criminalization?"

The next day they buried Patsy O'Hara up in Derry. And the man who organized the farewell to Costello would have been proud of his own send-off. The Catholics of Derry turned out in their tens of thousands, taking two hours to climb the hillside to the cemetery. The INLA provided a guard of honor of thirty-two masked men, six firing the farewell volley over the coffin. At the graveside his older brother, Sean, called for unity between the IRA and INLA to drive the British out of Ireland.

The INLA's Army Council, at a meeting after Patsy's death, resolved by a closely fought vote to call off their hunger strike, as a waste of life and effort. But word came back from the Kesh that their men were continuing regardless.

Inside the Kesh, Bik was battling with the problem of Brendan McLaughlin, who had been transferred to an outside hospital in agony, showing the symptoms of a bleeding stomach ulcer.

Liam Og from Bik Monday 25.5.81 4.30 P.M.
. . . just on Brendan—is there any medical treatment he can receive for his illness which is non-vitamin based? If so, can we get him to accept such treatment? I'm distracted thinking about him. What a bloody catastrophe . . . Those reports about the McCreesh family must have distressed them greatly. Those Brits are the world's worst. I heard also that the peelers [police] played themselves when handing over Patsy's body. Nothing need be said about such activity. It is indescribable . . .

"Happy Wagon on the air." Dinnertime.
"Stew on the air and Ciste Bui."
Groans went up and the prisoner wrinkled his nose. Minced stew, two potatoes, black carrots and boiled kale. "Cail" in the Irish, he mentally recited to himself, "to discard or throw away." Low-grade cabbage. Pig swill. And Ciste Bui for pudding: "Yellow cake"—the tag given to it since word had filtered through from the Cages in 1979 that there was uranium mining going on in Donegal. Slabs of processed uranium 289. "Enough of that and you'll blow your way out

of here." Veterans claimed to have counted it in fifty-two varieties—with currants, seeds, jam . . .

Today it was plain sponge. The portions were inevitably unequal; the screws never stopped trying to get them fighting. Half of one portion of the Ciste Bui was missing. Don Quixote's greyhounds would probably be blowing their way out of their kennels tonight, he thought. Carefully the two men redivided their portions, the prisoner automatically swopping his pudding for half his cellmate's stew.

Dinner finished and the tea ceremony over—dashing the dregs from their cups against the ceiling to ease the reflected glare of the neon tubes—the two sprawled on their mattresses as the screws signaled their departure with the clanging of the distant grilles.

After a few minutes of silence his cellmate ambled to the chamber pots and peered into them in turn.

"They won't last," he said.

"Aye, better ask the Ceannfort."

"Ah, hell." The sentiment didn't need expressing—the hope that they were not the only ones. The prisoner nodded, thinking of the stench when they had to try and pour it out of the window, dripping down on to the hot pipes.

"Listen, we've two pots full," his cellmate called to the commanding officer.

"Can you not hold out till three?"

"No, they're full."

"Anyone else want to slop out?"

To their relief they heard two shouts.

"OK, all slop out . . . fire it out there, lads."

The prisoner hurriedly tended his bread dam while his cellmate prepared the paper funnel. He would almost welcome a wing shift with this cell; the gap under the door and depression in the concrete floor outside made it one of the worst he'd had in three and a half years.

"OK?"

The splashing had already started down the corridor. He gave the dough a last tentative squeeze and nodded. His cellmate started tipping.

As they went back to their mattresses a beginners' class in Irish was signaled with a call of "Right lads, we'll start with a greeting. D for delta, I for indigo, A for alpha. New word. I for indigo . . ."

"Here, slow it up"—from a pupil battling to keep up, scratching on his makeshift blackboard amidst the brown smears on the wall.

"For fuck's sake, write it down and toss it over to him."

"Any chance there, lads?" from the teacher, aimed at a couple gossiping between cells near the grilles.

"Right, yo, knock it on the head, there's a class," called the commanding officer.

The prisoner dozed lightly, wakening to the curses from the circle as the ammonia stench hit the screws returning from dinner and a midday drink. The routine of the head count began again, boots splashing through the pools, followed by the tense ten-minute wait.

The squeegee sloshed its way past his cell and the prisoner was beginning to relax when the cry went up: "They're putting it under the doors." He hurried to check his bread barrier. But a quickening in the strokes of the squeegee, matched by the scrapes of two chamber pot lids as two other prisoners with a bad door battled to hold back the tide, signaled the trouble was down the corridor. He heard a door opening, a smack of flesh on flesh and scuffling and then the pounding of boots as other screws rushed down from the Circle. The yelling began.

"What's happening?"

"Don't know."

"It's 8 or 16."

"You bastards, open this door and I'll take the fuckin' heads off ye."

The door boomed again followed by the shout of: "PO, one for the Boards," and a babble of voices, mixing obscenities at the passing screw with shouts of inquiry and reassurance to the condemned man.

"They hurt you bad?"

"My eye—think it'll be a steaker."

"You'll be sound."

"You'll be back in a few days."

"Just keep your head."

For the fifteen minutes that the wing waited to hear the arrival of the van in the yard, the prisoner's imagination wandered. To 1978 and the scalding, when buckets of near-boiling water had been hurled into cells. Denis the Menace had gone apeshit about the blisters on his back. Then the battle of the buckets, when the screws had started hurling the urine back into the cells. And the forced baths, the deck brushes scraping their balls: that had been the day Governor Miles's name had been sent out. They'd caught him at his home off the Antrim Road. His wife had answered the knock on the door and when her husband joined her to see who it was they had pulled out their guns and opened fire. Neighbors tried to give him artificial respiration, but he had had no chance. "There's many more MILES to status" went the joke in the Kesh at the time. And the time Danny had bust the screw's nose with his head; for that they pinned him up against the grilles, two standing on his feet, two holding him, batoning him in relays and putting a cigarette out on his back. Do anything, but don't hit a screw. Though it would be worth it to land a few on the Pervert, after he'd played with the Wee Lad's foreskin. The obscenity of that story brought the prisoner's mind back to the present and the grinding of the van's gears in the yard.

"C Wing, send him out."

The locks slammed open. Sounded like half a dozen screws—taking no chances. The prisoner peered through the *crack, catching a glimpse of the naked figure being pulled at a run by one arm and his hair. Just past him there was a splash and shouts: "Get up, you bastard." Grunts from cell 26 as he was kicked down over the mirror. A gloved finger probing his arse and his mouth. The clang of the grilles, the wing listening for sounds of a beating in the Circle. Warnings were shouted across to the adjoining wing to watch out for signs of injury as he was loaded into the van. The engine roared as he was taken off to the Boards, the small punishment block of windowless one-man cells with their concrete tables and chairs and wooden strips on concrete beds. Naked all day. A generator whining day and night nearby. It would be an icebox now. At least they'd beaten the silence rule. But it was the continual fear of the place; fear bred of isolation, fear of imminent violence, fear ultimately of the straitjackets and padded cells.*

The wing quieted down as the screws finished mopping the corridor.

SIX

*"Broadcasters cannot be impartial about the
activities of illicit organizations."*

—Annan Committee on the future
of broadcasting, 1977

*"The people involved in the shootings are playing
into the terrorists' hands."*

—Secretary of State, Humphrey Atkins,
commenting on a spate of Protestant
killings of Catholics, November 5, 1980

He was wearing corduroys and a brown jacket and sipping
tea out of a plastic cup as he walked across the car park of
Long Kesh towards them on that sunny Tuesday.

"Lynch?" he asked, through the window. "Are you going
in to see Kevin?"

"We are."

The IRSP man climbed into the back seat of Paddy Lynch's
beach-colored Ford Granada, under the eyes of the sentry
boxes nearby.

"Times is bad," said Paddy.

"They are," said the IRSP man, adding: "Raymond
McCreesh could be dead tomorrow and Patsy O'Hara on
Friday—Kevin's taking Patsy O'Hara's place."

Bridie Lynch stared at him speechlessly. Paddy burst out
swearing: "Fucking hell, why don't you go on it?"

When they went into the visiting area, the IRSP man in
tow, Kevin was already sitting at the table. Bridie saw immediately that her son was in distress. She had never seen him
looking so bad. They sat down.

"Daddy, I'm going on hunger strike and I need your help,"
said Kevin.

"You're going on no hunger strike," retorted Paddy. They
started arguing, Kevin repeating that he knew what he was
asking them, but that he had to think of the other prisoners.
Some of them were doing sentences of twenty-five and thirty
years and had wives and children outside. Somehow they had
to bring an end to the dirty protest, he said.

Then Kevin leaned over to his mother, took her hands and
said: "Mammy, you've never let me down. I never needed you
more than I've needed you now. I'm asking you one thing,
will you please stand by me?"

Bridie was near tears. "Kevin, I've never let you down.
Whatever you want, I'll stand by you."

The tranquility of the Lynches' lives, in their luxurious double-story house in the Co. Derry village of Dungiven, had been
shattered four years previously by a hammering at the door
at 5:40 A.M. on the morning of December 2. Paddy pulled
on his slippers and opened it, to find a throng of police and
soldiers in the snow outside.

There was little in Kevin's background to suggest he would
become the target of that early morning knock on the door.
Paddy's family had lived for three generations in the village of
Park. He was a builder like his father and grandfather before
him, although for a while he owned a pub in Dungiven. All
five of the boys followed him into the construction business.
The family was Nationalist, but then who wasn't in Dungiven.
Kevin's middle-class and religious background made him a
more obvious candidate for the hustings with the SDLP, if
he had had a yen for politics. But anyone following young

Kevin on his way to Mass in St. Patrick's church on a Sunday morning could have guessed at his political allegiance, from the way he paused, devoutly, at the gravestone of O'Carolan and Kilmartin, two IRA men killed in the area in 1922. "It is not those who can inflict the most, but those who can suffer the most who will conquer," the obelisk quoted MacSwiney.

Liam Og 2.5.81
Comrade, Bik [McFarlane] has asked me to give you a rundown on my past so here goes. I was born on 25.5.56 in a little village called Park, Co. Derry. That's about five miles from Claudy. I am the youngest of a family of 8—five boys and three girls. My father and mother do not come from Republican families, or were Republicans themselves. We moved from Park to Dungiven to live when I was 4 years old. Our present address is 14 Chapel Road, Dungiven. I went to Dungiven Primary School and on to St Patrick's Secondary, Dungiven. I was mad about sport and liked history a lot although I wasn't too good at it. I won a lot of medals in the school football and hurling teams and represented Derry County on a lot of occasions, the most treasured is being captain of Derry Under-16 hurling team which won the all-Ireland final. While at school I joined the Sticky Fianna n h-Eireann [the youth wing of the Official IRA]. I was 14 years old then. I moved up into the Official Army in 1971 when I was 15 years old. Around that period the Brits were giving most of the young lads a lot of harassment and we often got stopped coming home from record bop about 2 A.M. in the morning and messed about, with them pulling wires out of my mate's ear. I think that's what started me off. I left school and worked for a short period in my father's pub before I went out to serve my time as a bricklayer working for my eldest brother, Michael. When the Sticks called their cease-fire I, along with a lot of other men left

the local unit, but we never joined up with anyone else. We just stayed Independent. I left this group in 1973 when I went to Bedford, England. First I went for a holiday and I ended up staying, working again along with my eldest brother who had just moved over. I joined the GAA club in Luton called St Dympna and played for Hertfordshire County minor team which won a trip to Ireland to play in the Connacht Championship. I went to a few marches with my mates in London, but that was all the connection I had with the Republican Movement over there. I got fed up with that stinking country and came home early in 1976. A couple of weeks after that I joined the INLA. I was never lifted except for a few hours on a couple of occasions. However at 5 A.M. on December 2, 1976 I was taken from my home to Castlereagh and spent 3 days there. I didn't lodge any brutality case and I was charged with robbery in Limavady Court on December 5th 1976. I spent a year and a week on remand and was sentenced on 13th Dec. 1977 to 10 years. All my charges were two counts of robbery for arms; a kneecapping and conspiring with others to disarm members of the security forces. I got 10 years for each job to run concurrent. I entered on to the blanket protest on arrival at the blocks on 15th Dec. and from that I have been here in H3.
Kevin Lynch H3.

The robbery charge was for stealing shotguns from the home of a clay pigeon enthusiast. The conspiracy related to a planned operation, never carried out, to ambush a carload of soldiers or policemen—using the shotguns, their cartridges loaded with ball bearings—to try and get more badly needed weapons for the INLA. The kneecapping, with a .22, was of a man accused of "antisocial activities": fighting in pubs in the Dungiven area. Kevin confessed to the offenses during interrogation at Castlereagh—after another member of his active service unit had already made a statement giving details—saying: "Right lads, I blow the gaff on myself, but I'm not mentioning anyone else's name."

Inside the Kesh he was nicknamed "Barabbas," because he was said to look like a caricature of an Orthodox Jew, with hooked nose and heavy beard. He had demonstrated his ability to endure suffering while on the blanket, at one stage being hit by a tooth abscess and enduring the horrific pain of it for two weeks, rather than put on prison uniform to see the dentist. But he appeared nervous of confrontation with warders and on his return visits was often greeted with cries of "grow a pair," because inevitably he had failed to smuggle anything back with him. So many prisoners were surprised when he volunteered for the hunger strike, although he had shown himself increasingly interested in the IRA political lectures.

He started his hunger strike on the morning of Saturday May 23, replacing Patsy O'Hara. It looked as if another replacement would be needed soon: Brendan McLaughlin, who had taken over from Hughes, was in a bad way. He had a perforated ulcer and was bleeding internally. The Movement was agonizing over what to do: the hunger strike was a protest action, aimed at putting maximum pressure on the Government through a slow and lengthy buildup of publicity. That was why Sands and Hughes had been so concerned not to catch cold. McLaughlin was tough and committed. Like Hughes he had refused to take food or water during a rough interrogation after being captured and like McCreesh he had refused to take his monthly family visit, rather than wear the prison uniform. The effect of the ulcer had begun to show after only seven days, when he had been moved to the prison hospital, and then straight out to the military wing of the Musgrave Park Hospital in Belfast. He allowed doctors to carry out an X-ray, which confirmed the ulcer, but he still refused to eat. With the likelihood that he would die within days—from blood loss and oxygen starvation to the brain as well as from gangrene—it was decided he would have to come off. A lawyer was sent into hospital to tell him. McLaughlin looked at the lawyer as if he were a British agent, come to fool him into pulling out, and refused. The lawyer eventually persuaded him.

Inside the Kesh, McFarlane had been becoming increasingly worried about strategy. The deaths of Sands and Hughes had provoked a high point in emotional reaction outside, but had failed to force the settlement. Would the repetition of their deaths do anything more to move the Government? In mid-May he had written to the outside leadership proposing a dramatic escalation—putting about thirty men on at once. He had the volunteers who would go through with it—in fact there were a couple, like Pat McGeown, whom he believed they'd need to shoot to get them off. Of course what was worrying him was the possibility that the whole thing was not going to work anyway—that Frank and Bob had died for nothing; that if Raymond and Patsy died and there was still no movement they would be forced to reassess and call a halt. And that would wreck him. But the outside leadership had cooled him down; they had a longer view and the first hunger strike had demonstrated the dangers of going on en masse.

Now, with Ray and Patsy dead, and McLaughlin off the hunger strike, there was a breathing space, which had McFarlane anxiously looking around for another way of forestalling the next round of deaths.

To Brownie [Gerry Adams] Wed 27.5.81 10.30 P.M.
Comrade Mor, Just heard that Brendan ended his hunger strike. He must be wrecked. Anyway, back to your comm and escalation. I went ahead and informed M. Hurson to embark on hunger strike on Monday next, but I think maybe we should bring him forward to Saturday as a replace for Brendan . . . The situation will now become

somewhat relaxed while we wait until Joe approaches the crucial stages. We must hold the position now. These Free State elections will give us a good opener. We talked here also on the 'balance of power' aspect. If we are successful enough we could pose a formidable threat to Haughey alright. I accept what you say about 'no magic formula' and I realize that hard work on the ground is the only answer. Perhaps I expect too much too soon, but it's just that I'm anxious to get a settlement here as quickly as possible, hence my push in all directions at one time—just getting the boot into anything that moves and isn't on our side. The revolutionary effect would not manifest itself quickly anyway regardless of inability to exploit the situation. It would still take time to build and mould our people into what is necessary for a successful push forward. The Free State does present difficulties. There is really no comparison between the people down there and those in the north. I think they need a rude awakening which I believe we are presently doing. Once the swing has started then we are on our way, remembering of course the 'hand-crank' at all times. We'll see how it goes down there shortly. Just thinking there (dangerous pastime indeed)—if Martin goes on Saturday, what about commencing escalation say next Friday with another man. I'll get back to you on this again, once I have the list of Vols [volunteers] sorted out. I really do sympathize with your problem of those wishing to kill dead things. They're at it in here. God Bless. Bik.

Liam Og [Sinn Fein official] from Bik 27.5.81
Comrade, . . . A lad named 'Bosco' Doherty, H7, informs me he is going on hunger strike and is just waiting on my clearance which, if he doesn't get, doesn't really matter as he 'bends the rules to suit', sez he. Now, comrade, I did a quick IO [intelligence officer] job on young Bosco and I

feel he needs gentle, but firm, sensible treatment as he is somewhat erratic (mildly put). To give you a clear picture of him might help—he eats razor blades!! . . . I've sent him a comm, but would suggest our people in Derry have a yarn with his parents. God knows what he's likely to do. I can just see your face right now. Dear Lord help us!!
PS I just heard that Brendan ended his hunger strike today. I've a wee comm for him enclosed. He's probably wrecked. Also a statement from us for release if necessary. Reckon people like the 'Menace' [Fr. Faul] have now conclusive proof that no one is committing suicide here. Hope he exploits this to the full. Can we contact M. Hurson to take Brendan's place, say Saturday instead of waiting till Monday . . .

McFarlane's problems were Britain's advantages. The Prime Minister, having demonstrated with the help of four deaths that she was not for bending—and, with Brendan McLaughlin's collapse, seeing the first possible chink in the hunger strike—decided it was time to grab the headlines with a surprise visit to the Province. It was her third trip to the north of Ireland in three months and the routine was well set; for the sake of security not a hint was to be given to anyone until her actual arrival. This posed something of a problem for her civil servants, because Mrs. Thatcher had decided it would be appropriate if, during her few hours in the territory, she were to meet the church leaders. But could they break security and tell the man from Crossmaglen who he would be meeting when they issued the invitation? They decided not, so on the Wednesday afternoon, the day before her arrival, the cardinal's secretary got a phone call from the Northern Ireland Office inviting him to a meeting the next day with the Secretary of State and the leaders of the four other main churches. The cardinal had already planned to be in Dublin that Thursday, so he declined. Later that night the telephone rang again. This time it was the Secretary of State himself.

He would very much appreciate it if the cardinal would come. The cardinal was becoming perplexed: the church leaders all lived in the Province so there shouldn't be any difficulty setting another date. Was anybody else attending? he asked Atkins. No, said the Secretary of State. Well, in that case, there was no great urgency about it and he was afraid his appointments in Dublin could not be postponed. At 10 A.M. the next morning the Northern Ireland Office called again. They had decided the cardinal should be taken into their confidence: the Prime Minister would be there. It was no great act of confidence—the large press corps was also being briefed by then. The cardinal said he would need a few minutes. Half an hour later he called back, explaining he had not been able to cancel the appointments. In the circumstances he would have to go to Dublin.

"Good morning, good morning, good morning," said the Prime Minister to the crowd as she busily shook hands. "I didn't know there would be so many people in Marks and Spencers at this hour of the day. I'm not going to get any shopping done. Good morning, good to see you, good morning." In the middle of the crowd, being buffeted by her bodyguards and other government officials, a local radio reporter, Eamon Mallie, was battling to get a question in.

"Mrs. Thatcher, why are you here, could you say why you're here, Mrs. Thatcher?" he called out, brandishing his microphone.

"Good morning, good morning, to see these people, good morning . . . we've got too many cameramen around here, good morning, how are you."

Mallie turned in frustration to women in the crowd who were chanting "Good old Maggie" and "Keep up the good work."

"What do you call good work?" Mallie asked one.

"Ohhh, stand firm against the H-Block crowd. God bless her."

"She's a bitch, that's what she is, a bitch," cut in another woman.

"Why do you say that?"

"Because she's just a bitch."

Mrs. Thatcher had lunch at Stormont and held a press conference. She said that the hunger strikers had been "persuaded, coerced or ordered to starve themselves to death." She also said: "Faced with failure of their discredited cause, the men of violence have chosen in recent months to play what may well be their last card." Afterwards Mallie was granted his own short session with her, because he represented the local commercial radio station, Downtown.

"Prime Minister, in your statement, in your speech, you said the IRA may have played what you said was their last card. How sure are you of that and why, indeed, did you say it? Couldn't it be tantamount to provoking them?" asked Mallie.

"I don't think so. And I came today to demonstrate my commitment to the future of the Province, to all of the people of the Province, to give them reassurance about that, to give them the reassurance that we will uphold law and order, we will do everything to help them help themselves," said the Prime Minister.

"But Mrs. Thatcher, can I ask you with respect, why did you say they may have played their last card? Does that mean you think they're defeated, beaten?"

"Because they have played almost every other card and it has not happened. And the fact is that the people of Northern Ireland, the leaders of all religious communities and people almost everywhere have rejected violence. The Provisional IRA are the men of violence. Violence is practiced by people who cannot persuade and therefore have to resort to fear and intimidation. I believe the community has rejected that and the Provisional IRA know that . . . everyone has rejected violence and no one—and I stress this very much indeed—no one in any responsible position in any religion has urged me to give either political status or anything like special category status."

"But they haved asked you to compromise, haven't they?"

"One moment, one moment. No one has asked me to compromise on any of those things."

"Are you saying that you haven't been asked to actually find a solution?"

"May I answer your questions? No one. Now let's get this absolutely clear. No one has asked me to compromise on any of those things. Now what I am saying is we will uphold the law, we will continue to uphold the law. We will do everything to help the people of Northern Ireland to help themselves out of this difficulty. I cannot pull solutions out of a hat. I will not depart from upholding the law and the position of constructive help. But I am saying we can do all this, we are doing it, we are winning out against violence. Now I am saying to people you too must combine to help yourselves."

"Prime Minister, may I remind you that twenty-two people have died since Bobby Sands died in prison. Can you guarantee that another twenty-two and possibly more won't die if this question is not solved and solved quickly?"

"And who killed them? The men of violence killed them."

As Mrs. Thatcher was calling on Ireland to abjure the men of violence, a member of one of the world's most highly trained groups of killers, the British army's SAS, was patrolling the streets of Londonderry in his Opel Ascona. Sergeant Oram was going north, along Cromore Gardens, when he spotted a brown Ford Escort going in the opposite direction. There were four men in it, which was faintly suspicious, so he reached for his microphone and radioed base for a vehicle check. He drove a little further and was about to turn right when he heard a horn beep behind him. As he slowed for the turning he looked over his shoulder, to see the Escort pulling alongside him, the four men inside now wearing masks. They braked across his front side, blocking the right turn. The two nearside doors of the Escort swung open and two of the men got out, each carrying an Armalite rifle. One took a position at Oram's front right wing, the rifle pointed at him from the hip. The other stood at his rear offside door, Armalite also pointing at him from the hip. What followed was just a blur. Oram pulled out his 9 mm Browning pistol, fired at the gunman in front of him, pivoted in his seat and shot through the window at the gunman behind. He turned to the front again, to see the first gunman rolling along the side of his car. Oram stuck his pistol out of his now smashed side window and fired at him as he rolled past. Then he let out his clutch and shot into Lonemoor Road, heading for the Strand Road police station. At the police station he handed in his Browning, first checking the chamber. It had been loaded with twenty rounds and he had fired eleven in those brief seconds. Back at the scene of the shooting both gunmen—Charlie Maguire and George McBrearty of the IRA's Creggan unit—were dead. McBrearty had been hit seven times and Maguire twice in the head.

Brownie from Bik Friday 29.5.81 1 P.M.
. . . Terrible episode that in Derry yy [yesterday]. Not much chance in setup like that. God rest our comrades. Sometimes I feel our lads are trying too hard—possibly over-anxious for a score. Just an observation, OK? . . .

Mrs. Thatcher flew back to London that evening and the cardinal returned from Dublin to find a letter waiting for him expressing her regret that she had not seen him, but inviting him to come and see her at Downing Street if he happened to be in London in the near future. He immediately sent a reply, saying he would have to be in London at the beginning of July, to attend centenary celebrations of the martyrdom of St. Oliver Plunkett. The saint, a predecessor of O Fiaich's as Archbishop of Armagh, had been hanged, drawn and quartered by

England in the seventeenth century, on a trumped-up charge of treason. It would be a piquant occasion for a Primate of All Ireland to see an English Prime Minister.

> Liam Og from Bik Friday 29.5.81 8 P.M.
> ... In answer to your query re my comms while on the no-wash protest I chewed them into unidentifiable mush and spat them at the wall. At one stage I even contemplated drawing a dart board to amuse myself through idle moments. Today, however, finesse has replaced crudity and I tear them into thousands of minute particles and play weddings in my piss pot. Poor little dears don't last long. I suppose you have filed all mine for future reference when I get charged with mutiny and all such other trivialities RA [IRA] men face from time to time ...

Others hurried to emulate Mrs. Thatcher's example. David Steel flew over on the Friday followed by the Archbishop of Canterbury, Dr. Robert Runcie, and Princess Alexandra. Steel went into the Kesh and asked Joe McDonnell how conditions compared with those in the remand prison, Crumlin Road. "The food wasn't as good," said McDonnell. The Princess went to Belfast's Anglican cathedral, St. Anne's, and listened to Runice thanking God there were still men and women with the courage to put their own lives at risk by defending the community.

About two miles out of Newry early that Sunday morning, May 31, the bomb disposal squad was called to examine a suspect car. Sgt. Major Michael O'Neill, a thirty-four-year-old father of two, was inspecting the vehicle at 7:50 A.M. when it blew up. The blast threw him down the roadside embankment and he had become the seventeenth bomb disposal expert to die in the north. Later that evening police reservist Colin Dunlop, aged thirty, was guarding a patient in the Royal

Victoria Hospital in Belfast. He was standing outside the intensive care unit when, shortly after 7 P.M., he saw a woman walking down the corridor towards him with two men just behind. The woman stepped aside, revealing that the men were carrying leveled guns. Dunlop had four children. The youngest, Michael, had had his second birthday on Saturday, the day before he lost his father.

At Westminster the House of Commons was busily throwing up ramparts against a repeat of Fermanagh–South Tyrone— processing a bill to prevent prisoners from standing for Parliament. It was called the "Representation of the People Bill."

The Independent Broadcasting Authority (IBA) was worrying about what the people should be allowed to see: on June 1 they had demanded the censorship of a current affairs program on the hunger strike, produced by the Granada television company, on the grounds that twenty seconds of footage showing Patsy O'Hara in his coffin represented Republican propaganda. Granada withdrew the program completely, in protest. They replaced it with a program on smoking.

Down in Dublin, meanwhile—where the people were still allowed to be represented by whomsoever they wanted—the National H-Block Committee was announcing that nine prisoners, including the four hunger strikers, were standing for the June 11 election. There had been internal ructions between the IRSP and Sinn Fein over who was going to stand and where, so the campaign was getting under way a week late. The pundits were already predicting humiliation for the prison candidates. As the announcement was being made in Dublin, up in Co. Donegal Charlie Haughey was wiping off his face the remains of an egg thrown at him by an H-Block supporter.

The H-Block committee set up their campaign headquarters in the basement of an old Georgian house in Mountjoy Square, Dublin, the front door of which was kept under

constant surveillance by Irish special branch men in a car
outside. Inside Mrs. Thatcher enjoyed pride of place on a
wall in reception, on a wanted poster declaring her a fugi-
tive from justice for "murder and torture." A black flag of
mourning dangled over the secretary's desk and the walls
were plastered with black-bordered posters of prisoners, a
scrawled "RIP" identifying the four dead hunger strikers.
The prisoners' chances did not look good. The organizers
were short of funds—they had previously been banned by
the Government from collecting money—and were unlikely
to get time on the airwaves, because the Irish broadcasting
act prohibited interviews with Republican extremists. The
hurried decision to contest the election was reflected in poor
organization; Bernadette McAliskey, who had wanted to stand
herself but had been vetoed by the H-Block committee, was
racing around the country in a battered old car, limping to
platforms on crutches—reminders of the nine bullet wounds
in her—and complaining that, without even a constituency
map, the only way she could figure out what constituency she
was in was by reading the roadside posters. The bickering
within the Republican Movement had not been resolved by
the decision to fight the election either; in one constituency,
Clare, the chairman of the H-Block committee and some of his
supporters had flatly refused to campaign for their candidate,
INLA prisoner Tom McAllister.

Liam Og from Bik Sun 31.5.81?
. . . Re: names for hunger strike—I still haven't received
any names from H4 and H6, but I'm expecting these
tomorrow. You already have those who were original
replacements and I reckon that the first men for escalation should come from these. Some of them have already
answered the AC [Army Council] comm and confirmed
their intention. I've the names for this block and H5,
but I want to be able to present you with a list of 20 or

so men whom I have vetted (if you like). Can I have the
'Big Boys' attitude to escalation as soon as possible and
clarification on Tom McElwee as first man. The OC IRSP
has forwarded his own name and two others only: Liam
McCloskey Dungiven H3 and Tom McAllister H4—when
is it proposed to phase their man in? I was thinking of him
coming in either with our third man or else by himself
after our second man. You can let me know the crack on
this as well. Also how many men do we envisage using
for this escalation? For example four more weeks takes
us to the crisis period for Joe McDonnell and if tragedy
occurs (God forbid) we are then faced with replacements
again. God knows what will occur by then. These elections may prove beneficial if we touch lucky and play our
cards right . . . I see the Brits dirty tricks dept are getting
blamed for that business with the explosive in the Fianna
Fail offices [an unprimed bomb found in Castleblaney,
south of the border]. Personally, I go for Free State dirty
tricks dept i.e. if the INLA really didn't do it . . .

McFarlane got agreement from outside for a small escalation in the fast, bringing a fifth man on. The choice was
another man from Tamlaghtduff Francis Hughes's cousin,
Tom McElwee.

The McElwees lived in a small farmhouse a few hundred
yards across two fields from Deed View House—the Hughes
home—outside Bellaghy. Tom himself was said to take after
his grandfather, James McElwee, who had left Ireland as a
teenager to go prospecting for gold in Mexico and the United
States, also working on the railroads. James was in his forties
when he returned with a small nest egg and a suitcase full
of guns. He got into an argument in the local butcher's shop
shortly after his return and, family stories have it, when the
police came to see him about it, it took six of them to drag him
off to the barracks for questioning. He hated cops. He used his

money to buy a farm and on the day he bought it—walking back to Bellaghy—he saw a pretty woman at the doorway of a neighboring farmhouse and said: "That's the woman I'm going to make my wife." Which he did ... before the week was up. He was a big, tough man in the heroic tradition of the rural Irish, and Tom grew up in his image.

Tom's father was a builder and himself constructed their three-bedroom home on five acres of land in Tumlaghtduff. They had sixteen children, four of them dying in infancy. Tom was the fifth of the twelve survivors, born in the small house on November 30, 1957. Like his cousin, he showed himself to be mechanically minded, always busying himself as a child with his Meccano set and, as a youth, nursing a passion for stock-car racing, buying himself an old banger at one stage and racing it. When he left school he wanted to become a telephone engineer, but it was tough at the time for a Catholic to get such a job. He went to a training center as an apprentice motor mechanic instead, but gave that up in the face of harassment by Protestant workers and ended up taking a job at a Bellaghy garage.

He had been a signed-up member of the Republican Movement from an early age, joining na Fianna Eireann—the youth wing of the IRA—at the age of fourteen. He subsequently joined Frank Hughes's "Independents" and followed him into the Provisionals, but, unlike his cousin, was never forced to go on the run. He ended up in Long Kesh with one of his brothers, Bennie, as a result of an incident on Saturday, October 9, 1976.

There were four of them in the orange Toyota Corolla: Tom, his brother, Benedict, who was just over a year younger than he, Colm Skullion and Sean McPeake. It was midday and they were on their way to the town of Ballymena. Inside the car were four bags of Frangex commercial explosive attached to creosote—sticky and highly inflammable wood preservative—mixed with petrol in a can. They were classic incendiary bombs which were to be planted in shops in the town as part of a coordinated "commercial bombing" attack, masterminded by a local IRA commander, Dominic McClinchey, and involving several active service units.

The traffic was heavy—Saturday was the day of the local fair—and the journey was taking longer than they had planned. The teenagers had been at a disco in the town of Dungiven the night before and were exchanging cracks about it as they pulled into a car park in the town, near the shops they had targeted. Tom, who owned the Toyota and was driving, turned in his seat, reaching for one of the three bombs in a duffel bag on the floor between Skullion and McPeake in the back. As he turned he told Bennie to put another cassette in the car's tape player. Bennie reached for a country and western tape. There was a white flash.

"Get out. The fuck. The whole blasted lot will go up," yelled Tom. Skullion's one leg was hanging by a piece of flesh. Bennie felt as if he was floating. The two in the back were yelling: "Get the fuck out." There were only two doors. Bennie managed to get his open, but was too stunned to get out. He leaned forward as Skullion and McPeake scrambled over him. The calf of Sean McPeake's leg dangled on the ground. Bennie stumbled out. Tom was standing at the back of the car, covering his face with his hands, blood mixed with creosote pouring between his fingers. He shouted: "For Christ's sake, somebody lift me." Sean began hopping between the rows of cars, before he collapsed. A crowd was gathering, staring in amazement. Someone took Bennie's shoulders and lowered him to the ground. A tarpaulin was pulled over him.

They paid heavily for the explosion. McPeake of course lost his leg, from above the knee; Skullion had two toes amputated and Tom lost one eye. Bennie got away with a perforated eardrum, bruises and abrasions.

An hour after the explosion in the car park a local baker, Hugh Leith, was strolling along Bridge Street in Ballymena, on his way to the chemist shop. As he passed the Alley Katz Boutique it rocked to an explosion. A nine-year-old boy, Denis Dunlop, came running out of the door shouting hysterically that his mother was in the toilet. Behind him the boutique was a roaring inferno. Leith sprinted to the back of the shop, spotted the toilet window and smashed it with a brick, shouting: "Anyone in there?" There was no answer.

Yvonne Dunlop, mother of three sons of whom Denis was the eldest, had been incinerated doing her own mother—the owner of the boutique—a favor; standing in for her while she was away on holiday. Her killing was a blunder: a ten-minute warning had been telephoned to the local operator, but it was insufficient time for the affected shops to be cleared. A list of the shops targeted was found in a coat in the McElwee car. Tom, in the forlorn hope of enabling the others to beat the charges, claimed the coat and bombs were his and, after an appeal, he got twenty years' jail for both the killing and possession of explosives. A girl was caught running away from the Alley Katz boutique and broke under interrogation, naming Tom's girlfriend, Dolores O'Neill, as an accomplice. Dolores, a petite girl, 5 feet 2 inches tall, also got twenty years. Bennie got five and a half years.

The two brothers did not see much of each other after that, in the Kesh. Tom won a reputation for fighting warders; another childhood passion had been boxing and he was dubbed "Punchie McElwee" by one senior warder. Standing 6 feet 2 inches tall, with his one eye, he was a formidable figure. He had also shown himself devoted to Irish; when the hunger strike started Irish lessons had been suspended, but he had insisted on continuing his studies. He was already fluent in the language; often he would refuse to speak to other prisoners in English.

To Ogloigh na helaronn. Vol. T. McElwee H-Block 3
Comrade, ref comm J. O'Neill received Saturday 23rd
May. On receiving your comm I have again reaffirmed
my position in myself and now request permission to continue. I am fully aware of the pain and suffering that I
will have to endure and I know that at the end I may and
most likely will have to forfeit my life. This I am prepared
to do because I believe that it is only in a continuation of
the hunger strike that the pressure needed to break the
British criminalization policy can be obtained. I understand to the full the extent with which my action involves
the whole overall struggle for Ireland, freedom and self-
determination. This . . . because criminalization was introduced to break the freedom struggle. The weapon of the
criminalization policy must be removed from the British
by achieving political status for Republican POWs. Thus
would recognition of the flight of our people be obtained
and support for the struggle at home and abroad consol-
idated. Victory is to be got. The Brits' stand can be and
will be broken. I am ready to give my life to help in its
breaking. In a few months my body might be no more,
but like Bobby, Francis, Patsy and Raymond I will not be
dead. So long as one Irishman resists the occupation of our
country and fights for the establishment of a democratic
and socialist republic.
Is mise le meas Tomas Mac Suialli. Bhius.

In his cell McFarlane had problems, as usual. There was
the ever-present worry of choosing the next to face death.
There was the possibility that one of those he had already
chosen, Paddy Quinn, might be suffering from a kidney ailment, which posed the danger of a repetition of the Brendan
McLaughlin episode. And, more confusingly, there was the
problem of Kevin Lynch. McFarlane had heard about the blunt
way the IRSP had broken the news to Lynch's parents and was

also worried that the organization was not giving their man
the support he needed. He knew the Lynch family as solid
and middle-class representatives of the values of "constitutional" Nationalism and likely to be susceptible to pressures
from the Church and the SDLP. So it came as no surprise
to learn that they were trying to persuade Kevin to agree to
another initiative through the European Court, being devised
by an American lawyer with known Republican sympathies,
Paul O'Dwyer, with what appeared to be SDLP help. But, in
addition to that, the Catholic Church was moving in, with an
appeal from its "Irish Commission for Justice and Peace" for
specific compromises from both sides over the five demands.

Liam Og from Bik 1.6.81
... Now Tish [Sinn Fein official] expressed some concern
about some lads who put their names forward in H4 being
a bit young. Truth is, comrade, I had a look at the list today
and discovered that all but two are YPs [young persons],
many of whom have been in prison since they were 17, so I
feel I'm bound to give them a miss. It's not just a question
of commitment or resolve, as you well know yourself. It's
just not right firing young lads into the front line of a
hunger strike. Now I got a comm from Jim McCann H5
withdrawing his name from hunger strike list ...

Liam Og from Bik Wed 3.6.81 9 P.M.
... Re the IRSP. Due to withdrawals they are now left
with M. Devine, their OC [officer commanding], and L.
McCloskey in this wing ...

An Bean Uasal from Bik Fri 5.6.81
Comrade, I didn't get the comms which were sent up today
and when I heard shy young Gerard didn't get them on his
visit I nearly tore the door off its hinges—Gerard's head as
well. Apparently his girlfriend was loaded with 14 separate

comms, most of which were personal letters. Also there was a parcel of tobacco. He managed to get the tobacco and five of the comms, but was spotted by the screw and couldn't operate after that. He was searched and possibly his girlfriend was searched going out . . . I was expecting comms today that would finally confirm our escalation strategy and when I heard that my stuff couldn't be got I just erupted . . . the doctor sent for Paddy Quinn (he's my second man for escalation) yesterday and asked if he'd undergo certain tests to establish if he has a kidney disease which is apparently hereditary in his family. It seems his father died of the disease and just three months ago his brother was admitted to hospital suffering from an illness directly attributed to the kidney disease. He made a full recovery however. Anyway, the family doctor [wants to run] tests on Paddy, which involve blood samples and X-rays. I told him to bang away, but he's not fussy at all and maintains he is fine. He is as I said the second on our escalation squad which means that he would be on hunger strike before any results were obtained. Now what I propose is that we move him to fourth place and bring L. McKeown forward to second place. This means that a period of four weeks will elapse in which he would have the results of the tests . . .

Brownie. Bik Sat 6.6.81
. . . Kevin is just back from visit with Paul O'Dwyer—here goes. Entire visit taken up with pressing Kevin to take case to European court on seven points. I've just banged down the gist of the points as you should get a copy of the document presented to Kevin this morning. 1. Inhuman treatment by the regime. 2. Discrimination between himself and other prisoners held on similar charges. 3. Lack of

remedies to complaints forced him to hunger strike action.
4. Brit Govt failure to safeguard his life and humanity. 5.
Brit Govt failure to respect family life and correspondence
with them. 6. Brit Gov. failure to satisfy recommendations
of Euro Court re complaints in case of Tom McFeely etc.
ends. That's the heap. Now, comrade, P. O'Dwyer had a
meeting with H. Logue (SDLP) on Thursday and Logue's
name appears on the document as a nominee to act on
Kevin's behalf. O'Dwyer maintains that the entire exercise
is solely his doing and is not connected with anyone else.
He even said that Kevin could delete H. Logue's name if
he wished. Now mate, you should already be aware that
J. Hume has had a few meetings with the Lynch family.
So this is obviously another move to mush in the Commission. Kevin will have another visit with O'Dwyer this
afternoon. I told him to take the line that we don't see
any value in this at all. That had there been any chance
of a settlement or friendly settlement then it would have
materialized with Bob and also a couple of weeks back.
I told him to say he wasn't interested in pressing this any
further—at least not until he sees his own signer [solicitor]
and will leave it like that. I also told him to name you
and Bangers as those we have nominated to speak on our
behalf and that if O'Dwyer wants to contact the signer he
can do so through H-Block information centre by asking
for Pennies or Tish. That's about it, comrade. Now I sent
word out to our people and INLA a couple of days back
that P. O'Dwyer was coming up, but no one made an effort
to contact Kevin's people prior to this visit. The IRSP did
not see them at all OK. Also, O'Dwyer asked Kevin if the
man in charge of the blocks—i.e. me—would request a
visit with him to see the crack. I will not be doing this at
all OK? No point in lending credence to something that
may pull the carpet from under us . . .

Sunday 7.6.81
Here's a short general run-down on Kevin Lynch. His
weight today was 56 kg ... most of the days he reads
which doesn't tire him at all and for about half an hour he
walks each day. He likes walking and feels good when he is
walking. He does not sleep much during the day. At night
he sleeps soundly, although it takes him a while before he
dozes off. Apart from the first few days he has not had any
headaches or dizzy spells except upon awakening, then it
takes him 10 minutes or more before he feels fully awakened. For that short period he feels weak and sluggish. He
feels a bit of discomfort around his hips with being in bed
so much. The food does not bother him, he does not feel
anything like that, but from time to time he gets a strange
feeling, but it's nothing much. He's generally in a good
mood although at times he feels bored and when he feels
like that he doesn't want to talk to anybody. That's about
it, though as I said overall he's in pretty good condition ...

An Bean Uasal from Bik Sun 7.6.81
You should know also that Kevin is coming under heavy
pressure from his family to adopt O'Dwyer's proposals.
Also, please note that there is a very strong SDLP alliance
hanging over his family—i.e. regular visits by J. Hume
and contact (permanent) with H. Logue. Strong Church
connection with Fr McIldowney so you can see the difficulty with the family. They would not doubt men of such
high integrity. Furthermore O'Dwyer being acceptable in
Republican circles adds credence. I had a long yarn with
Kevin at Mass today explaining that such a move could
only undermine us and pointed out carefully the political
situation in Free State and us being a potential danger to it.
Now he understands, he says, but still believes O'Dwyer is
genuine. I pointed out that he could be alright, but that he
was being taken advantage of and used, because if he got

us to take a formal case to Europe, we would let all those clients off the hook and run ourselves into a brick wall. He has agreed to stick to the terms of reference laid down to him i.e. Brownie, Pennies and myself as advisors, in case someone else moves on his behalf. OK? Now, he is sound enough, but family pressure may have an effect on him. A visit to the signer [lawyer] would do a world of good, but he won't be available for a week or so . . . on to another point—the IRSP—there is no way I am pleased with them not contacting Kevin's family prior to his visit. Also there appears to be a complete lack of effort in trying to cut out the SDLP involvement. Can we get Tish to ask them to try and get on top of the situation. Kevin has had no contact with them for over a month. Neither has the OC IRSP contacted him in a month. I've kept him up-dated, but I don't want him losing confidence in his own organization. It could be psychologically damaging . . .

Thoughts for Thought [a column written for the *Starry Plough*, the IRSP newspaper] 7.6.81, by Kevin Lynch
. . . I saw a photo of Charlie Haughey recently and the remnants of an egg were dribbling down his face. Not the way forward, definitely not the way forward . . . anyway I read the article which accompanied the picture and a distressed Charlie remarked—and I paraphrase—that his father fought for Ireland's freedom and he wasn't going to allow anyone to interfere with his democratic right to meet people, or allow anyone to besmirch his father's cause. Good on you, Charlie. Does this mean an end to undemocratic State censorship? Are you going to withdraw Irish troops from England's border and stop stabilizing partition? Unless I'm mistaken Charlie's father was an IRA man who believed in violent struggle to attain freedom. Was he wrong, Charlie? If he had been captured by the

British, Charlie, would he have been entitled to political status, Charlie? Charlie must reckon the people of Ireland are all right charlies . . .

I wonder how the electorate of Waterford are doing? Maybe if I lavished ye's with praises, or did something gimmicky ye's would vote for me. That's not my score really. But I still hope and pray that ye's vote for me. I pray like I never prayed in my life and 400 other political prisoners pray and the families and half a million Irish people. People who need you now more than ever.

Feeling sound enough today. It's starting to get a bit difficult going to sleep at night. A wee bit weak in the morning. Otherwise strong enough. Went to Mass today. I was the only one that had a chair. Everyone else was sitting on the floor. Such is life in the best prison in Europe! Kevin Lynch.

Pennies [Danny Morrison] from Bik Tue 9.6.81
. . . Now those EC [European Court] chappies were here today and saw Tom who referred them to me. Apparently they were delighted they could get talking to the main man, but when they asked the Governor for my cell he refused them permission to speak with me, saying they didn't recognize the command structures and therefore could not permit the EC chaps to see me in the capacity. There was a bit of an argument and then they left. During this period I was having a rather wonderful cold shower . . .

Meanwhile, in the Irish Republic the election campaign was moving towards its climax, still with little hope held out for the prison candidates. The apparent lack of public interest in their intervention on the hustings was reflected in the country's four national Sunday newspapers the weekend before polling day—between them they devoted barely a paragraph to the

H-Block candidates. But then, on the eve of the election, came an electrifying, morale-boosting development.

On Wednesday, June 10, in the basement of the Crumlin Road remand prison—looking like a decaying fortress across the road from the Belfast Crown Court—five solicitors were murmuring to their clients across the formica-topped interviewing tables. It was hot in the room; the prison boiler was just the other side of the wall. Eight IRA prisoners were taking part in the confabulations. They were facing a series of serious charges, including complicity in three murders. They had been captured a year before, in a dramatic siege of a house less than a mile from the prison where they were now being held. During the siege a captain in the SAS had been killed—that was one of the charges.

The search box giving access to the big visiting room was being manned by Prison Officer Richard Kennedy on that Wednesday. At about 4 P.M. Kennedy was searching a prisoner carrying a paper bag with sweets from the prison tuck shop. Finding nothing, he checked through the flap in his wooden door that everything was all right in the visiting area and slid the bolt, letting the prisoner and accompanying warder go through. He was just closing the door when it was slammed open again and he found himself face to face with one of the eight, Angelo Fusco. Fusco was carrying a warder's baton in his left hand. Behind him was a second of the eight, "Fats" Campbell, carrying a small automatic pistol. Campbell pointed the gun at him, cocked it and said: "Kennedy, this is no fucking joke, we are taking you as a hostage." Campbell asked for the keys. Kennedy said another officer had them. Campbell grabbed him by the lapel and pulled him forward, repeating that he was going to be their hostage. He was pushed into the big room ahead of the two prisoners, feeling the pistol jabbing in his back, just below his right shoulder. As he got to the middle of the room Kennedy spun around and hit Campbell twice on the left side of the head with his baton. Campbell stumbled away, but Kennedy was hit on the head from behind and knocked to the ground. Dazed, he felt himself being kicked and punched—he was hated by the prisoners—before a calm, authoritative voice said: "Don't shoot him, or we won't get out." He was dragged out of the room, down the passageway, and locked in a cell.

The eight rounded up the other warders in the visiting area together with the solicitors who were down to see them and other "ordinary" prisoners who were not taking part in the escape. Two of the eight, Joe Doherty and Peter Ryan, pulled on warders' uniforms and a third, Tony Sloan, put on clothes taken from one of the solicitors. They had only 200 yards to reach the road outside where IRA support units were waiting with getaway cars. But there were three heavily guarded gates between them.

Prison officer Tom Perritt was on duty at the inner gate. He saw the group coming towards him. It looked like a solicitor, carrying a black briefcase, followed by prisoners and prison officers. As they came up to him the "solicitor," Sloan, waved a brown lawyer's pass at him and then tried to brush past him. Perritt realized something was wrong. He shoved Sloan back. Then one of the men in prison officer's uniform stuck a hard object in his back. "Don't make a noise," he said, ordering him to open the gate. He opened it and was shoved into the airlock between it and the second gate, the group crowding in with him. One of the prisoners shoved a 9 mm Walther into his face, shouting: "Keep that door locked, or I'll blow you away."

Prison officer Thomas Killen was doing some admin work in his little office at the outer gate when he heard the commotion. He went over to the inner gate to investigate and recognized one of the prisoners, Mike McKee, carrying a baton. Killen turned and ran for his office. He slammed the door behind him and, holding it shut, pressed the alarm button.

McKee, chasing him, smashed the glass panes in the door. Killen jumped back to avoid flying glass and McKee burst in, closely followed by Fats Campbell waving the Walther pistol. Campbell cocked the gun, held it at Killen's neck and shouted: "Touch that bell and you're dead." There were shouts outside to the two prisoners: "Come on, to fuck." They ran out of the office, heading for the outer gate.

Outside, in the Crumlin Road, three detectives were sitting in a Ford Escort patrol car, waiting to pick up a fourth officer from the court house opposite, when they saw men tumbling through the prison gates. It looked as though a group of prison warders was chasing a bunch of prisoners. Sergeant Robin Herron, in the driver's seat, accelerated towards them. The men hurtled over a low wall surrounding a car park adjoining the court house. As Sgt. Herron braked to a halt shots began to ring out and a bullet hit the bonnet of his car.

McKee jumped into one of two getaway cars waiting for them in the car park. Police bullets shattered the back window as he lurched into gear and crashed into a wall. He reversed and screamed off after the other IRA car ahead of him.

All eight prisoners had got away.

An Bean Uasal from Bik Wed 10.6.81
. . . Here, we just heard about our comrades in the Crum— super. All the boys are over the moon. A terrific boost at just the right time. Bloody marvellous altogether . . .

To Mary in Cork 12 June 1981
As I am sure you know, I have joined the hunger strike. This is my fifth day. Time is going on reasonably fast. I thought myself that it would drag, but it doesn't. My health as of yet is sound, extremely good according to the doctor. I get a run over from him every morning. Weight and all taken. Weight today was 64.4 kg. I started off at 67.35, but on the second day the Medical Officer thought a mistake

had been made the first day . . . I hear from Dolores quite often. I got a letter from her yesterday. She's a good girl, the best. Like yourselves she'll be worried at present, but for worry there is no call. I will be OK. Just place it all in the hands of God, that is what I have done; and do all you can down there to let the people understand our plight. We are waiting patiently here for the result of the elections. I'm expecting about two of our lads in. I'd be disappointed in the people if we fail completely. Tom [McElwee]

The euphoria over the breakout carried over to the election, the results of which astonished observers, if not the prisoners themselves. Two of the nine prisoners, Kieran Doherty, who was on the twenty-second day of his hunger strike, and Paddy Agnew, found they were full-blooded Irish MPs. Agnew— serving sixteen years for a gun attack on a Royal Navy Patrol boat in 1977—had actually topped the poll, on first preference votes, in Co. Louth, while Doherty in Cavan-Monaghan was only pipped by the Minister of Education by some 300 votes. While pollsters had been predicting they would get a fraction of 1 percent of the vote, they gained 2.1 percent—about 15 percent in the constituencies they contested. But even more significantly, the battle for government between the two major political parties had turned out to be virtually a dead heat, with Fine Gael taking sixty-five seats, the coalition partners Labour fifteen, Fianna Fail seventy-eight and Independents (apart from the two prisoners) six. If only theoretically, two convicted felons languishing in jail in northern Ireland held the balance of political power in the south.

But as Dr. FitzGerald and Mr. Haughey began their frantic efforts to negotiate their way to government with the real power brokers—the minority Labour Party and a handful of Independents who, unlike the prisoners, could get to Parliament and therefore vote for a new Prime Minister—the prisoners found their unexpected success accompanied only by

renewed pressures. One of them came in the form of the inde-
fatigable Dungannon priest, Fr. Faul—"Denis the Menace."

Brownie Sun 14.6.81 9 P.M.
. . . We have certainly caused a stir. Looks very like Garret
would form a government, depending of course on his
relationship with Cluskey's boys [Labour]. Regardless of
who forms a government it will be extremely shaky. Well
we have effected the political change you spoke of. Congratulations, oh wise one!! Must press on here with some
business. The Menace was in today for Mass. Just before
he arrived one of the lads read me out an article he published in yesterday's Irish News. I tackled him at Mass and
asked what his crack was with the 'ping pong' business.
Well, as you probably know, he was referring to O'Dwyer
arriving here and being directed to you lot immediately.
He said the man was confused, as were a lot of people. I
told him that O'Dwyer got our answer and thoughts on
Euro Comm and was only referred to you for a broader
appreciation of overall situation. I told the Menace that he
had levelled criticism at us which wasn't based on a full
appreciation of the facts surrounding O'Dwyer's visit and
in doing so had left the door open for 'people' to suggest
that the hunger strikers and prisoners were being manipulated by the RA [IRA] and in fact were being ordered to
die. He said he never said this at all, but I told him that
someone like my mother who doesn't fully understand
the situation would take it at face value and interpret it
that those outside the prison were directing operations
and manipulating etc. We had a long yarn about trivial-
izing the sacrifice of the hunger strikers. I explained that
our strategy was designed to both maintain and increase
pressure on the Brits and that we aimed for a settlement
as quickly as possible with as little loss also. I did however
agree that the people would eventually look on a hunger

striker's death as he had described it in his article. I drew
a comparison with the 12 years of war and the acceptable
level of violence that people had become accustomed to.
His argument is a logical one and I admitted that I saw his
point. He then asked me to clearly state our position on
negotiating publicly. He said people don't know where they
are at all and we should make a statement to clear the air.
I said the Brits already knew our terms of reference—who
will speak on our behalf. He boned me then and said that
if I thought the Brits would entertain you and Pennies then
I was mistaken, because they'd never talk to you two. We
should be more flexible in our approach to this, he said.
He then referred to mediators and named J. Hume and
the Cardinal. I said we and those who nominate are more
capable of talking for ourselves. He then gave me the line
of there must be room for all to save face. Says I, if the
Brits genuinely wanted a settlement here and I asked for
James Connolly then they'd go out of their way to resurrect
him to ensure we'd arrive at a solution to the issue. He
then referred to the Irish Commission of Justice and Peace
proposal opening the way and why hadn't we responded.
Only Sinn Fein and the H-Block Committee had mentioned
it and were vague about it. I said that I'd have said exactly
the same about J. Hume's utterances about the proposals.
I told him they did not contain a settlement and were far
from our five minimum demands. I said I appreciated the
concern of the Commission in trying to save lives and find
a way out of this situation, but no way would I accept a
non-solution. I referred to the four lads dying also and
said I wouldn't settle for less than they died for as it would
be a gross injustice. We went all around at the pointers
about three times. God knows how long we were at it. If
you judge by the amount I write and multiply it by the PR
system formula it might give you a rough idea in terms of
weeks!! He said—if the Brits came tomorrow and said, let's

talk about a solution, would you ask for the two efforts
to be brought in? I said that Bob had made it abundantly
clear when the European Commission was here, that he
would only be prepared to talk when those he nominated
were present. That's how it was and that's how it stands.
I said No Change!! He also mentioned the Free State. I
don't think he's too happy with Haughey getting knocked
out. He said at least he [Haughey] was concerned about
the H-Blocks, to which I replied by cutting Haughey to
ribbons. Anyway, dearest, flexible thinker, that was the
heap between the Menace and I. He wasn't too happy at
all. He really is very sound, but now and then he doesn't
half let fly at us, even in subtle articles about 'ping pong'
games. Now just thinking on the overall situation—if there
is a general feeling that decisions are being made For the
prisoners and not by the prisoners, then this should be
rectified because of the inherent dangers. If it is not, then
the Movement will find itself on the firing line instead
of the Brits. Hunger strikers' families will obviously be
a big danger if they feel that their sons are being kept on
hunger strike by outside influences. I feel we should answer
the Irish Commission rather than just leave it open. For
instance, Big Tom got a letter from his family saying that
the proposals should be accepted. They had been talking
to Father Crilly who saw Tom during the week. I explained
to Tom that there was nothing in these proposals except a
suit of clothes and if we were ever to open the door to the
Brits to talk on these points we'd get murdered, 'cause they
could say they accept the Commission's recommendations,
but the prisoners are refusing them. Anyway, we ought to
make our position clear in regard to the proposals. We
sent out a statement which was thought not to be strong
enough . . . I've enclosed another one here and if there is
anything out of line Pennies can doctor it and let me know
the crack. Now, if you still feel that we should not release a

statement can you let me know. I realize it's a red herring as Pennies said, but it appears to be cropping up everyday all over the place and among hunger strikers' families which may be bad crack. I don't want us getting nailed as inflexible on this effort. You can let me know the score . . .

The dangers of being wrong-footed by the Church were becoming increasingly apparent, and the pressures for action were steadily growing, although from the British press one might have assumed that the cardinal—"the wretched Cardinal Fee" as Auberon Waugh in the *Spectator* described him—was backing the IRA men wholeheartedly. The *Express* newspapers were being particularly vituperative, the *Daily Express* describing him as "the Cardinal who is like a recruiting officer of the IRA," the editor of the *Sunday Express,* John Junor, referring to him as "Chaplain of the IRA" and the cartoonist Cummings depicting him as mouthing "Why can't the British show some Christian charity to someone carrying a cross?" while behind him three masked IRA men carry a crucifix made up of crossed rifles, a placard urging "Let us prey," with a masked, pistol-packing priest taking up the rear.

On Monday, June 15, Fr. Murphy went in to see McFarlane for half an hour on the cardinal's behalf, asking for an indication of the prisoners' attitude to the Irish Commission for Justice and Peace. McFarlane gave him his stock answer: the Commission's proposals did not offer a basis for a settlement, because they fell too far short of the five demands. The priest carefully wrote down his words. But even more worrying for McFarlane were reports reaching his cell of the families ganging up with the priests.

Brownie Tue 16.6.81 8 P.M.
Well, child, it's me again to add to your headaches as usual. The following you probably know with possibly one exception—firstly Liam McCloskey (IRSP) had a

visit today with a Fr McGinn from Dungiven from whom came the following—he told Liam that there was a meeting the other week you, Pennies, B. Browning etc. and the hunger strikers' families. The Lynch family intimated to that sagart [priest] that the impression they got from you, Pennies etc. was that you were very unfeeling towards the hunger strikers and that you didn't care whether they died or not. Now the sagart also told Liam that another meeting took place on Sunday past, but before this meeting (with you etc.— notice how I chop these other efforts down to the status of the etc. ha!) the families had a private meeting themselves. They discussed the proposals of the Irish Commission (Rose Dugdale was present) and that Paddy Quinn's brother is purported to have stated that he was speaking for his brother and if the proposals were granted then they would be accepted. Apparently all the families agreed with this. The sagart then asked Liam for his view and Liam promptly hit him with the 'Bik McFarlane pocket book of ready-made answers for nosy sagarts'!! Seriously, though, Liam gave him a straight run-down on our position and that he didn't see a settlement in the Commission's proposals. Now the sagart has just seen Tom McFeely who gave the same run-down as Liam—sagart also referred to remission during his yarn with Liam. That was the heap old chum. Just by the way, Liam got a comm from his centre [IRSP] today. They had someone up seeing Kevin's family and apparently they are wrecked and don't know why he is on hunger strike. They think he was brainwashed and they don't understand what it's all about . . . I believe the Menace is not (as Tish said) being used, but that he has taken up stance with the other side. He's a shrewd man and I don't underestimate him one iota, even in spite of his sometimes reckless manner. I now feel he may have got more out of me on Sunday than he should have. I have a habit of just banging away and speaking my mind, sometimes forgetting that discretion is the better part of etc. etc. Anyway when he said to me about Haughey being concerned at least, I got stuck into dear Cathal and said what I believe he could do to pressurize the Brits. The Menace said that what I was talking about was the next thing to a declaration of war on the British. Sez I, Sure, what do you think we're all about? Every Irishman should be at war with the Brits and the sooner the better!! Ricky reckons I went too far. Perhaps I did anyway, above everyone else the Menace is probably the most dangerous man we could find on the opposite side . . . I know he is a very sound man. I know a brave few sagarts who are in his league—very strong nationalists, but that's where it ends . . . I think we need to get those families on the right line of thought. Now it won't be easy, I know. I have boxed the hunger strikers to ensure they are 100 per cent sound on our position. That they leave no one in any doubt that we make the decisions and they get the points across to their families and bring them round. I believe in my heart that all the lads are sound enough. I don't believe there was any problem with Joe or Doc's family, was there? . . .

In Belfast police found a 3 lb. booby-trap bomb lying on the pavement in front of the university. It seemed a funny place to leave a booby trap . . . until it was realized it had fallen off the car of the former Lord Chancellor, Lord Gardiner—the man whose Commission of Inquiry back in 1975 had led to the introduction of the criminalization policy. By a stroke of luck the IRA had been robbed of a prize kill. Lord Gardiner, who had gone to Queen's University to chair a law seminar, only heard of the attempt when he got back to his home in north London, where reporters found him happily working in his garden. He shrugged the news off with the comment: "I am eighty-one."

But Constable Neal Quinn, whose name was to become a new landmark in the territory's bloody history, was only fifty-three. The father of three children, he was having a quiet beer in a Newry pub on the Saturday afternoon when two men in black leather jackets and carrying motorcycle helmets walked in and pulled out pistols. Constable Quinn ran out the back, but the IRA gunmen followed and shot him nine times. He was the hundredth member of the RUC to be killed in the "Troubles." And he was a Catholic.

Constable Quinn was being buried, 5,000 people were gathering at the Bodenstown Cemetery in Co. Kildare. They were Republicans, come for the annual commemoration of Wolfe Tone, the eighteenth-century Irish revolutionary. The "Republican Party" was not there—for the first time in its history Fianna Fail had decided not to make an appearance: after losing an election because of the prisoners, they were in no mood to remember a Republican who had died in a prison cell. During the ceremony a man in disguise walked up to the rostrum and pulled off his dark glasses and cap, revealing himself—to cheers from the crowd—as Dingus Magee, one of the Crumlin Road escapees. As word filtered out from the cemetery, troops and police rushed to the area and threw up road blocks. But he had escaped again.

While the priests were scuttling in and out of the Kesh, delivering messages, getting involved in argument and bringing out their impressions, the Catholic hierarchy decided it was time for a public, frontal assault. The Irish bishops, meeting at the Maynooth seminary in Co. Kildare, issued a stern statement, imploring the hunger strikers "and those who direct them to reflect deeply on the evil of their actions and their consequences." They were not unmindful, they said, "of the injustice in Northern Ireland over the years" which had created a climate for paramilitary organization. Nor did the impasse in the gaol arise suddenly. But "if the present efforts were to fail the consequences throughout the whole island could be very grave indeed." They implored both the prisoners and the British Government to compromise and settle on the basis of proposals made by the Church's Irish Commission for Justice and Peace. "We ask people to persevere in prayer always. What our Lord says to us is that 'We ought always to pray and never to lose heart.'"

The prisoner's stomach lurched as he heard his name shouted from the Circle. He pulled off the blankets and wrapped the towel around his waist.

"G'luck," said his cellmate.

The door was swung open and he walked out, looking hurriedly down the corridor past his two-man escort. No screws lounging outside 26 so maybe he was lucky, perhaps they'd had enough for the day. But you never knew, there might be four inside. He picked his way around the remaining damp patches, a screw behind and the second in front, and walked into the search cell.

It was piled high with the white cell lockers stacked there since the prisoners started breaking up the furniture. But only two more screws, so he looked safe. Wordlessly he pulled the towel off and routinely reached for the rumpled prison uniform. Just as routinely the screws murmured: "Search." He offered no resistance as his legs were spread-eagled and the mirror, mounted crudely on its sponge mattress, slid between his legs. As the two screws holding his arms pressed with their boots at the back of his knees and he automatically sank into the requisite crouch he smothered a smile at a memory from H6: the four screws—used to "crims" and new to the formalities of dealing with non-conforming prisoners—desperately trying to make him bend, jumping up and down with all hands on his shoulders.

The search was over quickly, a hurried glance at his reflected anus, a quick look into his mouth and up his nostrils with the torch, fingers dragged tentatively through his hair. No check on his foreskin, but he had felt fairly safe about that. He pulled on the regulation striped shirt, denim trousers, coat and clumpy shoes.

Out to the first set of grilles. The class officer was taking his time opening them.

"As usual," the prisoner shouted in Gaelic, reassuring the wing.

"Give her my love," came an echo, but he couldn't place the voice.

Through the second grilles, down the passageway, past the classrooms. The third grilles and into the Circle.

"Name?" asked the screw, bringing the prisoner's book from the control room.

"Number?"

"Next of kin?"

"Date of birth?"

The prisoner muttered the formal replies, skipping the number as usual. The screw ignored the omission, grabbed his right hand and went through the motions of comparing fingerprints with the smear at the back of his book. The prisoner repressed a twinge of irritation.

There was a Park Ranger—stranger—at the grilles and he studied the prisoner's photograph with exaggerated care before unlocking. Then he was out of the block and into the yard. The prisoner took a deep breath of fresh air, feeling the snow crunching underfoot. The best moment of the month.

"Hey," came the shout from the wing.

"Look at the size of that dog."

"Where'd y'get that wee dachshund."

"You not got a lead for that and all?"

"Take him down to the bottom, to that wee lamp and let him have a piss."

"Go on, turn round and beat the balls off him. Give him a tanking."

He waved them off with a clenched-fist salute.

The obstacle course of gates began. The screw at the second gate muttered: "Why the fuck does anyone want to visit you? Look at the state of you!" The prisoner ignored him.

At the third gate a screw from the Cages recognized him from the old days.

"Fuck, what about ye?" The prisoner stared him out.

"What's wrong with ye?"

The prisoner was beginning to feel the cold and it was with reluctance mixed with relief that he was ushered out of the fresh air into the Portakabin. Inside, the waiting inmates were gathered in two small clumps. He joined the Republicans, greeting two comrades from the Ardoyne days.

"Give me a bit of cover," he murmured to one of them. Shielded by the other man from the screw at the door he reached through the torn crutch of his trousers, eased out the packet and, with a camouflaging cough, slipped it into his mouth, his tongue pressing it into his favored place where his left lower wisdom tooth had left a gap.

He reentered the hum of conversation. Then he caught the eye of one of the men in the second group and nodded a greeting which the other man followed up by walking over.

"Ah, fuck's sake, what about ye? Still sticking it?" asked the Loyalist.

"Aye," said the prisoner. "What about ye? Goin' to join us again?"

"No way. Once is enough. How long are ye on now?"

"Three years."

"Fuck's sake. Who's up to see you?"

"Aagh, just a friend of the sister."

"Aha! Well, tell Jimmy I was asking."

The man's hand bumped the prisoner's. "See ya." They shook hands awkwardly, the three needle-thin cigarettes slipping into the prisoner's palm.

As the other man walked away the prisoner mentally shook his head. The Loyalist was doing time for bombing an IRA volunteer's funeral, killing one mourner and badly injuring another. He was a hard man, reputed to have had links with the Shankill Butchers who had taken delight in carving up their Catholic victims with meat cleavers; torturing and slashing throats. They had been in adjoining cells in 1978, when the Loyalists had briefly joined the blanket protest. The shared experience had left a residual, if perverse, sense of camaraderie.

"Here, bangle this," he said, slipping the cigarettes to one of his Republican comrades as his name was called from the door.

A cursory frisk in the small search room and then into the visiting area, with its vinyl floor tiles and low partitions. She was not there when he was ushered to the box. So he savored the atmosphere as he lounged in his chair, acknowledging the greetings of former neighbors with calls of "How's about ye's" and "Say hello to . . ."; listening to the buzz of domestic confidences; the squeals and giggles of children, impatient with enforced inactivity. His eyes drifted to the younger women; after a month he thought they'd gone the way of the dodo. Gazing at a brunette in stretch jeans he suddenly switched his eyes to the visitors' door, feeling a momentary anxiety at the delay. She shouldn't have been caught—she was experienced and would probably use her vagina. But it wasn't foolproof. Then a young girl walked in and he recognized her from the way her eyes flitted, trying to spot him in time to play out greetings for the screws' benefit.

SEVEN

KING: . . . *you have planned*
To put a voice by every cottage fire
And in the night when no one sees who cries,
To cry against me till my throne has crumbled
And yet if I give way I must offend
My courtiers and nobles till they, too,
Strike at the crown. What would you have of me?
—The King's Threshold, *by* W. B. Yeats

"The Government will not negotiate terms for
ending the hunger strike either with the prisoners,
or their representatives."

—Margaret Thatcher in a letter to
Labour MP, Ernie Roberts

The priest went down on his knees on the green carpet next to his bed. He began to recite the Prayer of Abandonment of Charles Foucauld, the nineteenth-century French dilettante and explorer who became a holy man beloved of the nomads of the Sahara desert: ". . . Do with me what you will. Whatever you may do, I thank you. I am ready for all, I accept all. Let only your will be done, in me, and in all your creatures—I wish no more than this, oh Lord . . ."

The prayer finished, Fr. Oliver Crilly clambered into his bed, in his double-story house in South Dublin, and tried to sleep. Usually he slept easily, but on this night of Monday, May 4, 1981 he tossed and turned. Eventually he drifted off and awoke in the morning to hear the news on the radio: the man for whom he had been praying, Bobby Sands, had finally died.

The hunger strike was a particularly poignant episode for Father Crilly, not only because of the moral conflict it provoked in him—like many others in the Irish Church, faced with such a sharp choice between Christian principle and instinctive sympathy for Nationalist sacrifice—but because he was personally related to two of the hunger strikers.

He had been born near Bellaghy, the home of both Francis Hughes and Tom McElwee, and was a second cousin to both men. His father was a particular friend of Tom's father, Jim McElwee, and since childhood he had been a regular and frequent guest at their home in Tamlaghtduff. Of course his own life had followed a very different course from that of the Hughes and McElwee boys. Taking a degree in Celtic studies, followed by a Master's in the Irish language—he was as fluent in Irish as in English—he was at the time of Sands's death what might be described as a senior civil servant in the Irish Catholic Church: Director of its Commission for Communications, which had responsibility for the Church's publishing and other media operations, including a television training center. He had been a member of the Commission for thirteen years and Director for about eight, and it was to some extent ex officio that he had also been appointed, at the end of 1980, to the Irish Commission for Justice and Peace. That commission was one of eighty established around the world after Vatican Two, under the leadership of a Pontifical Commission in the Vatican, which were intended to help national hierarchies assess what the Church's position should be on human rights issues.

As a newcomer to the ICJP Fr. Crilly had felt constrained from active participation. But at its AGM in May 1981 he had been elected to its executive committee. Taking this as a vote of confidence, he had begun to think about what role the commission could play in trying to resolve the hunger strike.

So the weekend after his election he had gone up north to see his father and had taken him around for a visit to the McElwees. From there it was only a short walk to the Hughes home.

He found both families receptive to the idea of the ICJP's intervention which he floated so hesitantly. Frank's brother, Oliver, had just arrived back from a visit to the Kesh and said he had the impression that the prisoners were very open to a fair settlement. So when he got back to Dublin he telephoned the president of the commission, the Auxiliary Bishop of Dublin, Dr. Dermot O'Mahony, with the proposal.

A series of meetings and trips up to the north followed as the commission members tried to find a route for intervention. Another member of the commission from northern Ireland, Hugh Logue—a prominent figure in the SDLP and a close friend of the Lynch family—joined enthusiastically in the task. Fr. Crilly himself made another personal visit to Bellaghy, driving up in his VW to attend the wake for his cousin, Francis Hughes. And while he was driving along the Slane Road, through the rain and the thunder which marked that day, he switched on his car radio and heard the voice of Fr. Joe Dunn—his predecessor as head of the Commission for Communications, who happened to be in Rome on a film assignment—describing the scene in St. Peter's Square where the Pope had just been shot. It was with all this violence and death in mind that Fr. Crilly arrived at the Hughes home that night, went in to see the coffin and was struck by the coincidence—and symbolism—that the unusually long index finger of Frank's left hand was crooked as if around a familiar trigger, but threaded with a set of rosary beads.

The ICJP held back on any public moves until the excitement of the first round in the hunger strike ended, with the deaths of McCreesh and O'Hara on May 21. Then, on June 3 they issued a tentative statement suggesting that as the women in Armagh already had their own clothes this should be extended to the Maze; that there was room for greater freedom of association in the prison without tolerating military activities like those pursued by the inmates of the compounds; and that penal work with demeaning overtones could be avoided if emphasis were placed on work with cultural and educational value.

The statement was well timed, although it was given little immediate publicity as Ireland tried to recover from both the bruising events of the previous month in the north and from the general election in the south. But as politicians began looking around for straws to cling to in the face of the threatened renewal of the crisis, with the next round of deaths looming, attention began to focus on the ICJP. The bishops in England and Wales, as well as the Irish hierarchy, issued statements backing the proposals. They were raised in the House of Commons, where Labour's backbench committee on Ireland appealed to Mrs. Thatcher to approach the crisis along the lines suggested by the ICJP. The prisoners themselves issued a cautious statement, expressing appreciation for the efforts of the commission while stressing that the proposals fell far short of the five demands. Both Haughey and FitzGerald, still fighting each other to form a government, called them in—Garret demonstrating the importance he was attaching to their initiative by giving them one and a half hours of his time on the day he was frantically choosing a putative cabinet. And the commission itself began to press forward, with feelers into the Maze and a request to the Secretary of State, Humphrey Atkins, for a meeting.

Brownie [Gerry Adams] from Bik [McFarlane] Mon 22.6.81 P.M.
Comrade Mor, Big Tom had a visit with Fr Crilly (Irish Comm) this afternoon and had a lengthy yarn with him on our position and 5 demands. Main points that arose were as follows. Firstly the sagart [priest] says they were very pleased with the statement we released in response to their

proposals. Says that he understands there is no settlement
in 3 proposals and he recognizes our five basic demands as
the settlement, but their intention is to open up dialogue.
Secondly he told Tom that they have a meeting with Atkins
tomorrow. Now the crack is that they have what is termed
a 'three column programme' i.e. 1. To establish whether
or not we are genuine in seeking a solution. 2. To establish the same in respect of the Brits. 3. To get dialogue
in motion so that settlement can be obtained. Now, re
column 1, they are satisfied we are genuinely pursuing a
solution. Re column 2, if the Brits do not satisfy them,
they will release a strong statement on Brit intransigence.
He also said they would be meeting our people tomorrow
afternoon as well . . . although Tom believes that the sagart
is genuinely interested in getting a solution he agreed with
me when I told him that that may be the case, but he was
being used and his strings were being pulled and therefore
Tom should not trust him one iota . . .

Brownie from Bik Tue 23.6.81
. . . [Paddy Quinn's] brother spoke to Fr Crilly and H.
Logue who told him their intention was to find an opener
for dialogue . . . They maintain they are trying to find
common ground between us and the Brits to forge a solution or to at least [create a] situation so that the onus lies
squarely with the Brits. Paddy's other brother attended
a meeting of relatives recently—bad atmosphere existed
against Sinn Fein. Resentment and a feeling that SF were
not prepared to allow any other groups to take part in
getting a solution—that SF were deliberately excluding
these groups from playing a part . . . I can see the Menace
is up to his tricks again—a dangerous man at times. I've a
good mind to tell him where to get off, but I don't suppose
he'd pay too much heed . . .

Fr. Crilly had been nervous about meeting Tom McElwee, who had already started his own hunger strike. He was worried Tom might see the commission's intervention as time-wasting interference, another ploy encouraged by Britain to give "an illusion of movement." But he was relieved to find Tom was still treating him as family and an old friend. For the first time Fr. Crilly was given an insight into what the prisoners meant by the five demands and he had the impression that there was room for movement. But at the same time he got from his cousin an almost frightening sense of obduracy in so far as the hunger strike itself was concerned: it was clear not only that the motivation for the fast came entirely from inside the prison, but that the hunger strikers had an immense sense of conviction and saw themselves as representatives not just of the others fasting, but of all the Republican prisoners.

Two meetings were held with the Minister of State responsible for prisons, Michael Allison, at which the two sides sounded each other out, the Northern Ireland Office stressing—and the commission accepting—that there was no question of "negotiation," it being an exercise in "clarification." Semantics are important in the Northern Ireland context.

But as the initiative developed it was, inevitably, creating unease inside the Kesh. Superficially such initiatives may appear to be harbingers of hope, but to the prisoners—or at least the leadership—they were simply tactical problems. Believing that the power to settle the hunger strike lay purely in the Government's hands, they saw outside initiatives as little more than public relations exercises: there might be a chance that the Government, in allowing outsiders to get involved, was looking for a vehicle for compromise, but it was far more likely—they believed—that it was a maneuver to outflank them, to shift all-important public opinion against them. Ever since 1921, when Lloyd George had foisted Partition on

Ireland with one of the most brilliant but brutal exercises in negotiation in the annals of diplomacy, British government duplicity had been an article of faith with Irish Republicans. And of course the ending of the first hunger strike had only reinforced the prejudice.

Brownie 28.6.81 9 P.M.

... Now on the situation and possible near certain Brit move on Commission's 3 proposals as major undermining exercise. First of all it is my belief that the alien elements (Church, SDLP and Haughey) have already succeeded in undermining our position greatly. Families of hunger strikers appear ready to grab what comes as a feasible settlement. It will, I believe, be attractive enough to satisfy the Church etc. of Brit flexibility and in time they will look to us for a response i.e. terminate the hunger strike . . . if we choose to continue with the hunger strike we will be faced with a situation whereby Joe will die, followed by others and after X amount of deaths public opinion will hammer us into the ground, forcing us to end hunger strike with nothing to show but deaths that could have been avoided and a shattering defeat into the bargain . . . if we can combat the undermining successfully and eliminate the prospect of a crushing defeat after further deaths then I feel we should at least maintain our position. I know this could well mean Joe's death and possibly others before we reach a settlement, but if a settlement is obtainable we should try for it. It has been a horrific price to date and maybe worse before we finish. Now if we cannot negotiate this hurdle successfully and all the dangers start looming overhead then we must, I believe, give consideration to terminating the hunger strike and salvaging something from Brit concessions. A point Jake made to me I thought was important to mention and that is, whereas concessions are not important in themselves to us, they are important to our people who will see at least some fruit of their labour and give them a certain sense of achievement. Anyway cara, it's a deadly situation and I just don't know what way it's going to leave us . . .

In Dublin the last hours of the government of Mr. Haughey were ticking away; the vote in the Dublin Parliament on the election of a new prime minister was scheduled for the afternoon of Wednesday, July 1. On the Tuesday, in a last-ditch effort to swing the votes of Independents, Haughey moved to present himself as the man to solve the prison crisis. Disclosing that he had called the British Ambassador in for talks, he issued a statement saying: "The consequences of further deaths are so serious and far-reaching that a solution which will prevent them occurring must be found and I am convinced that the time to find such a solution is now." London immediately retorted by issuing a five-page statement—which was being prepared in response to the ICJP initiative, with Mrs. Thatcher's personal attention—summarizing the British Government's position. The statement concluded, depressingly for Mr. Haughey, that proposals for change in the prison regime should be "fully and carefully weighted," but that "this process cannot proceed further while the hunger strike places the authorities under duress." The ICJP, however, said the statement was encouraging to them.

Brownie from Bik Mon 29.6.81 9.30 P.M.
Comrade Mor, just a quickie here for you. I suppose everyone is shooting in the dark at the moment and can only speculate as to what Brit move will be. You should have received a comm from me today looking an attitude on our overall positions. Tish gave us a run down today on certain aspects. There's no way am I happy with the situation with the families. I have this nasty feeling that someone is sitting poised with a ready-made statement for them to initial. If

Brits don't meet with Commission approval and forward a
very watery offer, can we cope with the families i.e. prevent
their disintegration if we refuse. Do your people (i.e. yourselves) feel we could bear up under concerted pressure from
the elements pushing Commission? Here, you may forget
about all the above questions—I've just heard the Hump's
[Humphrey Atkins] statement—'no changes'!! Are they
serious? What sort of people are we dealing with? I just
for the life of me can't fathom their logic at all. Surely they
must pull the greatest condemnation yet upon themselves.
It appears they are not interested in simply undermining us,
but completely annihilating us. The church etc. must surely
cut the water out of them now. Haughey made a right balls
of himself today—you'd imagine the Brits were trying to
do him damage deliberately. It doesn't make sense—well
not to me anyway . . . The question is, can we hope to
move those people at all? They are insane—at least Maggie is anyway. I'm beginning to believe that, cara, and it's
greatly worrying me. Just looking to the days ahead—Joe
is a cert to die. What way will the families react now?
What's more important—what way will the hunger strikers
receive the news? Now, I know Joe is sound, but I'd need
a good appreciation of the attitude of the other lads in the
hospital. As for these lads here in this wing—they are very
sound indeed and I have no worries about them. They were
very quick in grasping the situation with Commission and
understand it alright. I feel confident that their resolve is
sound. If all hunger strikers prove to be on same lines and
are determined to press forward and if we can honestly
see our objective being achieved, then we should maintain
our position. I realize that as long as our resolve holds fast
then the Brits are always the losers. However if they are
prepared to continue to be losers without conceding our
demands, then we can only go so far . . .

To Brownie Tue 30.6.81 10 P.M. [From Bik]
Comrade Mor, I feel somewhat isolated just now. Got
your comm today. Also got copy of Atkins statement
and heard Commission's response—so I know why the
dampers are on signer and Angel. I am even half expecting
a block on our visits tomorrow if a big push is coming.
Anyway, here's the opinions you were after, though it's
not based on a totally informed footing, as you know.
(Firstly find enclosed a statement in answer to Atkin's five
page document. Everyone got copies tonight at 7.30 P.M.,
though the hunger strikers received them at 3.30 P.M.
Having read the document a few times I am of the opinion that it contains nothing we haven't heard before—a
run-down on the regime—a refusal to grant status or five
demands—continuing review of prison conditions with
a hint of improvements on a similar line as Commission
proposals 'someday'. The impression can be taken that
they are contemplating a settlement of sorts. But such
an impression I believe is there to mislead people into
believing that the Brits are genuine. Anyway, cara, it is a
very dodgy situation, especially with response from Commission etc. welcoming the statement by Atkins. Commission mentioned 'certain clarifications', which obviously
leaves everyone to believe that there is something there
alright. That is bloody annoying, because it's going to
increase the hopes and expectations of the families and
subsequently their distress will be all the greater, which
means trouble as you know. I got a quick opinion from
Tom, Paddy and Lorny [Laurence McKeown]—just to
feel out their thinking. They compared the statement to
the December 18 one i.e. at face value nothing there. An
attempt to dishearten us, especially hs'ers—a trick to
create impression of movement. As far as five demands are
concerned, Brit statement is well off the track. That's just

some of their comments, OK. Each of them knows to ask for me if approached by anyone . . . If this development is the major undermining effort we've been expecting and we are not able to combat it then we should seek a way out of this situation, saving lives and as much face as possible. If it doesn't appear that the Brits will be forthcoming with a feasible settlement, then we should get in before public opinion swings against us, forcing us to halt after say six or seven deaths, which would be a disaster. I do not want the war to suffer any setbacks like public condemnation of the Movement. We have made major gains to date, which is what we are all about. To detract from those gains would be disastrous and a terrible waste. So let's hope we make the right move at the right time and do the right thing. Easier said than done!! There are some overriding factors which will play a major part in what way things go—the families; pressure from all the 'do-gooders' and the lads on hunger strike . . .

While McFarlane was agonizing over the implications of the ICJP intervention, the Church's commissioners were preparing the final thrust of their initiative and Charles Haughey was finally surrendering power in Dublin, Cardinal O Fiaich was scheduled to have his compensatory appointment with the Iron Lady. His visit to 10 Downing Street was scheduled for 8 P.M. on that Wednesday. As usual, he stayed in London with Cardinal Hume, but had breakfast at 8 A.M. with the Archbishop of Canterbury, Robert Runcie. It was a pleasant meal, with nothing particularly serious discussed—the vexed issue between the two churches, of mixed marriages, was only touched on once. In the afternoon the cardinal was chief celebrant at an open-air Mass on Clapham Common to mark the martyrdom of St. Oliver Plunkett. In the procession, after Mass was completed, he was mobbed by an enthusiastic crowd of London-Irish and was startled by their numbers. He later took a taxi to Downing St., with his Armagh auxiliary, Bishop James Lennon, arriving to find the lady was late; she was with the Queen, having missed her regular prime ministerial meeting with the monarch on Tuesday because she had just returned from a trip to the Middle East. The two churchmen were put in a waiting room downstairs and summoned at 8:15 P.M. Mrs. Thatcher was waiting for them at the top of the stairs, on the first-floor landing, and gushed a welcome.

They followed her into a drawing room where they were joined by Humphrey Atkins. They were offered a drink and the cardinal asked for an Irish whiskey, but that omission had still not been rectified since John Hume's visit and he had to make do with a Scotch. They started with the usual pleasantries, but quickly moved on to the prison issue.

"Will someone please tell me why they are on hunger strike?" asked the Prime Minister. "I have asked so many people. Is it to prove their virility?"

The two clergymen had agreed beforehand that Bishop Lennon would take notes and the cardinal would do most of the talking. But at this remark from Mrs. Thatcher, Bishop Lennon solemnly put pen and paper down.

The bishop launched forth with a lecture on the effect that the hunger strike was having in alienating Irish youth both from the Church and from moderate politicians and leaders, citing the attitudes of his own nephews and nieces and grandnieces as examples. The cardinal asked her for some changes in the prison regime which would allow the hunger strike to end without loss of face. Mrs. Thatcher said it would be wrong and dishonorable to give any concessions to murder and violence, quoting the Pope's abjuration to the men of violence to abandon their evil ways. The cardinal sidetracked, complaining of the treatment he had been receiving in the English media. He immediately regretted it as Mrs. Thatcher brushed him aside by pointing to the criticism and ridicule she had to suffer at the hands of journalists and cartoonists.

Her performance made her authority within the Government on the Irish issue clear—the Secretary of State for Northern Ireland was hardly getting a word in. Her voice was high-pitched and strident, but nevertheless it was a bravura performance—she was showing herself more than capable of taking on two highly intelligent and articulate people single-handedly in the cut and thrust of argument.

"Why can't the Irish be friendly?" Mrs. Thatcher demanded. "We fought against the French, we fought against the Germans, and they are friends, why must the Irish be exceptions?"

"Because you're no longer in occupation of the Ruhr," retorted the cardinal, with satisfaction at getting at least one thrust home.

She began to paraphrase a letter which had appeared in the *Daily Telegraph* a few days before: Mexico would have as much right to seek Texas back as the Irish Republic to seek the Six Counties. The cardinal launched into a historical and geographical account of the issue. He emphasized the artificiality of the border, pointing out that no one had even been able to find an adequate name for the northern state: it was not Ulster, because that ancient kingdom had been made up of nine counties, not the present six; it was not "northern" Ireland, because the most northerly part of the island, Donegal, was part of the Republic. He explained how the border cut right across the most ancient territories in Ireland—the parish and diocesan borders, dating back to the twelfth century. His own parish had three churches, two north of the border and one south. When the parish priest passed from one church to another, no one would persuade him that he was passing from one country into a foreign state. He told of a house in Armagh which was actually divided by the frontier: the householder ran a small shop, moving it from time to time between the kitchen and the front room, depending on whether cigarettes were cheaper at the time in the north or south. But it was all to no apparent avail. It was clear that Mrs. Thatcher was not only Prime Minister of the United Kingdom, but a fervent believer in that union. It did not matter how many were going to die on hunger strike, she was not conceding. At 9:55 P.M. she gave a gentle hint: she had to be in the Commons for a vote at 10 P.M. They parted at the top of the stairs. Outside the front door the journalists were conspicuous by their absence. The press had not been alerted by either side and had missed the story.

In Co. Tyrone, in the little village of Sixmilecross, the Rev. Ian Paisley was still trying to gallop down the Carson trail. Addressing 900 men who had paraded military-style before him in the village, he bellowed: "We shall fight them in the lanes and on the highways and we shall never surrender." He demanded to know whether Loyalists were going to wait to be murdered by the IRA, "or shall go out to kill the killers?" Afterwards he told reporters he was speaking purely of a defensive role.

On Friday, July 3 the five members of the ICJP piled into the red Volvo of the secretary to the commission, Jerome Connolly—packing an overnight case each—and started the familiarly bumpy journey up to Belfast. With Connolly and Crilly were Bishop Mahoney, president of the commission, Auxiliary Bishop of Dublin and the holder of a doctorate in canon law; Brian Gallagher, the chairman and a Dublin solicitor, and Hugh Logue, the SDLP's spokesman on economic affairs. For a while they had thought it was going to be a trip to London—the Irish Government had had the Prime Minister's executive jet fueled and waiting at Dublin airport to fly them over to see Atkins, who was in the English capital. But the Northern Ireland Office had decided that Atkins's deputy, Michael Allison, could handle them and so they went north, stopping off at a shop to buy a new Irish translation of the Bible—to present to the prisoners if, as they hoped, they were given a chance of seeing them—and tarrying a while for lunch at a roadside hotel; not eating too much, because they wanted to be alert.

They arrived at Hillsborough Castle, official residence of the Secretary of State, shortly after 2 P.M., and Allison was waiting together with civil servants from the NIO. They always found him an affable man, easier to relate to than the Secretary of State himself. There was the usual polite chatter, Allison pointing out the huge rhododendron in the garden as the largest in Europe; an impressive sight, if slightly spoiled by the policeman in bottle-green uniform, toting a submachine gun, peering around it.

They got down to detail, going over almost every aspect of the prison regime at the Kesh. At one stage Allison had a huge plan of the H-Blocks brought in and they all went down on their knees on the carpet and began poring over it, arguing over whether the cell doors could be left open at certain hours and what would happen if something was stolen from a cell—the principle would have to be "operational flexibility and common sense to safeguard prisoners' privacy and possessions," said Allison. He pointed out that the blocks could not be converted into compounds, because they had been specifically designed to frustrate any compound-type regime. The commissioners accepted that changes would have to be made within the context of continued overall control by staff. Allison argued that an incremental approach would not work, because what they were discussing was light years away from what the prisoners wanted, but the commissioners insisted it was the only way to try and close the gap between the two sides, repeating the old penal truism that prisons were communities not only of restraint, but also of consent. At one stage Allison hinted that he would have liked to be more concessionary, but that there was always the "lady behind the veil"—which the commissioners took to be a reference to Mrs. Thatcher.

The meeting lasted nearly eight hours, during which they had only some coffee and shortbread made by Mrs. Allison. They finished with Allison agreeing to consider overnight their request to be allowed into the Kesh for discussions with the hunger strikers. The five left Hillsborough and went on to the home of the assistant prison chaplain, Fr. Murphy, outside Belfast, talking with him and the prison chaplain, Fr. Toner, until 2 A.M. There was not enough room in the house for them to stay, so Fr. Toner telephoned the Greenan Lodge Hotel in West Belfast. The hotel was full, but the staff moved four beds into a first-floor sitting room and cleared out the storeroom down the passage for Bishop O'Mahoney. They did not know it then, but it was going to be home for one of the most trying weeks in any of their lives.

Brownie 3.7.81 5.30 P.M. Bik
Comrade Mor, got your comm today and was somewhat relieved to learn that hunger strikers are all pretty stable. I had a fair idea the Brits would take the Commission on a mystery tour. It keeps pushing the deadline right on top of Joe's critical period. I hope you succeeded in getting them to attack the Brits. They should have done so at least a week ago. Surely they must realize that the Brits are only having them for "ould eejits." Tom and Paddy went to hospital this morning. Both are very sound indeed. The screws let me in to see Tom for a short yarn (5 or 10 minutes). I was glad of the opportunity. Anyway, he has a copy of that point by point assessment I sent you out and he was very pleased with it as were Paddy and Lorny. If there is any problems with the four lads in hospital Tom should straighten things out. He has a visit on Monday so Tish [Sinn Fein official] will see him then. Lorny had a

good visit with his mother today and tells me she is very sound indeed . . .

Brownie from Bik Fri 3.7.81 9 P.M.
. . . Re hunger strikers' resolve we now believe that Commission has absolutely nothing in their so-called clarifications. The lads don't expect much to come of their efforts and proposals so perhaps we'll get some sort of condemnatory statement from them against the Brits which would help us . . . I'll write to IRSP O/C asking him to endorse Owen Carron [for Fermanagh-S. Tyrone] but I reckon I'll be wasting a skib, because I reckon the IRSP will push Bernie [McAliskey], outside and inside. There's a danger of causing internal friction, I realize they are a minute grouping here and would present no problems. I take it they are being swallowed up by our Movement outside and are struggling very hard for individual identity and prestige. Can they not fit in the broad base Movement a hundred per cent? Anyway I'll contact their O/C, but God knows when you'll get a reply . . .

On Saturday morning the ICJP met the Minister of State at the Northern Ireland Office, Michael Allison, again and found him in a conciliatory mood; they had their permission to go into the Kesh—it seemed the lines to London had been buzzing overnight. They left for the Kesh at about midday. As they went through the front gates in their Volvo they saw a television crew lounging nearby, looking bored; through his rearview mirror Connolly saw them frantically mounting the camera as the car disappeared. They parked their car and went into a security hut, having their security photographs taken with a Polaroid and then clambering into a minibus for the trip to the prison hospital. Then they were searched, the commissioners feeling antipathy from the warders going through their belongings, one of them inspecting Connolly's notes until pulled up by a senior officer. They were led through several gates—the fencing, topped by rolls of razor wire and overlooked by watchtowers, bringing home the grim reality of life in the Kesh—to the room where the hunger strikers were waiting for them.

There were eight of them, in dressing gowns, pajamas and slippers. The commissioners shook hands with each of them. Two formica-top tables had been pulled together to form the semblance of a conference table. The hunger strikers were carrying small jugs of water and there were several bowls on the tables for them to spit into. There was something awful about the jugs, the bowls, the bareness of the room, the harsh scratching of the chairs as they took their places—a terrible finality. Bishop O'Mahoney led them in a short prayer. Mickey Devine, now officer commanding the INLA prisoners, ostentatiously turned aside, making it clear that he was not partaking of the opiate of the masses. Devine was sitting at one end of the tables, the others sitting down the one side, in order of seniority on the hunger strike, with Joe McDonnell at the other end. Joe was in a wheelchair. He had greeted them with the others, but looked far gone, his head sunk forward, chin on his chest, looking sightlessly down. As the discussion got under way Kieran Doherty repeated the important points in a whisper into Joe's ear. 'The commissioners kept glancing at him. His impending death was the immediate reality; his life what they were now fighting for.

Joe was thirty years old. He was born, the fifth of nine children, into the family of Robert McDonnell, a construction worker, in Belfast's Lower Falls area, the cockpit of Republicanism in West Belfast. The ninth of the children, a little girl called Bernadette, was adored by Joe. Her death of a kidney complaint when she was three was something he never fully got over. He started his own family when he was only nineteen. His wife, Goretti, was eighteen. She was from Andersonstown;

attractive, with a striking figure. She had two children in quick succession. The first was a girl and Joe gave Goretti no choice about the name: it had to be Bernadette. His little sister had been born again. Within a few months Goretti was pregnant again, with Joseph. Little Joe, everyone called him, to distinguish him from his dad. As tends to happen with marriage at that age, Goretti was totally dependent on Joe, who was working as a furniture upholsterer. So when, in 1972, the troops raided the house where they were squatting and hauled Joe away for internment it was as if her right arm had been amputated. It was a traumatic period—the frantic visits to the Kesh, staggering along with babies and bottles. When he was interned again the following year she was becoming more used to it—the fear of his not coming home: like the night she had news that there had been a bomb in his upholstery shop and Joe's boss had been blown into so many pieces and was such a huge man that they had thought the bits of him left were the remains of two men and she had had to wait until Joe finally came home at 10 P.M. after walking aimlessly in the rain, his swarthy face drained white, he was so upset by it all. And so was she.

So by 1976 she was the fully fledged wife of an IRA activist, although even that did not prepare her for what was to come.

It was in October that Joe was arrested, along with Bobby Sands after the bomb attack on the Balmoral furniture store. They had all been great friends, Bobby, Joe, Goretti and the others. In fact they all met at Joe's house before the operation. Joe was one of those drafted in from the Andersonstown operational area to help Bobby's fledgling active service unit in Twinbrook. Like Bobby, Joe refused to recognize the court and so they both got fourteen years—along with two others—for the single pistol found in their car when they were captured. It always seemed unfair—fifty-six years between them for one pistol—but then everyone knew they had taken part in the bomb attack, even if it could not be proved.

By this time Joe was a veteran and a tough character. Nothing was particularly sacred to him and he was fond of "winding" others up, making "eejits" of them. His wing in the blocks had a core of characters like himself, cynical old hands: if anyone suggested a lecture they would as likely as not be met with a raspberry from Joe; if an Irish class were called the cry would come up from him of: "None of that Paddy Irishman caper here, we want to get a kip at lunchtime." But they were reliable, at the end of the day the staunchest wing of the lot. If the command was having trouble with a screw who was knocking around one of the younger lads the word would go down to Joe's wing to "fill in" the offending warder and at the first opportunity they would do it, laying into him with feet and fists and . . . what the hell, the Boards were just a break from the bloody Irish classes.

When Joe went down Goretti did the calculation that every wife makes: fourteen years with fifty percent remission, that's seven years, less two years on remand, that's five years to wait. Of course Joe might go on the blanket which meant no remission, but then nobody believed that the blanket protest could go on much longer; sooner or later they must surely get status.

It is a terrible thing to be married, and jailed for a long time; even more so when you go "on the blanket," which Joe did. There is always that fear, of "What is she doing now?" the awful images that flit through the mind at unguarded moments. And to try and sustain the relationship through censored letters pawed over by the screws, or in those tiny comms! Seeing each other once a month made it almost worse—trying to pack a month of lovemaking, talking, arguing, laughing into a quick kiss and half an hour's yearning across a table. Different men try to handle it in different ways. The dramatic thing to do, of course, is to make the magnanimous gesture, to turn your back on it all and tell the lady: "Look, forget about me, you're still young and you've got a lot of life to live, so get on with it." Which is what Joe did, sending an early comm out to Goretti, telling her he wasn't planning to take regular visits and not to wait for him. When she got it she felt something close to relief; the momentary relief of thinking that a world of problems can just be waved away by a single gesture. But of course when she started to think about it, he was her Joe and it would, after all, only be five years. So she wrote back and said, no, she would wait and, yes, she agreed with him about the visits—it did not seem worthwhile putting on the uniform for a miserable thirty minutes a month. And instead she tried to keep it going with comms; locking herself in her bedroom and endlessly etching out tiny letters, to be carried in noses, mouths, anuses and vaginas to tell a man he was still loved. Later Joe confessed to her that he had not really meant it when he told her to forget him; he was only testing her. Which was fatal, of course, because it was a confession that he didn't trust her. And gradually the mistrust was fed, by those midnight fears, by the gossip in the blocks, the stories of the women who had failed to wait. Wasn't the husband always the last to know? And finally it all erupted, first in comms full of questions and then accusations—someone had told him at Mass that she had been seen with another man. She couldn't take it any more. So she wrote a comm saying yes, it was all true, everything he was accusing her of—if that was what he wanted to hear he could have it. He wrote back, calling her every name in the book. She didn't reply. A long silence followed; they had no contact for about six months. Then suddenly she got another comm from him, a chatty letter, saying nothing about the row. She wrote back in the same vein and gradually the relationship was reestablished, but on another plane now, quieter and more restrained. And so it went on, until the day the boys came to see her and warned her: Joe was going on hunger strike, it would be on the telly soon, so she'd better tell his family and her kids.

She nearly left it too late to tell Joe's mother. The news was broadcast on television that night, that Bobby Sands was going to be replaced by another prisoner, Tom Loudon. "God, isn't that awful, that's news going to somebody's house tonight," Joe's mother said to a friend as she heard it. Later that night Goretti arrived at her mother-in-law's house and took her into the kitchen to tell her. "No, no way, Goretti," said Mrs. McDonnell, "Goretti, I heard it on the news, Goretti I heard it, it was Tom Boy Loudon." Goretti insisted it was Joe and said: "Do you want me to ring Sinn Fein and check?" Mrs. McDonnell said "Yes." She heard Goretti say on the phone: "So it was a mistake?" and of course she thought it meant that Joe was the mistake. When Goretti turned to her and said that the news announcement was a mistake, Mrs. McDonnell squealed blue murder.

Goretti told the kids last, calling them into her bedroom that night. Bernadette took it hard—at that age little girls idolize their fathers. She cried: "He's going to die, he's going to die, I know he's going to die, they let Bobby die." Little Joe cried as well, of course, but he did not say anything and somehow that was worse. His absent father had been troubling little Joe for a long time. He had only been four when his dad disappeared into jail so he didn't have much in the way of memories. Instead he used fantasy. He used to say to his mates: "God, you need to see how me and my daddy used to play football over there." But they never had. It came out in his schoolwork as well. In one composition he fantasized about his father escaping. A knife had been smuggled in to him and he had stabbed a screw in the hand and snatched his keys, opening all the other cell doors. The essay ended: "And now all the daddies are home with their children."

The hunger strike ended Joe's moratorium on visits and the card duly arrived from the prison, notifying Goretti of the day that she was expected up with the kids and with Joe's mother and sister. It had been five years since he had gone to jail and with all that had happened in between it was a traumatic visit. Joe had obviously gone over it in his mind, again and again—he even described to her, in one comm, precisely how they would all sit in the visiting room. And so it was to be. When the day of the visit came—May 12—Goretti set out with her mother-in-law, her sister-in-law, twenty-eight-year-old Maura, and the two kids. Maura took charge, telling the children as they walked to the visiting room: "Now when I go in, the man I go towards, that's your daddy." They ran into his arms and Maura was startled to see tears in his eyes as he swept them up: it had been a characteristic of Joe as a kid that you could beat him from end to end of a room and he would not cry. It was the first time she could remember seeing his tears.

It was just as he had outlined in that comm: he balanced Bernadette and little Joe on his knees and Maura sat opposite, their mother next to her and Goretti furthest away. Maura did most of the talking, chattering away. Mrs. McDonnell said: "It can't happen, Joseph, she [Mrs. Thatcher] can't let no more die." Joe said: "Mummy, she let Bobby die and Frank is on his way out. He's singing his way out and he can't sing a note," he laughed.

Goretti had much to say to him, but she found she could not say anything. She wished to God, as she sat there, that she could be anywhere else in the world. He didn't look too bad, although he kept fidgeting and they kept catching each other's eye. Then, at last, the thirty minutes were over and he fumbled a goodbye, just holding her arm for a brief moment, and she was out in the open air with a sense of relief.

As they headed home the McDonnell family was worried, but not overly so. Sands was dead: there was no point in more dying, or being allowed to die. In fact some of Joe's friends had said, when they heard that he had been chosen to go on next, that it meant the IRA was signaling the end of the hunger strike was in sight: everyone knew Joe McDonnell would not be dying on hunger strike; he was married, wasn't he, with that pretty wife and don't forget how much he adores his kids. No, they wouldn't have chosen Joe McDonnell if they meant the hunger strike to go on . . . But when they got home and heard the news, Joe was right: singing Frank had gone.

A week later Goretti had a second visit, this time to the hospital. For some reason the prison authorities had decided to move Joe into the hospital far earlier than the previous hunger strikers. The routine was different, visiting the hospital. The minibus in which they took her there was the worst part: the windows were completely blacked out and there was a stench in it that she was later to associate with death. After the search—far more intense than for a normal visit—she was taken into his room and found him in bed. He was angry when he saw her.

"I don't want a visit here," he exclaimed, obviously not wanting her to see him as an invalid.

"But you must have been bad," she said, assuming he had suffered some sort of collapse.

"I'm still mobile, I can still get about," he said.

An argument started with the warder. She went to see the principal officer and eventually Joe was allowed to get up and go through with her to another room. The sense of having fought together—against "them"—and won broke the ice between them. He took a chair and she sat on his lap, giggling. It was magic. Somehow the warder keeping watch from a chair at the other end of the room receded into the distance; it was as if she were seeing him through the wrong end of a telescope. They talked and laughed. All was right with the world. Except Joe was going to die.

Between the visits, which came with ever-increasing frequency as Joe steadily deteriorated—one a week, then two a week, then three a week, then one a day—Goretti threw herself into the publicity battle to save the hunger strikers. Her life became frenetic, particularly after Joe was put up as a general election candidate in the Sligo Leitrim constituency, down on the west coast where Yeats was born. Her days were made up of frantic dashes, to the hustings, to lobby the politicians, to Belfast to take part in marches, demonstrations, and torchlight parades and to the Kesh to see Joe. She showed a purposeful confidence. During one meeting with Charles Haughey—with meek Mrs. Doherty in tow—she gave the Irish Prime Minister a tongue-lashing for claiming he did not know what the prisoners wanted. Mrs. Doherty broke down in tears.

And Goretti was good value for the media; not only an attractive figure for the cameramen, but—with the exception of Geraldine Sands, who had been separated and was never seen—the first wife of a dying hunger striker. The children only added to the pathos and Goretti, knowing this, tried to take them everywhere with her. She was courting criticism. Irish Republicans, for all the socialist rhetoric, are a conservative community as is most of Irish society, and Goretti was seen by some as flaunting herself and exploiting her children. Tensions were also developing between her and Joe's family. Goretti, having known Bobby and other IRA men well, was determinedly sticking to the prisoners' formal line. But Joe's parents were suspicious that the prisoners were being manipulated by the external leadership and wanted Goretti to intervene regardless, to take Joe off. Word began to reach her of secret meetings of relatives to which she was not being invited.

She was worried about the children—even Joe was questioning the need to take them on the election road. There had been an offer from a family in the United States to have them over there and she asked them if they wanted to go. Bernadette was enthusiastic—she seemed to understand more clearly than her little brother the horror of what was happening—and Goretti got passports for both of them. But the day before they were due to leave little Joe said no, he wasn't going. His life had been dominated by the absence of his father, he couldn't miss his presence now. So Bernadette went on her own and took the battle across the Atlantic, going on television to plead with America to save her father's life. Little Joe, meanwhile, went with his mother on the pilgrimages to the Kesh. Until one day his father, lying in his bed, asked Goretti to hand him the ashtray because he could no longer see it. And Goretti fetched the ashtray and handed it to Joe and saw little Joe looking at his father's eyes, saying nothing. When the next visit came little Joe said no, he wasn't going to the Kesh today, he was going to go and play soccer with his mates, because his dad wasn't too well last time and he'd prefer to wait until he was better.

The ICJP spent three hours in the Kesh with the prisoners on that Saturday, July 4—Joe's fifty-seventh day without food. Maura was up that day on a visit, with her eldest brother, Robert, and a sister-in-law, Mary—the wife of another brother, Patsy, who had come over from Canada to help the family. When they arrived at the Kesh they were told that the visit had been called off because the ICJP was coming in to see the hunger strikers. But eventually they were allowed in, with the warning that as soon as the meeting with the ICJP was due to start they would have to leave. In the hospital an orderly touched Maura by the arm and said: "Don't be getting alarmed when you get in." She could feel sweat breaking out. As usual she was the first into the room—she always rushed ahead of the others.

"He's dead," she thought when she saw him, lying still and pale with hands clasped on his chest. "He's dead and they've sent me in here." She went to the bed and put a hand on him. He opened his eyes. "Yes?" he said. Maura told him that they could not stay long, explaining what was happening with the commissioners. Joe argued with her, saying he wanted them there to tell him what was happening. She reassured him that they would be meeting the commissioners anyway, afterwards, and would be able to tell him everything.

"What are you thinking?" she asked him.

"I'm not thinking of anything."

"Well I'd like to think you were thinking of something," she teased him. "What are you thinking of?"

"I can see a whole lot of fields and a big house."

"What else?" she asked. Then she saw he was choking. "It doesn't matter, Joseph, don't be telling me what you're thinking of . . ." Maura said. She had realized what it was: the old grief. He was thinking of their house when they first moved into it. There were only four bedrooms, for eleven of them, but it had seemed so big because they had moved to it from a two-bedroom house in the Lower Falls. And when they had moved the area had not been built up and there were fields all around it . . . when his kid sister, Bernadette, was alive. On his own deathbed he was still mourning the lost Bernadette.

An orderly came in and said: "We're going to have to cut your visit short."

"Joe, we're going to have to go."

When Maura and the other two came out they were taken to meet the commissioners. A priest with them said: "We think everything's going to be all right."

"What do you mean?" asked Maura.

"Everything will be all right," repeated the priest. Her brother, Robert, started crying and so did Maura.

At home they were phoned by the commission and invited to a meeting at the Greenan Lodge Hotel. There they and the other relatives were briefed on what was happening. The commissioners tried not to raise their hopes too high: the hunger strikers themselves had seemed hopeful, but the main obstacle was their obviously deep distrust of the authorities.

Hopes were encouraged on Saturday, July 4, when the prisoners issued their most conciliatory statement of the whole hunger strike, saying that they were not looking for any special privileges—as against other prisoners—and that Britain could meet their demands with no "sacrifice of principle." They added that from statements made by the Secretary of State it appeared that he had misunderstood what they were asking for and they appealed to him to reexamine the precise proposals which they were making.

Joe was worried about birthdays again. Deep down, despite all the cynicism, there was a childish innocence in Joe and it showed in his passion for birthdays, Easter and Christmas. Goretti's birthday was in a week's time and Bernadette's on the following Friday. He was worried he did not have anything to give them. So he hummed a song for Goretti, as her present. It was Dr. Hook's: "We Never Got to Hear Those Violins."

On Sunday the commissioners were back into the Kesh again for another hour-long session with the hunger strikers. This time Joe McDonnell didn't make it; his colleagues had decided he was too far gone to follow the discussion. Afterwards three of them were allowed to visit McFarlane. There had been argument with the authorities over that, and eventually the concession was made that if McFarlane named three of them as "visitors" they could see him. The bishop, Fr. Crilly and Hugh Logue were chosen—Connolly and Brian Gallagher waited in a side room, praying.

While the commissioners were occupying center stage, at least in their eyes and those of the media, the hard bargaining was in fact going on in the wings. The Foreign office had relaunched the "Mountain Climber" initiative. While the commission was busily negotiating—or "clarifying the situation"—between the prisoners and the Northern Ireland Office, the Foreign Office was talking directly to the external leadership of the IRA, through the medium of the same middleman as had been used in December.

The channel had been reopened by the Foreign Office in the wake of the conciliatory July 4 statement by the prisoners, in which they had insisted that their five demands could be met without any departure from "principle" on the Government's part. The Mountain Climber had told Adams, through their middlemen, that provided it led to an immediate end to the hunger strike, the Government was prepared to issue a statement setting out agreed concessions. The Foreign Office, in its first offer, had conceded the prisoners' main demand of their own clothing—all prisoners in the north would get it, irrespective of the reasons they were in jail, so that the Government could claim it was no recognition of any "special" status. Visits and other such privileges had been agreed: the protesting prisoners would have them all restored on the ending of the hunger strike. But the prisoners were sticking on work, association and the restoration of lost remission. On work the Foreign Office was prepared to fudge the issue, suggesting that the main prop would be domestic tasks, such as cleaning, laundry and kitchen duties, together with "constructive work" such as building a chapel in the prison—the proposal put forward by Cardinal O Fiaich to Roy Mason so many years before—making toys for charities and studying for the Open University, or other educational courses. The prisoners wanted self-education to be the main prop, while being prepared to do maintenance work. The Foreign Office was offering nothing new on free association, arguing that the prisoners were already allowed to mix during leisure hours, in the evenings and at weekends, and that what they were demanding was "unsupervised" association, which would create unacceptable security problems—paramilitary activities like those which went on in the Cages. The prisoners had retorted that they only wanted free association in the wings and that there was no requirement that control be restricted—they would not interfere with the supervisory duties of warders. The Government had made a vague offer to restore a proportion of lost remission; the prisoners wanted it all back—for some of the men it meant an extra year or more in jail.

The Mountain Climber also offered to arrange for a Sinn Fein representative to go into the jail to discuss the negotiations with the hunger strikers and McFarlane. The IRA, in order to test the authority of the Mountain Climber, nominated one of the best-known Republican figures, Danny Morrison. Nicknamed "Pennies" or "Bangers," Morrison had been allowed into the jail in similar circumstances during the first hunger strike, but after its collapse had been banned from the prison. The Mountain Climber demonstrated his authority not only by overriding the ban, but by getting him on a Sunday—when visits are anyway not allowed to the prison. So while the Irish Commission for Justice and Peace were hurrying in and out of the Kesh, under the public spotlight, Morrison was inside the jail engaged in a completely separate, secret initiative.

To Brownie Monday 6.7.81 11 P.M. from Bik
Comrade Mor, I couldn't get writing to you before now as I was out of the block . . . Anyway Pennies will have filled you in on main pointers. The Bean Uasal has a time table of meetings, OK. At them all the same line was pushed by the Commission. You should have the main points from Pennies. They have maintained to myself and hunger strikers that principle of five demands is contained within the stuff they are pushing and that Brits won't come with anything else. I spent yy [yesterday] outlining our position and pushing our Saturday document as the basis for a solution. I said parts of their offer were vague and much more clarification and confirmation was needed to establish exactly what the Brits were on about. I told them that the only concrete aspect seemed to be clothes and no way was this good enough to satisfy us. I saw all hunger strikers yesterday and briefed them on the situation. They seemed strong enough and can hold the line alright. They

did so last night when Commission met them. There was nothing extra on offer—they just pushed their line and themselves as guarantors over any settlement. The hunger strikers pushed to have me present, but NIO refused this and Commission wouldn't lean hard enough on NIO. The lads also asked for NIO representative to talk directly to them, but the Commission say this is not on at all as NIO won't wear. During the session H. Logue suggested drafting a statement on behalf of hunger strikers asking for Brits to come in and talk direct, but lads knocked him back. A couple of them went out and made a phone call to NIO on getting me access to meeting and on getting NIO rep. They didn't really try for me, according to Lorny, because when asked they said they didn't want to push too hard and been put off by the Brits' firm refusal. Meeting terminated about midnight and Bishop O'Mahoney and J. Connolly paid me a short visit just to let me know the crack. Since then I haven't seen anyone except Lorny and Mick Devine on the way back to the block this morning. Requests to see hunger strikers and O/Cs have not been answered at all . . . I'm instructing Lorny to tell hunger strikers (if they are called together) not to talk with anyone till they get their hands on me. OK? By the way Joe was unable to attend last night's session. There's not really much more I can say at present. I sincerely hope you have been successful in all your efforts. I couldn't let other blocks have the full crack in writing in case the comm was lost . . . This comm will likely be ancient history by the time you receive it. I'm hoping and praying that we all do the right thing. Love to all. Take care and God Bless always. Bik.

Brownie from Bik Tue 7.7.81 10 P.M.
. . . I don't know if you've thought on this line, but I have been thinking that if we don't pull this off and Joe dies then the RA [IRA] are going to come under some bad stick

from all quarters. Everyone is crying the place down that a settlement is there and those Commission chappies are convinced that they have breached Brit principles. Anyway we'll sit tight and see what comes . . .

The ICJP initiative had placed the IRA leadership, both inside and outside the prison, in an agonizing dilemma because the Mountain Climber had set a strict precondition for the secret talks: if there was any public reference to these negotiations they would immediately end and the Government would deny they had taken place.

The difficulty for the IRA was that the Mountain Climber appeared prepared to offer more for a settlement than the commission seemed to be getting from the Northern Ireland Office. The danger for them was that, if the commission persuaded the Government—as they appeared to be close to doing—that they had a chance of getting the prisoners to settle on the Northern Ireland Office's terms, then the Mountain Climber would shut down his negotiations. So they desperately needed to get the commission out of the way. But they were bound by the confidentiality clause with the Mountain Climber—he might break off contact if they broke confidence. And any attempt they made to block the commission's initiative without explaining this background would look like obstructionism—would fuel the suspicion, already planted by government pronouncements on hunger strikers' deaths, that the IRA leadership did not want a settlement. And anyway there was always the possibility that the Government would use the commission as a face-saving device to deliver the settlement, whichever way it was agreed.

But, outside the IRA leadership and the Foreign Office, everyone was now waiting on the commission and the tension was almost unbearable. Garret FitzGerald had announced he was canceling holiday plans, because the situation was too critical for him to be away.

The commissioners came out on Sunday night, feeling they had the basis for a settlement. The only question was whether they could get the guarantees. The prisoners were insisting that someone senior from the NIO had to go in to confirm the details of what was on offer; to "get the fine print from the horse's mouth." On Monday morning the commissioners worked on a written summary of what they believed was the Government's position. Then they received word that Adams wanted to see them.

Two of the commissioners, Fr. Crilly and Hugh Logue, slipped out by a back entrance of the hotel, through the downstairs bar, jumped into a battered old blue Sinn Fein car and raced off to a safe house where Adams and another Sinn Fein official were waiting for them. Adams had decided they had to take a chance and let the commission know about the contacts with the British Government—for no other reason than to explain why the Commission should withdraw. He told the two men what the Government had been offering—more than had been offered to the Commission—explaining that he believed the authorities were merely using the ICJP as an intelligence feed, as a cross-check to construct a strategy to win, or at least settle, the dispute. The commissioners were stunned by the disclosure. They returned to the Greenan Lodge Hotel to tell their colleagues. It was decided to confront Allison. They telephoned the minister, who reluctantly agreed to meet them, but only on condition it was private—that no word of the meeting got out. Logue telephoned his sister, who was living in Belfast, and asked her if she would pick them up and take them to Stormont. Connolly and Gallagher went downstairs and told the press that they wanted to give them a briefing and while the journalists crowded around them the other three slipped down to the bar, grabbed Logue's red-haired sister who was waiting for them, jumped in her Mini and drove off to Stormont to see Allison. The minister appeared genuinely surprised by the disclosure of the Foreign Office contacts with the Republicans. The commissioners pressed him to send a guarantor into the Kesh to confirm the deal. Allison said he would have to make a phone call. He returned and announced that he had approval. The guarantor would go in the following morning. It appeared that the disclosure by Adams and Morrison had embarrassed the Government into a final concession. The commissioners returned to the Greenan Lodge and telephoned the Kesh with a message to the chaplains to tell the hunger strikers an NIO official was coming in.

Adams, meanwhile, had received a rocket from the Mountain Climber—a message, through the middleman, that the Foreign Office was "deeply disturbed" by the abuse of confidence by which Allison had become involved. The message said that the line of contact was unknown to "the most senior of their people" and if the confidentiality was abused the secret initiative must be put at risk. But it seemed that the contact had not been broken.

By late on Tuesday morning the commissioners still had no word from the chaplains that the official had arrived. At 11:40 A.M. Bishop O'Mahoney telephoned Allison to find out what was happening. Allison said he wanted to see them again. The bishop refused, saying the only issue now was whether the official went in. The call was broken off part way through. Reconnected, Bishop O'Mahoney told the minister he was shocked, dismayed and amazed that the Government should be continuing with its game of brinkmanship. He said: "I beg you to get someone into prison and get things started." The call ended at 12:18 P.M. They decided to call a press conference for 1 P.M. to release a summary of what had been agreed by the Government and explain how they had failed to honor it. Five minutes before the press conference was due to start the Northern Ireland Office phoned and said the official would be going in in the afternoon, so they called off the press conference. At 4 P.M. the Northern Ireland Office said the official would be going in, but the document was still being drafted. At 5:55 P.M. the commission phoned Allison again to express concern. And again at 7:15 P.M. At 8:50 P.M. they were told an official would be going in shortly. At 10 P.M. Allison phoned to say no one would be going in that night, but that the delay would be to the prisoner's benefit. He reassured them that Joe McDonnell would hold out.

Joe was semi-comatose, saying nothing, just lying there making grunting noises, clearing his throat. The dribble bowl was at the side of his face, on his shoulder. He had been calling for Bernadette. The family did not know if it was his daugher or his sister, but, just in case, they phoned America and said Bernadette had better come back.

Maura dozed off for a while, sitting on the chair with her head resting on the bed next to Joe. The orderly shook her awake and said: "We want to change his bed." Maura said he was getting very cold and the orderly said: "Aye, we'll put another blanket on him then."

Gerry Adams was in a safe house in West Belfast, waiting by the telephone for more messages from the Foreign Office contact, the Mountain Climber. The calls usually came through in the early hours of the morning—deliberately timed, the Republicans assumed, to try and catch them when they were tired—so he had taken a break on Tuesday evening. When he got back in the early hours of the morning the Sinn Fein official manning the telephone in the parlor said: "Nothing, he's gone quiet."

At 2 o'clock on Wednesday morning the commissioners said Mass together in their makeshift bedroom at the Greenan Lodge. Fr. Toner had lent them a traveling Mass kit. Bishop O'Mahoney led them, the others sitting around on the four beds. It was a moving experience—they were all prayerful men and found they had been closely bonded by their shared experience. They went to bed at about 3 A.M. Shortly after 5 A.M. they were awakened by the telephone ringing.

The family was not really worried. They knew a deal had been done, the Church had shown once again that it could be relied on. It was quite fun, in fact—Fr. Murphy was teasing Maura that it was time she got married. They kept saying everything was going to be all right, the official was coming in tonight, Joe had a couple of days left in him, plenty of time. Then they got the message that the official couldn't make it that night, but would be in the next morning, at about 7:30 A.M. And it was decided that they should leave Joe alone for a while, just in case their presence was disturbing him—they wanted him as strong as possible for the morning. They went into the waiting room and Mrs. McDonnell climbed into the bed, the other two dozing off in chairs. At 4:50 A.M. Fr. Murphy woke them up. "Joe's passed away," he said. As they ran for his cell they saw Fr. Toner coming down the corridor, pulling on his trousers. Maura ran up to the body and began shouting: "Joseph, you're not dead, you're not dead, don't give in to them," shaking him by the shoulders. Their mother said: "Maura, leave him alone."

Bernadette, rushing back from America, was met at Dublin airport by Goretti's sister, who drove her up to Belfast. They turned off the motorway, into the Andersonstown Road, to find themselves facing burning barricades. "What's happening?" the sister asked a passerby through her window. "Don't you know? Joe McDonnell's dead."

To Brownie Wed 8.7.81 10.30 A.M. from Bik
Comrade, Just got confirmation that Joe died this morning. God rest his soul. No. 1 Gov. and NIO rep. called Lorny [Laurence McKeown] out to their office and read out a document (it was presented to all prisoners this morning about 9 A.M.). In brief, the document covers the NIO position

and says that nothing has happened since they issued their document on June 30th to lead the Secretary of State to think that anything in that document should be changed.

Norah McCabe, the mother of three small children, left her sister's home in West Belfast to get some cigarettes at a shop in the Falls Road. Two police Land Rovers were driving down the Falls. Nothing was happening, but as they passed the entrance to Linden Street one of the officers took a pot shot through his gun port with a plastic bullet and Norah McCabe was dead, aged thirty-three.

Further down the Falls Road, at 5:10 A.M., ten youths in a hijacked van crashed through the gates of a bus depot, hurling petrol and acid bombs at two soldiers guarding the premises. The soldiers opened fire and John Dempsey was dead, aged sixteen.

To Brownie Wed 8.7.81 from Bik
Comrade Mor, I'm just back from the hospital this minute. Couldn't get a comm done this morning; I was shipped out in the middle of a comm to you. Now I had a yarn with all the hunger strikers. They are all strong and determined. Very angry about Joe's death, as we all are. I emphasized the point of staying solid and keeping their clanns [families] in line . . . 'Pennies' had already informed them of 'Mountain Climber' angle and they accepted this as 100 per cent. They accept the view that the Brits, in trying to play us too close to the line, made a blunder and didn't reckon on Joe dying so quickly . . .

Brownie from Bik Wed 8.7.81 9.30 P.M.
Comrade Mor, got your comm today alright. I was wrecked when I read it. The whole thing could have

been settled now. You must be worn out cara. I know that what happened surprised the Brits. I sat here this morning and cursed them from the high heavens. I had a good idea they were operating every bloody angle they could lay their hands on to outflank us someway and take Joe to the brink. What a tragedy. I told you I was up in the hospital this morning. The boys were all very sound and strong. That's 100% though I'm worried about Kevin. His family as I told you got a special visit today and he is coming under pressure from them constantly. I told him to be gentle with them, but firm in getting the points across. You can let me know how the families are in general. Big Doc [Kieran Doherty] pulled his girl into line and says she's now sound. I gave them all another warning about Index [Fr. Toner] etc. No problems there at all. I have to tell you that after talking to them I felt somehow strengthened myself. Those men are an inspiration and that's the truth. I've never seen the likes of them. I only met Joe for the first time on Sat. past. He was in a dreadful state, cara, and could hardly hear me talking. Paddy had to repeat it to him occasionally. He couldn't see me clearly and couldn't raise his head. It wrecked me looking at him propped up on his wheelchair. Yet for all his suffering and weakness he was the first man to raise a row about making sure I had a good place at the table so that all the lads could hear what I had to say. When the medical orderly came in to hand around the blow [cigarettes] Joe was again making sure I wasn't left out. He didn't say much, but his few words touched me deeply. 'I might have a week or maybe only two days. Then again I could go tomorrow.' That was Sunday evening. Big Doc asked him how he felt about hanging on. 'No problem,' said Joe 'no problem.' He made a terrific impression on me and no mistake. Well cara, not much else just now . . .

They brought Joe home to Lenadoon, laying his coffin with its open top lengthways under the lounge window. Little Joe was broken. He ran up and down the lounge, moaning and crying. And then, in the tradition of the Irish wake, comrades, friends and neighbors filed in to say their last goodbyes. And of course some of the kids joined the queue two or three times, curious to see a dead hero. And little Joe spotted one of them and began shouting at him: "You've been through once, why are you coming again?" And then he went upstairs and fetched his football and took it across the road and began kicking it against a wall. And he kicked and kicked and kicked . . .

The prisoner stood with a loud "hi." They embraced and she used her body with confidence to block the line of sight from the control booth, her hand nudging into her jacket pocket. The tobacco. Their mouths met and he tongued the small package to her. No problem. They sat opposite each other, heads close together, and he began the monologue in Gaelic.

"There's a comm for Brigade and a letter. The O/C says to make sure . . ."

The time raced. The screw got talking to a colleague, giving the prisoner—sitting deliberately on the edge of his chair—a chance to grab the package from his pocket and slip it into his backside, talking all the while. It felt like tobacco and a pen. She said there was also a letter from his Ma and five letters for Ginty from his girl.

Her Gaelic was better than his; she said she'd learned it doing time in Armagh—two years on a possession charge. He had to ask her to repeat herself twice, once when he got confused by her pronunciation, the second time when he lost himself in the movements of her mouth and eyes. She was small, with mouse-colored hair, but attractive to a young man who had been without for so long. She knew the story of the wife and filled him in with some of the gossip. He would pass it on at Mass, it could not be shouted between the wings.

"OK," said the hovering screw.

"So, take care," she said. She looked into his eyes and the prisoner wondered for a moment if she was attracted. Or just sympathetic?

"Yourself, too," he said.

She was asking the screw for the toilet as they walked off, for a quick, early switch.

On the way back to the block they passed a group of conforming prisoners playing soccer in the snow and the sight started his screw off on a monologue. "You don't have to do the protest, you know, you's should go to your work—look at them young lads out there playing . . . athletic young lads, you're going to have arthritis and lumbago and what're you going to do when you're thirty, you'll be a physical wreck. Haven't left that cell for three years, you'll be an old man before you're thirty . . ."

The prisoner's mind wandered to his mother, worried she would not understand why he hadn't sent her a visit. The last was three months ago, when she'd brought her customary half ounce of tobacco up. It was chancy that day—the screw guarding him had been a right animal. In the middle of their conversation she had sat upright and openly flicked the parcel across the table at him.

"What the fuck d'ye do that for?" he had hissed when his heart had slowed down again.

"He looked away," she had whispered.

A yell in Gaelic reminded the prisoner that his monthly excursion to the fringes of the outside world was over: "D'ye get any?"

"Yo," he bellowed back at the window.

He stripped quickly in cell 26, tossing the uniform on the floor. He had a moment's worry that the package was not in deep enough, but the mirror search was cursory again and he had made it, wrapping the towel around his waist. As he came through the grille the chattering started.

"*So what's she like? What's she like?*"

"*She's gorgeous.*"

"*You make a hit?*"

"*Tell the O/C everything's fine,*" the prisoner shouted.

He gave his cellmate a quick rundown as he pulled his blankets on and then went to the door to enjoy some of the chaff.

"*How much you got?*"

"*About half an ounce. Would've got an ounce, but Ginty's got five Gettysburg Addresses in it from his girl. Hey, Ginty, next time I get a visit why don't you stick Elizabeth Regina on the back of my neck, then they'll know I'm a postbox.*"

"*Aww, shut up and get them over.*"

"*Take it easy, you'll get them tonight. Here, ask Hector how his other nose is doing.*" Hector's vanity was a byword: he routinely carried a comb inside himself.

"*Wha . . .?*"

"*She said he was growing another nose last time she saw him.*" Bellows of laughter.

"*Pimply eejit.*"

"*She say anything about the kitten?*"

"*She said the kitten came back to the Center after seeing the Elephant, sank into a chair and said: 'You should have seen him.'*"

"*What's she mean by that? Probably meant Paul Newman.*"

"*You're jealous, Herr Moo.*"

"*Yeah, she wore a fur coat to see me,*" said the Elephant. "*Hinkey says she wore a duffel coat for you, Moo.*"

"*Gentlemen, gentlemen. You belong to a disciplined organization. Besides, how can an elephant make it with a kitten?*"

"*A declaration of intentions is called for, methinks.*"

"*Ahh, shudupp.*"

The banging of the grilles as screws left for tea signaled 4 P.M. and a quiet hour. The wing settled down again, another

Irish class starting down the corridor. The prisoner pulled his mattress flat and started telling his cellmate about the tobacco from the Loyalist. The conversation drifted inevitably to the girl.

"She wasn't bad. Dead right for you."

"Na, doesn't sound my style . . . Let's see what you got."

The prisoner slid his packet out and began carefully unpeeling it. Half an ounce of tobacco with a plastic pen refill buried in it, the small clump of letters for Ginty and the smaller one for himself. Popping his mother's letter in his mouth, in case of a sudden cell search, he undid the package he had given to his cellmate earlier and began repacking it. The point of the pen he buried into the tobacco—it could rip his insides otherwise—with a ball of cigarette papers, a lighter wheel, spare flints and a tiny blade bound up in sponge and bread. "At least I don't have a radio," he thought as he rammed the completed package back inside himself. He tongued his mother's letter out, peeled it open and began reading.

EIGHT

*"In the blackmailing battle to achieve political
status for thugs, they had ordered him to starve
to death. To the IRA Joe McDonnell is worth
far more dead than alive. The men with the guns
are weeping no tears. For them the funeral was
no more than another well-managed melodrama,
another notch on the gun barrel in their
propaganda war."*

—Daily Mail, *July 11, 1981*

As Joe McDonnell's coffin was carried out of his house, on
July 10—Bernadette's birthday—little Joe, who did not want
his father to go, clung on to it, weeping. It was the most
heart-breaking public spectacle of the entire hunger strike and
somehow it was a turning point in the whole tragedy. It was
almost as if, having got so close to reconciliation through the
offices of the ICJP, the island lapsed back into a mood of sullen
confrontation; a mood which could erupt in violence at any
moment, as it did during the McDonnell funeral procession.

Adams arrived late for the funeral; he had been attending
the earlier burial of a youth shot dead by the army. As he
walked with the mourners down the Shaws Road, in West
Belfast, he began to have a niggling feeling that something
was wrong. He could see a police Land Rover on high ground
a couple of hundred yards away; they were closer than usual.
And the hovering helicopters: as one left, probably to get
fuel, it was immediately replaced, which was also unusual.

The procession came to a halt outside the Busy Bee shopping center for the salute. It was close to the spot where the salute had been fired for Bobby Sands, which was perilous: repetition always poses danger in northern Ireland. As the photographers pressed forward to get the gunmen into their viewfinders Adams found himself hemmed in, facing the coffin. A former IRA Chief of Staff, John Joe McGirl—who was under an exclusion order, subject to arrest on sight north of the border—was standing near him. "Isn't this dangerous?" Adams asked him. "No, it'll be OK," said McGirl.

Above them in the helicopter Detective Sergeant Gilmore Brown was watching with a pair of high-powered binoculars. He saw three men in black berets and paramilitary uniforms materialize from the crowd, line up alongside the coffin and raise rifles to their shoulders. Three puffs of smoke came up from each barrel.

On the ground the coffin was loaded into the hearse and the cortege started to move again. Adams called to the organizing steward to hold it, he wanted to make sure the firing party was with them. But when he turned back the gunmen were already heading off for their prearranged safe house.

In the air Sgt. Brown was tracking the gunmen's path with his binoculars and an Ordnance Survey map, radioing their movements down to police and army units waiting at the side. He saw the gunmen walking along the side of a house in the Andersonstown Road and into another house backing on to it, 20 St. Agnes Drive. He shouted a message for an army unit to go for number 20.

The message was received by a nine-man army unit on standby a few streets away. They roared down to St. Agnes Drive in four Land Rovers, the soldiers leaping off and sprinting to cover the exits at number 20. Lance Corporal Mark Adams ran around the back. A man came running past him, but simultaneously he saw another man carrying a rifle clambering out of the kitchen window. "Army. Stop, or I'll fire," shouted the corporal. The gunman tried to turn, still holding the rifle, and Corporal Adams triggered one shot at him. The gunman fell backwards. The corporal ran to the front, to report it to his color sergeant, then tried to break the front door down. Hearing noises at the back he started to run around, only to find his color sergeant clutching his hands which he had cut trying to open the side door. Corporal Adams forced the door himself and rushed through into the kitchen. There was a rifle lying on the windowsill, the barrel sticking out of the window, and a man on the floor, clutching his side. The wounded man was a namesake, Patrick Adams— younger brother of Gerry Adams.

Shots rang out outside, as other soldiers opened fire on two men running with rifles. Both stumbled and fell, as if hit, but recovered and ran on. The soldiers raced after them, straight into a barrage of bricks and bottles being hurled by the mourners, which forced them to retreat. Screams and shouts went up to the thump of plastic bullet guns. An ambulance arrived to collect Adams, but the military insisted he would have to go in a Saracen armored troop carrier. An uncle of the wounded man lay down in the road in front of the Saracen, to prevent it getting to the house. Eventually the troops departed with their captives and the funeral procession reformed, making its way down the Andersonstown Road to Milltown cemetery.

McDonnell was buried next to his colleague in that attack on the Dunmurray furniture store, Bobby Sands. John Joe McGirl, who had acted as Joe's election agent down in Leitrim, delivered the oration, quoting Padraig Pearse: "He may seem the fool who has given his all, by the wise men of the world; but it was the apparent fools who changed the course of Irish history."

Funeral parades were held for McDonnell in towns and cities around Ireland, but it was noticeable that the crowds were smaller than previously. In Sligo, where Joe had so nearly become the local MP, an estimated 300 turned out, compared with some 8,000 at the time of Sands's funeral. In Dublin, where there had been appeals for "the biggest possible mobilization," a mere 400 marched from the General Post Office to Parliament. Outside the GPO, where the bullet holes from 1916 still stud the classical columns, another former IRA Chief of Staff, Daithi O Conaill, told the crowd: "The British Government understand only one thing: force."

At the Greenan Lodge Hotel in West Belfast the five men from the ICJP were disconsolate. On the night of Joe's death they had staged a press conference in which they made a furious attack on the British Government, detailing what had happened and accusing London and the Northern Ireland Office of having failed to honor undertakings and of "clawing back" concessions. Britain shrugged it off, Michael Allison conceding he had received medical advice that McDonnell had longer to live; the Northern Ireland Office declared bluntly that ministers were not interested in engaging in public exchanges with the commission.

The commissioners waited for a few days, to see if there was any chance of resuming the initiative, filling in time giving interviews. Fr. Crilly had a chance to demonstrate his linguistic ability, when the BBC asked for an interview for their Welsh-language station and he was able to deliver it in Gaelic. Jerome Connolly had a go at French for a Canadian television crew. But in the middle of the interview he broke down, tears streaming down his cheeks. Brian Gallagher and Hugh Logue drove to Dublin to brief Garret FitzGerald on what had happened. FitzGerald dispatched his Minister of Foreign Affairs to London to urge Britain to reopen contacts with the ICJP. But the commission's role was over, as McFarlane was making clear inside the Kesh.

Brownie [Gerry Adams] from Bik Fri 10.7.81 10 P.M.
. . . No one will be talking to them [ICJP] unless I am present and then it will only be to tell them to skit OK. More

than likely you lot have already done a fair job on them this evening. Sincerely hope so anyway. If we can render them ineffective now, then we leave the way clear for a direct approach without all the ballsing about. The reason we didn't skite them in the first instance was because I was afraid of coming across as inflexible or even intransigent. Our softly softly approach with them has left the impression that we were taking their proposals as a settlement. I'm sorry now I didn't tell them to go and get stuffed.

An Bean Uasal from Bik Fri 10.7.81
Comrade, got your comm today alright. Find here a statement attacking ICJP as requested. Also tribute to Joe. We held a parade this evening . . .

Brownie Sun 12.7.81 from Bik
. . . Talking to Pat [McGeown] this morning and he reckons we should not have cut out Commission. I explained the crack in full, but he's one for covering all exits no matter what the score is. Just thought I'd mention that OK? . . .

Michael Allison, meanwhile, had flown off to Washington on what was described as a fightback against Republican propaganda. It was badly needed. Staff at the British Consulate in New York's Third Avenue were complaining bitterly of the harangues they were being subjected to in the street. "When I go to work I am called a bastard and a murderer and a liar and again when I leave," said one. Republicans in the U.S. were also jubilant over an announcement that a scheduled visit to America by Princess Margaret during the weekend had been called off on security grounds. "It's the first time a member of the Royal Family has been afraid to visit a friendly country," exulted one leading Republican in Washington.

Allison went on television to tell America that the ICJP were a bunch of well-meaning amateurs and that "the Irish

terrorist suicide" was like the Japanese Kamikaze pilots of
the Second World War. He added: "We have another week
or fortnight before the next suicide takes place and we hope
we might be able to make a bit of progress in that period."

The medical advice he was receiving was proving of doubtful value: he had been wrong about Joe McDonnell and he
was about to be proved wrong again because on Sunday, July
12 the Hurson family got a message from a priest who had
been in prison, warning them that Martin was in a bad way
and they had better try and see him.

Well Liam, here is a few details about myself . . . Name
Edward Martin Hurson, address Cappagh Road, Dungannon, Tyrone. D.O.B. 13.9.54. Next of kin: Father called
John. Nine of a family: 6 sisters—three brothers, that's
counting myself. Date arrested 9.11.76. Held for three
days in Omagh, Cookstown and Clougher police station,
beaten up in Omagh until I signed. There was a good few
marks and bruises on my body. Four others who were
jointly charged along with that fellow Jimmy Rafferty from
Dungannon that had the tribunal against the [Special]
branch a few weeks ago. Was arrested the same morning
as myself and he was beaten up by the same branch men
in Armagh barracks. So his case and mine were tied up
together. My barrister fought my case by using Jimmy's
brutality case alongside my own. He was being questioned
about the same things as myself. He came to the court
to give evidence for us. I was charged on the 13th Nov. I
had four charges, the first one was attempted murder of
UDR men when a land mine went off—the jeep fell into
a crater. The second charge was blowing up a van when
a land mine went off. The lads who were in the van both
got injured, not bad. This van was mistaken for a Brit
Land Rover. The third charge was planting bombs in a
rock quarry and wrecking a lot of equipment. The fourth

charge was IRA membership. I was in the Crum[lin Road prison] on remand for about two weeks then I was moved to the Cages, Long Kesh. I was there for one year before the trial started in November 1977. When the court case started the five of us refused to recognize the court but as the trial went on the barrister told us to change our plea and fight the case, because the barrister got more medical evidence on my case. Then when trial began things were looking [up] for myself as my medical evidence was the best of the five. But after the trial was over the judge gave me 20 years for the attack on the UDR, 20 for the van attack, 15 for the quarry bomb and 5 for membership. I then put an appeal in early in 1978 which took two days, then got the verdict on April 1 1979. Got new trial. On remand for six months, trial again in September, got one of the charges dropped—UDR one—but got sentenced to the same again on the other charges. Put another appeal in, but got beat back. I am on the blanket three years. Got a good few beatings. I was in the prison hospital for a month in December '78 after I got force-washed and badly beaten up by the screws. No medical complaints. If you want any more details let me know. From Martin H5.

20.3.81
Well, Liam Og [Sinn Fein official], Sent you out a few details yesterday, Thursday the 19th. Hope you got them alright, so I have another few for you here. I was never in jail before, but when I was outside the cops and Brits were always lifting me. I never had any past connections. The names of the school I went to were St. Joseph Primary School and then on to St. Patrick's School, Dungannon. Before I came into jail I was working for Powerscreen International Coalisland, Dungannon doing fitting and welding. Spent a couple of years working for McAlpine. I was at a lot of Sinn Fein marches, GAA etc. . . . I was in

H3 on the blanket where I got all the beatings. The wing
moves were very bad at that time . . . my father is over 70
now my mother is dead. So I will finish off now . . .

The home outside Dungannon where Hurson was born and
raised was a small farmhouse perched on a hillside which his
father had bought some forty years before. It was a smallholding: ten acres of land on which they grew potatoes and kept a
couple of dairy cows and the occasional pig. Martin's father,
John, earned their main income as a laborer working for the
local county council while his mother, Mary Anne, kept a
vegetable garden and some chickens—selling eggs to the local
grocer. There were nine of them in the three-bedroom house.
Meat was a luxury, usually only to be found on the kitchen
table at Christmas. And in Martin's childhood there was no
electricity or running water. But they were not starving and
the children were adequately clothed. Martin himself grew up
into a 5 foot, 10 inch gregarious and good-looking youth, who
was very close to his mother. She died suddenly when he was
thirteen and the trauma cost him his memory—he recovered
it after a week when he overturned a tractor on a steep slope.

McFarlane did not know Hurson at all. His place on the
second hunger strike was in a sense a posthumous choice by
Sands, who did know him and had him listed as an early
replacement on the first hunger strike—enough of a recommendation for McFarlane. In fact Hurson already had a small
place in the history of the "Troubles," as a bit-player in a
case which became a *cause célèbre*, over police interrogation
techniques in the mid- and late-1970s.

He was picked up in 1976 after a wave of IRA attacks in the
area, including the killing of a postman delivering letters—a
part-time member of the Ulster Defense Regiment—and the
wounding of two police reservists in separate gun and bomb
attacks. At the time a new police chief, Kenneth Newman—
later to head Scotland Yard—and a newly appointed Secretary

of State, the "Barnsley Brawler" Roy Mason, were engaged in
a particularly tough crackdown on terrorism; toughness which
included, whether or not it was sanctioned, police brutality
in interrogations. Hurson was taken to a police station in
the town of Omagh, beaten up and confessed. Transferred
to another police station to be charged, he complained about
the earlier beatings. He was promptly interrogated a second
time—this time without any beating but, he was later to claim,
under threat of being returned to Omagh—and confessed
again. A series of court cases ensued, in which the Omagh
confession was eventually thrown out, but the second confession was upheld and his sentence of twenty years confirmed.
Another man arrested with him on that day in 1976, James
Rafferty, was more fortunate, at least in the longer term: after
being badly beaten up at Omagh he was released without
charge and went on to fight a lengthy and widely publicized—
although eventually unsuccessful—legal battle to get damages
from the police.

Hurson was well liked in the Kesh: you would have to
be hard-pressed to dislike Martin with his jocular humor.
"How're you doing . . . how's things . . . aaah 100 percent,"
was his invariable greeting. His famous quip was: "Jesus,
but this is a great wee protest." He had the rude health of a
country boy; he was young, at twenty-four, and while he had
suffered jail conditions for five years there was no reason to
believe that he wouldn't go "the distance" on hunger strike:
Hughes, after all, had lasted fifty-nine days, and he had been
badly injured, while Sands had made sixty-six. So the Hursons
had no reason to believe that weekend that Martin—after
forty-two days—was in any immediate danger.

On that Sunday Martin's two brothers, Brendan and Francis, were away at H-Block rallies—Brendan in Camlough,
South Armagh, and Francis on the other side of the island, in
Donegal—when they received a message from the priest that
they should get into the Kesh. Brendan jumped in a car with

Bernadette McAliskey and Martin's girlfriend, Bernadette Donnelly, and dashed for Belfast.

Martin's father had already gone in with his twenty-one-year-old daughter, Rosaleen, and a son-in-law, Paddy McElvogue. They had been stunned when they walked in the room: Martin was flailing his arms around in the bed, his head and eyes rolling. Rosaleen was so frightened at the sight of him she was taken down the corridor by a warder for a drink of water. She returned to the room where her father and Paddy were standing gazing from the foot of the bed. She walked to Martin's side and called out her name, her father's and Paddy's. There was no response. She repeated them and then shouted them a third time. Martin at last responded, whispering the names of Brendan and his wife, and then theirs. They were called out and taken into a doctor's room. The doctor went to see Martin and came back after a few minutes, to tell them it was too late to do anything; if they tried to save him now he would be a cabbage. The three returned to Martin's room and stood there, looking helplessly; then they could not take it any longer and told the warders they wanted to leave.

As they got out of the minibus near the gates they walked into Brendan, who had been allowed in, but without Bernadette Donnelly or McAliskey. The warders said they would have to get back in the van if they wanted to talk, so they climbed in and the doors were closed on them. Rosaleen, a 5 foot blue-eyed brunette, was in tears and their father looked ashen-faced. Both of them said they couldn't face going back. Paddy said he would, but the warders wouldn't let him. So they said goodbye and Brendan went in alone.

In Donegal Francis had just walked into a hotel for a bite to eat before the evening H-Block rally when a receptionist came in and said there was an urgent message to phone the Kesh. As he walked to the phone Francis ran into the SDLP leader, John Hume, and told him about the message.

"I think Martin's dead," said Francis.

"God, he's not," said Hume.

They went to the phone together and Hume telephoned the Kesh for him. He was told that there was no crisis, but that if Francis could get to the prison before the gates were locked, at 8 P.M., he could have a visit. It was about 100 miles—a two-and-a-half-hour drive on the twisting roads—and there was no chance of getting there in time, but Francis got into his car and started the journey. He arrived at his home at Carrickmore at about 9 P.M. and called the prison again, to be told he could not get in, but there was no cause for panic.

Sitting in the back of a minibus, trundling down to the prison hospital, Brendan felt both lonely and a little scared. He was taken down the corridor to Martin's room, past the rows of cell-like wooden doors. An orderly in a white coat accompanying him slipped back the peephole on one, looked in and then unlocked the door and swung it open. They walked in. Brendan was shocked: Martin was swinging his arms from side to side, and his head was heaving. On one side was a heart monitor, but it was not connected. Brendan grabbed his hands and shouted: "Martin, can you hear me?"

"Br . . . bu . . . bu," was all Martin could say, his eyes rolling. Brendan tried to hold his arms still.

Later a doctor came in and inspected him. Brendan asked what would happen if they tried to save him now. The doctor said there would be permanent brain damage. He connected the heart monitor.

At about 2 A.M. Fr. Murphy came in and joined Brendan. Martin was still thrashing around. The priest said the last rites and from that moment Martin seemed to calm down—the heaving and swinging of the arms stopped. At about 4 A.M. the blip on the heart monitor became weaker and weaker and then flattened out and a red light went on.

"Is it all over, then?" Brendan asked the doctor.
"It's all over," agreed the doctor.

Brownie from Bik Mon 13.7.81 1 P.M.
Comrade Mor, we heard around 11 A.M. about Martin's
tragic death. In all honesty it has been the biggest shock
to date and has left me shattered. No way was anyone
even thinking on Martin as anywhere near the danger
mark. I can only assume that the infection in his stomach
has somehow been the cause of his untimely death. May
God have mercy on his soul. I will have to move immediately with a replacement. It will be Matt Devlin (Tyrone).
He was on the second squad on first hunger strike. This
means that the usual clearance procedure will be skipped
over. You'll have to accept my judgment on him being
sound. He is fully aware of exactly what this hunger strike
means—i.e. that in a short period he stands to lose his
life. He understands the position clearly and yesterday he
reaffirmed his intention to embark on hunger strike. He
has from the outset volunteered for hunger strike and has
repeatedly forwarded his name when I asked for volunteers
to stand by as replacements. I have confidence in his ability to see hunger strike through to whatever it holds for
him . . . Now with Kieran and Kevin in the crisis I will need
to have replacements cleared and commed by A/C [Army
Council]. The IRSP replacement is Liam McCloskey (this
wing) from Dungiven (same charge as Kevin). I would ask
you to comm George Murdoch (St James) H5 as our next
replacement . . .

As Hurson lay dying on Sunday night, prisoners in the
Kesh could hear in the distance the thump of Lambeg drums,
the sound of Protestant Ulster on the march. July 12 is the
anniversary of the victory in 1690 of William of Orange over

the Catholic, King James II, at the Battle of the Boyne—a time when Loyalists pour on to the streets of northern towns in their tens of thousands to celebrate the defeat of Catholicism and reiterate their determination never to capitulate to the "Whore of Rome." Since July 12, 1981 fell on a Sunday, the celebrations had been delayed for a day. Brendan left his brother's body, to be met by his parish priest, Fr. McGuckin, outside. As they set off for Tyrone they passed carloads of Protestants driving around the prison, shouting "another bastard dead."

The mood of confrontation, not only with Protestant Ulster, was summed up by the battle standard of the 45 Marine Commando, flying from the army observation post on top of the "Planet of the Irps"—Divis Flats—in the Lower Falls. The post overlooked bent street poles and smoking rubble left by the early-morning rioting which had followed news of Hurson's death. Five soldiers, a civilian and a policeman were slightly injured in gun and blast-bomb attacks during the day.

They buried Martin at St. John's Chapel, near his Cappagh home. The pastoral setting provided a contrasting backdrop to the funeral procession: three youths in hoods and paramilitary uniforms walking behind the lone piper in company with fifteen priests to the freshly dug grave and then firing the final salute with pistols, as about 1,000 mourners waved fists and gave the V for victory sign to army helicopters clattering overhead. At the requiem Mass Fr. McGuckin echoed appeals of Irish priests down the centuries for a just and peaceful solution to the dreadful agony of Ireland. "May God grant that the death of Martin Hurson may be the last of its kind," he said.

"I am sure that Oliver Plunkett who was hung, drawn and quartered at Tyburn and Joan of Arc, the young French maiden who was burned at the stake, were among those who received Martin and placed him beside Ireland's glorious dead," said

Sean Lynch, Martin's election agent in the southern election, in the graveside oration.

In Washington, the Irish Embassy was trying to give effect to Fr. McGuckin's wish, at a lunch for the U. S. President. Ronald Reagan had been invited to the embassy for the conferral of an honorary fellowship of the Royal College of Surgeons in Ireland on Nancy's stepfather—who at eighty-six had been unable to make the trip to Ireland to fetch it. The Ambassador, Sean Donlon, used the opportunity to present the President with a letter from FitzGerald, appealing for U.S. assistance in bending the Iron Lady. Britain had already sent out signals to the White House that the Lady would not be bending on this issue and Reagan was to refuse the Irish plea. But it was all overtaken with the sudden announcement from London by Sir Humphrey Atkins of yet another intervention.

Kieran Doherty was in a bad way. On Sunday he had been in a wheelchair, his right leg had lost all feeling, his hearing was going, his vision was blurred and he was vomiting green bile. On Wednesday morning he was given the last rites. At 7 o'clock in the evening the eight hunger strikers were all called together in the prison hospital and addressed by the Governor, Hilditch, and an official from the Northern Ireland Office. The civil servant said he was not there to negotiate with them, only to read out a statement from the Secretary of State. The statement said the Government "has received an offer from the International Committee of the Red Cross to visit the prisons concerned in Northern Ireland under that part of its statutes which enables it to study the conditions of prisoners other than prisoners of war." The committee had made it clear the offer was "not on the basis of the Geneva Conventions of 1949, which deal with the conditions of prisoners of war, but in exercise of its right to take humanitarian initiatives." Atkins added: "The ICRC have made it clear to the Government that the sole aim of their visit will be to assess and, if necessary, to make recommendations to improve the conditions of imprisonment in Northern Ireland."

Despite the qualifications, the wording of the statement was transparent. The Red Cross had been trying to get into the Maze for five years and had been repeatedly blocked by the Government, partly because of the POW overtones such a visit would carry. But what with the Irish prime minister petitioning the American president there was an urgent need to fill the gap left by the ICJP. The only question was how the prisoners would react.

As soon as the statement had been completed the prisoners asked Hilditch for McFarlane. He was duly ferried over to the hospital and allowed a lengthy session with the hunger strikers. He told them immediately that it was simply another attempt to undermine them and should be treated as such. If the Brits wanted to bring in outside groups for a face-saving cover-up to a settlement that was their concern; as far as the prisoners were concerned they were only interested in direct contact with the Government. Any attempt at mediation by outsiders had to be blocked. If the Red Cross made an approach to them as individuals they should immediately be told that there would only be talks if the hunger strikers' nominees were present—McFarlane himself and Danny Morrison. The Red Cross could make all the inquiries, investigations or recommendations they liked, but settlement of the hunger strike would come only when the Brits talked to them. The hunger strikers agreed with McFarlane. Doherty was with them, in a wheelchair, but could hardly speak. Kevin Lynch was also looking weak. As McFarlane left, Doc [Doherty] whispered to him that he was sound—"no problem."

The Red Cross team flew in from Switzerland the next day. There were three of them: Frank Schmidt, the leader, Philippe Grand d'Hauteville and Remi Russbach. They stopped off at London's Heathrow airport, where they had brief talks with a government official, before flying on to Belfast. They were inside the Maze within two hours of their arrival.

To Brownie Thursday 16.7.81 10 P.M.
Comrade Mor, here goes with today's crack. These members of Red Cross were in with hunger strikers. The lads sent for me immediately and there was no problem . . . Basically they were here to examine prison positions thoroughly and to make recommendations to the government on improvements etc. They have rules of practice etc.—usual score. Now they said they hoped they could be of some help in bringing about a settlement to this issue. Though they would not ask us to terminate the hunger strike. I got in straight away . . . I said it had the appearance of a repetition of last week's catastrophe with the ICJP . . . I told them that Brits only using them to create illusion of movement and trying to sink us simultaneously. . . . I told them if they wanted to help they could make a recommendation to the Brits that they talk directly and that their talk is about a settlement based on our five demands . . . he [Schmidt] asked why they [British] wouldn't talk to date. I said they have a hang up about 'terrorist' organizations and criminals. Which was a load of bull because two NIO officials were in in the last eight days, though not negotiating . . . He then asked if I felt that a solution could be arrived at under the auspices of the Red Cross. I asked him to explain exactly what he meant and he said he was referring to some arrangement on mediation . . . I said that if he was referring to themselves as a sort of central power, pulling both sides together to negotiate directly, then that, if achieved, would be a useful role, but only if it were done on stipulations and terms of reference that I had . . . He then asked did I think that you and Pennies [Danny Morrison] could be brought in without public knowledge. No problem, sez I. Perhaps one or two screws

would see you, sez I, but that's of little consequence. Brits can cover any aspect like public face if they wish. I told them of Pennies being in last week, and not a word about it, except for minor rumour. If the Brits want to do it, I said, then they can do it. I told them that there was a great sense of urgency and that I would be expecting movement within 24 hours. They said they recognized the urgency alright. They kept looking at Doc—he's not a pretty sight and may as well not have been there. He's in a bad way, Cara. It's my opinion that Doc today is in a much worse condition than Joe was the Sunday before his death. By the way I did all the talking today—no one got a word in at all . . . Meeting lasted for an hour and a half. They then left for meetings with other prisoners. They had asked to see reps from each block, but Hilditch told them that reps were not recognized and they would have to make a random selection, which they did. I told them that no one would see them unless they happened to be the correct reps and even then I'd have to be there. The meeting was scheduled for 7 P.M. in this block. A guy from H5 weighed in by himself. I'll kill him when I see him!! . . .

An bean Uasal Bik Thur 16.7.81
. . . Mick Devine is now in hospital. All are in good spirits. Big Doc is in a bad way. Kevin is slipping also, though he was cracking jokes at me tonight. He is now on daily visits . . .

The Red Cross team had four meetings with the hunger strikers, all to no effect. The most the authorities would offer was to send an official in to "clarify" any of the statements issued by the Secretary of State: no negotiations would be allowed. By Saturday the initiative had obviously collapsed. Sinn Fein issued a statement offering thanks to the Red Cross, but declaring they were being used by the Government as part of its brinkmanship.

As the Sinn Fein statement went out a crowd of some 10,000 were marching on the British Embassy in Dublin, in the biggest demonstration seen in the Irish capital during the hunger strike. Part of the reason for the huge turnout was anticipation at the prospect of a repeat of events nearly ten years before, when a similar crowd—enraged by the events of "Bloody Sunday" when the paratroopers went amok in Derry, killing thirteen men— burned down the embassy. But the Irish Government was similarly aware of the precedent—it had had to donate the new embassy premises as compensation to Britain—and a police guard of nearly 1,000 men was mounted to protect the mission. The marchers were stopped several hundred yards short of the embassy. Sinn Fein officials tried to control the crowd, but stones began to fly. The police made a baton charge. A street battle ensued in which hundreds were injured—police alone claimed that 150 of their officers had to go to hospital for treatment. The televised scenes of violence horrified the Irish Republic. It seemed to be the realization of their worst fears, of the northern troubles spilling over the border.

The Red Cross continued their inspection of the Kesh for their routine report on prison conditions, also traveling down to Armagh jail, where Schmidt conceded in a meeting with the leaders of the IRA's women prisoners that "perhaps" they were being used by the British.

But while the Red Cross initiative had made no progress, behind the scenes Britain was once again trying for a settlement through the "Mountain Climber." On Sunday, July 19, again through their middleman in the north, the Foreign Office sent the IRA leadership a lengthy message incorporating a proposed statement which the Government was prepared to publish if it meant an end to the hunger strike. This statement contained little new, other than a placatory tone—the protesting prisoners would get their own clothes, the restoration of letter, parcel and visiting privileges and restoration of one fifth of lost remission, but no advances possible on association and more fudging on the work issue. But the message itself went on to try and persuade the IRA leadership that it would be a genuinely "new" regime, to the extent of telling them that the prison governor, Stanley Hilditch, would be replaced within eight to twelve weeks. The message stressed that there was a limit to which the Government could go—the Prime Minister must be able to defend her position at Westminster.

The Mountain Climber messages were being sent in a crudely coded form, apparently because the Foreign Office was concerned that the phone line they were using into the north might be tapped by the local security forces: the negotiations were being couched in the form of exchanges over an industrial dispute, prisoners being referred to as "the workers," the external leadership of the IRA as "the shop stewards" and the British Government as "management."

A fast series of exchanges followed. The IRA said that the gap between them on work and association was still too big. The prisoners were not prepared to do any work outside their own blocks—going to the workshops, prison kitchen or laundry, for instance. Association during leisure hours was not enough and in addition they would need specific assurances as to what they would be allowed to receive in parcels. They stressed that copper-fastened guarantees were needed, adding, plaintively, that the prisoners were quite determined to continue the hunger strike if they did not get them—that very day Kieran Doherty had sent them a message through his family that no one was to come near him unless they had the five demands. The Mountain Climber replied with a lengthy account of Mrs. Thatcher's political position: in her hard-line stance she had the support not only of her entire Cabinet, but of the leader of the Opposition, Michael Foot, the Liberal

leader, David Steel, and the leader of the new Social Democratic Party, Roy Jenkins—who, he pointed out, as Home Secretary had let Frank Stagg die on hunger strike. She had also
had the backing of all the European Foreign Ministers and
Presidents Carter and Reagan. It was against that background
that Mrs. Thatcher had agreed to the statement proposed on
July 19 which, the Mountain Climber stressed, was a genuine
attempt to get a settlement. She had agreed to the statement,
because she wanted a quick settlement—in time to announce
it at the summit of Western leaders which was then getting
under way in Ottawa. The Government had had the option
of trying for a settlement through members of the Irish establishment who had offered themselves as mediators—the ICJP,
John Hume, Cardinal O Fiaich and Garret FitzGerald himself.
But it had decided instead to deal directly with the "shop
stewards"—the external leadership of the IRA—despite the
fact that all the most powerful political forces in Britain were
opposed to such an approach. The Government was aware,
from its own sources, that the "shop stewards" were genuine
in saying more had to be offered in order to persuade the
prisoners off the hunger strike. But all that the Government
could now offer was an assurance of goodwill and honorable
intentions to make the changes that the prisoners were asking
for. They believed that their demands could be met in terms
of that statement and they could not afford to go any further
in giving guarantees. It was possible that circumstances might
change and the Government might eventually be forced to go
further, but no politician in England could afford to gamble
his political future on that assumption. That was the political
reality that lay behind the present impasse.

The IRA replied in similar vein, after expressing appreciation for the Mountain Climber's "frankness." But they too had
practical difficulties. The prisoners were associates, comrades
and personal friends whom they could not undermine, not least
because if they did so they would themselves be rejected by

them. Their collective prison experience was that prison warders, up to the most senior level, would enforce written rules
and regulations vigorously and literally. Therefore anything
which was not written down or publicly explained—despite
all the goodwill and verbal assurances of the Government—
would not be adhered to in the prison. The prisoners would
not accept anything less than the substance of their demands.
They (the external leadership) were as surprised as anyone
else by the continued readiness of the prisoners to die. It was
but one indication of both their resolve and the extremities
of the regime under which they had suffered. If the hunger
strike ended in confusion, or resulted in a regime which was
less than what the six men had already died for, it would
perpetuate the jail protests which could become impossible
to resolve. If this were to happen as a result of pressure put
on them by the external leadership it would be disastrous for
them. That was the reality of their position. They wanted
the prison protests to end. Any political advantage reaped
from the hunger strike by the Movement was neither planned
nor anticipated. The Movement could not plan strategy on
the assumption of men's willingness to die on hunger strike.
They had tried to prevent the hunger strikes, but had been
forestalled by the lack of foresight and imagination of both
the prison administration and the Government.

The Mountain Climber replied almost sadly, expressing
appreciation for their forthrightness and sincerity and regret
that there seemed to be no way out of the impasse. His initiative must now end. The "shop stewards" retorted with their
regret that the Government was unable to take the reasonable
and commonsense steps which would have ended the whole
dispute.

Brownie from Bik Sun 19.7.81
. . . Kevin wasn't out last night, was very sick this morning,
but wasn't too bad this afternoon. He is only managing to

drink one pint of water per day now. He's very weak but strong in spirit. The rest of the lads are all sound . . . he [Doc] reckons he has a couple of days left. Told me that if Brits were going to move they'd need to do so pretty soon, otherwise he wouldn't be around to keep the pressure on them. He's a terrific person altogether . . .

Dublin, meanwhile, together with the Catholic hierarchy and the SDLP, had been pressing the British Government repeatedly to have direct talks with the prisoners. Shortly before midnight on the Monday after the collapse of the Red Cross initiative, Kieran Doherty's father, Alfie, and brother, Michael, were summoned from the hunger striker's bedside by the prison governor. They were told that the Government had received a message through an unnamed priest, saying that Kieran and Kevin Lynch wanted someone from the Northern Ireland Office to explain the last statement by the Secretary of State. Alfie said he did not know anything about it. When he got back to Kieran's bedside he checked with his son, who also knew nothing of it. But a few hours later two Northern Ireland Office officials arrived and the Dohertys and Lynches were called out to meet them. They started with their "clarifications," but Alfie told them they should be talking to the hunger strikers and McFarlane. The officials said they were not prepared to speak to the prisoners with McFarlane present. Alfie told them not to be bothering Kieran, anyway. So the officials went to see the rest of the hunger strikers, only to be told that they were not interested unless McFarlane was there. The officials left.

The confused and abortive meeting had little apparent meaning, until the next day when Garret FitzGerald issued a statement saying Britain had satisfactorily discharged its responsibilities by sending officials in; that the prisoners' conditions for meeting the officials were unrealistic and that responsibility for finding a solution now lay with the prisoners.

The Irish Government also appeared to be washing its hands of the affair.

In prison McFarlane was anxiously asking the external leadership for news of the Mountain Climber. Details of what had happened were sent in to him.

To Brownie Wed 22.7.81 9 P.M. from Bik
Comrade Mor, I got your comm today. Quite a revelation I must say. I lay on my bed for a couple of hours, trying to weigh up everything. Almost dashed out of my cell once or twice. I even toyed with the idea that their 'very frank statement' was a master-stroke linked to a super brink tactic. It was then that I wised up and started looking to the future (immediate and distant) and began moving to a positive line. Firstly I'd like to say I believe you lot have done a terrific job in handling this situation and if we can take the opposition's 'frank statement' as 100% (which it does appear to be) then in itself it is quite some feat, i.e. extraordinary such an admission from them. Then again I suppose it is something we have all known already (or at least suspected). Anyway, to be going on, I fully agree with the two options you outlined. It is either a settlement or it isn't. No room for half measures and meaningless cosmetic exercises. Better be straight about it and just come out and say sin e—no more!! Now, to maintain position and forge ahead, it looks like a costly venture indeed. However, after careful consideration of the overall situation I believe it would be wrong to capitulate. We took a decision and committed ourselves to hunger strike action. Our losses have been heavy—that I realize only too well. Yet I feel the part we have played in forwarding the liberation struggle has been great. Terrific gains have been made and the Brits are losing by the day. The sacrifice called for is the ultimate and men have made it heroically. Many others are, I believe, committed to hunger strike action to achieve a final settlement. I realize the

stakes are very high—the Brits also know what capitulation means for them. Hence their entrenched position. Anyway, the way I see it is that we are fighting a war and by choice we have placed ourselves in the front line. I still feel we should maintain this position and fight on in current fashion. It is we who are on top of the situation and we who are the stronger. Therefore we maintain. In the immediate this means that Doc and Kevin will forfeit their lives and as you say the others on hunger strike could well follow. I feel that we must continue until we achieve a settlement, or until circumstances force us into a position where no choice would be left but to capitulate. I don't believe the latter would arise. I do feel we can break the Brits. But again, as you say, what is the price to be? Well, Cara, I think it's a matter of setting our sights firmly on target and shooting straight ahead. It's rough, brutal, ruthless and a lot of other things as well, but we are fighting a war and we must accept that front-line troops are more susceptible to casualities than anyone. We will just have to steel ourselves to bear the worst. I hope and pray we are right. You can give me a run-down on exactly how far the Brits went. Did 'Tish' [Sinn Fein official] see the lads in hospital? I boxed the three lads here with a general picture of the situation. OK? I am going to comm all O/Cs and give them a general outline of things. I will impress upon anyone who forwards his name for hunger strike that he will only have two months to live. I think that's about all I have for you now. Hell, I forgot to tell you that Doc told me on Sunday that Nixy [an INLA prisoner] was talking about pushing his people outside to call a halt to the hunger strike. This is bad crack and could cause problems. They have one man left as replacement for hunger strike. Also, very reliable sources inform me that there is every chance of me being moved to H4 . . . Silvertop [Fr. Murphy] explained that neither he nor Index [Fr. Toner] were involved in that episode when NIO reps weighed into hospital. It was Fr McIldowney who had visit with Kevin on Monday. I don't know how he got in touch with NIO, but he managed to somehow. Yet he maintains that he stated our terms of reference twice. Silvertop checked with Germans [British], they said that the sagairt had not made this clear at all. There you are now. Silvertop sent word this morning to Amadon II [Fool II—FitzGerald] via Fr Crilly that NIO meeting with hunger strikers was not the honourable venture they were claiming it to be. He also informed him that himself and Index were not involved. His main worry was that Amadon II would accept that the Brits had fulfilled their duty in 'talking to hunger strikers' ...

An Bean Uasal from Bik 22.7.81
... We heard the Duke of Bedford and some other article were prowling around the camp today. No sightings reported. I see the Brits are digging in. Deadly state of affairs. Keep praying ...

Paddy Quinn had started vomiting. He was sitting on the edge of his bed when his lawyer was brought in to see him.
"Some Duke or somebody came in," said Paddy.
"He was what?"
"I think he said he was the Duke of Norfolk."
"What'd he say? Did you send for him?"
"No, I didn't send for him. He just walked in."
"What'd he say?"
"Well, he said he was an English Catholic and that he didn't approve of the hunger strike and he said it was immoral and a waste of life and so on. And he said: come off it. And he just got up and went away."

In Dublin the Irish Government was tying itself into knots over the issue of who should have talked to whom. After getting Fr. Murphy's disavowal, FitzGerald met the families of the surviving hunger strikers and assured them the earlier statement had been a mistake: the Government was not backing out. But he was immediately embarrassed by the release, in London, of the text of a letter Mrs. Thatcher had just sent to the four leading Irish-American politicians, Speaker Tip O'Neill, Senators Ted Kennedy and Daniel Moynihan, and Governor Hugh Carey. The so-called "Four Horsemen" had sent a critical message to Downing Street earlier that month, accusing Britain of lacking commitment to resolve the hunger strike. The Prime Minister replied that she had done all she could, adding: "You will no doubt have seen that a spokesman for the Prime Minister of Ireland said that Dr. FitzGerald believed the British Government had met his suggestion that an official should speak to the hunger strikers; that he deeply regretted the hunger strikers had rejected the offer from officials to clarify which conditions would apply if the strike ended, and that in his view responsibility for finding a solution now rested with the prisoners." Dr. FitzGerald reacted to the letter by summoning the British Ambassador, Sir Leonard Figg, and demanded an explanation for what he claimed was a misrepresentation of his position.

Back inside the prison, McFarlane was busily holding the line, as usual. In addition to the INLA threat to pull out, he was facing the continued threat of rebellion from the Lynch family, with Kevin deteriorating. There were the usual pressures from the Church. And he was having some problems with one of the latest hunger strikers, twenty-five-year-old Pat McGeown, who had replaced Joe McDonnell.

McGeown had been jailed for fifteen years back in 1976 for, among other things, bombing Belfast's most prestigious hotel, the Europa. He was a "solid" Republican, his record dating back to the early 1970s, when he had been interned at the age of sixteen. Having been convicted before the cutoff date for special status, he had been serving his sentence in the

Cages. But in 1978 he was captured in an escape bid with McFarlane. Together with a third prisoner they had disguised themselves as warders and attempted to walk out. Sentenced to another six months and transferred to the H-Blocks, Mc-Geown had gone on the blanket immediately. Highly rated by the other prisoners—for a while he was Officer Commanding H6—he had shared a cell with McFarlane for some two years. He had volunteered for the hunger strike as far back as 1979. But on hunger strike he was continually questioning the leadership's tactics and handling of would-be mediators, criticizing their rejection of the ICJP on the grounds that all doors should be kept open.

An Bean Vasal Sun 26.7.81 10 P.M.
... Pat McGeown is having trouble with an internal wound and was in some pain last night, he couldn't sleep with it. Now apparently last year he was receiving treatment for a cut in his back passage. He went out to Musgrave for tests in September, but by then it had healed. He had been receiving medical treatment i.e. cream and tablets, but as I said it healed up. Anyway, he will inform doctor tomorrow and I'll let you know what happened. He asked me about treatment. I explained that so long as it was non-vitamin or glucose based, then that was sound enough ...

To Brownie from Bik Sun 26.7.81
... had a long yarn with Pat Beag [McGeown] this morning and impressed upon him the necessity of keeping firmly on the line. I explained that independent thought was sound, but once it began to stray from our well considered and accepted line then it became extremely dangerous. He accepted what I said alright. Also I stressed the need for all of us to have confidence in you lot. I think he is sound enough. Index was here yesterday twice. First time on behalf of our friend Mr Canning. If NIO reps were to

meet us all together would I refrain from attempting to negotiate? Apparently Mr Canning got it on the grapevine from Amadon II's people that I was hell bent on using any available opportunity to leap into negotiations the moment I laid eyes on a NIO rep. I gave Index an answer which he wrote down so as to avoid any confusion. I said that if reps came in then most certainly we would listen to what they had to say and if we felt it necessary then we would pose questions. We would also welcome meaningful dialogue. However if they ruled out negotiations then it is blatantly obvious that negotiations would not take place. That was it. I gave him our line again and told him to impress upon those concerned councillors etc. that they were only being used and abused!! The second session occurred because our old comrade, his lordship [Bishop of Derry] Ed Daly, sent in a proposal; i.e. would we now call a halt to the hunger strike and rely on the thousands of concerned individuals, among whom rate some people of power and influence, to ensure that the necessary pressure was brought to bear on the Government to engage in dialogue to bring about a feasible settlement in the immediate future? My exact words were 'Is he serious?' I told Index to tell him there was no chance of that in a million years. And who did Ed think he was kidding. I told him that Ed and Co. would be as well using all that power and influence now in pressurizing the Brits and in calling publicly for the granting of our five demands if he was so concerned about the situation. He said he'd be prepared to come in today to talk to me and the hunger strikers about his proposal. I told Index that he'd be as well not setting his foot across the front gate. That was about it. Index threw in one or two of his own proposals: 1. Why don't I appoint one of the hunger strikers as O/C for seven days, or 2. Why don't I go on hunger strike for seven days? I just said no to both as they were ridiculous suggestions. That's about all sunshine. I reckon that both himself and Silvertop are as pissed off as I am with all the recent running about. They know [it is] all going nowhere. Incidentally Mr Canning also believes they have little or no chance of succeeding. Anyway enough about them for now. We've been thinking in various ways of exploiting our situation to the full for maximum gain on the ground, especially in the Free State. The climate now is ripe to make significant progress and establish a firm base down there which is a necessity for future development and success in the final analysis. To allow opportunities to slip by (opportunities which may not present themselves again) would be a grave mistake. We are examining the possibility of contesting elections and actually making full use of seats gained—i.e. participating in Dail. Such an idea presents problems within the Movement. How great would the opposition be and what would be the consequences of pursuing a course which did not enjoy a sizeable degree of support? There are obvious dangers in promoting ideas that could and possibly would be classed as departure [from] policy. This again of course depends on the amount of awareness within the Movement of a need for progression in such a field if gains are to be made. It's all very well if the climate is right, but if the Movement isn't ready or geared for such a change then it could be a dangerous venture. Anyway, we are thinking along these lines at present. It isn't a universal line of thought as yet. In fact it's pretty much restricted to a few. But once I get a feedback from a few quarters we can pursue it further. To be honest, I only asked Jake last week to think on the Free State elections lines. I got a positive response from him, but he pointed out to me that we could be wasting a tremendous amount of time and energy pursuing something if the Movement is not ready or able to move on to this line. He recognizes it as our big chance at finding a permanent base, without which we'll never get to the end of the road. Anyway, he told me today he'd stick a load of thoughts together and bang you out a wee note. So I'll leave it there for the time being . . . By the way no one from this block of H4 retracted their names from the hunger strike list. That's a total of 33. Still waiting on word from 5 & 6. I'll get back to you tomorrow. Love to all. Take care. And God Bless. Bik.

To Brownie Tuesday 28.7.81 from Bik 10.30 P.M.
Comrade Mor, just back from hospital—fearful sight altogether. The boys sent for me and I had an hour with them. Firstly the Lynch family, in conjunction with the Menace [Fr. Faul], intend to release a public statement tonight or tomorrow calling for an end to the hunger strike. I saw Kevin but he couldn't talk, see or hear me. He was lapsing into unconsciousness every few seconds. Very bad state altogether. His brother was there, but I didn't get talking to him. I just nodded to him. He was looking [for] signs of hope from me I suppose. I saw Doc [Kieran Doherty]. He's somewhat delirious, but was able to tell me he's strong and determined and maintains the line. Now I spent the best part of an hour with the other lads discussing some points which arose today. 1. Paddy Quinn had a visit with his brother who told him that two SDLP boyos (McAvoy and some other efforts) had contact with NIO official who told them we could get clothes, something on remission and something on segregation, but that work remained the same. A load of balls as you can see. However Paddy said he couldn't speak for everyone, just himself and that personally he would be interested to hear what the SDLP boys actually had. The second pointer today arose when Tom had a visit with Fr Oliver Crilly who put a proposal to him—as it stands now, he said, both parties are almost at the peak of a mountain, but neither wants to make the first

move. We should make that move, he says, and terminate
the hunger strike, thus moving directly to that peak. From
there we can enjoy universal acclaim and support which
would insist in ensuring that a settlement is arrived at.
Now the whole business is along lines of Bishop Daly proposal. I tore it to shreds and pointed out that the moment
hunger strike stopped then cosmetic reforms would be the
order of the day and sin sin [that's that]. I told him straight
that the decision was theirs—either we pursue course for
five demands or we capitulate. No in-between solutions.
Tom then pointed out to me that he wasn't on about 'half
a loaf', but just a possible change in tactics to secure us
the five demands. I said that we should keep firmly on our
line and not deviate in the slightest, because to do so spelt
danger. They expressed concern about saving the lads'
lives if a way could be found through a change in tactics.
However they accepted that the offers floating about were
of little or no relevance at all. They all say they are strong
mentally and determined to carry on. They say they realize it could mean all of their deaths, but they understand
this. They expressed concern about the pressure swinging
towards us and the Brits using me as an excuse for not
talking. (The papers haven't been too healthy since last
week as you know.) They were thinking of a way to turn
the tables on the Brits and expose them as having nothing
to offer. They proposed that I take a back seat and allow
them to see NIO reps so they can get rid of this red herring
for good. I explained the position about my presence being
essential at any negotiations and that a break in the line
now would hammer us for the future. Also, that keeping
firmly on line weighed far heavier in the balance than a
propaganda exercise. I said that you lot were doing your
utmost to ensure that bad propaganda was warded off and
that you'd counteract Brit moves. The boys said you were
making heavy weather of it this last week. I then explained

how you were on the ball every day pulling Amadon II back into the firing line and that we'd gone through periods of unfavourable press coverage before. I told them that we could always expect things to run this way, but that we'd managed to get above the situation alright. I said that you lot were in the best position to advise and to read the situation and that you had agreed that my presence is a must at any talks. Also that you'd ensure 100% effort and more to steering the propaganda in the right direction. Paddy expressed the opinion that once Doc and Kevin died then we couldn't really expect further pressure to build on the Brits, even if they were all drawing close to death. He felt that there'll come a time when we'd have to make a move. I put our position straight to them all. Firstly, that cutting me out to gain a propaganda victory was dangerous and that it in itself would not save the boys' lives. Secondly that we had two options—1. pursue our course for five demands, or 2. capitulate now. I told them I could have accepted half measure before Joe died, but I didn't then and wouldn't now. I told them that the price of victory could be high and they might all die before we get a settlement. I said the Brits took a firm stand last week, but had also acknowledged that somewhere along the line they may be forced to meet our terms. I then asked them for an opinion and they each told me that they'd continue and maintain the line. They are strong, cara. I think the last week's propaganda had an effect on their morale slightly . . . Tom mentioned about the possibility of me going on hunger strike so that no matter what moves were afoot I'd be in the middle of things and could ward off Brit propaganda tactics. I just told him there was little chance of me getting permission and it wouldn't help things anyway. Once we get rid of one red herring the Brits would just fish out another one to suit. I had to explain to them all that I had been an advocate of hunger strike, only you lot or else Bob and Dark recognized me as disaster area. I told them I wanted to be on this hunger strike, but Bob wouldn't even listen to me. Tom knows the score as he was in the wing with me from [when] we came from H6 in '79. I told him I mentioned to Tish [Sinn Fein official] on a visit shortly after Bob died that I wanted to go on hunger strike and that he told me I was crazy. Anyway they all realize I would be a propaganda liability. If it makes any difference, cara, I don't believe I would be, not now anyhow. I no longer accept the argument that tore lumps out of me this last year. I've had more publicity lately than Prince Charles and not a word about it [his conviction as a multiple killer]. Propaganda-wise (good or bad) I'm burnt out. I've always wanted to be in that front line and I haven't changed one iota. I should have been there sin e and I still want to be there. I've no need to tell you what degree of commitment I have or how much understanding of the situation I have. You know I'd do my best and I know I'd die sin e. I'll abide by your decision as I can do little else. If it's negative just say no. Please don't forward any explanations. I just wouldn't accept them and that's the truth, cara. I'd appreciate it also if you'd refrain from giving me a lecture!! I think I've covered everything. I've told the boys they shouldn't send for me unless it's urgent, as numerous visits don't really help that much. It's not that I don't want to be up there. That's the truth, cara. Though I must be honest and tell you that tonight's episode wrecked me. But I'm sound enough now. Please don't think my request for place on hunger strike has only come [now]. I was boxing it off last week only Rickey cut me to shreds and convinced me I'd be wasting my time . . .

An Bean Uasal from Bik 28.7.81
. . . I asked the Big Lad about men with ulcers and if they'd be in danger even if they received treatment in non-vitamin

based tablet form. I used Pat Mullan as an example. He
is on my list and has ulcers himself. If it's too big a risk
factor then I'll have to drop such men. But could you let
me know as soon as possible . . .

An Bean Uasal Tue 28.7.81
. . . Was up in hospital tonight. Kevin's in a bad way. He
wasn't able to talk or hear me or see. On the point of a
coma I'd say. Breathing heavy. He slipped into unconsciousness two or three times in the five minutes I was with him.
A frightening sight altogether. Doc was able to talk, but
became delirious and told me he was 'talking to Bik earlier
on and had a yarn with Bobby'. He's practically blind and
has great difficulty in hearing. His spirit is strong and he
is very determined. Paddy Quinn was rough looking. Just
can't hold the water down. Liver isn't taking it in—just
rejecting it. He was pretty miserable looking. The rest are
sound OK? . . .

On that Tuesday, July 28, Fr. Faul had been down in Dundalk,
saying Mass in the Dominican church. As he was strolling
back to his father's house, enjoying the sun on that balmy
summer's day, he was thinking of Mrs. Lynch; of the woman's
fearful hopes that the Church and prayer would save her son.
Something had to be done to realize her faith, Fr. Faul thought.
And then he decided—it was time to move on the families.

Fr. Dennis Faul is one of those contradictory beings that
the Catholic Church is adept at producing from time to time,
often to its own mortification; a fierce individualist who
is nevertheless totally subordinate to his faith, in different
areas simultaneously a stubborn conservative and a social
progressive.

The name was originally Fawl and the family claim to be
able to trace it back to Neil of the Nine Hostages, a High King
of Ireland who ruled in the fourth century. It is a boast which

Fr. Faul is apt to couple with the tart remark that it all goes to show "this Elizabeth woman in England is only an upstart," lightening it with the observation that of course everyone in Ireland boasts a high king as an ancestor . . . that's why none of the Irish find it necessary to work.

He was born near Dundalk, just south of the border, in 1932, his father a doctor and mother the daughter of a customs and excise man. It was a fiercely Catholic home, nurturing middle-class values of family life, order and service to the community. Fr. Faul, the second eldest, was the only one to enter the Church, but his older brother was to become a consultant physician, one sister a doctor, a second a teacher of retarded children and the third married an American professor, while his two other brothers became respectively an assistant bank manager and the secretary of an investment bank. There is no Republican tradition in the family—to some extent they despise it, certainly the military strand.

If one were to look to his ancestors for the personality traits which were to make Fr. Faul a public figure during the "Troubles," they could probably be found in his mother. She was fond of saying that when the first Jew was knocked down in the streets of Munich in 1933 and kicked and spat upon, that was the time everyone should have protested, not after they had been hauled off to the gas chambers. It was a principle which Fr. Faul clung to, through his ordination at Maynooth in 1958, a year's study in Rome and his years as a teacher at St. Patrick's Academy in Dungannon.

He joined St. Patrick's in 1958, teaching Latin, then ancient history and of course religion . . . together with football. And he has been there ever since with little apparent prospect of moving on to higher things within the Church, nursing a cynicism for the Catholic hierarchy shared by many lowly priests who—often being earthy men, particularly in Ireland—can sometimes be heard muttering behind closed doors observations such as that the only qualification for ecclesiastical promotion is to keep one's mouth shut and arse open.

Keeping his mouth shut was never one of Fr. Faul's attributes. It began to open, in public, back in 1969 when he was incensed by the conviction of a young Dungannon boy on charges of throwing a petrol bomb, by a jury which included several members of the hated and notoriously sectarian police reserve, the B Specials. He wrote an article attacking the judiciary as lackeys of the Protestant ascendancy and distributed it to local Catholic newspapers on the pretext that he was about to deliver it as a public lecture (he never did). It created a furor, drawing the wrath of no less a personage than the then Prime Minister of Northern Ireland, Sir Robert Chichester-Clark. The head of the Irish Church, Cardinal Conway, was highly embarrassed by the publicity and sent instructions to the priest, ordering him to make no more public statements about matters in the north. Fr. Faul's reaction was typical. He summoned a friend who worked for a local newspaper.

"Ask me a question," he demanded of the reporter.

"What question should I ask you?"

"Ask me what do I think about Chichester-Clark, the Prime Minister's, attack on me for criticizing the judiciary."

"What do you think about the Prime Minister's attack on you?"

"I can't answer the question, because I'm not allowed to speak by Cardinal Conway."

The resultant publicity achieved Fr. Faul's goal: he had a phone call from the cardinal's secretary, informing him he was free to make any public statements he wished.

With internment in 1971 he began to turn his attention from the courts to the interrogation rooms, playing a substantial role in exposing Britain's use of sensory deprivation as well as detailing more straightforward brutality. When the Kesh could no longer hold all the internees and the overspill was moved into Armagh women's prison, Fr. Faul asked the

chaplain at that jail, Fr. Murray, for help in taking statements. They became a team. Fr. Murray, it turned out, had a
natural bent for the publishing business and the two of them
began churning out books with self-explanatory titles: *The
British Army and Special Branch Brutality, The Black and
Blue Book of the RUC* [Royal Ulster Constabulary] and *The
Castlereagh File.*

He volunteered, in 1972, to go into the Kesh to say Mass,
on a weekly or bi-weekly basis to help the official chaplains.
And down the years he became a familiar figure to the prisoners, with his chubby, rosy-cheeked, usually beaming face. The
attitudes of Republicans towards him were mixed: respecting
him for the work he had done and turning to him for help
with cases of brutality in the jail—he had published a book-
let, *The Burning of Long Kesh,* which detailed the brutal
way the security forces handled that particular episode in
the Cages in 1974. They enjoyed his irreverence towards the
establishment—whether it was Church or Government—and
yet knew his hostility towards the IRA.

He had not been very deeply involved with the hunger
strike, other than making a half-hearted attempt to postpone
the fast in January and then getting involved in those theological disputes with Bobby Sands. Essentially he supported
the prisoners in their five demands and nursed a particular
antagonism towards the Catholic hierarchy in England—
personified by Cardinal Hume—for its insistence that hunger
strike deaths were suicide. It showed that they were English-
men first and Catholic Christians only second, he would say;
there was one theology for the rich countries, and another
for the poor. But he found the suicide argument increasingly
persuasive as the coffins kept coming out of the Kesh. Protest
by hunger was developing into protest by death, he argued
with himself and then with the prisoners. He had a couple
of furious rows with McFarlane over the issue when he came
in to take Mass.

But until that sunny day in July he had been content to leave it to others in the Church to try and resolve the dispute, although he felt somewhat hurt that Fr. Magee, whom he had known personally, had seemed to ignore him during the Sands mediation bid and that the ICJP had taken little notice of him. He had thought that the ICJP would settle the dispute. In fact he had gone away to France for a break just as the ICJP initiative moved to its climax. He was staying in Paris, on the Left Bank, attending a French language course at the Institut Catholique. But inevitably he paid little attention to lessons and spent much of his time trying to find out what was happening back home. He heard the news of Joe McDonnell's death on his radio on the morning of July 8. Someone tipped off French television that an Irish priest closely connected with the Kesh was in town, so he was interviewed in front of the cameras that night. Then he saw the film of the fighting at Joe's funeral and he could not bear it any more—it was just the sort of incident which had become his life blood, sending him scurrying around, collecting affidavits and lodging complaints. He had an excursion ticket and was only due to return towards the end of the month. So he paid the difference, abandoned the French course and flew back to Belfast, arriving just in time to attend Martin Hurson's wake and pay his respects to the family. Then he went to see the Lynch family. And so it was that he fell to thinking about the duty of the Church to try and ensure a mother's prayers were answered.

When he arrived back at his father's house outside Dundalk on that Tuesday he began telephoning around the north, arranging for relatives of the surviving hunger strikers to meet him at the town of Toomebridge, on the River Bann. He was told that they were already going to a relatives' meeting at the Lake Glenn Hotel in Belfast that night, so he asked them to come on to Toomebridge when they were finished. He invited others as well. In fact there was quite a crowd gathered at the Toomebridge Hotel, including Bernadette McAliskey—who claimed the right to attend because she was related to one of the latest to join the hunger strike, Matt Devlin.

Fr. Faul told them that there was no point in the hunger strike continuing: Thatcher was not going to make any concessions and there was nothing to be gained by further deaths. It was time the IRA called it off. An argument started as to whether the IRA could call it off—Fr. Faul insisting that as they were an army, with a command structure, they could be ordered to stop. In fact, he said, McFarlane had indicated to him recently that the buck really stopped with Gerry Adams. It was decided that the issue should be put to Adams. Laurence Quinn went to telephone Sinn Fein headquarters. They were told that Adams could not make the trip there, because of security considerations—the telephone was no doubt bugged and he could be set up for assassination. So they all agreed to go and see him and piled into their cars and drove off to Belfast.

They met Adams downstairs in the Republican headquarters, together with some other Sinn Fein officials. They argued for a couple of hours, Adams insisting that the IRA could not order an end to the fast and that it had in fact been staged in the face of opposition from the Army Council. Because the prisoners had been adamant, the Movement had no alternative but to give them their backing and help organize it. Asked if he would request the Army Council to try and order them off, Adams pointed out it would take days for its members to get together and consider it. But he said he would pass on the request. Fr. Faul decided to try some flattery, telling Adams that he was as persuasive a speaker as any politician or barrister he had ever heard—it was a genuine compliment, Adams was a formidable debater—so he was the obvious man to go in and persuade the hunger strikers off. Wouldn't he go in and tell the prisoners what the stark reality was? Adams asked rhetorically why Fr. Faul could not do that.

The next morning Fr. Faul received a call from Adams, saying that in view of the concern of the relatives he was prepared to go in and explain the position to the hunger strikers. Fr. Faul rushed over to Cardinal O Fiaich's house to get his help in obtaining backing from the Northern Ireland Office. They quickly obtained permission for Adams to go in together with Owen Carron and an IRSP representative, Seamus Ruddy.

The three men met six of the hunger strikers—Big Tom McElwee, Paddy Quinn, Laurence McKeown, Pat McGeown, Matt Devlin and Mickey Devine—in the hospital canteen, together with Brendan McFarlane. Kieran Doherty and Kevin Lynch were too ill to join them. Adams was nervous as he walked in, both as to the condition the men would be in and the effect the visit might have in raising hopes. They looked bad, prison-pale skin stretched across paradoxically young skull-like faces with what Bobby Sands had once described as "that awful stare, of the pierced, or glazed eyes." Big Tom McElwee reached for the water jug.

"Would you like a drop?" he asked Adams in Irish.

"I would," he said.

"Go ahead, there's a lot of water in this place," he said, grinning.

Adams took a swig. "Hold on," said McElwee. "It costs the British Government a lot of money for that stuff." They roared with laughter.

They got down to business, Adams telling them of the flak they were taking outside, explaining he had come in to set the record straight. The decision was the hunger strikers'. As far as the Movement was concerned, if they decided to call it off altogether they would welcome the decision. The same would apply if any individual decided to come off—his decision would be respected. He spelled out in detail—based on his direct contacts with the Mountain Climber—what was on offer from the Government. Prison uniforms would be abolished, they would get their own clothes. Their demands would be met on visits, letters and parcels. There would be effective, although unofficial, segregation. Work would be ambiguously defined, to include educational courses and handicrafts. There would be free association throughout weekends and for three hours every weekday. And the Government would phrase the deal in conciliatory terms. He said he did not believe that the Government would concede any more at present. "You eight could be dead and another five or six could be dead and you still might not get your five demands." Tom McElwee, who was effectively the leader of that batch of hunger strikers, replied: "If there was some other way [of getting the five demands] then I would be the first to take it. If we stop now they'll make us crawl."

As he listened to Carron and Ruddy making their contributions, Adams's eyes strayed and, looking under the table, he saw how scrawny their legs looked. They were smoking in relay—no matches were allowed past the search point. Adams had emptied two jugs of Tom's spring water. "We're not letting you in again," said Tom, as he went for another refill.

Paddy Quinn was having trouble hearing what Adams was saying and the others had to repeat it. He could not see Adams properly either, just making out his beard. After a while he said he had better be getting back to bed, he did not want to pass out. He called Brendan over and said to him that he did not think he had more than a week to go, but to wish all the lads in the blocks all the best from him. Trundling in his wheelchair down to his cell he felt strangely contented: he was going to die, but the fear of it seemed to have gone.

In the canteen Adams and Carron got up with McFarlane to go and see Kieran Doherty. McFarlane greeted him in Irish as they went in: Doherty was massive in his gauntness and obviously had trouble seeing them, his eyes moving to their voices.

"I've a week in me yet," he said. "How's Kevin?"

"You'll both be dead," said Adams. "I can go out now, Doc, and announce it's over."

"Thatcher can't break us," said Doherty. "I'm not a criminal."

They said their goodbyes, Doherty telling Adams not to worry—they would break Thatcher in the end.

They had been told that Kevin Lynch was in too bad a condition to see them, but they went through to see his father and brother, Pat, in the waiting room. The old man was in a state and demanded bitterly of Adams: "You'se are responsible my son is dying there . . . Why don't you take them off it?" Adams replied: "I can't take him off, but you can."

"To raise a son and see him die like this!" said Mr. Lynch.

To Brownie Thur July 30 10.30 P.M. from Bik
. . . Firstly it was great having a yarn with you last night, though the circumstances were pretty dire . . . I don't know how you felt about last night, but that was really rough—a deadly experience, cara. Such a contrast between both clanns. I could have cried both times, but for different reasons. Doc's father and brother made a terrific impression on me. I realize they must be heart-broken, but their strength really amazed me. They seem like very understanding people. Our meeting was brief, I know, but I gained from them warmth and strength of spirit . . . Kevin's shattered me. I've never experienced anything like that in my life. How can you get people to understand and view things in a clear light? Looking back I realize you were right in not pursuing the conversation, but I just felt I had to try to get them to see things in a true light. But then what can one say in such a situation? Dear Lord, what a place!! I pray for them all. Yet I feel it is I who need prayers more than most . . . Tell Owen and Seamus it was a pleasure meeting them . . .

While all these meetings were going on yet another mother was facing her moment of truth.

Mrs. Catherine Quinn was a widow. Her husband, Jim, had died twenty-four years before, of a kidney ailment. And life since then had been a battle for her. They had a farm of thirty-two acres outside Camlough, in South Armagh, keeping pigs and both dairy and beef cattle. She kept it going after Jim's death with the help of her two eldest sons, Paddy, then aged nine, and Seamus, aged seven—both of whom had to take turns milking the cows for her and helping around the farm.

Theirs was an old Republican family, one of her uncles boasting a bullet wound in the neck resulting from a shoot-out with the Black and Tans. Mrs. Quinn's mother, who was to live to the age of ninety-one—two years past the hunger strike—used to regale the boys with stirring tales of the old IRA. So it was inevitable, in a way, that Paddy should join up. Which made life even rougher, because both he and Seamus became prime suspects to the security forces and their farmhouse seemed to be the target of daily raids. Eventually Catherine gave up and moved into a council house in Camlough, leaving the farm empty.

Paddy was captured a month after the move to Camlough, in that same shoot-out as Raymond McCreesh, in 1976. The McCreeshes lived only about four miles away from them. Paddy was sentenced to fourteen years for attempted murder and of course went straight on to the blanket. Seamus subsequently went on the run, taking refuge south of the border, near Dundalk.

Paddy, like Raymond McCreesh, refused to take visits for the first fourteen months. When his mother finally did get in to see him she hardly recognized him.

Down in the Republic, meanwhile, Seamus was suddenly taken ill with intense headaches. He was admitted to hospital in Dublin with a suspected brain hemorrhage. But he was found to have polycystic kidneys. It was the same thing which had killed his father—dozens of cysts which, if they become active, replace the normal kidney tissue, eventually causing renal failure. Seamus recovered. But the condition was hereditary and the doctors started testing the rest of the family. Word was sent in to the prison medical staff and Paddy was asked if he wanted tests, but he knew at that time he would be going on hunger strike and he refused—he did not want to give them a weapon to bring extra pressure on him once his fast had begun.

Paddy was among the prisoners who joined the first hunger strike en masse, for the final four days. And when Raymond McCreesh went on the second hunger strike Mrs. Quinn had little doubt her son would soon be joining it. Early in June she went up on a visit and he confirmed it. He was starting on the 15th.

15.6.81 from Rickey
. . . Paddy Quinn went on hunger strike today. He is directly across from Big Tom McElwee and he'll probably be moved into a cell on his own tomorrow. I lay on my bed today thinking of the night we had our parade for Raymond McCreesh. Paddy gave the oration that night and I asked myself today 'will there be a parade and an oration for Paddy? . . .'

Paddy weighed in at 140 lbs. He found the first four days easier than he had during the 1980 hunger strike. This time they were taking salt separate from the water, instead of in tablet form with the water, which made it easier to drink. But by the weekend he was feeling sick and struggling to keep down the five pints; then on Monday it eased. One governor irritated him by coming in every day and asking questions such as: "Are you not tempted yet, Quinn?" pointing to the food on the table.

Down in South Armagh the McCreesh family had told Mrs. Quinn that she would not see much difference in him for the first month or so. But when she went to the Kesh the first time he was looking bad. The second time he had to be helped into the visitors' room by a warder. The third time he was in hospital.

Brownie from Bik Tue 23.6.81
Comrade Mor, just a short note for a change. Paddy Quinn had a visit with his family this afternoon. Very bad visit altogether. His mother was shattered and hardly spoke through the visit except to say that things can't go on like this and Maggie will never give in. She told Paddy to walk back slowly after the visit in case he took a heart attack. Such is the measure of the poor woman's distress, cara. Paddy was naturally a bit upset, but he is sound as a bell . . .

Paddy was in the same wing as Tom McElwee and they were moved to the prison hospital together; Paddy had done twenty-one days, Tom twenty-seven. Paddy was again having trouble keeping the water down by then. But the condition of the others in the hospital was much worse. There was Joe McDonnell, in his wheelchair, hardly able to hear, see or keep his head up; Martin Hurson and Kieran Doherty throwing up green bile with their water.

Every morning those who could do so went out into the yard for some exercise—usually they merely sat down, conserving energy and enjoying the sun if there was any. Paddy pondered the irony that, after four and a half years locked up, he should be given the opportunity of exercising when he could not do it. They were finding sitting difficult as well— the bones hurt. A request for comfortable armchairs in the canteen was refused, so they brought their pillows to sit on.

It was after thirty days that Paddy's eyesight began to go. It started one morning, after he had had a hot shower, when he started seeing double. He began to find it difficult to walk straight. Getting out of bed and standing up became an effort. The doctors, who were examining him every morning, tried to explain what was happening, although they did say little was known about the medical effects of hunger-striking—most knowledge which did exist emanated from the Nazi concentration camps. But they said that losing control of the eyes was a sign that the body was beginning to feed off brain protein. On visits he started wrapping himself carefully in his dressing gown, so that his mother would not be too alarmed by his loss of weight.

Mrs. Quinn was making the trip to the Kesh almost every other day towards the end of July. She very much wanted to take Paddy off, but the trouble was timing. She was encouraged by Fr. Faul, and had been to the Toomebridge meeting with another of her sons, Laurence, and the other relatives.

Paddy was starting to throw up the water, with green bile. He had been moved, after Hurson's death, into Martin's cell. The nausea became steadily worse—he could scarcely keep water down at all. The smell of the bile was sickening in itself. His mouth felt dried up, and a thick scum formed which stank. He seemed to be heaving all the time. Now and then, when there was no water to vomit, he threw up traces of blood. One of the doctors said it was like chipping away at a high chimney: it would reach a stage when it needed only one more chip to go and it would all collapse. And if there was a weak spot in the body then the effects would concentrate on it; he meant the kidneys, of course, but Paddy tried to ignore it, which was not easy; lying in the bed in which, he was told, Martin had died. Death. It was scaring. Terrifying.

The battle to live was the battle to take water. If he did not hold it down the kidneys would not get flushed out and poisons would begin to accumulate in his bloodstream, reaching his brain and killing him. But water had never seemed so revolting; he could smell it in its jug, as well as the ever-present food at the bottom of the bed. He tried to drink half a pint, then lie down on his bed and concentrate on holding it down. But up it would come. As soon as he tried to get up the heaving started. He tried going over to the food and smelling it, then quickly drinking the water, but that did not work either. Jesus, but he hated that water. His hearing was going as well. The doctor had said that the buzzing noise came from inside his ear, but it seemed to Paddy to be outside his head: like a bluebottle fly buzzing around, up against his neck, then his ear, his forehead, his temple and even the tip of his nose. Around and around it went, sometimes settling on his chest.

It was about 11 P.M. on the Sunday night when he started thinking he was going mad. He had just downed a pint of water and was lying there with it in his stomach, saying to himself: "This time it'll stay down." Then the room went all weird, like a film in which the director was trying to imitate the vision of someone drugged to the eyeballs. Paddy got out of bed and began to wonder who he was. He was standing on a mat, about a foot away from the wall. He knew his name, but he could not identify with it, saying to himself: You are Paddy Quinn. No, I am Paddy Quinn. Who the hell is Paddy Quinn? What is Paddy Quinn? It's only a name. It's your name. No, it's my name. I am Paddy Quinn. You are on hunger strike. That food on the table you will not touch. You won't let the lads down. You won't let the people down. You are not mad. Am I Paddy Quinn? I am. Who am I? And all the time he was rubbing his stomach. He saw the flap in the door was open. Someone was watching him. He went on rubbing his stomach, pondering the name of Paddy Quinn. Then everything went black. Maybe I'm dying, he thought. Maybe I should look upwards.

He awoke on the floor, his head propped against the wall, to the sound of keys jangling in the door. His mind was clear. They lifted him on to his bed. "Must prefer sleeping on the floor," said one. Another called his name three or four times. He ignored it. They left and he dozed for a few minutes, waking to find his mind was absolutely clear. His mouth was no longer dried up, instead it had an oily taste in it. The nausea had gone and the water stayed down. He felt like having a piss, which he hadn't done for a couple of days. It was great. But the next morning the doctor said it all marked a further deterioration in his condition. And sure enough he found he could not walk—he had to start using the wheelchair. His hand was shaking and he kept spilling the water and the urine bottle. His heart seemed to speed up when he was out of bed. On Monday night, coming back from the canteen in the wheelchair, he felt the heartbeat going faster and faster and faster until he passed out.

On Wednesday, July 19 Mrs. Quinn did not make it to the prison, but one of her daughters, Roisin, went. Just before Roisin left her mother called out: "You tell him to come off, because I'm not going to let him die." But Roisin did not pass on the message—she knew what Paddy's reaction would be.

Mrs. Quinn did not have a telephone. But the next night her neighbor brought a message that she was wanted up at the Kesh urgently. So Laurence drove her. She was met by Fr. Murphy who explained, apologetically, that Paddy had gone into a delirium and had asked for food, so they had called her for a decision, but since then he had come around again and was now insisting he did not want any food, so her trip was wasted. She went in to see him with Laurence and found Paddy fully coherent. They begged him to come off but he would not hear of it, urgently whispering to her not to even talk of it—that the screws were listening and it could harm Kieran Doherty and Kevin Lynch, who were near death. Mrs.

Quinn could not understand what Paddy was talking about; how could it do them harm?

After lunch on Tuesday a fifty-four-year-old widow came out of her house in a side street around the corner from the Andersonstown police barracks in West Belfast and paused for a moment to admire her yellow and red daisies, the pale purple and mauves of the asters. It was a peaceful scene: a comfortable, semi-detached house with a monkey puzzle tree in the front, roses, fuchsias and chrysanthemums as well as the beloved daisies and asters coloring the flower beds with the former convent teacher, Mary McDermott, standing there in her light summer dress with its low neck, drinking it all in. But it was time to go and she climbed into her new, pale silvery-green VW Polo and headed for the Kesh.

Mrs. McDermott was feeling nervous. Not that it was new to her. Her own father, an ardent Republican, had died down in the Republic when she was a child, his health destroyed by a series of prison hunger strikes. She had always been a Republican—not a member of the IRA, or anything like that, just feeling that this was her country and the British had no place in it. In 1976 the Irish conflict brought another death home to her when the third of her six sons, Sean, aged twenty, was killed. He had been part of an active service unit which carried out a bombing attack on the Conway Hotel in Dunmurray. Afterwards they had gone to a nearby house to try and hijack a car. They did not realize that the householder was a police reservist. He had led Sean upstairs to get the car keys, but instead had pulled a pistol out of the drawer, turned and shot her son dead. Anyway, that was the story as she had heard it in the media. She had never talked to the others involved in the mission, always wondering who they had been—not that she would ever be told. Anyway, she had joined a Relatives Action Committee, campaigning for the prisoners, as her contribution to the cause. And on visits to the Kesh for the committee she had met and become friendly with Kieran Doherty.

Damn, she felt nervous. She had seen Kieran a week before and he had looked bad. What would he look like now? "He'll be dying, Mary, there's no use going in as a moaning minnie and saying it's terrible, you have to take up face," she said to herself.

She had to pull herself together mentally as she walked through his door. He looked frightening, propped up slightly with a pillow; a skeleton with skin on. Sunken face, eyes staring, Adam's apple sticking out, ribcage showing in the gap of his pajama jacket. She bent over him, taking his hands, and said, forcing her silvery voice to brightness: "Oh hello, Kieran, how are you today?"

"Don't know you," he said, but he kept holding her hand as she sank back into her chair. His eyes turned to her voice, but she knew he could not see her.

"I'm Sean's mother," she said.

"Oh yes, Sean. He was a fine soldier."

Mary McDermott said nothing.

"He was shot dead beside me," added Kieran after a moment.

"Oh?"

"Yes."

"Do you want a drink, Kieran?" she asked.

The orderly came over with an invalid's cup and tilted water into his mouth. It went down like the Niagara Falls; she seemed to hear it cascading through bones and emptiness.

"That's lovely," he said.

Time used to fly so fast, on her visits with Kieran, but this time it crept by. Eventually the warder said the half-hour was up and she hearkened back to the old visits in her goodbye: "Well here he comes again, Kieran, I've got to go again."

"Oh well," he said, "don't worry about me."

She looked back from the door, before turning and walking down the corridor, still not knowing the full story of her son's death.

The next day Paddy Quinn's mother had arranged to be taken to the Kesh by Roisin's husband, Eugene. She was waiting for him at Roisin's house in Camlough. He was late home and Mrs. Quinn was getting agitated, because she knew they closed the gates at the Kesh at 3:45 P.M.

When Eugene finally came home and they arrived at the Kesh the gates were closed. So they rattled and banged on them until a warder came out and they explained that they just had to get in, because Paddy might be dying. The warder went away to telephone for directions and came back and said it was OK, they were allowed through. At the hospital they were met by Fr. Toner, who said Mrs. Quinn could not go in, Paddy's condition was too bad. He had been having fits since 11:30 in the morning. But Eugene was allowed in and came out again looking ill. He said perhaps he should go home and fetch the rest of the family.

Mrs. Lynch and Mrs. Doherty were in their waiting room and could hear screaming coming up the corridor. Mrs. Doherty covered her ears. Mrs. Lynch went into her son, Kevin's, cell and told him Paddy was praying hard. She persuaded Kevin to say prayers with her and she said them as loudly as she could, to try and stop him hearing Paddy's agony. When it quieted down she came out again and she and Mrs. Doherty started the rosary.

Twenty blue and silver gas-filled balloons bounced above the horse drawn carriage. More than 100 palace staff threw confetti and rose petals as it trundled its way through the huge iron gates to the roar of the waiting thousands. The Princess was dazzling, in pale coral pink tussore with matching bolero, a white silk organza collar edged with frills and cummerbund sash around her waist. The Prince was dapper in a gray flannel suit.

In Halcombe Street, in Protestant East Belfast, the kids were guzzling sausage rolls, jelly and ice cream. Each of them was presented with a souvenir mug and pensioners received a wedding keyring. Across the north the scene was repeated under waving Union Jacks and bunting, the young and the old fingering their souvenirs, watching fancy dress parades, "wedding" processions, pipe bands, donkey derbies, stunt riders and the occasional figure lurching under the burden of celebratory, cut-price beer. "This is great fun and puts the seal on a great day for everyone," said thirteen-year-old Lynn Watters, as her friends tucked into lemonade and buns up the Ballysillan Road in North Belfast.

Mrs. Quinn and Eugene were taken to see the prison doctor. Mrs. Quinn asked what would happen if they intervened now. He said it was 50/50. Mrs. Quinn said: "I'm taking him off." Fr. Toner's face broke in a smile of surprised delight.

Kevin Lynch's sister walked into the waiting room where her mother and Mrs. Doherty were praying.

"Is Paddy dead?" asked Mrs. Lynch.

"No, he isn't dead, his mother's taken him off. They've taken him to an outside hospital," said Mary.

"Thank God," said Mrs. Lynch, thinking of the widow-woman's agony.

"So who's next, who's next to take their son off?" demanded Mary, frantic to see her brother saved.

"Well it'll not be me," said Mrs. Lynch. "I gave Kevin my promise and I'll not be breaking it." Mrs. Doherty echoed her. Mary stormed out.

Paddy had quieted down, meanwhile, and Mrs. Quinn was allowed in to see him. His eyes were open, but it was obvious he was not seeing anything. She leaned over and kissed him and he immediately went into convulsions again. They told her an ambulance had been called. The wait for it seemed to go on for ever. She was asked to sign a document confirming her decision.

Paddy was rushed by ambulance to the Royal Victoria Hospital in West Belfast, the Quinns following in their car. They were kept waiting for about one and a half hours before being allowed in to see him again. He was wired up to machines and drips. An aggressive-looking warder was standing over him. Paddy was in a delirium. He was imagining that he was looking at three people behind a sort of glass barrier. He knew one of them: it was a cousin, an American called Brian who lived in Delaware in the U.S.A. Brian used to visit them in Ireland and go out with Paddy, to dances and the Pub. But in 1976 he had been paralyzed in a car accident in America, eventually dying of his injuries. And now he was behind that barrier in Paddy's mind. Paddy thought he could recognize another of the men behind the barrier as well; maybe it was "Blessed" Noel Quinn, another cousin serving time in the Kesh. All the time a voice was saying: "Perpetual sufferers shall have eternal life." It seemed to be Brian's voice.

"Is that Brian, is that Brian, what are you doing here, Brian?" asked Paddy.

Mrs. Quinn peered at the grumpy-looking warder. "Are you Brian?" she asked hopefully. The warder shook his head.

To Brownie from Bik Friday 31.7.81
. . . Now, re a protracted hunger strike. A few months back this is what we spoke of in dread and did not visualize . . . I've always understood why we would need a big sacrifice to shift the Brits. A climb down here is a major coup for the movement. As Roach 90 (that's 'Hole in the Head') said to me—it's the greatest political victory of the past 12 years. Before the first hunger strike started I

was talking in terms of between five and eight men dying before achieving settlement. (Yet once it started and things began to build, I thought we'd do it without loss at all) . . . I told you before that as far as I was concerned it is the hunger strikers who are the front-line troops—the human Armalites, as Frank said . . . Also heard about Paddy in hospital, though I'm not too sure as to the exact position . . .

It was a couple of days before Paddy became lucid again. He thought he had taken himself off the hunger strike and was obviously upset. His mother discussed it with her priest and he advised her to tell him herself what had happened. But when she went up to see him again—by now he was in the military wing of the Musgrave Park Hospital—he already knew and he was mad as hell with her. So she took him in her arms and said in that Irish brogue: "Now sure, Paddy, aren't you glad to be alive today?"

And he said, "I don't know whether I am or not."

"Hey, here comes Henry VIII—happy wagon on the air." The kitchen van with its familiarly bulky and bearded driver had been spotted coming into the yard. A heated debate followed as to whether it was chicken tonight. There was no sound of the kettles, so they could count on the urn and hot tea. The debate ended with the yell from the end cell: "Bangers on the air." It was already getting dark and the screws had switched off the cell lights. But in the beam from the passageway, as the orderly swung the door open, they could see it was two sausages, a piece of potato bread and beans. The prisoner drained his tea, luxuriously, and reached across to the pipes for an appleseed kernel; dried, they tasted like desiccated coconut—the prisoner's after-dinner mint. They hadn't needed to shred apple stalks for a couple of weeks, now, he thought, tobacco supplies hadn't been too bad since the last consignment along

the main supply route from the Cages. Twelve ounces in one delivery! They'd smoked themselves silly.

The prisoner yawned and stretched. His cellmate was down in the corner at the pipes, murmuring to next door: "Are you listening . . . are you listening?"—the continual refrain of blind conversation. He could feel the day's tension ebbing out of the jail.

From the Circle came the sounds of filing cabinets being slammed shut, the banging of chairs being moved, the movements of lock-up time. The wooden door leading from the Circle out of the block thumped. The prisoner visualized the screw's movements from the sounds: the reverberating crash of the huge corrugated iron gates leading into the caged walkway; the rattling as he tested the lock and the ringing of the bell in the Circle as he pushed the red alarm button in its blue box. The smaller, second gate into the exercise yard clanged, followed by rattling and ringing. At the third, smaller gate the rattle of the keys and then the clatter of the lock reverberated into the rustling of the wire fencing running parallel with the cells. The repetitive sounds faded slowly and then grew louder again as the screw made steady progress along the loop through the gates. The thump of the wooden door again marked his return.

"AB grille."

"Numbers . . ."

"D Wing numbers."

"Check."

The rattle of the brass handles as the screws, checking each side of the wing in tandem, twisted and pulled. The third screw clicked the button as they reached the end, activating the clock alarm. If the night guard failed to hit it every hour it would be triggered.

"D Wing, sir. Thirty-three, sir. Correct, sir."

"Parade." The prisoner wondered if the scene matched his imagination of it: the day guard lined up, beer bellies with

colic faces, the Brit recruits with shoulders pulled back, the
wee Senior Officer with his rodent's face, too-big hat and
high-pitched voice struggling for authority.
   "Fuck away off," came the inevitable shout from the wing.
   "Peewade, deehsmiss!"
   The barracking started from the other side of the wing, the
men crowding the pipes and taunting the departing screws.
   "Fuck, look't that Billy, he's really putting on weight."
   "Fuck, he's got terrible fat, terrible old looking."
   "Holy Jesus, look't the state of that eejit there."
   The boots clattered away into the night, through the clash-
ing of the gates, and the prisoners reluctantly climbed down.
   "Everybody ready for the rosary?"
   "Hold on, I'm rolling a fag."
   The murmuring started, "Blessed" Noel leading.
   "Open my lips, O Lord."
   "Thou O Lord will open my lips."
   "And my tongue shall announce your praise."
   "Incline to my aid, O Lord."
   "O Lord, make haste to help me."
   ". . . The first joyful mystery . . ." Between the shit-covered
walls the prisoners contemplated the annunciation of the
Blessed Virgin.

NINE

With hindsight it was the beginning of the end, when Mrs. Quinn eagerly told the doctor she wanted Paddy off. It had always been the Achilles heel of the hunger strike and one which the prisoners themselves had recognized from the beginning: a mother wanting her son to live and the law saying that once consciousness was lost one's life was in the hands of the next of kin. The chubby priest from Dungannon had tumbled to it and now he was knawing at the tendon, arranging more meetings and going to see relatives; "educating" them as he was to describe it to himself. But it was too late for the mother whose prayers had originally motivated him. Too late for others, as well.

Kevin Lynch was lucky, if one wants to see it as luck, in that the prison allowed the family a twelve-day bedside vigil. His mother and father took turns, Mr. Lynch doing the night shift, Mrs. Lynch the day, waiting for their son to die or for something, or someone, to give. They had so much time with him, because he lasted so long. He had started his hunger strike on May 22, the day of Raymond McCreesh's funeral and the same day as Kieran Doherty. By the time Paddy Quinn had been taken off they had gone well past the sixty-six days that Sands lasted; in fact they only had Terence MacSwiney's and Joseph Murphy's records to beat.

They were terrible days for Mrs. Lynch, thinking, thinking, thinking about Kevin; she could not bear to eat, herself: suffering a weight loss from 161 down to 126 lbs. She was desperate to save him, but he was as adamant as any that had gone before him. At one stage another son, Patsy, who could not bear the sight of his brother lying there dying, asked him: "Kevin, is there no other way than this?"

"If that's all you have to say you had better go home," said Kevin.

Patsy couldn't sleep that night. He was not due to go up the next day, but he did anyway, to say he was sorry. Mrs. Lynch resignedly asked Kevin where he wanted to be buried, in Park or Dungiven. He said Dungiven.

He was obviously upset by his mother's distress and he said to her: "You were talking about Granny living until she was ninety; well that was three months." She did not understand what he was talking about and did not reply: there seemed to be a lifetime's difference between the two to her.

She saw him for the last time on the Friday. When she reached the Kesh, Fr. Murphy was waiting impatiently and told her Kevin had been calling for her. They went in and the priest said: "Mammy's come." Kevin, who was blind by then, shook his head in acknowledgment. They sat there on the bed, holding hands. During that long day an orderly came in with a mouthwash, to treat the mouth ulcers he was suffering. But Kevin clenched his teeth shut. "Do you not want it, Kevin?" He shook his head.

The Lynches' other two sons, Frank and Michael, would not let their parents in for the end. They took over for the final hours and watched Kevin die, peacefully, at 1 o'clock on Saturday morning.

To Brownie [Gerry Adams] Saturday 1.8.81 1 P.M.
Comrade Mor, we heard about 10 A.M. of Kevin's death. God grant him rest . . . the next man for hunger strike is Liam McCloskey IRSP (Dungiven) . . . he will commence hunger strike on Monday. Our future strategy of replacements will be that men embarking on hunger strike will do so one week apart. This means that if the Brits allow Doc to die then Pat Sheehan will not start on hunger strike until Monday week, the 10th.

An Bean Uasal 1.8.81 Sat 1 P.M.
. . . heartbreaking news about Kevin. May he rest in peace. We will all pray for him and for his bereaved family. Who can really understand their sufferings? . . . We are in a very bad way for cigarette papers. Just to give you an idea—I would use 30 [to write on] in two days and the hunger strikers are both smoking about a dozen per day . . .

To Brownie Sat 1.8.81 from Bik [McFarlane]
. . . the pressure appears to be hardening in the direction of the A/C [Army Council] to call a halt. Do you want a statement from us outlining the position in regards to hunger strike? I've just told Ricky to get down a paragraph or two on A/C moral obligation aspect and if you feel it helps then bang it out. Don't mean to jump the gun by us stating A/C policy. Just felt a need to say something . . .

As Kevin's body was being wheeled out of his room an elderly couple down the corridor listened to its creaking despairingly. Alfie and Margaret Doherty knew it could only be a matter of hours before their son made the same journey.

And then not only would they have to live with the tragedy, but with the bitterness of a girl who loved him dearly.

Wed 20.5.81
Full name Kieran Gerard Doherty, D. O. B. 16.10.55. I was born and raised in Belfast (Andersonstown) where I attended both primary and secondary school (St Theresa's primary, Glen Road, CBS secondary). At 15 I played football for St Teresa's GAA and for a while St Johns. At the same time I worked as an assistant bar man at a pub by the name of Drinian—top of Alcover St—part time. After leaving school (no great features) I got a job as an apprentice heating engineer. This didn't last long, the firm being made redundant after that—early 1972. I laboured for M & J Gallaghers . . . for a few months then I received an apprenticeship as a tiler (floor layer) for J. P. Corrys, Corporation St. I worked there until my arrest in 1973 (Feb. 15th). During the time I was working I wasn't associated with any trade union.

I joined the Republican Movement as a member of Na Fianna Eireann [youth brigade of the IRA] in Oct. 71. I spent several months in Na Fianna Eireann until I joined Oglaigh na Eireann [IRA] March '72. Feb. 15th, '73 I was arrested and interned. My brother Terence had been released from Internment the previous March. His arrest had taken place in October. Shortly after my arrest my eldest brother Michael was lifted, April, and also interned. He spent 14 months inside. I was released from internment on the 7th November, 1975. I forgot to mention that I had been arrested in a hijacked motor in November '72, but was released having been charged with taking and driving away and no licence. I was fined £32 at Lisburn Court January '73. After internment I immediately re-involved myself in the Movement. On the 25th August 76 I was arrested while walking down Balmoral Ave by a police patrol who later identified me as the person who they saw abandoning a hijacked motor in a side street near . . . There were three members in this . . . patrol. I was also identified by another SPC man who claimed that he recognized me as being one of a number of men who while being chased by the police on the Malone Rd area fled from one of two motors that came to a halt in a cul-de-sac. However I was charged with possession of firearms, explosives (bomb) plus hijacking, likewise four other men namely John Pickering, Terence Kirby, Liam Whyte and Chris Moran were also charged, three of whom had been caught after being surrounded in a house by police, the other Liam Whyte was caught at the scene. I fought the case as ID was the only evidence against me. We were not sent for trial until 17 months after our arrest, during which time I applied for bail, but was turned down. We were all found guilty Jan. 24 and sentenced. J. P., T. K., and C. M. received 26 years L. W. got 18 years and I 22 years. On arrival at the Kesh we all joined our comrades on the blanket protest. During my time on the protest I was assaulted twice, July '78 and Oct. '78. Both cases are in the hands of my brief [lawyer], O. Kelly. These assaults resulted from my refusal to comply when first introduced to the mirror search. I appealed my conviction which wasn't heard until more than two years later. Thrown out. I also forgot to mention I had another motoring offence during 1976. I was fined £40 for driving without a full licence and without the owner's consent. That's it.

He was on a bombing mission in Belfast when he was caught, with four others, in a saloon car and a van carrying the explosives. They were spotted by a plain clothes police patrol which got suspicious and followed them, radioing ahead to have them stopped. There was a short chase, until the IRA vehicles ran into a cul-de-sac. They had set the bomb in the back of the van to explode and they fled. Three of them ran into a nearby house, with a machine gun, taking the occupant hostage. After several hours a priest was brought in and persuaded them to surrender. Kieran, meanwhile, had almost got away, hijacking a car and dumping it about one and a half miles away. But he was spotted by another police patrol and, as a known IRA suspect—despite protestations that he had merely gone for a stroll to buy himself a lollipop—was arrested.

Kieran's family were solid Republicans. They were related to the well-known Maguire family. Ned Maguire had taken part in a famous IRA escape from the Crumlin Road prison in 1943. His son, also Ned, was part of a mass escape from Long Kesh in 1974. Two women in the Maguire family, both members of the Cummann na mBan—the women's wing of the IRA—were shot dead by British troops in 1971. Another relative of the Dohertys', Gerry Fox, escaped from the Crumlin Road jail in 1972. Alfie Doherty, Kieran's father, a floor tiler by profession, was manager of the Andersonstown Social Club, one of the best-known Republican drinking clubs in Belfast where a pint could be bought for a few pence less than in commercial bars and drunk to the accompaniment of rousing rebel songs. Alfie had got the job after his predecessor as manager, Jack McCarten, had been shot by a sniper outside the club—widely suspected, in Catholic West Belfast, to have been an assassination by a British undercover squad. Kieran's mother, Margaret Doherty, was Protestant, converting to Catholicism when she married Alfie. She was a warm and gentle woman, lacking a Republican background and almost naïve where the harsh realities of the Irish conflict were concerned, but fiercely loyal to her menfolk and whatever they believed. There were two other sons and two daughters.

Kieran himself was a tall—6 feet 2 inches—quiet, reassuring presence. "Big Doc," his friends called him. He was something of a fitness fanatic, doing hundreds of press-ups in his cell every day. He was an intensely loyal member of the IRA, although not particularly political, and intolerant of anyone in the Movement who showed weakness, who signed statements or recognized the courts. While on remand in the Crumlin Road prison he had even tried to have the "touts' table" reinstated—the ostracization of anyone who had broken under interrogation which had been the rule in the days of internment. But if you were sound by Kieran's standards there was nothing he would not do for you.

He was good-looking and, in the short period between his release from internment in November 1975 and his arrest in August 1976, started dating a local Catholic girl, Geraldine Scheiss. She was a tiny thing, 5 feet 1 inch, but very striking with green eyes and dark brown hair. They met at a dance, at the Road House in West Belfast. She was working as a tele-ads girl at a local newspaper. Her family were middle class; her father, who was Swiss, had died when she was a child and there were no links with the Republican Movement in the family. Geraldine was fairly naïve and had no idea that Kieran was in the IRA—to her he seemed too gentle for that—until the day of his arrest.

At first Kieran, like many other IRA men in the early days of the blanket protest, refused to take visits. But they used to write a lot to each other—the formal, censored letters and the smuggled, more intimate ones. They were not formally engaged. Kieran insisted that he did not want to tie her down. But they might as well have been.

Kieran was among those who went on en masse at the end of the first hunger strike. So when the second one started there was a fair chance he would be on it. But it was not much of a worry to Geraldine, because there was no way she could imagine the British Government allowing even Sands to die, much less others—there would be civil war before it got to her Kieran, surely. Then she went to the Kesh on May 2—her birthday—on a monthly visit. Kieran told her that Bobby was not too well, but that he did not think he would die. He added, off-handedly, that he had volunteered to go on at some stage. The next time she saw him he was in the prison hospital, well into his own hunger strike. She was terrified before that visit—wondering what he would look like. And it was pretty bad when she did see him. He was thin and gaunt; with his height he seemed to go on for ever. But he was light-hearted and told her everything was fine, not to worry. At the end of the visit he took her by the hand, laughing, and said: "Come on, I'll walk you to the door." Four were dead by then, but she still did not believe that her Kieran would follow them. It was just too unthinkable.

Monday 8th Kieran Doherty
Comrade, just a brief note to inform you of my condition. Firstly physically I'm not having any problem at all. So far I haven't had a headache. I try to drink five to six pints of water per day . . . the priest pays me regular visits. Strictly religious. Mr Toner read me part of a letter he received from the Pope's envoy . . .

Geraldine got into an argument at her office one day with a colleague who said of course it was not the decision of the hunger strikers—they had been ordered to die by the IRA. She told him he was talking nonsense, how could anyone be ordered to die? But as Kieran's fast dragged on and her worries started to grow she began to get suspicious. Then, before one of her visits to the prison hospital, she was asked by Sinn Fein to smuggle a letter in for him. She took it, but opened it and read it before going up. The letter was a formal request to Kieran for his approval for statements to be issued in his name without consultation. It was a practical step in the circumstances. There was close coordination between the prisoners and the Movement outside, through the enormous quantity of comms smuggled back and forth, but at the same time it was not always reliable: a "pilot" could always crash, his comm be intercepted by the "Germans," and there might well be a time when a statement had to be issued in too much of a hurry to wait for it to be drafted and brought out from the prison. But to Geraldine, who did not have the experience of the Republican Movement to understand that, it indicated her Kieran was nothing more than a pawn. Her suspicions were fueled by the fact that whenever she did talk to Kieran about the hunger strike he reeled off his answers as if he had memorized them. And as she got to know relatives of the other hunger strikers and heard them relate what their men had told them it struck her that they all seemed to use the same terminology, almost as if they had been programmed. Her suspicions grew.

She kept writing to Kieran, even in the censored letters, trying to reassure him not to be worrying, that she would make sure he survived. Until he protested: "For God's sake will you stop telling me it's all right and not to worry—these guys will think I'm up to a 100 [scared]." But her fears continued to build up until one day she was sitting there with him and he was reading a newspaper and on the back of the page he was looking at she could see an article arguing that it was time the hunger strike ended, that there was nothing more that could be achieved by it. And Geraldine could hold it in no longer and she burst out: "Look, Kieran, will you come off this!" Kieran exploded. "Get out of here and don't come back," he shouted. She sat there, shocked and silent. She did not budge, but she was terrified that if she said any more he really would throw her out. "I don't want to talk about it," he said. She said nothing. But she told herself that he did not really mean it, that it was not him saying these things. How could anyone really mean it? How could they voluntarily die?

The worry was terrible. She developed shingles, which also made Kieran annoyed, because it was obviously a nervous reaction. Outside she was becoming more and more alienated from the Republican Movement. One day, at a meeting of relatives organized by Sinn Fein in a West Belfast hotel, the Lake Glen, she burst out: "I don't think decisions are being made inside the prison. I think decisions are being made by people present in this room." When the Irish Commission for Justice and Peace got involved she was convinced that they would resolve the whole thing. She had always had great faith in the Church and there was, after all, a bishop leading the commissioners. Surely he could solve it. Driving down to the Republic to take part in the campaign for Kieran's election in Cavan-Monaghan, she talked to a senior member of Sinn Fein—one of the Old Guard, who was highly respected in the Movement—and was astonished and excited to hear him say that he thought the commission's proposals should be accepted. On her next visit to the Kesh she eagerly recounted the conversation to Kieran, who seemed impressed as well. When nothing came of that and the initiative collapsed she became even more convinced that the IRA was making these men die.

It was just after the collapse of the ICJP initiative that she was asked by her sister to be godmother to her baby. But on the day of the christening they received word from the Kesh that Kieran was very ill. Would they come in full-time? In terms of prison regulations Geraldine was not really allowed in on these visits, because she did not belong to the family. But Alfie had obtained special permission for her through the prison chaplains. They were a bit worried about telling Kieran that they were starting the vigil—in a way it was telling him he was about to die. But he did not seem affected; he told Geraldine to make sure she wore comfortable clothes, to put on her old jeans. She did dig out her denims, but when she put them on found they were much too big for her, she had lost so much weight. She tried on a pair of black trousers, but they were worse, so she put the jeans back on again and her favorite blue blouse with white spots.

That night she slept on a hospital trolley, in a room put aside for her and the Dohertys just down the corridor from Kieran's room. She tossed and turned all night, the trolley squeaking and shifting on its castors every time she moved. She woke up feeling awful. She had no toothbrush and it was oppressively hot in the hospital. She and the Dohertys discussed how they would organize a rota and agreed she would come in during the days with Margaret, Alfie taking the night watch.

It was a curiously happy time, those days waiting for Kieran to die. Margaret, his mother, gave them lots of time to be on their own—"to let them hold hands," as she put it to herself. Kieran had his radio next to his bed, and of course they listened to every news broadcast in the hope of hearing some breakthrough. Otherwise they just talked and Geraldine found herself getting to know Kieran like she had never done before. She would sit there, with one of his brothers or sisters, listening to them chatting about their childhood, and to Kieran reminiscing about his days when he worked as a central heating engineer. She had been to the U.S.A. a little more than a year before and he made her tell him all about it. Sometimes he teased her, one day making her recite her Latin and French verbs. It was difficult to believe what was happening and once even he had to remind her. She knew the others were in the canteen watching television and she said to Kieran: "Are we keeping you back? You can be down there, you know." And he said: "Geraldine, I'm not down there because I'm very ill, you know."

Steadily he deteriorated. One day she brought in her precious picture of herself meeting the Pope. She had gone to Rome the previous year on pilgrimage and had met the Pope at his summer residence, Castel Gandolfo. The Pope had given her a rosary and had blessed her own beads. She had given hers to Kieran and made sure she was wearing the Pope's rosary throughout the hunger strike; she had to do everything to save him. She had always wanted to show Kieran the photograph, but you were not allowed to take pictures into the Kesh normally. Now that he was in the hospital she could. But the day she did bring it in Kieran's sight had gone. She gave it to him anyway and he sat there clutching it, his face yellow with jaundice, while she tried to describe it.

Fr. Faul was busy outside, trying to "educate" the families. His insistence that the IRA had the power to order an end to the hunger strike had worried the Dohertys—Margaret in particular. So together they confronted Kieran and asked him whether he wanted to come off. Kieran was adamant: "If we get the five demands—the July 4 statement—and my mind's away, you can take me off." So the Dohertys announced they were having nothing more to do with Fr. Faul, because he was trying to break the hunger strike against the wishes of the hunger strikers. But Geraldine kept seeing the Dungannon priest and attending his meetings.

Kieran began drifting in and out of consciousness, hallucinating at times—saying one day that he had been talking to Sean McDermott, his old friend who had been shot dead by the security forces.

After seventy days he said to his father: "I'm going to break records here." He was determined to last longer than MacSwiney. His mother asked him hesitantly if he wanted to see where he would be buried. He said he did, so she brought a photograph in of the Republican plot at Milltown cemetery. He said it looked beautiful.

On the night of Friday, July 31 Geraldine was sitting on Kieran's bed, listening to screams down the corridor. It was Paddy Quinn and it seemed to have been going on for hours. A warder came in and said that everyone had to stay where they were; Geraldine was not to leave the room. Then there was silence and she thought Paddy had died. But shortly afterwards Mrs. Doherty came in looking distracted and said that Mrs. Quinn had taken Paddy off. Later she heard that there had been something of a row when one of Kevin's sisters had suggested to Mrs. Doherty and Mrs. Lynch that it was time for them to follow suit.

Geraldine went home that night feeling a new surge of hope. If Paddy Quinn was off, surely that was the end of it. But in the middle of the night she was awakened by the telephone ringing. Her brother, Eugene, answered it—her family always raced to the telephone nowadays to answer it before she did, just in case. It was to say that Kevin Lynch had died. Outside Geraldine could hear the crashing of dustbin lids starting, as the women of West Belfast began to signal the death and the beginning of the rioting.

Next day Geraldine went up to the Kesh as usual with Mrs. Doherty. In the hospital the Lynch family was no longer there to share the waiting. It made Kieran seem terribly alone. He used to send messages to Kevin, the two of them asking how the other was, comparing their conditions. Kieran was confused today. He could not swallow water and they tried to wet his mouth with a soaked handkerchief. Then suddenly he said: "Geraldine, would you get me some tablets?"

"What do you want tablets for, Kieran?" she asked breathlessly.

"Geraldine, get me tablets."

"Why?"

"I want tablets, I want tablets for my body."

There had, of course, already been the experiences with Raymond McCreesh and Paddy Quinn and they had been warned that it could happen, but that of course it would mean nothing because they were simply delirious. But Kieran was looking straight at her and she told herself he was lucid. His brother, Terence, was in the room, so she made Kieran repeat himself three times. He seemed annoyed that she wasn't understanding him. "I'm going for your mammy," she said, decisively. And she went down to their rest room and told Mrs. Doherty: "Kieran wants tablets." Mrs. Doherty said: "He's raving." Geraldine said angrily: "He's not raving, now will you get the doctor?" Mrs. Doherty said: "Get out, it's none of your business." Geraldine ran out, down to the security grilles, crying. The warder at the grilles took her through to a waiting room where she sat until a principal officer came through and took her into his office. Still crying she recounted what had happened. The warder said: "Geraldine, Kieran's been asking for something to eat and for cups of tea, but we were afraid to give it to him, because of what happened to McCreesh." The warder telephoned the prison chaplain, who arrived shortly afterwards. She repeated the story. The priest went in to see Mrs. Doherty, but she said she wanted Alfie there before any decisions were taken. By the time Alfie arrived Kieran was in a coma. After discussing it with the doctor, Alfie said it appeared Kieran had been delirious, so his son's last wishes still stood and would be respected.

The warder asked Geraldine, in his office, if she would like to go and say goodnight to Kieran. She said she couldn't bear to face the Dohertys. Fr. Toner took her home.

On Sunday morning Geraldine went to Mass and on her way home she ran into Mrs. McDermott—the dead Sean's mother—and talked about the row with Kieran's family. When she got home she decided she had to see Kieran again and telephoned one of the priests at the Kesh. It was arranged and Mrs. McDermott drove her up with her mother, dropping her off at the prison. Inside the hospital the duty officer told her that Kieran's brother and sister were in with him, but that they were going to tell them that he needed to have his bedclothes changed, to get them out of the way. So Geraldine slipped in. She found that the room had been moved around and a heart monitor brought in. Kieran was unconscious. She talked to him, but he did not reply, just made a croaking noise. He had told her once that if it got to that stage and he seemed to be in a coma it was possible that he knew she was there, even if he could not tell her. If it happened she was to squeeze his hand and if he knew what was happening he would squeeze it back. So now she took his hand and squeezed it and he squeezed it back. Then the orderly said it was time to let his brother and sister back in, perhaps she should go. But she defiantly told him to let them in. They looked surprised and angry. And then Geraldine leaned over him and kissed him and said: "I'm away, I'll see you later."

As Geraldine walked through the grilles and the gates Kieran died. The news was broken to her when she reached home. He had missed MacSwiney's record by just a few hours.

To Brownie Sunday 2.8.81 9 P.M.
. . . I've just heard about Doc. God rest him. He was bloody marvellous when we spoke to him on Wednesday. Dear God this is fierce altogether. We'll have to break these bastards right. Sin e . . . PS Nixy [one of the 1980 hunger strikers] is pushing IRSP to cut Owen [Carron] out of election.

An Bean Uasal Sun 2.8.81 3 P.M. from OC H5
A radio was lost this morning in this block. The man whom it was found on (S. McVeigh S. Strand) has been taken to the boards. Could you inform H6 of what has happened. I will let the other blocks know. Will have to wait now to see what repercussions there be from the screws . . .

Within one hour of Kieran's death the IRA launched a rocket attack on an army Saracen in the Falls Road. A twenty-one-year-old soldier, Corporal Phillip Hartley, lost both legs in the explosion. He had just returned to northern Ireland after recovering from injuries suffered on an earlier tour of duty.

Earlier in the day two policemen had died when an IRA unit triggered a 600-lb. bomb under their car in Co. Tyrone. The dead officers had six children.

On Monday the flags on government buildings in Dublin were flown at half mast for Kieran. Government officials were quick to point out that it was the custom upon the death of a parliamentarian, but even that did not detract from the sight of the Irish political establishment mourning the death of a jailed IRA man.

There was a mood to match the flags, inside those buildings. The memory of the clashes outside the British Embassy were still fresh, a bomb had hit a power plant in Monaghan on Saturday night while on Sunday 100 demonstrators had attacked a police station in the county and a petrol bomb had been thrown at another police station in Co. Kildare. There would have to be a by-election to fill Kieran's seat. The other prisoner holding an Irish seat, Paddy Agnew, was threatening to resign. The seats would probably go to Fianna Fail, weakening FitzGerald's fingerhold on power yet further and possibly forcing another general election. John Kelly, the acting Foreign Minister, lamented in a radio interview that the IRA was taking no notice of his government's denunciations, while the British Government was scarcely more responsive. Charlie Haughey said: "Like many other people in the country, I am becoming increasingly angry that the situation is being allowed to continue indefinitely."

They buried Kevin on Tuesday, in Dungiven as he had asked his mother—just a few dozen yards from that monument where he used to pause on his way to Mass, for O'Carolan and Kilmartin. It was an important occasion for the IRSP, but the Lynch family had not forgiven them for the way they had been handled over the hunger strike. The family refused to allow the INLA to mount its customary guard of honor over the coffin in their house, asking friends to do it for him instead. Six masked gunmen did fire a volley of pistol shots over his coffin in the churchyard, which infuriated the parish priest, Fr. John Quinn, who had been given assurances that no such military display would be made. In protest he refused to wear his ceremonial vestments at the graveside. But a piper played the lament which had sounded Sands to his grave: "I'll Wear No Convict's Uniform."

Kieran's funeral followed on Tuesday. He was buried in Milltown cemetery, in the Republican plot—the place his mother had shown him in the photograph.

The deaths of Kevin Lynch and Kieran Doherty had swamped the earlier speculation that Mrs. Quinn's decision heralded the end to the hunger strike. But if the authorities had known about the trouble McFarlane was having inside the Kesh they would have been more optimistic than they were at this stage.

McFarlane's biggest worry was still his old friend and co-escapee, Pat McGeown, who had replaced Joe McDonnell. McGeown's had been a challenging voice since the start of the hunger strike; in the "kitchen cabinet" around Sands earlier in the year he had played the role, to some extent, of a devil's advocate—putting the suggestions which nobody else wanted to voice, like ending the blanket protest and abandoning the hunger strike. He had always been worried about the blanket protest, the hearkening back to Tom MacSwiney and those who endure the most. He felt that it was not a practical approach: sure, you came out of it with a moral superiority, but the Movement already had that, he thought, and so did not need to do it. What the prisoners had to do was win the battle and in order to do that they needed to be more flexible, to adopt a two-pronged approach—try to destroy the system by working within it while at the same time standing outside it. He had been overruled, of course, and on the basis of that majority decision he had made the personal decision to join the hunger strike himself. It was rough for him, from an early stage. On about the eighteenth day he went down with a bout of flu and was moved to the hospital early. He also had an infection in his nose and was suffering from internal bleeding—he had spent three weeks in Musgrave Park Hospital the previous year undergoing tests to establish the cause of the bleeding, without success. But it was his nose that was worst—streaming dark green mucus, making it even more difficult to drink. The doctors wanted him to take medicine for it, but he refused.

At Mass on Sunday morning, between the deaths of Kevin Lynch and Kieran Doherty, he confided to McFarlane that he doubted whether he would go through with the fast. It was a major blow to McFarlane. McGeown raised the same points he had before and some new ones. He felt that a settlement was achievable, if without the propaganda impact they had previously hoped. He was critical of the outside leadership's handling of the Mountain Climber initiative, feeling that Adams and company should have been more flexible and met the Foreign Office negotiator half way. He also complained that the Church representatives had not been given enough of an opportunity to mediate before being rejected. McFarlane countered by arguing that it would have been madness to compromise before the British had crossed the base line, into true negotiations. The Mountain Climber episode had not gone that far and in retrospect it simply looked like an attempt to undermine them. The British knew full well what a flexible settlement amounted to, but they were just not willing to cross the line. McGeown retorted: "How can the Brits know what we want—I don't even know." McFarlane asked why he had not raised these issues with Adams when he had come in the previous week. McGeown said he had been too worried that the room was bugged. It all made McFarlane a very worried man. He did not have time in Mass to finish the argument, so he sent a long comm to McGeown, going over the points again and adding that his doubts could be highly damaging to the morale of the other hunger strikers if they spread. It all smacked of the disastrous ending of the first hunger strike. If McGeown could not see it through, then would he please make a decision to come off before being transferred to the prison hospital, otherwise it could lead to catastrophe.

To Brownie Wednesday 5.8.81 9.30 A.M. from Bik
Comrade Mor, top of the morning to ye. Just after reading Pat boy's [McGeown's] comm to you, I got one in similar vein. There's an air of relief and a degree of contentment in his words. It appears he has conquered his problem alright, but I just can't make a 100% judgement on that at all. To be sure in myself I'd need a yarn with him to broaden out on things and this is just physically impossible as we are at opposite ends of the wing. It's impossible to say if he has truly won the inner battle or not. It certainly appears so, because the tone of that comm is one of a very much relieved mind. He has been truthful with us to date which has caused him much pain. It couldn't have been easy to open up like that. Anyway, I just don't know now. As it stands I feel I must accept that the inner conflict has ended and has ended favourably. Who can read minds eh? I can say little else at this stage. I'll get back to you later. Love to 'Roach 90' and 'Tish.' Take care and God Bless—Bik—xoxoxo

To Brownie Wed 5.8.81 from Bik
. . . Just on Padraig Beog [McGeown]—I can't really say more than I said today. All I can do is to let you know that he has come through a pretty rough week or two of internal conflict which he appears to have risen above yesterday . . . [but who] can be certain? Only himself, I suppose. Every man must face similar problems and each must overcome inner conflicts. I have had plenty myself, but then I'm not on hunger strike so I have more time

without that type of pressure to work things out. Anyway my heart goes out to him, cara, and to them all. This is really a titan struggle . . .

It was a depressing time for McFarlane. The problem with McGeown was followed by a message from Musgrave Park Hospital that Paddy Quinn would not be reembarking on hunger strike. McFarlane decided he must write a note to him, reassuring him. He was a good lad, Paddy. And then two of the block OCs sent him comms warning of morale problems.

To Brownie Friday 7.8.81 9 P.M. from Bik
. . . I answered them telling them both not to allow a feeling of despair to creep in. I've commed all the blocks to that effect, urging the lads to stand firmly together and fight back. There is obviously a certain feeling of helplessness seeping into some men and I can understand because they've taken a fair hammering this last while back . . . Make them see that we can in fact break the Brits if we believe in ourselves . . .

The IRA commander in H6 had done a straw poll among his men, estimating about thirty percent wanted to call a halt, believing the hunger strike had become hopeless; another thirty percent were not confident of winning, but believed they should continue as long as they could, the remaining forty percent demanding no compromise.

Not only the prisoners were being sapped by the struggle. On Thursday police released figures on violence accompanying the hunger strike: fifty-one dead, ten of them policemen and thirteen soldiers; over 1,000 injured and 1,700 arrested.

Desultory attempts to find a way out of it all continued. In Dublin the acting Foreign Minister, John Kelly, passed a message to the British Embassy suggesting that if the prison reforms hinted at were introduced immediately for conforming prisoners London would be able to give both a practical demonstration of what was on offer and at the same time avoid the charge that it was capitulating to the protesting inmates. It was specious and London politely rejected it. Jerome Connolly, of the ICJP, telephoned Fr. Murphy at the Kesh with a message suggesting that the prisoners make a written complaint to the Northern Ireland Office that their request for clarification of the Government's position and meaningful dialogue had not been met. Perhaps this would open a channel for fresh moves in which the commission could be brought in as witnesses—or even the English Commission for Justice and Peace, which was annoyed at the way their Irish counterparts had been treated by the Government. Fr. Murphy passed the message on to McFarlane apologetically, anticipating the response, which he duly got: Tell Connolly to either call for the five demands, or get lost.

Inside the prison hospital Tom McElwee was granted a rare privilege by the authorities. At the time of the premature explosion back in 1976 which resulted in the capture of him and his brother, Benedict, police had arrested Tom's girlfriend, Dolores O'Neill, in follow-up operations. Dolores had subsequently been sentenced to twenty years. With Tom on his sixty-first day on hunger strike the NIO decided to grant a request from Dolores to make the trip from Armagh prison to see him.

The next day Mrs. McElwee was in to see Tom with his big sister, Enda. They had not started a bedside vigil, because he had insisted that he was too well for that. He did not seem too bad that day, although he had stopped smoking the cigars he had taken to smoking since going into hospital. And he did confess that he had felt bad after Dolores had left him—as if his stomach was falling out. Mrs. McElwee was wearing her new light-blue raincoat which she had bought for a trip she had made to the U.S.A. in June, trying to whip up support for the hunger strikers. She was to meet some Congressmen on that trip, but had called it off early when she had heard of Martin Hurson's death and had come back to be with Tom. As the visit came to an end and she walked to the door with Enda her son called to her: "Mummy, that's a nice coat." She smiled and he waved goodbye.

That night Tom and Pat McGcown got talking. They were old friends, having shared a cell together in the blocks about two years before. In those days a favorite topic of conversation between them was the difference between country and city attitudes; comparing notes, they had been intrigued to find that the Irish divide in the country was more political and in the city more sectarian. Tom would tell how many of his neighbors were Protestants and Loyalists, yet friendly with the family—a rarity in the cities, at least in the ghetto areas. Now Tom said he had written to some of those Protestant neighbors, trying to explain the hunger strike to them. They also talked about Mickey Devine's condition—Mickey had just hit the "sickness" phase which all of them had suffered, around the forty-day mark, with the puzzling exception of Tom. They agreed that it must have been because Tom only had one eye. Tom said he was finding it difficult to read now; he had got half way through an Eilis Dillon novel, but had given up. Pat asked if he could borrow it, he didn't think he had read that one. Tom told him about Dolores's visit, saying it had been good, but too short—he felt he had so much more to say when she had left. Pat told him he would probably be given another visit with her before he hit the crisis. And then it was lock-up time.

They were awakened as usual at 7:30 A.M. The mobile machine with its seat was rolled in on castors to weigh them and they had their blood pressure taken. Then the doors were locked and they listened to the radio, waiting for the doctor to do his rounds, ignoring the breakfast of cornflakes, milk and tea dumped at the bottom of their beds. During slop-out

Pat wandered into Tom's cell to return the book, which he had read after all. . . .

Mrs. McElwee had suffered the fears and doubts of most of the hunger strikers' mothers, although they did not talk about it much on these visits. At one stage early on in Tom's fast she had got very worried about the stories that the IRA was ordering the men to die and she had written to him, asking about it, but he had written back saying it was nonsense—that if anything they were forcing the IRA to allow the hunger strike. She had accepted that. But she had never really believed that it would reach the point where he could die. Now, with over sixty days gone, that point was obviously fast approaching.

On the Saturday she and her husband decided it was time for a family conference to make a decision on what they should do. They wanted an outsider's advice, so they asked their doctor from Bellaghy to come out and join them. And they were sitting there, in their sitting room, listening to the doctor talking about what the medical effect would be if they took Tom off now, when the telephone rang. The younger boy, James, picked it up, listened and then dropped it.

The hunger strikers had been allowed out for exercise. Tom could not make it. The medical officer was standing at his door, chatting with him—they got on quite well. Pat joined Lorny—Laurence McKeown—in the exercise yard. It was a beautiful, sunny day. They walked around the perimeter of the yard for about half an hour, then shortly before 11:30 A.M. they heard a noise coming from the wards, sounding like someone battling for breath. Lorny said: "That's Tom." His window overlooked the exercise yard. They walked on, the heavy breathing getting worse, then there was a gasp. "Tom's died," said Lorny. The two men were feeling exhausted in the heat, so they sat down on the tarmac, resting. Two "crims" working as orderlies in the hospital—one a Catholic, the other a former member of the Protestant UVF—came and joined them. Then Lorny had a weak spell and keeled over and they had to carry him in. The hospital was quiet when they went in. The doctor rushed past, looking worried. The medical officer whom they had last seen chatting to Tom was looking white and shocked. "What's wrong?" Pat asked him. "Big Tom has died." "Aye," said Pat. They were locked in their cells. In the silence of the hospital they could hear the trolley trundling down the corridor, to collect the latest body. Later they learned that Tom had asked the medical officer for a light for his cigarette. The officer had gone to fetch his lighter and been delayed a few minutes by the arrival of the chaplain. By the time he had let the priest in and got back to the cell with the lighter Tom was dead.

Inside H-Block 4 Benedict McElwee had only seen his brother, Tom, briefly on the hunger strike. Since being jailed five years before they had seen each other sporadically. Initially Tom went into H5 and Bennie into H3. Then for about a year they had both been in H4, in adjoining wings, and had met a few times, mostly at Mass. Subsequently they had both been moved to H6 in the abortive attempt to isolate the IRA leadership. For most of that time they had been forced to take separate visits with their family. About half way through Tom's hunger strike they had met coincidentally outside the visiting area, each of them waiting to see different members of the family. The warders were hurrying them on, but they had snatched a few words in Irish, Bennie asking Tom how he was, Tom saying OK, telling each other to keep the chin up. Bennie had asked twice for permission to see Tom during the hunger strike, but had been told he would only be getting it when his condition was serious.

On that Saturday morning Bennie was lying on his mattress, staring at the ceiling, when his cell door swung open and the warder said: "You've a visit to the hospital." He was led down the corridor to cell 26 where he pulled on the uniform. And then it was through the grilles and out of the block. The blue Transit van was waiting for him. The screw with him, nicknamed "Gusty" after the famous Protestant paramilitary leader, was usually a jovial man, but today he was quiet. It was the first time Bennie had been into the hospital, but the procedure was familiar to the H-Blocks—the wait at the grilles as the warders went through the formalities of prison security. When they reached the Circle he saw Fr. Toner waiting for him. The priest walked towards him. "I've sad news for you," he said. "Thomas has died." Bennie could feel the warders watching him and he fought back the tears. He was taken into a side room. The family had been told, said Fr. Toner. But would he go in and see Tom, just to identify him for the record—it would save his family. So Bennie said OK and was taken through to Tom's room. He was still lying in his bed, his bones sticking up sharply, as if they were about to break through the skin. He looked totally different from the brother he had last seen.

Bennie walked out of the ward with only one thought in his mind: that come what may the screws were not going to see his tears. It was a battle with himself, as he was led out once again through the grilles, locked in the Transit van, back into H4, undressed in cell 26 and then naked back down the corridor. As the steel door slammed behind him he lay down on the mattress, pulled the blanket over his head and started to cry.

To Brownie Sun 9.8.81 from Bik 10 P.M.
Comrade Mor, the news yy [yesterday] of Big Tom's death greatly stunned us here. It came suddenly and left us pretty numb. He was a terrific character—a pillar of strength here with the deep respect of every last blanket man. He was fearless and never knew despair. It is indeed a very great loss. I think he made a fair impression on you the other

week. It's hard to properly describe such a man. You need to meet him, cara. His spirit was marvellous, God rest him . . . Also would you get an A/C comm to B. Fox (St James) H5 re hunger strike replacement. I will phase him in on Monday 24th to bring our number back to 8. Also IRSP have no further replacements, so I intend to use our men, unless you feel we shouldn't for some reason or other. Dark was telling me this morning he got word from Cleaky that UVF were told by outside to make contact with me to discuss our five demands. Apparently Harold McCusker and others are pushing a line for them on segregation and clothes and they want to thrash out some pointers with us. But no way does Harold want to pursue five demands. They've probably studied our documents and are trying to hit a feasible compromise line with the Brits . . . Personally, cara, I don't particularly want to set eyes on any of them at all. I've no time for them. They are only wasters and robots sin e. My feelings are not sectarian. Believe it or not, I never really was that way inclined . . .

It was ten years, to the day, after the introduction of internment in the north, an anniversary which was always marked by violence, redoubled this year. It was estimated that 1,000 petrol bombs were thrown in the course of rioting on Sunday morning. Two people died during the weekend, one a forty-year-old man killed by a plastic bullet, the other a sixteen-year-old Catholic boy shot dead from a passing car while walking with friends in North Belfast.

There was more trouble with the clergy at Tom McElwee's funeral, in St. Mary's church in Bellaghy. The priest, Fr. Michael Flanagan, took the opportunity to get a few points off his chest, chastising the Government for showing such indifference to the ICJP, but adding: "It is similarly disappointing when those who called the hunger strike should not end it, particularly when they achieved electoral victories in both

DAVID BERESFORD

families and the community continuing suffering." Several
women in the congregation, including Bernadette McAliskey, stormed out of the church in protest. On the way to the
cemetery the McElwees broke with an Irish tradition, his
eight sisters helping carry their brother's coffin. The graveside
oration was delivered by Sinn Fein's Danny Morrison, who
told mourners that at the end Tom had repeatedly said "that
he longed for the day when the Protestant and Catholic people
of this land would live together in peace and harmony." Morrison added: "We do not claim to be perfect, nor do we claim
the certainty of God's blessing on our work. But we stand
over this, that as sure as there's a sun in the sky and as the
earth turns on its axis, then there can never be moral wrong
in an oppressed people using force against their oppressors."

The McElwee funeral was not the only gathering to be
disrupted. In Magherafelt, near Bellaghy, a council meeting
was scheduled two days later. As it opened Frank Hughes's
brother, Oliver—one of the Nationalist councillors who held
a one-person majority—walked up to the chairman, Patrick
Sweeney, and said: "Chairman, this meeting is not going on
tonight."

"Why not?" asked Mr. Sweeney, also a Nationalist.

"Look, I've lost my brother and I've lost my cousin and
it's time we closed this shop down," said Hughes.

Sweeney duly proposed that the meeting be adjourned, as
a mark of respect for Tom McElwee, as well as for a former
councillor who had died recently, of natural causes, and—as
a conciliatory gesture to the Unionist councilors—for a local
man who had been killed by the IRA.

Among the Unionist councillors was a clergyman, the Rev.
William McCrea, famous as the most popular gospel singer in
the north and notorious as a hard-line Protestant extremist.
McCrea stood up and said it would be an insult to couple the
dead councillor's name with that of "the murderer McElwee."

Furious exchanges ensued, the Unionists denouncing the hunger strikers as murderers and terrorists, the Nationalists shouting that the real terrorists were in policemen's uniforms. A Unionist took a swing at Sweeney, knocking him flat. Hughes picked up a chair and belted McCrea over the head. A pitched battle followed, civic leaders scrambling over the furniture to get at each other, punching and kicking. The police were called to break it up. Hughes loaded the battered chairman in his Renault 18 and drove him to the local hospital, arriving to find it was visiting time. They put on a fine performance, Hughes holding up Sweeney as he limped into casualty, moaning and groaning with his £30,000 gold chain of office dangling from his neck like a cowbell. Then Hughes saw an ambulance draw up and the Rev. McCrea being unloaded in a wheelchair. So he charged at him, grabbing him by the lapel and dragging him out of it. He was himself grabbed and thrown off the premises. The next day he was back visiting Sweeney when a television crew arrived. Hughes posed tenderly, mopping Sweeney's brow.

In New York staff had hauled down the Union Jack flying outside the British Consulate and bundled it away in a cupboard, to await better times.

Ireland's Deputy Prime Minister and new leader of the Labour party, Dick Spring, went on national radio to say: "It is my personal opinion that this matter could have been settled if there had been any other prime minister in Britain." Cardinal O Fiaich said on radio that he shuddered to think what would happen if it was not stopped. Recalling his meeting with Mrs. Thatcher in July he said: "I would not like to say that I was convinced she did not care. While she would like to see this problem solved it did not impinge very much upon her political activities, nor did she look upon the Northern Ireland situation in general as one of her priorities. If the same thing were happening in Yorkshire or Kent or anywhere else across the water, there would certainly be some greater sense of urgency in seeking a solution." Garret FitzGerald went on television to accuse Mrs. Thatcher of inflexibility: "All I can hope at the moment is that on further reflection, over a somewhat longer time scale, the British Government will recognize its position." He added that he was puzzled by the decision of the British Government to call the Fermanagh–South Tyrone by-election to fill Sands's seat, given that it did not usually hold elections in August. "It seems a singularly unhelpful time to have an election from the point of view of moderate forces in Northern Ireland."

The by-election had been set for August 20. The writ had been moved by a Welsh Nationalist MP, Dafydd Elis Thomas, amidst accusations that the Government—already seen to be tampering with democracy, with the new legislation banning prisoners from standing—were stalling for fear of another humiliation at the hands of the Catholic electorate.

Unable to put forward a hunger striker, the Republican Movement had considered various options, including the candidacy of one of the Crumlin Road escapees who was still on the run. But in the end they decided to play safe, putting up the little man who in a way had started the whole electoral hare in the constituency, Sands's election agent, Owen Carron. There was some unhappiness in the Movement: they had, after all, "borrowed" the seat for Bobby Sands, now it seemed to be becoming a habit.

There was some opposition from the IRSP, loath to see Sinn Fein pulling off another coup. They tried unsuccessfully to get McAliskey to stand. And after that it did look very much like a repeat of April. The SDLP agonized again over whether to stand. The executive committee decided, by eleven votes to seven, that they should. But then the constituency branch in Fermanagh–South Tyrone voted by forty-eight to forty-four that they did not want to take part. The executive accepted this, issuing a statement in which they said: "This decision reflected the strong feelings about the circumstances in which this election was called and, in particular, the contempt shown for the electorate in Fermanagh–South Tyrone by hurried changes in the electoral law and the unusual timing of this by-election, to say nothing of the highly emotional atmosphere in which the by-election was called."

The Unionists had made a deal, agreeing on a former B Special and major in the Ulster Defense Regiment, Ken Maginnis, as a unity candidate. Carron faced competition on the Catholic side. Sinn Fein the Workers Party—previously the political wing of the old "Official" IRA, which was trying to escape its own history by name changes—put up a candidate, as did the Alliance Party, an essentially Unionist grouping which nevertheless had some support in the Catholic community, drawing nearly twelve percent of the Northern Ireland vote in the 1979 general election.

The rhetoric was much the same the second time round, Maginnis declaring: "If the Catholics vote once for a hunger striker that is bad enough. If they do it again, it will appear that they are condoning all the violence that has occurred since Sands's death." And the Nationalist population answered him in much the same way as they had to Concannon back in April, returning Carron with an even bigger majority than Sands. As the graffiti said on a school wall in the constituency: "Fuck 1690—we want a replay."

Harold McCusker, the Unionist MP for neighboring Armagh, gave a press conference to tell of his disgust at Republican impersonation at the polling booths. He had had two of them arrested himself and saw another two get away. Thousands of votes had been impersonated, he said. "Between 5,000 and 10,000."

A Sinn Fein official, Danny Morrison, butted in: "Tell them about the four Loyalists arrested in Moygashel. I hope you're talking about that! Tell them about how the village of Rosslea was sealed off to prevent Catholics voting."

"I don't talk to the associates of murderers," said McCusker.

"Get that down and we'll have a smoke," said his cellmate as devotions ended to be replaced by the buzz of conversation along the pipes, between windows and across the corridor.

The prisoner pulled the package out again and, squatting on his mattress, started the rolling. Fourteen in the wing smoked; a couple each would do for the time being. His fingers worked delicately, flattening the paper, and laying the thin trail of tobacco. His cellmate joined in the work. They made them needle-thin, one normal cigarette the equivalent to nearly half a dozen prison roll-ups.

"Who's had a visit, then?"

"I'm rolling," shouted the prisoner.

"Yo," came a shout to the left. The prisoner listened absentmindedly as the recital started, of comrades captured, Paisley's antics, clerical denunciations ... When the rolling was done the prisoner took half the cigarettes, fumbled for the long thread among his bric-a-brac store in the mattress and, tying the cigarettes to the end of the thread to make a pendulum, clambered on to the pipes.

"OK," he called as he started swinging them in the well created by the perspex window box. It was hard work, but he finally felt the tug of fingers from the next window and he let the string go slack, hauling it in as it dropped free after a few seconds, fumbling with the knot next door.

At the door his cellmate was shooting a button across the corridor, flicking it out and drawing it back on the attached thread, to shouts of advice from a prisoner squinting through the crack in the opposite door: "Harder and to the left ... more to the left, more to the left ... now a bit right." A shout of triumph as the scooper on the other side finally made contact with his paper shovel and they started ferrying the second batch of roll-ups.

The prisoner pulled a small piece of thread out of his towel, fluffed it out, flicked the tiny lighter wheel four times against a piece of flint before getting a flame. He ignited another piece of plaited thread, wet and then dried stiff on the pipes. The two men, heads together, gently blew their cigarette alight and then sent the smouldering thread across the corridor on the cotton bridge before hauling the line in. Down the corridor to the right the training officer called a lecture.

"Right, lads, the lecture tonight is on the five 'isms,' that is the five separate strands of philosophy which go to make up what we know as the ideology of Irish Republicanism— which make Irish Republicanism distinct and unique as a philosophy . . ."

The prisoner and his cellmate angled their mattresses against the wall and drew deeply, enjoying the smoke in silence, half listening to the lecture.

"The next of the 'isms' is nonsectarianism. That's how it is laid out in the formal lecture. But rather than being non-sectarian we are antisectarian. The Republican Movement recognizes sectarianism and all its ugliness as being a tool of imperialism . . ."

The prisoner tried a smoke ring, which lazily curled up towards the brown-stained light in the ceiling.

"The next 'ism' is socialism. In socialism and nationalism we have the most important of the five 'isms.' Socialism is our belief that the ownership of Ireland is vested as of right in the people of Ireland and that the individual right of any person within the nation is not good as held against the right of the nation to prosper . . ."

"Can I ask you a question there?" It was a country accent, one of the new lads in last week. The prisoner gave a thumbs up to his cellmate, who shook his head before taking a last drag on his smoke.

"What happens, like, you take a situation: My father got a farm from his father whose grandfather farmed it and whose great-grandfather farmed it. And it's only a small farm and it's not doing no harm. Is there no private ownership at all allowed here?"

The training officer, who had fought over the ground innumerable times during the great debates back in the Cages, sounded a little testy as he replied.

"Look, there's no hard and fast role for the advent of socialism in a country. Socialism in any country is a product of the nation's history, the cultural background of its people. There's no hard and fast rules, no absolute blueprint for bringing about socialism in a country. All that you can lay down are guiding principles and those guiding principles should be that private ownership and private enterprise are held to be invalid as soon as they begin to infringe on the rights of others, or as soon as they begin to manipulate the labor or wealth of others."

"Well, I can see all that, but when we get through all this argument and fancy talk, will I have my farm or will I not?"

A hubbub of voices signaled the start of another of the interminable battles between the "rosary beads wrapped around the .303 brigade" and the Young Turks. Except the Young Turks were getting older, the prisoner thought to himself. The training officer was a youngster and likely to flare up, but he had an OK background—that's why he had the job: a stint in the Cages as a teenager, operational experience and a rough time in Castlereagh without breaking.

Castlereagh! The prisoner's mind went back to his own time in the police interrogation center. He breathed heavily in reflex, at the recollection of the wet towel suffocating him. What did that Special Branch man say about Doirend?

*Christ, but they must have been watching him carefully.
The cop had been right, of course, she had found someone
else. He wished she had waited. Waited? For twenty-two
years? Well . . . Ah, for chrissake. Wonder what she'd be
like when he got out. Say ten years, if the protest ended.
If . . . Well, then he'd be thirty-five. Would he look her up?
Maybe he'd run into her. Where? At the Andytown social
club.* "Excuse me. Oh!" Shit. *The sound of the training
officer—calling for quiet in the argument over the countryman and his granddad's farm—brought him back to his cell.*
"OK, cool it. You're objecting very strongly, so what we'll
do is have a debate on it tomorrow night. You can pick a
crew of fellows and we'll put up an opposing team and have
a proper debate . . ."

"Does you want to call a few singers?"

"On your bike, we had a sing-song last night."

*The argument was ended by a voice launching into the
ballad of McIlhatton's brew that had the birds in the burrows,
the rabbits in the sky and the fox out chasing the hounds.*

"Quiet, lads, there's a concert going on in H4." *The chatter gradually petered out as they tuned in to the distant chorus
of "The Provo's Lullaby."*

It was cold.

"D'yuh remember the Christmas of '78?"

"'77, y'mean?"

"No, '78, I was in H4." *His cellmate grunted agreement.*

"Christ that was cold," *said the prisoner.* "Me and Jimmy
made forty ice bricks on the window, with those trifle cartons
we got for dinner. They looked like frosted bullion bars."

*The two of them lay staring up at the ceiling, thinking of
Christmases past and Christmases to come. Nineteen more
of them, if the protest goes on, thought the prisoner. Nearly
1,000 weeks, 7,000 days. Into jail at twenty-two out in his
forties.*

Through the perspex lid of the window box the stars sparkled sharply in the black sky. The snow on the ground had thawed a little and then frozen hard again into ice. Across the way in H4 the chorus had ended and a solo started. The lone voice echoed the ancient lament across the empty yards, wire fences and steel gates with absolute clarity.

TEN

"We were not just comrades, we were blanket men."

—Ex-prisoner, Long Kesh

They called him Red Mickey. It was a pun, really: he was a member of a revolutionary socialist INLA, and he had red hair. "A typical Derry lad," one Republican publication was to describe him. And maybe he was. But he was a very untypical hunger striker.

Michael Devine was born on May 26, 1954, about a mile outside Derry in a place called Springtown, a housing slum made up of prefabricated Nissen huts which had been occupied by American servicemen stationed in the Province during the Second World War. The house had two bedrooms, a kitchen and a toilet, with a tin bath to wash in. At least it was not cramped: unusually for a Catholic family of that generation, he had only a sister, Margaret, who was seven years older than he. In 1960 they were moved to a flat in a new housing estate, the Creggan, just above the Bogside. Some of the other kids in the flat saw Mickey as a bit odd—sort of stand-offish. But it was there that he met Noel Moore, who was to become his lifelong best friend. Noel, who lived in the flats with his parents—a family of fifteen—was an easy-going, happy-go-lucky lad and together they had great fun, playing catch-and-kiss with a couple of local girls down in Brooke Park—it was more of a rubbish dump, really, than a park, although it had a big fountain, slides and some bushes to hide in. They got their first job together, as well: a paper round. They had seen a sign in a newsagent's in the Strand Road and Mickey was peering at it shortsightedly when a bird flew overhead and shat on his head. Which was good luck of course, in the Irish tradition, and sure enough within ten minutes they had the job, sharing it between them, the money and the work.

At home life was not so good for Mickey. He was eleven when his father died, of leukemia. Shortly afterwards Margaret married a local coalman, Frank McAuley, and Mickey was left with his mother and grandmother.

In Derry at this time the Civil Rights agitation which gave birth to the present troubles was moving to a head. The so-called Maiden City had long been a symbol of conflict in Ireland. Founded as a religious settlement by St. Columba— Derry, or "Doire," means oak grove—it was granted by James I, in the early seventeenth century, to the Irish Society of London. They built the hilltop fortifications still surrounding the commercial center of the city and appended "London" to the ancient name. The famous Catholic ghetto of the Bogside grew under its wall, taking its name from the marshland on which it developed. In 1689 the garrison town, siding with the Protestant William of Orange, held off the Catholic forces of King James II in a famous siege which gave Derry a central place in Loyalist mythology. Today the very choice of name in conversation—Derry, or Londonderry—is a cipher by which the user identifies with one or other side of the political divide.

Cut off from the farming region of Donegal by Partition, starved of capital development by the Stormont government and kept under the control of Protestants by gerrymandering of municipal boundaries, the city had long been a hotbed of Catholic discontent when the waves of the Civil Rights movement from America and the continent began beating against Irish shores in the 1960s. Then on October 5, 1968 a march was staged in Derry which, it was later to be said, changed the course of Irish history. Organized by a fiery young socialist orator, Eamonn McCann, and banned by Stormont, it was attended by only a few hundred demonstrators led by, among others, John Hume and the Belfast MP, Gerry Fitt. The police, with no provocation other than the technical illegality of the gathering, attacked them with batons. The scenes which followed—including Fitt bleeding copiously from a head wound—were televised and catapulted the territory to British and international attention and into the mayhem which was to follow.

Mickey Devine was fourteen at the time. He did not attend the march, but saw it on television and joined the other youths from the Creggan and the Bogside in the rioting which followed that night—smashing shop windows and stoning the police. Within a month every youth in Derry seemed to have become a political activist. For Mickey politics offered him a comradeship which he eagerly embraced, attaching himself to the left-wing radicals who gathered around Eamonn McCann and joining the Young Socialists.

He later joined a Trotskyist organization, the Young Socialist Group—the youth wing of the Northern Ireland Labour party—which later became the Workers Revolutionary Party, made famous by the membership of the actress Vanessa Redgrave. But as the barricades went up in the Bogside the drift towards Republicanism was denounced as "sectarian" by the Young Socialists, who thereby cut themselves off from the community. Mickey opted to man the barricades and joined the Official IRA.

On January 30, 1972 he took part in another demonstration in the city which ended even more violently than that of October 1968: in Bloody Sunday, the day on which British paratroopers ran amok and killed fourteen demonstrators. Mickey was not hurt, but it confirmed him even more deeply in the comradeship of arms. It was not a comradeship which always made Mickey happy, however. One day, short of cash, he broke into a shop on the edge of the Bogside and raided the till. The comrades in the Official IRA found out about it and they held a disciplinary inquiry. It looked, at first, as if he was going to be kneecapped. But instead they chose to humiliate him. He was ordered to clean the streets for a couple of hours, with a sign around his neck saying: "I am a thief."

In September 1972 he received one of the biggest blows of his life, when he came home to the Creggan flat one day and found his mother dead on the sofa, his grandmother desperately trying to revive her. It had been a brain tumor. She was only forty-five years old.

Mickey went to live for a while with his sister, Margaret, and her husband. But after a while he had a fight with Margaret and moved out, taking a room with an old Republican family, the Walmsleys. Norman Walmsley had a daughter, also called Margaret and Mickey started taking her out. She became pregnant. A story went around that Mickey was not responsible, but it was not true and one day he came running over to his old buddy, Noel Moore.

"Would you do best man for me?"

"What?"

"I'm getting married, would you do best man for me? I've no money."

"Well, how're you going to get married?"

"I'll sort that all out."

"Wait'll I tell you this, Mickey, I've no money either. How're you going to get married, what're you going to do about the drink?"

"I'll sort that out."

"Where're you going to hold the reception?"

"I've sorted that out, in a house over in the Bog."

"What about a meal and all?"

"Sandwiches."

And so they were married, Mickey at the age of nineteen, Maggie seventeen. He and Noel put red roses in their

buttonholes and on their way to the church Mickey said he
needed a drink and they stopped off to get a bottle of vodka,
taking a few shots. Afterwards they posed for a wedding
photograph and there, perched behind the legs of Mickey and
Maggie and Noel and the bridesmaids and Norman Walmsley,
can be seen the bottle of vodka in its carry-out bag. The reception was a great carry-on, with much drinking and singing of
songs. Mickey had not invited his sister, Margaret. She found
out about it later and reproachfully took a present around to
him and they made up.

It was not a happy marriage—they rarely are in such circumstances; a couple too young to have formed their own
personalities, the feeling of having been trapped. Mickey was
off to the pubs a lot, usually in the Frying Pan on the edge of
the Bog. They began to fight, physically as well as verbally.
She was a skinny little thing, 5 feet 1 inch tall with long hair
and bony face. Mind you, he was no Atlas—5 feet 8 inches
tall, tubby, with thick glasses, a slight turn in his left eye,
shoulder-length bright red hair sometimes parted down the
middle, and a habit of holding his head a little to one side. He
had got a steady job, working as an assistant in a draper's shop
owned by a Protestant up in the old city. And of course he
was still in the Official IRA, although his "war" was limited
largely to slipping out of his bed in the middle of the night
to go painting slogans on Derry walls with some of the other
lads. "Going out with your Teddy gang, then?" Maggie would
taunt him as she watched him go.

In 1974 Mickey left the Official IRA together with many
other Derry members—tired of the ceasefire which had lasted
two years and suspicious of the "Stalinist" direction in which
they believed it was heading—to join the new IRSP and its
then military arm, the People's Liberation Army. In 1975 he
became a founding member of the INLA and on September
26 of the following year his short military career ended with
his arrest.

It was an incompetent mission. Deciding they needed some weapons, he had set out to raid the home of a gun collector in Lifford, Co. Donegal, with another member of the INLA, John Cassidy. They took a Fiat car for the raid and were accompanied by Patsy O'Hara on a motorcycle, acting as scout. When they reached the bungalow the gun collector was out and they broke in quite easily. Their haul was seventeen firearms—including old Krupp and Winchester shotguns—and assorted ammunition, seven telescopic sights, four bayonets and six copies of *Guns and Ammo* magazine.

By the time they arrived back in Derry an alert was already out and the security forces had a full description of them: tan-colored Fiat, John Cassidy driving, Michael Devine, "ginger hair and wearing silver-framed glasses," in the passenger seat. They did manage to off-load the weapons before they were picked up, but they still had a pair of binoculars stolen from the Lifford house in the car.

They were taken to the Strand Road barracks for interrogation. The police did not have to ask the Secretary of State for the usual extension to seven days; Mickey broke after three hours. Cassidy was tougher, trying to protect Mickey by claiming that he had hijacked the car and, seeing Mickey walking down the street, had given him a lift without his knowing it was hijacked. But Mickey had signed a 1,000-word statement, telling the whole story, and, faced by that, Cassidy cracked as well.

Mickey was sentenced to twelve years' jail in 1977 and went straight into the comradeship of the blanket. But within that comradeship he remained, relatively, an outsider. Some prisoners sharing his wing did not even know that he was married, which, in such a close-knit community, was an extraordinary measure of how withdrawn he was. He listened to discussions and debates, but rarely—for a representative of the most ideological of the Republican organizations—took part. But he was eager to join in. He had been listed as the first replacement in the 1980 hunger strike—he would have taken John Nixon's place if he had died. He was appointed officer commanding the INLA in the Kesh when Patsy went on hunger strike, which amounted to a statement that he would be next. The appointment and his choice as a hunger striker came as a surprise to many—it was almost unheard of for a man who had made voluntary statements to police to win a leadership position within the jail. But they were short of candidates and Patsy, who had known Mickey well in the Bogside and had been on the Donegal operation with him— escaping capture—had recommended him. With hindsight it was a shrewd choice, because it is often true that there is no one quite as dedicated as a revolutionary who has failed the revolution and then been given a second chance. And it was with a fierce determination that Mickey refused his breakfast on June 22.

There was another factor behind his determination: Maggie. It was rough for her, of course, at that age seeing her husband going inside for a long stretch. She found herself a boyfriend, Seamus McBride—a local ice cream man—and began skipping visits to Mickey in jail. It was traumatic for Mickey, she was really the only woman in his life, a replacement—however badly he had treated her—for his beloved mother. He wrote out to her, desperately declaring his love, pleading with her to come and see him and to bring the kids—they had two by now, a little girl, Louise, born in 1976, had joined their first-born, Michael, Jr.

Gradually the relationship between Mickey and Maggie soured into hatred. Her affair with Seamus was a local scandal and the INLA stepped in. Two "heavies" were sent to teach them a lesson, knocking the two of them about and shearing off their hair—Maggie's beautiful silky hair, cascading down to her waist. In December 1979 Maggie had another daughter, which obviously was not Mickey's. He started divorce proceedings in February 1981.

So it was a deeply unhappy young man who refused his breakfast on that Monday morning: one who had little to live for, but much to die for—for Bobby, Frank, Raymond, Patsy, Joe, Kieran, Martin and Tom, for the lads in the blocks and of course for the cause. It was a death which he was now not prepared to allow Maggie to share. He had a power of attorney drawn up in favor of his sister, Margaret, to make sure that Maggie had no part in his funeral. The INLA decided to create some family for him. Teresa Moore, a Derry housewife who worked for the IRSP as a "welfare officer"—helping dependants of INLA prisoners—was appointed his "aunt" and her husband, Patsy, his "uncle." The authorities accepted the masquerade and they were allowed in on "family" visits.

He refused to allow his wife to come in at all and a distressing dispute broke out between them. Maggie wrote to him, begging him to see her. When he received those letters his eyesight had already gone and another hunger striker, Paddy Quinn, had to read them to him. He was adamant: not only could she not visit him, but she was not to be allowed at the funeral. She tried, tentatively, to use the children as a lever, declaring she would not let them in unless she could go along with them. The IRSP sent one of their men in Derry to see her. He arrived to find that she was redecorating her house. She explained it was in anticipation of Mickey's wake—this was where the coffin would lie. She was told Mickey had specifically asked that he be buried by his sister and she was told to have the kids ready for a farewell visit to their father.

The children said their farewell just before the McAuleys and Moores started the final vigil. It was a traumatic visit. Mickey's eyesight had almost completely gone. Margaret lifted Louise, aged five, on to the bed first. The girl was rigid with fear. Then it was eight-year-old Michael's turn. Tears coursed down his father's face as his hands fumbled over his son, feeling the shape of him.

*   *   *

In the Falls Road in the early hours of Sunday morning youths
were commemorating the anniversary of internment, ghost-
ing their way in and out of side streets, hurling missiles at
army Saracens which occasionally roared through makeshift
barricades, firing plastic bullets from their portholes as they
passed. At 2 P.M. a Land Rover swung into one of the side
streets, Iveagh Parade, and policemen jumped out to grab a
young man. Women in their dressing gowns watching from
their front gates began to scream and the police opened fire
with plastic bullets, narrowly missing them as they ducked for
cover. The youth was bundled into the Land Rover and driven
off. As the excited talk in the street among the small group of
neighbors began to die down, an army foot patrol pounded
out of the dark at the lower end of the street. Their faces
blackened, they rushed through the scattering and screaming
crowd, one soldier firing a plastic bullet up the road from the
waist. Obscenities shouted by the soldiers were matched by
the civilians, one man shouting "hoppity, hoppity"—taunting
them over the fate of Corporal Phillip Hartley, the twenty-one-
year-old who had had his legs blown off by an IRA rocket.
A few minutes later troops in another Land Rover took up
positions on the corner of Iveagh Parade. Two young men
walked up to a group of them and a heated argument started.
One of the civilians was pushed in the chest and then a soldier
swung his rifle, grazing the man with the barrel. The two
started running across the Falls Road and a piece of waste
ground. Half a dozen soldiers gave baying chase and one fired
a plastic bullet at their backs. One of the fleeing men screamed
and the troops pulled up, letting them go. As they returned
to their position a soldier stepped into the middle of Iveagh
Parade and, facing the crowd, spread his legs, slightly bent
his knees, and mimicked masturbating, mouthing words at
the same time.

*   *   *

Later that morning Fr. Pat Buckley took Mass in the hospital and went in to see Mickey, who had been too ill to make it. There was an awful smell—almost cancerous, of the eating away of flesh—mainly from his mouth, but so pervasive that his whole body seemed to be breathing it. Mickey confessed that he was scared, afraid to die. Buckley asked him why he was afraid—he was a free agent; if he was not happy he did not have to do it. Mickey said he felt it was the right thing to do, but he was still scared. His eyes were wet and Buckley, taking out a handkerchief to mop his cheeks, could feel tears in his own eyes. Mickey asked if he could take his confession. Buckley put an arm around him and listened. Red Mickey was finding comfort in the ancient faith.

The McAuleys and the Moores sat with him on the usual shift basis, the women doing the days and the men the nights. There was some good crack, despite the tragic circumstances and Mickey's quick deterioration. Even his failing eyesight was good for humorous exchange, Margaret complaining that she had wasted £15 having her hair done for him and he couldn't even see it. And telling him he wouldn't be allowed to die, because he had borrowed £2 from her and he was not going anywhere until she got it back. But then his voice began to fade and he seemed to have difficulty in opening his jaw, as if his teeth were locking. He had told them he wanted the last rites and as it became obvious that the end was approaching they started praying with him.

On Tuesday, in Strabane, South Derry, the District Council was in session. John O'Kane, the chairman and local under-taker, turned up wielding a baseball bat and wearing a crash helmet. They were troubled times.

*   *   *

On the Wednesday night Frank and Patsy took over from Margaret and Teresa as usual. The men were desperately tired, having hardly slept since the previous night. Shortly after midnight Patsy could not keep going any longer and he lay down in the room set aside for them, falling asleep.

Down the corridor Pat McGeown was in trouble. It was only his fortieth day, but he could not keep the critical water down. And he couldn't get comfortable in his bed, tossing and turning. It was warm and he was sweating. He could hear talking in the corridor, the medical orderly's voice going up and down and, whenever Mickey's door opened, groaning. He drifted off for a while and awoke to see the sun was coming through outside. He could hear moans from Mickey again, across the corridor, and the mumbles of priests giving the last rites. He dozed again.

Patsy awoke shortly after dawn to find Frank asleep in the room with him. He got up and went down the corridor to check on Mickey. The orderly said he looked bad and perhaps it was time for the priest. And he rang the bell for the doctors as well. Frank was called and the two of them stood at the foot of the bed, watching the heart monitor as a doctor examined Mickey and the priest prayed. The line on the monitor got flatter and flatter and then went straight as the built-in alarm went off. Mickey's battle, for life and with life, was over.

Pat McGeown woke to the sound of a trolley trundling down the corridor for the latest body. His mind drifted. A priest came in and talked to him, but he could not make out what he was saying. Later he made out the doctor and medical orderlies having a confab in the corner, but again he could not hear them. Dinner was brought in. Later his brother and wife stood next to the bed and then his mind was off again, drifting, dreaming of standing on the edge of something and falling towards it, then floating back. It was so peaceful, then suddenly he felt tense and uptight. He felt something cold on his head and registered that it was a priest giving him the last rites, before he drifted off. He awoke again and there was a female nurse bending over him with an injection needle.

To An Bean Vasal from Bik [McFarlane] Fri 21.8.81 1.30 P.M.
... They told me that Pat McGeown had been sick for a few days and was sinking rapidly. He took a bad dip last night and his wife came in and signed the papers. That's about it ...

It was a critical blow for the prisoners. The hunger strikers in the hospital had been planning to call McFarlane in to discuss the situation once the Fermanagh–South Tyrone result was in. But what with Mickey dying and McGeown coming off, they decided not to wait and asked to see McFarlane the following morning. He was brought over and Lorney began firing questions: Had the Government's hand been strengthened by McGeown's withdrawal? Would it encourage them to hold out even longer in the hope of breaking the prisoners? What impact would the election have—win or lose? McFarlane agreed that if family interventions went any further, setting a pattern, the whole action would be jeopardized. But he said the election result should come as a major boost. The hunger strikers assured him they personally had no hesitation about continuing and that they had got reassurances from their own families that they would not intervene; but who could say what would happen when the moment of truth arrived? Pat Sheehan confided privately to McFarlane that he believed his family would intervene, even though he made his opposition to that very clear to them. McFarlane told him to repeat himself to them, as firmly as possible.

Mickey was buried on the Saturday. Outside Derry the funeral went almost unnoticed. The wake was at his brother, Frank McAuley's, house, and Mickey's wife Maggie was told that she would not be allowed to view his body, or attend the funeral. The children, Michael and Louise, did attend, though, clutching red roses by their father's grave.

In the Kesh and Belfast intense discussions were under way, as to how they could overcome the families. One option considered was for the hunger strikers to sign a legal document, stating their wish to be allowed to die and forbidding intervention. But it was doubtful what legal force such a document would have and there was the danger that the authorities could exploit such a move propagandawise—underlining, as it did, family opposition to the hunger strike. On Saturday, August 30 McFarlane was allowed into the hospital again and once more he went through the options. The hunger strikers said they were prepared to sign a document. Barney Fox had in fact already signed one which the prison doctor had presented to him, absolving medical staff from responsibility for not giving him treatment. Liam McCloskey said his cousin, Fr. McIldowney, had told him that he would ensure he did not die, that he would force his family to intervene. Liam had told his family he was going to send them a legal document forbidding it. But it was agreed that the document was not the answer. It would be far better to persuade the families to make a public declaration of support for the hunger strike. If it was necessary, in order to persuade the relatives, they would tell them that in future if there was intervention they would go back on the fast as soon as they recovered consciousness. The hunger strikers appeared determined to continue, the families were the only problem.

To Brownie [Gerry Adams] Monday 31.8.81 10 P.M. from Bik

. . . I think we have done everything in our power to combat this, so we can only wait and see. It wrecks me to think that the breaking power lies with those who haven't a clue

what our struggle is all about. I'm serious—I'm shattered
even thinking about it. I only pray we can overcome it.
The boys are 100% sound as you know yourself. A general
consensus of opinion (i.e. from about 4 of us) is that we
face a very dangerous period with the clanns [families].
In fact it could well prove disastrous if it isn't rectified. A
precedent has been set and followed once. If a trend were
to set in, heaven help us!! ...

To 'R 90' [Sinn Fein official] Monday 31.8.81
... Not much I can say on the clann problem which hasn't
already been said. To tell you truth it has me wrecked ... it
certainly appears that the Germans [British] will sit tight
to test the clanns. Deadly state of affairs altogether ...

But if the prisoners had their problems, so did the Government. In the Cabinet there was growing dissent over the handling of the hunger strike. Reports had been coming in steadily
from the Foreign and Commonwealth Office of the propaganda gains being made by the Republican cause abroad. The
French Foreign Minister, M. Claude Cheysson, had gone so far
as to speak of the "supreme sacrifice" of the hunger strikers
and to declare that their "courage" demanded "respect." At
the time of the royal wedding his government had even made
an offer to the Irish Government (which declined it) to boycott
the ceremony, if Dublin felt the gesture would help. It was
even worse in America: the British Consulate in New York
was complaining that they could not fly the Union Jack, for
fear it would be pulled down and burned. Surely something
could be done to stop the deaths.

The dissent in Government focused on an anticipated Cabinet reshuffle. Atkins was seen as the Prime Minister's poodle.
What was needed, it was argued, was a stronger Secretary of
State who could impose his own judgment. The man whose
name was being canvased was James Prior.

Prior belonged to the old Tory tradition—something of a country gentleman. The son of a prosperous Norwich lawyer and tea merchant, educated at one of England's most famous public schools, Charterhouse, and a Cambridge graduate, he became a land agent and a farmer. Elected to the Commons in 1959, he became Minister of Agriculture in 1970 and Leader of the House in 1972. At the age of fifty-three he inevitably had his eyes on the premiership itself, but his hopes of that had been checked by the steady entrenchment of the Thatcher faction, with its own harsh, confrontationist approach to government. As part of the Old Guard surrounding the former Tory leader, Ted Heath, Prior had been identified as one of the leading "Wets" in the Thatcher administration. But he was a powerful figure in the party and, as part of the trade-offs which inevitably accompany the formation of a new administration, had landed the Key Cabinet post of Employment Secretary. Demonstrating a fine ability, for a Tory, to get on with the unions—a convivial soul, he is always "Jim," never "James"—he proved a success in the job; too much so for Mrs. Thatcher, who was aching to "take on" organized labor. So the idea of transferring him to Ireland was attractive to her. But not so to Prior who, when he got wind of the planned reshuffle, informed Mrs. Thatcher that he would rather resign.

For McFarlane, problems also came in more mundane form, like the loss of a "Mrs. Dale"—a radio, the continued demands of Boscoe Doherty to go on the fast, and suspicions about whether the Brits were fighting dirty.

To Brownie Wed 2.9.81 from Bik
. . . PS It is now approximately 10.30 A.M. You won't believe this, but 'Crazy Eyes' Tomboy has just been to the toilet and back in a rather dozy mood. 'Mrs. Dale' has gone for a little trip to Greencastle!! . . . I'll stiff him when I get him . . .

To Brownie from Bik Thursday 3.9.81 9.30 P.M.

. . . Do you reckon the Brits are controlling the rate of deterioration in the boys? I felt that Lorny's particular case was somewhat abnormal and I was beginning to suspect a similar move to that which we suspect (almost certain) took place at the time of the Bonnie Prince's wedding—i.e. vitamin boosters. This would mean that they can control things to suit a particular political climate or a given or suspected set of circumstances. You've probably discussed this anyway before now. Just for your info one of the lads here who drinks about a gallon of water every day (a connoisseur) tells me that of late he has noticed a change in taste!! He maintains that the water has a 'sweet' taste to it. I also just discovered today that Liam McCloskey, when he was here told one of the boys that he tasted lime or something of that nature in the water. This was over two weeks ago. So this guy today forwards me the theory that he reckons the Brits are treating the entire water supply to suit whatever end they have in mind . . . Anyway no matter what the Germans are at, we can't very well start screaming the place down about it, can we? It's bad news though when they are controlling the rate that men deteriorate. What about a subtle leak that this is what occurred at Charlie's wedding??

To Brownie Friday 4.9.81 8.30 P.M.

. . . Boscoe Doherty—Derry lad doing 18 years. Arrested end of '76. Was on blanket about six months and left round May '78. When first hunger strike started he went on lock-up protest. Did the same again when current hunger strike started. After Bob's death he wrote to me asking me (actually demanding) for place on hunger strike. Near the top of the list. He informed me that if I gave a negative reply that it wouldn't really matter as he usually did his own thing anyway. He was just letting me know that he

was ready to bang away on hunger strike. He wrote to me
again two days ago asking again for place on hunger strike.
I had answered his first comm explaining the situation
and thanking him etc. etc. and I put him off in as nice a
way as possible. When dealing with this lad a super subtle
approach is necessary as he is probably the most erratic
individual in captivity. He's all heart and acts totally on
impulse. Regardless of the consequences. I don't believe he
weighs up the consequences. Apparently (though I can't get
this confirmed) he, along with a couple of others, went on
hunger strike in '78 in H1 or 2 to get moved to H7. I don't
believe they got their move. Then, last year, Boscoe made
a meal of a handful of broken-up razor blades and spent
a little time in hospital. I've been informed his motive was
again to get a block shift . . .

The hunger strike was by now staggering under a series of
blows. Pat McGeown's coming off had its inevitable effect on
the families. On September 4 Matt Devlin was taken off by
his relatives and two days later Laurence McKeown's family
followed suit. McKeown had done seventy days—the third
longest of the entire hunger strike, after Kieran Doherty and
Kevin Lynch—but the pattern of family intervention was being
reinforced. On the same day, across the border in the town of
Dundalk, an emergency conference of the National H-Block
Committee was staged and a sense of demoralization was
apparent among the delegates. A statement was issued at the
conference on behalf of the INLA, saying that, with only
twenty-eight of their protesting prisoners left in the Kesh,
they were cutting back on the frequency with which they
would replace the hunger strikers. In fact they had run out
of volunteers.

The Republican Movement, meanwhile, was trying to
cash in on Owen Carron's by-election win. He made a formal
request to 10 Downing Street, as a Member of Parliament,

for a meeting with Mrs. Thatcher and a similar request to FitzGerald in Dublin. FitzGerald, who was holding a crisis meeting with his ministers and civil servants on the H-Block issue, emerged to announce he was refusing it. Mrs. Thatcher followed suit, but—to meet the parliamentary convention that MPs should have access to ministers—told him that Atkins's deputy, Michael Allison, would see him. The meeting duly took place, and lasted an hour. But inevitably nothing of significance happened—Allison reiterated that there would be no negotiations, and Carron accused the Government of intransigence.

The episode underlined once again the handicap under which the Movement had placed itself by its abstentionist policy. Carron's victory, like Sands's before him, was bringing home to many Republicans the need to take their war into the political arena. One such man was a prisoner in the Kesh, who decided to write directly to the Army Council on the issue.

To P. O'Neil A/C 10.9.81 9 P.M.

Comrade, just a couple of thoughts of my own on the hunger strike and the war. After 12 years of war we (the Movement) have made more gains in the past six months than at any other period of our struggle. We have generated a considerable amount of support, but our most significant gains have been our election victories. We can, technically speaking, claim to have took over from the SDLP as the representative of the population due to the fact that we have a seat in Westminster and the SDLP have none. The decision of Sinn Fein to fight W. Belfast elated me as I am firmly of the opinion that in order to achieve a socialistic republic we will have to go into politics seriously. However it is my opinion that a lot of people feel they must have some sort of representation at parliament and therefore the abstentionist policy may not attract them. I don't think Owen Carron going to

Westminster would be damaging to our struggle. If he went he could confront Thatcher openly and her death policy in the H-Blocks and the plastic bullets issue. Of course nothing may be actually achieved as he will most likely be shouted down as our only support among British MPs would appear to be amongst the left wing only. However no matter what actually happens in the House of Commons it will be a psychological victory to our struggle due to the fact that a Republican has stood in the Brits' own Parliament and raised contentious subjects about the Brits' occupation of our land. If he is booed and heckled then it will be another exposé of the so-called democratic system. It will show democracy for what it is, a euphemism for a dictatorship of the capitalist minority over the oppressed majority. As long as Owen Carron makes noise he will draw more support to us. I don't know the man, but if he has the potential to be a demagogue then I feel we should make full use of his position. Demagogy is a very powerful weapon, as the victory of Begin in the last Israeli election clearly shows. Further, if the next Brit government finds itself in a precarious position (like FitzGerald's at present) then two Republicans will be in a powerful position for bargaining. In relation to the Free State my views are the same. If we can get seats in the Dail then we should take them and use them for the benefit of the struggle. This can be done under the auspices of the prisoners, but the main objective should always be the socialist Republic. Prisoners must never take a more important position than our final objective. We are secondary to the war. Well comrade, sorry if I caused you any form of indigestion due to views on the old abstentionist policy. I used to be the same myself and at that time talk like this gave me the creeps. However now I think we should fight the war on as many fronts as possible and if the support is there, well we may well use it!

In London, meanwhile, the political wheels were grinding on, slowly but surely, for Jim Prior. Mrs. Thatcher had called his bluff on his resignation threat. He accepted the post on September 12 on the conditions that he be allowed to remain on the Cabinet Economic Committee—enabling him to retain his influence on the economic policy issues which are the matrix of political power in London—and to take three of his closest political friends to Belfast with him, including an Anglo-Irish peer, Earl Gowrie, as his deputy. It was, he announced, his "duty to the nation" to go.

Across the Irish Sea on Monday, September 14 twenty-five-year-old police reservist John Proctor had been both mourning a death and celebrating a life. He had just been acting as pall-bearer at the funeral of a friend and UDR soldier, Alan Clarke, who had been shot three times in the back on Saturday. Immediately afterwards he went to visit his twenty-two-year-old wife, June, in the Mid-Ulster Hospital in Magherafelt. She had just given birth to their second son. As he left the hospital and was climbing into his car, 150 yards from the door, waiting gunmen opened fire, killing him.

Across the Atlantic, Britain was taking a hammering over the H-Blocks from Fidel Castro. Delivering a two-hour speech in Havana to parliamentary and congressional representatives from 100 countries, he described the IRA as heroes and likened the treatment of the prisoners to the Spanish Inquisition. The British Ambassador, David Thomas, walked out in protest. At the Liberal Party's annual conference in Wales, Stephen Ross MP said: "Fidel Castro calls these people heroes; I call them cowardly bastards."

In Belfast the first duty for Prior was an obvious one: to end the hunger strike. Not only for the nation's sake, but for his own. Although a Secretary of State for Northern Ireland exercises power in Northern Ireland, under direct rule, beyond that enjoyed elsewhere by any other member of the Cabinet, the post was seen as something of a stagnant position, at least so long as the political process was deadlocked. But if, by some miracle, an incumbent could break the deadlock—starting the territory on that so-elusive road to a resolution of the Irish question—the gains for his or her political reputation would be incalculable. For a man with an aspiration to the premiership, it was an obvious goal. But there was no hope of such an advance in reconciling the two communities while the hunger strike, with all its polarizing effects, continued. So on his arrival in Belfast—assuring journalists that Ireland was close to his heart; after all, he had kissed his first girl there—he set about ending the prison dispute.

The timing could hardly have been better for him. McFarlane had duly put two more men on to replace Laurence McKeown and Devlin, who had been taken off by their families. But one of the replacements, John Pickering—who had been in hospital only a few months previously with stomach and ear problems—fell ill almost immediately with a suspected ulcer. Fr. Faul immediately went on the attack, claiming the IRA was "scraping the bottom of the barrel" by allowing a man on like Pickering, who was previously known to have been in poor health. And there were other problems, as McFarlane was to find out on a visit to the hospital.

To Brownie Thur 24.9.81 7 P.M.
Comrade Mor, just after getting a short note from Big Gerry [Gerard Carville]. He informs me that he now realizes that there is no way could he die . . . he asks me to replace him asap. Now there's no way I would try to talk him round. What I will do is to get him to stall for a few days till we pick our best moment to replace him.

To Brownie from Bik Thur 24.9.81 10.30 P.M.
Comrade Mor, just back from the hospital about 10 minutes and I've been informed of a news bulletin which says
that Barney [Fox] came off hunger strike. Well he isn't off
hunger strike, although he will be tomorrow or Saturday.
He has an ulcer and it's murdering him altogether . . . he
called the meeting to let me know his position. I arrived
in the hospital approximately 8.45 P.M. and was there till
10.05 P.M. . . . I had a general run-down with the lads on
the situation. Liam [McCloskey] is in a bad way—blind—
but his spirit is strong. The others are all in good spirits. Big
Gerry told me he is now uncertain, but will let me know
by Sunday how he stands. OK? 'Pickles' [John Pickering]
blacked out during the meeting and I had to call an MO
[medical orderly] to revive him. He was sound within about
two minutes. He just felt his head going and sin sin . . . We
discussed the legal document and although all the boys
agreed to use it they had reservations about effectiveness.
Pat Sheehan says if we are going to move on it we'd need
to move now as Liam is almost on the brink. Jackie asked
me why Pat McGeown was not allowed back on hunger
strike by the [I]RA. I told him the truth—just said that it
was the opinion of all concerned that he did not want to
re-embark on hunger strike at all and sin e. It looks certain
that Liam's clann will intervene. He believes so himself. Pat
says that with Barney coming off and Liam's clann doing
the deed it will be hard for his clann not to intervene. He
reckons they'll do the deed . . .

On his second full day in the Province Prior paid his
first visit to the Kesh. Accompanied by his wife, he spent
three hours inside chatting to some of the Republicans in
the H-Blocks and seeing the hunger strikers themselves, but
not talking to them. It was, significantly, the first visit to the
prison by a Secretary of State for over two years.

To Brownie Sun 27.9.81 from Bik

Comrade Mor. 'Keep smiling at troubles, 'cause troubles are bubbles and bubbles will always blow away.' I'm told the author of that little piece is none other than 'Fat' Campbell, escapee extraordinaire, currently resident in Portlaoise. So there you are now . . . You should have received my comm informing you that Gerard Doherty H5 will commence hunger strike on Monday October 5. Following him will come Jack McGary, Martin Livingstone, Rab Kerr and Harry Murray in that order . . . Now where was I? Yes—'troubles and bubbles, etc.'. There is a growing feeling among those with what I would call a bit of savvy that our present troubles may prove insurmountable. I have been asked to consider terminating the hunger strike. Now that I will only consider when I believe we have no chance of regaining the top position and pushing forward towards a feasible solution. I don't believe we should allow the action of a few clanns to dictate such action by us. We do face a critical few weeks, but I believe that we can overcome the problem. However, if we cannot, then the reality of the situation would dictate an entire reappraisal. The Brits' hand has obviously been greatly strengthened, but we can reverse this situation. I don't really blame the lads for having a pessimistic outlook. We've been taking a bit of a hammering lately . . .

But time had run out for McFarlane. On Saturday, September 26 the prisoners issued a statement attacking Fr. Faul as a "treacherous, conniving man," but hard words had never been enough to put the tubby Dungannon priest off his stride. The next day he called another meeting of relatives. Representatives of five of the six families attended and agreed, albeit with varying degrees of conviction, that they should not allow any more prisoners to die. The following day at Faul's request Lord Gowrie—to whom Prior had given responsibility for the prisons—met the families. He stuck to the government line, that it would not make changes while the hunger strike continued. But the emphasis he gave to the Government's commitment to reform encouraged them.

Prior was busying himself seeing community leaders, including Hume and Paisley and Cardinal O Fiaich. Fr. Faul went along with the cardinal to Stormont, on Wednesday, September 30. The cardinal told the Secretary of State that there had been plenty of Priors in Ireland . . . in fact the name itself demonstrated celibacy had not always been practiced by monks and clerics, because the Irish rendering of it was Mac An Phrior, "son of the prior." It was the sort of crack which went down well with Northern Ireland's new ruler, who had a dry sense of humor. Faul harangued him on the importance of remission to the prisoners, urging him to restore all the remission lost during the blanket protest. Remission was becoming a favorite issue of the Dungannon priest, who was developing the theory that the quickest way to end the conflict was to bribe the paramilitary movements—or at least the families—with offers of amnesty. Both churchmen came away from the meeting impressed by Prior, by his quick grasp of the situation and obvious authority.

On the same day Prior gave his first press interview, stressing the problems, economic as well as political, faced by the Province and declaring that without an end to the hunger strike "I do not see any other progress possible." Asked if he was seeking to defeat the prisoners, he said he would not talk in terms of victory or defeat. "I've been a trained negotiator for a number of years," he said. "I do not believe in talking in those terms, because I believe they always result in doing more harm than good. I am saying to the hunger strikers: Give up. When it is clearly established you have given up, we can amplify the statements that have already been made about prison reform, and progress in prison. If there is any doubt about that Lord Gowrie will, of course, amplify that and set things straight."

As he was speaking a former Labour Foreign Minister, Dr. David Owen, was visiting the prison hospital where he made a personal appeal to the hunger strikers to give Prior—"a humane and generous-minded man"—a chance to settle by ending the fast.

By then they were all pushing at an open door. At 3:15 P.M. on Saturday, October 3, after 217 days, the Irish hunger strike was officially called off by the prisoners.

To Brownie Sun 4.10.81 9 P.M.

Comrade Mor, where do I start here? How's about last Friday, eh? . . . The Germans [authorities] blocked me all roads on Friday and were obviously trying to exact a confirmation from me which I wouldn't disclose at all. I did see Pat Sheehan, at his request, for half an hour, and boxed him with everything. He's quite a lad. Anyway, I retired on Friday night with one ginormous headache. Saturday morning I stalled till 11.30 A.M. and then hit the Germans with a series of requests for O/Cs and hunger strikers, in that order. I told them I was confident of bringing an end to the current situation if I was facilitated. Things moved like lightning after this. I got to see all O/Cs for individual sessions (five minutes at a time) and boxed them on the position. I then headed for the hospital and saw all the hunger strikers together and covered all points with them. They got a sound breakdown on the situation and agreed to a man that the intended course of action was our only option. At approximately 3.15 P.M. they all terminated their fasts. Actually the way things went I cut it very fine, but it worked out sound enough. On reflection I should have gone for a collective meeting with the O/Cs, but I wasn't thinking when I submitted the requests—I was concentrating too much on making sure I got to see the hunger strikers asap. You should have received verbals on Saturday afternoon that I got all the meetings alright. So that was about the heap. We saw Silvertop for about 10 minutes or so and boxed him off also. I returned to the Block at around 4.30 P.M. The screws, generally speaking, are convinced that a deal has been worked out with NIO. So there ye are now. They're a rare breed!! The 'Menace' [Fr. Faul] arrived in this morning and I decided to see what reaction there was to the ending of hunger strike. He was happy enough himself and proceeded to give me a break-down on his and Sagairt Mor's [Cardinal O Fiaich's] yarn with J[ames] P[rior] the other day. This issue was top of the list and the Menace gave me his observations. He reckons we are in a strong position and that pressure is now fully on the Brits to make positive moves. He pushed the line of own clothes, full remission, wider range of activities with choice by prisoners. They told JP that POWs always had a command structure in jail and always will have and that the best way to establish a settlement was to work through representatives in here. He also suggested that the O/Cs should allocate the tasks and men to carry them out. I said that if I had a choice of work and could appoint my men to do specific tasks then that was sound by me. I used Cages as an example and held to the self-maintenance line plus education to bolster this up. Obviously the Brits are thinking of workshops etc. The Sagairt Mor raised the cultural and historical aspect. The Menace reckons the Brits will move as we terminated at a very opportune time—new SOS [Secretary of State]—both he and Gowrie have high political ambitions—Conservative Party confer-ence in four weeks or so. Plus, he apparently assured the Sagairt Mor that there would be no misunderstanding this time in regards to a successful conclusion (whatever all that is worth, of course). The Menace said that one of our lads had suggested bringing on the ICJP—this is true; it was one of the IRSP. I said that their proposals were a major dilution and would not provide a feasible settlement, so it was pointless talking about them. He also asked if I felt I'd like to see the Sagairt Mor—I said: No! He reckons Gowrie will see me personally in the near future to put some offers to us. I reckon he will alright, so we'll see what gives. OK? We shall just have to keep our cool and stay on top of the situation. Apparently JP has a team of Civil Slaves drawing up a plan for end of hunger strike. We had a fair yarn this morning (that's the boys and me) and cleared the air on a few points. Jake has a breakdown for Joe. In short we believe that we cannot hope to maintain a protest for a protracted period and therefore we must move asap to get ourselves above present level—i.e. dispensing with Blanket protest and trying to build up. We will need to cut out the penalty aspect for refusal to work—otherwise men just won't hold together. We reckon we can get segregation by fighting for it. The Brits may give us this anyway if they genuinely wish to avoid trouble in here. Before we can even begin to do or say anything, we will have to examine the Brit position and see exactly what he is at. Then we can start moving. Now what way will Armagh be fixed? Can we link in with them via Pennies [Danny Morrison], or someone to ensure that whatever is happening is done in unison? What do you reckon the chances are of conducting discussions with Armagh via special visits with Pennies etc.? Before any decisions are arrived at I will conduct talk-ins with as many of the lads as I can get around a table. Contact with yourselves may not be granted—i.e. special visits, so we will have to ensure good lines. We don't need to rush into anything, so we will just slow everything down and take days to talk things over if necessary. You can let me have an attitude to what way you lot view the situation. I have a visit with Joe this Friday OK? I think that's about all for now. Oh yes, some of the boys gave us a bit of stick about that statement we put out against the Menace. They reckon we ripped the clams out of it. I made no apologies sin sin. I'll slide off here now and get some other comms done. Keep the fingers crossed. By the way, I don't want to start running for meetings with O/Cs until there is something happening? Regards to all the boyos. Take care and God Bless. PS. I'm tired man!! xoxo Bik xoxo

POSTSCRIPT

"After they die, they will be forgotten, just as those policemen and soldiers who died are forgotten after a while, except by those who loved them."

—Mrs. Florence Cobb, widow of a police
inspector killed by one of the
hunger strikers, December 1980

Milltown cemetery is easy to find. Coming into Belfast on the main Dublin Road, it sprawls across a slight rise to the left. In one corner, overlooked by an ugly charcoal tip in the back of an adjoining scrapyard, is the Republican plot. It is the place where local IRA men are buried and which Kieran Doherty admired in that photograph his mother showed him on his deathbed.

Kieran lies there now, of course, under a low, black headstone stating only his rank—"volunteer"—and name. Alongside him are Bobby Sands and Joe McDonnell. Simplicity is the style of the Belfast Republicans. The final resting places of the other seven are remembered in different ways.

Mickey Devine lies with Patsy O'Hara on that Derry hillside, under a small wall with a marble stone inset which declares: "They died so that others may be free." Frank Hughes and his cousin, Tom McElwee, also lie together, in a new section of the cemetery at St. Mary's church, near Bellaghy. Their tombstone is inscribed in Irish, which Tom— battling to learn the language even as he was dying—would have particularly appreciated. And Frank would have liked the wording: "Among the warriors of the Gael may his soul rest." Raymond McCreesh lies in the bandit country of South Armagh, within sight of his parents' front door, and Martin Hurson under a huge Celtic cross up in Co. Tyrone.

Kevin Lynch is just a few dozen yards away from that monument to O'Carolan and Kilmartin where he used to pause on his way to Mass. Their monument has the MacSwiney inscription: "It is not those who can inflict the most, but those that can suffer the most who will conquer." So Kevin's tombstone of black marble has the words from St. John's Gospel which Bobby Sands threw at Fr. Faul: "A man can have no greater love than to lay down his life for his friends." But another even more telling statement about suffering and love is offered by the shiny white pebbles which cover Kevin's grave: once a year his father washes them, each and every one.

The families have handled the grief in different ways. Mickey Devine's widow, Maggie, has had to have psychiatric treatment. She could not take the guilt, the suspicion that he may have died because she had left him nothing to live for. She moved in with her boyfriend, the ice cream man, and had another three children by him, but refused to marry him. That would have seemed like another betrayal of Mickey. She insisted on calling all the kids Devine. The house is littered with pictures and mementos of Mickey and she finds herself hallucinating about him. She is not the only one haunted by the hunger strike.

Geraldine Scheiss dreams of Kieran Doherty. They are happy dreams. In one he walks into the room and his eyes twinkle and he laughs and he says: "Geraldine, you're an eejit." She remembers praying that he would never be alone, that he would always have someone with him. And now she feels he is with her all the time—her constant companion. She remains convinced that Kieran was somehow forced to die. "And are not these white arms and this soft neck better than the brown earth?" Fedelm demanded of the hunger-striking poet in Yeats's play, *The King's Threshold*. It is a question to which the beautiful Geraldine has still not found an answer.

Kieran's mother, Margaret, has to live with the decision that she and Alfie took. She gets much comfort from a collection of letters which she treasures. One is from Kieran himself, in which he broke the news that he was going on hunger strike. "I know I can rely on you both to be strong and steadfast in the long days ahead," it said. Another was written by Martin Hurson to a friend in the Kesh and sent out to her after Kieran's death. "It means a terrible lot on the hunger strike when the family are behind you 100 percent," Martin said. And a third letter was written to the couple by the prisoners themselves, saying: "We all admired your extreme bravery in remaining loyal to Kieran's wishes. To do that was far harder than anything that most of us had to do." But of course the memories never go away. And the regrets are there. When she was waiting for him to die she used to long to take him in her arms and cuddle him and nurse him. But he was such a big strong lad that she felt she could not baby him. And now that he has gone she keeps thinking to herself: "Why didn't I hold him and say I loved him and kiss his cheek with the bones standing out of his face so?"

Goretti McDonnell has also been haunted by Joe. She had a rough time after his death, losing her own father, her grandmother and an aunt in quick succession. Her father had cancer and she found herself spending another week sitting by a deathbed. It was all death, death, death. She went through a period of dreaming that Joe was with her, and was certain that he was. But she was determined to go forward in life and not back, and she is now remarried. The fading graffiti on the walls of West Belfast can still hit her, though: "Don't let them die—give them their rights, not their last rites." It was also tough for her children, of course. Bernadette cried a lot when fathers of her friends were released from the Kesh. And little

Joe has had to live with the knowledge that his father will now never take part in a great escape . . . although others would.

Other parents of the dead men dealt with the grief, for the most part, with a proud resignation. Paradoxically, though, the family of Bobby Sands, who went to his own death with such certainty, have apparently not come to terms with his sacrifice. "Apparently," because theirs was the only family which refused any cooperation in the writing of this book. Mr. and Mrs. Lynch never forgave the INLA for the way that the news was broken to them of Kevin's decision to go on hunger strike. The old man later apologized to Gerry Adams for his outburst as his son lay dying in the prison hospital, and he and Bridie became firm supporters of Sinn Fein. Bridie takes comfort, in her grief, from those words of Kevin's which so bewildered her at the time: that there was no difference between three months and ninety years. As time went by she came to understand that he was talking about the relativity of time, and of life spans.

For other players in those dramatic events of the summer of 1981 life went on . . . and death, too. The deaths included that of Sgt. Oram, the SAS soldier who shot dead those two IRA men with such efficiency in Londonderry. He was mentioned in dispatches for that particular tour of duty and returned to Ireland the following year, only to die in another shoot-out. Two IRA men died with him, one of whom—John Hogan— was emerging as another Francis Hughes figure in the Movement. Oram was awarded the military medal posthumously.

Fr. Faul continues to teach at St. Patrick's Academy in Dungannon and to say Mass at the Kesh. "The man who broke the hunger strike" is not an easy tag to live with in Catholic Ireland, but it does not worry him. He views it all with his customary cynicism, blaming churchmen in a way for what happened: saying that, after all, they taught people to imitate Christ, so the Church can hardly complain when they go out and do just that.

Many of the prisoners involved in the hunger strike are now out, including baby-faced Jake Jackson who wept at the memory of his granny and of Bobby Sands; Hector and Teapot, entertainers extraordinaire, and hunger strikers Paddy Quinn, Pat McGeown, Brendan McLoughlin, Jim Devine, Barney Fox, and Gerard Hodgins. Their release brings home the point that, with full remission, all of the dead hunger strikers would have been free in 1987 with the sole exception of Francis Hughes, who was serving life.

Bik McFarlane, who was also serving life, did get out of the "devil's tomb," in dramatic fashion. The strain of the hunger strike—the constant struggle to hold back his emotions—was enormous; having to remain cool and calculating while watching friends die in a nightmarish game of human skittles devastated him and he was allowed to stand down as Officer Commanding the IRA prisoners shortly afterwards. But in September 1983 he led thirty-seven of his comrades in the great escape from the Kesh. Nineteen of them made it—including McFarlane himself—bluffing and fighting their way to freedom. McFarlane disappeared for several months—not only from the security forces, who were hunting him assiduously, but from the IRA as well. But he resurfaced, after what was obviously a much-needed break, to offer his services once again to the IRA in lighting "the blue touch paper." After all, Camilo Torres had said: "The Catholic who is not a revolutionary is living in mortal sin." In January 1986 he was recaptured in Holland, apparently while on an arms-buying expedition.

McFarlane's confidant during the hunger strike, Gerry Adams—"Brownie"—had his effective leadership of the Irish Republican Movement publicly confirmed by his election to the presidency of Sinn Fein in November 1983. In the general election of that year he emulated Bobby Sands by winning the West Belfast parliamentary seat, displacing Gerry Fitt, who retreated into the bosom of the British establishment with a life peerage. In March 1984 Adams survived an assassination bid when Protestant gunmen ambushed a car in which he was traveling in central Belfast, pumping three shots into him.

Humphrey Atkins, who was moved from Northern Ireland in the closing stages of the hunger strike, became Leader of the House of Commons and was knighted for his services to the State in 1983. James Prior, who replaced Atkins as Secretary of State, proved himself probably the most capable politician to hold the post, but failed to make significant progress on the constitutional front. In November 1984 he left the Northern Ireland Office and retreated to the back benches where he sits with others of the Tory Old Guard, hopefully awaiting the fall of Mrs. Thatcher.

Mrs. Thatcher continued, Boadicea-like, to pursue the politics of confrontation, dispatching her chariots of war—or at least the ships of the Royal Navy—to deal a crushing defeat to Argentina in the Falklands and then turning on Britain's National Union of Mineworkers to inflict a similarly crushing, if less bloody, victory over the followers of Arthur Scargill. In October 1984 the IRA narrowly failed to exact a personal revenge for her part in the hunger strike, when they blew up Brighton's Grand Hotel while Mrs. Thatcher was staying there for the annual Tory conference. She had walked out of her bathroom just seconds before it was devastated by the blast.

In the immediate aftermath the hunger strike was hailed, at least by the English press, as a triumph for Mrs. Thatcher. The *Daily Mail* described Mrs. Thatcher's stance as "magnificent obstinacy"; the *News of the World* said the collapse of the hunger strike was "a humiliating defeat for the IRA at the hands of the Government"; the *Sunday Express* said: "It has been a victory for commonsense and firm moral purpose, over the confused, tortured mentality of appeasement . . ." Even the *Guardian*, long respected in Ireland for its understanding of the island's woes, said: "The Government has overcome the hunger strikes by a show of resolute determination not to be bullied." The British Foreign Office, among others, holds a different view: when young diplomats are briefed on contemporary Irish history, in preparation for postings to Dublin, the hunger strike is held up as an unmitigated disaster for the Government.

The five demands for which the ten died were largely met within a comparatively short time. Within three days of the ending of the hunger strike Jim Prior called a press conference to announce concessions. They included the right of all prisoners to wear their own clothes—abolition of the "badge of criminality" which, if it had been conceded by Humphrey Atkins a year before, would almost certainly have prevented the hunger strike. Prior also restored half of the lost remission—on condition of good behavior—and granted greater freedom of association among inmates. The demands for improved mail, parcel and visiting privileges had already been met. The major outstanding demand was prison work. After repeated incidents of sabotage and in the aftermath of the great escape—when it was decided that they were too much of a security risk—the workshops were closed down and that demand had also been effectively met. No formal recognition was made by Government of the prisoners' "political status." But then the 30,000 who gave Sands their vote in the Fermanagh–South Tyrone by-election had already granted all the recognition that was needed.

But, as Goretti McDonnell told me fiercely one day: "They died for a lot more than the five demands." And that is true, of course: the hunger strikers died for a cause far more ancient than the gray walls of Long Kesh prison.

It requires a historical perspective from a time far in the future to gauge with any certainty what they did achieve, or failed to achieve. But there is some evidence to suggest that one day the hunger strike may be seen as a watershed in the Anglo–Irish conflict. Most importantly, the success of their electoral strategy during the hunger strike nudged the

IRA in a new policy direction—into what was to become known as the "bomb and ballot box" approach to the age-old struggle. Winning ten percent of the popular vote in an election for a short-lived "devolutionary" council in 1982, and then over thirteen percent in the 1983 general election, the IRA—or at least Sinn Fein—began to develop a serious electoral challenge to the so-called "constitutional Nationalists," John Hume's Social Democratic and Labour party. As Sinn Fein's political activities became increasingly disruptive of what vestiges of a democratic system remained in the territory—with warnings from Jim Prior that the island could be rendered ungovernable and reduced to "a Cuba" of Western Europe—the British and Irish governments, at John Hume's instigation, launched a rescue operation for the SDLP in the form of the Anglo–Irish agreement. It is a document of compromise and ambiguity, notably lacking the vision and courage which is desperately needed. But—in that it implicitly gives a formal recognition, for the first time since Partition, of the essential indivisibility of Ireland—the agreement, despite heated denials by Mrs. Thatcher's Government, may prove to have been a first hesitant step down the road to an eventual reunification.

The constitutional issue has obviously lain at the center of the Anglo–Irish conflict since time immemorial. But there is a sense in which the centuries-old struggle, between two nations locked in an extraordinary love-hate relationship, goes beyond the mundanities of borders, constitutions and governmental systems. And in the same way there is a sense in which the hunger strike rises above the rights or wrongs of penal administration, or politicians' posturing on the criminality of "terrorism." The story of how those ten very ordinary men died—a draper's assistant, a mechanic, an upholsterer, a milkman . . .—belongs more to humanity than to a limited Nationalist cause, no matter how ancient. It is the stuff of tragedy, of Shakespearean proportions.

A moment evocative of that unique blend of history, tragedy and theater which is characteristic of the Anglo–Irish saga came in 1986 when Bik McFarlane appeared before a Dutch court to face the British application for his extradition back to Ireland. During the hearing a stooped and wrinkled old man took the witness stand to tell the foreign judges something of the story of the Anglo–Irish conflict. He was Sean McBride, winner of both the Nobel and Lenin Peace Prizes, former Irish Cabinet minister and one-time Chief of Staff of the IRA.

McBride was the son of John McBride—executed in the 1916 uprising—and of the most famous of Irish beauties, Maud Gonne. Maud was the great love in the life of W. B. Yeats, whose inner turmoil over the 1916 executions—his jealousy towards John McBride coupled with his admiration for their sacrifices—produced the famous poem "Easter 1916," and the line so redolent of that episode: "A terrible beauty is born."

Subsequently, following the death of Terence MacSwiney, Yeats rewrote the ending to his hunger-strike play, *The King's Threshold*. It originally had the poet, Seanchan, abandoning the fast and living on. In the rewritten version Seanchan dies, surrounded by his young apprentices who are themselves under sentence of death. And the poet's dying words are as fitting an epitaph as any for the great Irish hunger strike of the summer of 1981:

> *When I and these are dead*
> *We should be carried to some windy hill*
> *To lie there with uncovered face awhile*
> *That mankind and that leper there may know*
> *Dead faces laugh. King! King! Dead faces*
> *laugh.*

Johannesburg
September 1986